FOURTH EDITION

Introduction to
EDUCATION
STUDIES

STEVE BARTLETT and **DIANA BURTON**

Los Angeles | London | New Delhi
Singapore | Washington DC | Melbourne

Los Angeles | London | New Delhi
Singapore | Washington DC | Melbourne

SAGE Publications Ltd
1 Oliver's Yard
55 City Road
London EC1Y 1SP

SAGE Publications Inc.
2455 Teller Road
Thousand Oaks, California 91320

SAGE Publications India Pvt Ltd
B 1/I 1 Mohan Cooperative Industrial Area
Mathura Road
New Delhi 110 044

SAGE Publications Asia-Pacific Pte Ltd
3 Church Street
#10-04 Samsung Hub
Singapore 049483

Editor: James Clark
Editorial assistant: Robert Patterson
Production editor: Nicola Marshall
Copyeditor: Gemma Marren
Proofreader: Lynda Watson
Indexer: Silvia Benvenuto
Marketing manager: Lorna Patkai
Cover design: Naomi Robinson
Typeset by: C&M Digitals (P) Ltd, Chennai, India
Printed by CPI Group (UK) Ltd, Croydon, CR0 4YY

First edition published in 2006 and reprinted in 2006 and 2008.
Second edition published in 2008 and reprinted in 2009, 2010
and 2011. Third edition published in 2012 and reprinted in 2012,
2014 and 2015.

Library of Congress Control Number: 2015951205

British Library Cataloguing in Publication data

A catalogue record for this book is available from
the British Library

ISBN 978-1-4739-1899-3
ISBN 978-1-4739-1900-6 (pbk)

At SAGE we take sustainability seriously. Most of our products are printed in the UK using FSC papers and boards.
When we print overseas we ensure sustainable papers are used as measured by the PREPS grading system.
We undertake an annual audit to monitor our sustainability.

Introduction to
EDUCATION
STUDIES

Education Studies: Key Issues Series

In the last 20 years or so Education Studies has developed rapidly as a distinctive subject in its own right. Beginning initially at undergraduate level, this expansion is now also taking place at Masters level and is characterised by an increasingly analytical approach to the study of education. Several discrete study areas requiring in-depth texts to support student learning have emerged.

Introduction to Education Studies (4th edition) is the core text in this series and gives students an important grounding in the study of education. It provides an overview of the subject and introduces the reader to fundamental theories and debates in the field. The series 'Key Issues in Education Studies' has evolved from this core text and, using the same critical approach, each volume outlines a significant area of study within the education studies field. Each of the books has been written by experts in their area and provides the detail and depth required by students as they progress further in the subject.

Taken as a whole, this series provides a comprehensive set of texts for the student of education. While of particular value to students of Education Studies, the series will also be instructive for those studying related areas such as Childhood Studies and Special Needs, as well as being of interest to students on initial teacher training courses and practitioners working in education.

We hope that this series provides you, the reader, with plentiful opportunities to explore further this exciting and significant area of study and we wish you well in your endeavours.

Steve Bartlett and Diana Burton
Series Editors

Steve Bartlett and Diana Burton: *Introduction to Education Studies*, 4th edition (2016)

Diana Burton and Steve Bartlett: *Key Issues for Education Researchers* (2009)

Alan Hodkinson: *Key Issues in Special Educational Needs and Inclusion*, 2nd edition (2016)

Emma Smith: *Key Issues in Education and Social Justice* (2012)

Stephen Ward and Christine Eden: *Key Issues in Education Policy* (2009)

To our sons, Tom, Dan, Ed and George Bartlett with all our love.

Contents

The authors

Steve Bartlett is Professor of Education Studies and associate lecturer at the University of Wolverhampton. He has led the development of the subject at undergraduate and postgraduate level for many years, chairing the Subject Benchmarking Review Committee for QAA. A founder member and the first Chair of the British Education Studies Association (BESA), he is currently editor of the BESA journal.

Steve has a Masters and PhD in teacher professionalism and he has written a number of books and articles on education studies in the areas of research methods, lifelong learning, teacher development and gender. He has led education studies programmes at the Universities of Wolverhampton and Chester.

Diana Burton is Professor of Education and Director of the Centre for Developmental and Applied Research in Education at the University of Wolverhampton. She was formerly Pro Vice-Chancellor and Professor of Education at Liverpool John Moores University, where she was previously Dean of Education. She worked for many years at Manchester Metropolitan University leading teacher education programmes and was a secondary school teacher before that.

Diana has a Masters and PhD in the field of Educational Psychology. She is the author of a number of books and articles on pupil learning, teacher development, educating children with behavioural, emotional and social disadvantage and citizenship education. She is a fellow of the Royal Academy for the Society of the Arts and the Higher Education Academy and is an active member of the British Education Research Association.

New to this edition

This fourth edition has been fully updated to reflect relevant changes in the education landscape since 2012. This includes:

- New coverage of special education needs discussing how policy has evolved historically and in more recent times throughout the New Labour and Coalition governments.
- Analysis of the 2014 national curriculum in England and the political processes and ideologies underpinning it.
- An extension of coverage of Coalition government education policy to cover the full parliamentary term up to 2015.
- A focus on the education policies of the 2015 Conservative government.

In addition, a new Video Discussion feature has been added throughout the book; these are short video clips that explore important chapter topics in further depth. They can be found at the companion website for this book, alongside a range of free-to-access SAGE journal articles linked to chapter topics at: https://study.sagepub.com/bartlettburton4e.

List of abbreviations

AL	accelerated learning
APU	Assessment of Performance Unit
ASC	academic self-concept
BESA	British Education Studies Association
BSF	Building Schools for the Future
BTEC	Business and Technology Education Council
CACE	Central Advisory Council for Education
CASE	cognitive acceleration in science education
CCCS	Centre for Contemporary Cultural Studies
CHC	Confucian Heritage Culture
CSA	Cognitive Styles Analysis
CSE	Certificate of Secondary Education
CTC	City Technology College
DCSF	Department for Children, Schools and Families
DES	Department of Education and Science
DfE	Department for Education
DfES	Department for Education and Skills
EBacc	English Baccalaureate
EBP	evidence-based practice
ECM	Every Child Matters

EEG	electroencephalogram
ELT	experiential learning theory
EMA	Education Maintenance Allowance
EYFS	Early Years Foundation Stage
FE	further education
FSM	free school meals
GCE	General Certificate of Education
GCSE	General Certificate of Secondary Education
GIST	Girls into Science and Technology
HE	higher education
HEFCE	Higher Education Funding Council for England
HMI	Her Majesty's Inspectorate
ICT	information and communications technology
ILS	Index of Learning Styles
IQ	intelligence quotient
ISA	ideological state apparatus
ITT	Initial Teacher Training
LA	local authority
LEA	local education authority
LSI	Learning Style Inventory
LTM	long-term memory
MBTI	Myers-Briggs Type Indicator
MFL	modern foreign language
MI	multiple intelligences
MLE	mediated learning experience
NAEP	National Assessment of Educational Progress (US)
NAO	National Audit Office

NC   national curriculum

NCC   National Curriculum Council

NCIHE   National Committee of Inquiry into Higher Education

NEET   not in employment, education or training

NESS   National Evaluation of Sure Start

NVQ   National Vocational Qualification

OECD   Organisation for Economic Cooperation and Development

Ofsted   Office for Standards in Education, Children's Services and Skills

PBS   positive behavioural support

PEPS   Personal Environmental Preference Survey

PFI   Private Finance Initiative

PIRLS   Progress in International Reading Literacy Study

PISA   Programme for International Student Assessment

PL   personalised learning

PSE   personal and social education

QAA   Quality Assurance Agency

QCA   Qualifications and Curriculum Authority

ROSLA   'raising of the school leaving age'

SEAL   social and emotional aspects of learning

SEL   social and emotional learning

SEN   special educational needs

SEND   special educational needs and disabilities

SES   socio-economic status

SSLP   Sure Start Local Programme

STEM   science, technology, engineering and mathematics

STM   short-term memory

TAT   Thematic Apperception Test

TechBacc   Technical Baccalaureate

TIMSS   Trends in International Mathematics and Science Study

TVEI   Technical, Vocational and Educational Initiative

VAK   visual, auditory and kinaesthetic

WICS   wisdom, intelligence, creativity and synthesis

ZPD   zone of proximal development

PART 1

EDUCATION STUDIES – AN INTRODUCTION TO THE FIELD OF STUDY

CHAPTER 1
What is education studies?

Chapter overview

The first chapter will introduce you to the study of education. We examine the appeal of the subject for students and explain its rapid recent growth. While the significant contributions of the related disciplines of sociology, psychology, history and philosophy are discussed, we argue that it is the positioning of education as the central focus that provides education studies with its own identity.

Education studies: the subject

First encounters

As students of education studies, we have an interesting relationship with the subject since we are all products of education systems and thus have our own unique perspectives that are hewn from our different experiences. Education is, for most people, an integral part of our first 16–22 years of life and yet our understanding of it as a system or process, beyond experiencing it as more than a set of curriculum subjects and examinations, is often limited. The role we undertake as pupils is to experience rather than question the nature of the education system and its attendant processes. Education studies as a subject turns this on its head and asks us to question what education is, who it is for, who controls it and why; essentially, to think critically about every aspect of education and the societal and political structures it sits within.

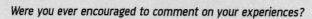

Reader Reflection: Your own educational history

Think back over the time you have spent in education.

Were you ever encouraged to comment on your experiences?

Should pupils and students be involved in decisions concerning their education?

The journals and books you encounter from the beginning of your course generally assume a level of understanding and knowledge about educational issues which you are unlikely to have at this stage. Thus, while there are many texts suitable for the knowledgeable student, there are very few which may be used by the novice as an introduction to the field. This present book aims to introduce the study of education and to provide a starting point from which to progress. It outlines several major areas of education studies and the key issues therein. In the text we refer, wherever possible, to current literature which you should be able to access. We are also aware that to deal with the overarching questions and issues in such a short space can actually do them a disservice and cause distortion by oversimplification. We want therefore to emphasise that the purpose is to introduce the study of education, outline the theoretical arguments and encourage deeper exploration.

The development of education studies

In the past education(al) studies has been seen as very much part of the education/training of teachers (Burton and Bartlett, 2006a). The study was effectively invented during the period of expansion in education post-Second World War, which created a demand for more high-quality teachers. To meet this demand the teacher training courses at the colleges of education were lengthened and the Robbins Report (1963) declared an intention to develop teaching into an all-graduate profession. This heralded the creation of the new Bachelor of Education (BEd) degree, which comprised both theoretical and practical study of education. The content of these new BEd courses was largely created from a range of subjects already in existence at the validating universities. Thus the academic study of education came to be made up primarily of the sociology, psychology, philosophy and history of education: the so called 'foundation disciplines' (McCulloch, 2012).

Rather than becoming a unified subject these disciplines generally remained as discrete units and were taught separately. For many students they were presented in isolation and did not sufficiently link with the other parts of their professional training courses to make them appear worthwhile. For such students their prime focus was on the subjects they were going to teach, the teaching practice itself and, particularly, aspects of classroom management and control. In an effort to make the theoretical and academic study of education more relevant to the needs of the student teachers, many BEd programmes began to create a more integrated approach. This involved the development of what became known as *curriculum, professional* or even *educational* studies (Lawn and Furlong, 2009). In hindsight this can be seen as a significant point in the development of a specialist study of education.

As a result of political and economic pressures in the 1970s and 1980s the theoretical study of education as part of teacher training courses fell into disrepute. Teacher education was criticised as being too removed from the classroom. It was perceived as largely ignoring the practical nature of teaching while also promoting progressive ideologies of education. It was from the 1980s onwards that the nature of teacher education changed drastically. With the emphasis becoming firmly placed on training, any traces of academic education studies were removed from Initial Teacher Training (ITT) programmes. However, shortly after the critical study of education disappeared from teacher training courses, new programmes called education studies began to develop in the rapidly expanding sector funded by the Higher Education Funding Council for England (HEFCE). We suggest a number of reasons for the rapid growth of this subject and its popularity among the student population (Bartlett and Burton, 2006a).

The increase in student numbers entering higher education (HE) and the concomitant development of modular degree programmes, allowing more flexibility in the choice of subjects studied, meant that education studies came to be seen as an important partner for a number of combinations. Thus students combine education studies with sports science, English, drama, religious studies, geography and the like. It took on a special significance for students planning careers that involved working with people in a variety of contexts. Teaching is often the first that springs to mind but there are also personnel management, welfare and health services, retail, publishing and a range of others.

The recent trend for many students who intend to become teachers to take a first degree and then a Postgraduate Certificate in Education (PGCE) rather than the traditional BEd has made education studies a more attractive part of that first degree. This changing landscape of teacher training has led to many schools of education seeking actively to diversify their portfolios, making education studies an obvious addition from an institutional point of view.

The nature of education studies

Whatever your eventual career decisions as an education studies student, you have chosen education as an academic area of study and will need to approach it in a critical fashion. You will be seeking answers to key questions such as: What is education and what are its purposes? How does learning take place and how far is achievement dependent upon natural ability or social factors such as income, life chances, gender and ethnicity? Your attention will also be drawn to educational policy and political issues surrounding education and to ways of researching these phenomena.

With the resurgence of the academic study of education and an increasing number of students with education studies in their degree title, the significance of the traditional disciplines from which it draws once again becomes apparent. Aspects of education are studied within various disciplines, specifically philosophy, psychology, sociology and history, as part of their particular interest in the human condition. However, education is also seen as a legitimate area of study in its own right by the Quality Assurance Agency (QAA) which considered that:

> Essentially, education studies is concerned with understanding how people develop and learn throughout their lives, and the nature of knowledge and critical engagement with ways of knowing and understanding. It offers intellectually rigorous analysis of educational processes, systems and approaches, and their cultural, societal, political, historical and economic contexts. (QAA, 2015: 6)

Reader Reflection: The nature of education studies

Consider your experiences of education studies so far.

How do they relate to the QAA view above of what the subject involves?

This means that education is at the centre of the study and therefore draws on the other disciplines as appropriate in an eclectic manner. Thus, while psychology students will study aspects of education as appropriate, for instance, in relation to cognitive development, education studies students will study some aspects of psychological theory when looking at the process of learning within schools or colleges. It is interesting to consider the status relations between these older and newer subjects, the longer-standing disciplines having a better developed theoretical base to consider as their own.

Davies and Hogarth (2004) were unable to identify a clear consensus about the nature of education studies, suggesting that there would be some value in exploring what might constitute its broad parameters.

Some features which, we would argue, characterise the subject are that:

- it is 'young' and developing
- it takes a critical, analytical and 'resistant' approach to the study of education
- it grapples with fundamental, contested concepts
- it explores a range of perspectives, not just those of teachers and schools
- it deals with multiple rather than singular explanations of phenomena.

Thus, the way in which education studies facilitates a critical engagement with educational phenomena contrasts sharply with the 'technical-rational' approach to teacher training described earlier. Even within non-teacher training programmes education studies is circumscribed to some extent by this pervasive culture since it must examine and describe extant education processes and systems in order to analyse them. However, the power to critique and rethink educational policies and processes is available to students of education studies in a way that is denied to ITT students. Education studies provides a set of analytical discourses that generate insights into educational phenomena as bodies of knowledge and societal conditions shift, develop and wane.

While the education studies benchmarks (QAA, 2015) provide a guide to those designing new courses, the structure and content of education studies programmes varies enormously. At the heart of each course, however, lies a critical analysis of key issues such as the nature of education, the content and development of curricula, teaching and learning, the relationship between ability, opportunity and success, and the policy issues impacting on all of these. It is a mistake to see education studies as essentially school-focused. This can happen due to its historical connection to teacher training but is certainly not the case as all aspects of education can be included. The subject has enormous scope from the development of young children, through learning in HE, to the workplace and the third age – a true study of lifelong learning.

We now turn to the interest education holds for a number of significant disciplines concerned with the study of people and society. The discussion will illustrate how the approaches and theories developed within these disciplines may be used by those students whose main concern is the study of education itself.

The traditional disciplines and education studies

Fundamental to any society, education and the processes it involves are of great interest to fields of study concerned with the human condition. In particular we refer in this book to philosophy, sociology, psychology and history.

Philosophy

Curtis (2011) suggests that philosophy and philosophers have been engaging with questions of education, learning and teaching for more than 3,000 years, since the beginning of formal thinking. The philosophy of education illuminates the ideas which underpin action and thought in education. The questions philosophers ask concern the nature and purposes of education, such as what makes an educated person, how knowledge is organised and what should be learned. They are primarily interested in the beliefs, morals and values which permeate education. These are very important questions which are at the heart of the whole process and therefore appear in every aspect of the study of education. They are key to discussions of the nature of curriculum which derives from different ideological positions on education and the structure of knowledge. Such questions are also apparent when analysing how beliefs are translated into policy or when looking at issues of individual development and progression.

Sociology

The sociology of education examines the wider social influences upon the individual in education and analyses the processes of socialisation. Sociologists ask questions about the influences of social class, ethnicity and gender upon achievement and these are seen in relation to various ideologies which shape education. Sociological analysis is concerned with power operating at different levels in society and how this influences outcomes. This explains the sociologist's interest in the creation of education policy and its implementation (Whitty, 2012). To understand modern education systems it is vital to study the relationship between prevailing ideologies and the societal structures and values they shape through the process of education.

Psychology

The psychology of education is mainly concerned with how people learn and develop. As such it asks questions about our maturation, intelligence, personality and motivation, as well as about the learning process itself. It is interested in the relationship between nature and nurture and the way they interact to influence individual development and achievement. A psychological analysis also involves philosophical issues of the nature of knowledge and understanding and shares an interest in sociological issues since the individual is seen to be part of wider social groups. An examination of pedagogy from a psychological perspective further reveals the link between psychological and sociological theory as well as the ideological perspectives which have influenced it.

History

The history of education may suggest causal explanations for changes which punctuate the political and social timelines of educational development. It helps us to understand the evolution of the educational system and structures to date. There are key dates and events within the development of the English education system that reflect the significant political and social issues of the time. While the scope of education has changed radically since the late nineteenth century, the pastoral, disciplinary and knowledge distribution functions of schools and other education establishments remain significant in modern Western societies. As Dufour (2011: 3) says, 'To study the history of education in any country with a formal state education system involves engaging with and unlocking the particular interplay of social, cultural, economic and political forces at work at any given time'. Goodman and Grosvenor (2009) point to the importance of a historical dimension in developing contextual understanding and strategic vision in those concerned with education.

Relating the four disciplines to education studies

Each of these four disciplines brings its own specific perspective to the study of education and each is interested in particular aspects as they relate to their own concerns. It is also clear that their areas of interest overlap. It is interesting that these four disciplines were the ones included in the initial BEd teacher training degrees (Dearden et al., 2009; McCulloch, 2002; 2012). Others may have been incorporated. The economics of education, for instance, would look at the importance of education and training in the creation of a valuable, high skills labour force, or at the benefits of state education systems compared to the competitive provision of schooling in the light of economic theories of monopoly and market forces.

Reader Reflection: The contribution of other subjects to understanding education

How might other disciplines or subjects, such as geography or political science, be useful to draw on when studying education?

When education itself is the focus for the student, as in education studies, it is important to draw from these disciplines as appropriate. This eclectic view can provide a richer picture of the whole process and may produce new forms of knowledge and new ways of understanding.

Conclusion

In this chapter we have outlined how students first encounter education studies as a subject and the way in which critical engagement with the subject brings new understandings. We have seen how the study of education has developed, and we have outlined its key features as a subject and how its constituent elements might be described.

Student activities

1. Find the education studies benchmarks on the QAA website (www.qaa.ac.uk) and read through the statements. How useful do you find these in outlining the subject of education studies? How do your experiences of education studies relate to them?

Recommended reading

Educationalfutures: The Journal of the British Education Studies Association (BESA). www.educa-tionstudies.org.uk/journal. This is the online journal for BESA. It is free to access and also part of the BESA website, which is well worth education studies students becoming familiar with. The journal and website will introduce you to articles on the subject and also provide contacts within the field that you may wish to pursue.

 Access the companion website to this book and find SAGE journal articles exploring this chapter topic in further detail: **https://study.sagepub.com/bartlettburton4e.**

CHAPTER 2
The nature of education

Chapter overview

This chapter considers the complex nature of education as an area of study, looking at the meaning of the term itself. It moves on to a discussion of the purposes and processes of an education system that can be seen from a number of different sociological perspectives. The key educational ideologies are outlined and a typology of ideologies is considered along with the component features that are said to characterise any ideology. The chapter concludes by emphasising the importance of a critical approach to the study of education.

The meaning of education

Education is an activity we all feel that we know something about, having had practical experience of it. In a systematic study of education, however, two fundamental questions will be posed:

1. What do we mean by education?
2. Why is education important?

Finding the answers to these two questions is a complex endeavour. As students of education, the answers we give are likely to vary over time. The meaning and purposes of the term 'education' are not universally fixed and are not the same for all of us.

Personal resonances of the term 'education' are shaped by a number of individual experiences such as coming top of the class, passing examinations, going on school trips, being made fun of by pupils or teachers, or being in the bottom set. Various groups of people are usually positioned differently in relation to education and its purposes. Political leaders, parents, pupils at school, university students, teachers, the police and factory managers will all espouse different views. These groups might themselves be differentiated: for instance, parents may be classified by income levels, marital status, age group, number of children in the family and so on. More specific questions about education help to elicit a deeper analysis.

Reader Reflection: The purposes of education

- *Is education a process?* Is it something which we go through over a period of years? Does this process vary over time? For instance, how is education for four year olds in nursery different from that for 20 year olds at university?
- *Is education a product to be consumed?* Can it be quantified? Is the product defined as what someone can do at the end of it, i.e. a demonstration of competence at something, or is the product about exam passes? Where does intellectual development fit in here? Does the product vary? For instance, is the education of an unskilled worker different from that of a nation's leaders? Should it be different?
- *What does education involve?* Is it about sitting at desks, learning important facts and answering questions? Does it mean being absorbed by interesting tasks or solving challenging problems? Should it make us happy or serious and should we be put under pressure and 'extended' to our limits?
- *Where does education take place?* Is it mainly in schools, colleges and universities? Can we do it at home using information and communications technology (ICT) and learning packages delivered 'online'? Does it carry on throughout life beyond school, college or university?

It is interesting to analyse our perceptions of education using such questions. Yet the range of responses, when we compare our views to those of others, can also be disconcerting. The complexity of the area of study becomes very apparent. Deciding what education is about may mean thinking of it as a process, as something to be consumed, or as a result or product. All of these possibilities are emphasised in various ways by different people when looking at the meaning of the term 'education'. We also need to ask if education has to be intended or if it can happen by accident in an unplanned and sometimes, perhaps, unrecognised manner.

Peters (1966, republished in 2015), a significant education philosopher, was well aware of the problems in attempting to define 'education'. He suggested that the term had been used in many different ways and, as such, was difficult to capture in any precise definition, though he was able to outline a range of 'normative' and 'cognitive' aspects associated with it. For Peters, education was deeper than just learning facts or how to do something. This more superficial approach he associated with training. Education involved a linking of concepts by the learner to gain a wider understanding of the world. In his view, for something to count as education it had to be regarded as worthwhile. In this way it was inseparable from judgements of value. It should also be learned in a morally acceptable manner; it should not involve coercion or brainwashing. This implies some agreement by the learner to take part (Peters, 1967, republished in 2010). This view of education could certainly cause us to question some of our own experiences within compulsory education.

Consider the life histories of convicts and the questions one could ask concerning their education. What has their education involved? Could it be that they learned different things than the teachers intended? What skills have they developed? Once in prison what do convicts learn and from whom? Do they go to education classes and listen attentively to the advice of the warders or do they 'pick up tips' from listening to and being with other inmates?

Using Peters' view of education unreformed convicts would see their learning of how to be criminals as useful. They entered into this voluntarily and so it is morally acceptable from their position, unlike their experiences at school where they had perhaps been chastised. It also fits with their wider view of the world and how they can survive in it.

In its broadest sense education is normally thought to be about acquiring knowledge and developing skills and understanding – cognitive capabilities. It can be claimed that as humans, we are identified by our capacity to learn, communicate and reason. We are involved in these things throughout our lives and in all situations. From the earliest times people have learned from one another in family and social groups. As society became larger-scale and more complex, so systems of education became formalised and expanded. We still learn from those around us but the education system now also plays a large part in all of our lives.

Formal education developed first for the elite minority and, over time, became compulsory for all. This is not to say that schools for the elite and those for the masses gave the same education or had the same purposes. Those being groomed to rule and those subject to being ruled have traditionally been educated in different ways and with different expectations. Steadily the time spent in educational institutions increased as children started younger and finished older than their predecessors. This trend of an increasing number of years spent in formal education continues today. The development of post-16 and higher education in recent years is testament to this while, at the same time, nursery and pre-school provision is also rapidly expanding. Since 2015, in England, young people must remain in some form of education or training until their eighteenth birthday, while in the rest of the UK the leaving age remains at 16 years.

Education has become a large industry employing many thousands of people in Britain alone. It is supposedly an important part of ensuring future economic development yet it also imposes a major financial cost. It is presented by politicians as an investment in our future, the 'our' referring to the nation as a whole as well as to the individual. Thus education plays a central role in society and also in all of our lives.

Reader Reflection: Education as a source of employment

Education is an important part of the economy. It is startling to note how many jobs are within, or rely upon, educational institutions.

Consider the broad economic effects of the expansion or contraction of one sector of the education system such as pre-school and nursery education, higher education or further education.

Sociological perspectives on the purposes of education

We may accept, then, that it is appropriate to take a broad view of the meaning of education. Turning our attention to why education is important may help us to understand more fully the meaning of the term. When looking at the purposes of education we are generally referring to the purposes of the education 'system'. It should be apparent from the previous discussion that this is likely to exclude a great deal of interesting material. While a wide detour may be made into education at the 'university of life', space does not permit this here. We will limit our concern to the 'official', or 'formal', processes of education.

The functionalist approach

The functionalist perspective views society as a system where interconnected parts function in relation to an integrated whole. Functionalism depends on the idea that social systems are significantly determined by fundamental human need. In this way it tends to be seen as a 'conservative' ideology. Functionalism also works with the idea of functional prerequisites: some social phenomena are simply there as they are necessary for the society to work for the benefit of all its different members. Some needs are common to all societies implying the idea of a general human condition independent of cultural differences (consider the seminal work of one of the founding sociologists who was writing in the nineteenth century and whose works have been republished several times, continuing to the present day, such is his influence – Durkheim, 1947 [1893], 1964, 1970, 2014; also Davis and Moore, 1967; Parsons, 1964). Thus education is seen alongside other social institutions as working to create and maintain a stable society. The functionalist analogy compares society to a machine or a living organism. The different social institutions, such as the forces of law and order, the political system and also education, function to maintain the whole society. In the same way that the different parts of a machine or a body contribute to the working of the whole, if one of the parts does not function properly then this affects the whole society and may even lead to a breakdown. The main functions of education may be listed as follows.

Development of basic academic skills: In order to participate in a modern society certain skills are seen as very important. Most notably we need to be able to read, write, perform basic arithmetical tasks, reason and problem solve. These are needed in all areas of modern life. Consider how many times you use reading skills in any one day. You could conclude that life as we know it is virtually impossible to live without them. It is amazing to think that some people do actually survive without highly developed reading skills but they are at a distinct disadvantage and need to seek help frequently. This is not easy for them because of the social stigma attached to an adult being unable to read proficiently. The ability to use ICT is now also regarded as an essential skill. The importance of, and increasing emphasis on, the acquisition of what are variously called 'transferable', 'key' or 'core' skills is part of the rhetoric surrounding the development of an adaptable, flexible workforce for the 'skills economy'. Thus interpersonal, communication, problem-solving, literacy and numeracy skills have been promoted up the educational agenda particularly within post-16 learning.

Socialisation: Functionalists see this as the way in which we become human. It is a process which begins at birth when we start effectively as blank slates. We develop our 'selves' as we learn what we need to know to live and operate with others in social groups. This includes language, right and wrong, expectations of ourselves and others, how to behave in different situations and so on. It is, of course, a matter of debate as to how much our development depends upon social learning or biological processes. Socialisation is a process of induction into society's culture, norms and values. This ensures a level of social cohesion necessary for society to be sustained. It is a process which continues throughout life but which is certainly of central importance in our early years. Thus the family and schooling have a crucial role in the socialisation process.

Social control and maintaining social order: For us to live our lives and for established social life to exist we must be assured of a level of order and safety as we go about our daily business. This involves the rule of law but also certain expected ways of behaving. These may be seen as norms of behaviour or manners. Consider how we behave in an orderly manner for much of our lives without really thinking about it. We queue up for things in shops or when waiting for public transport. We say 'please' and 'thank you' in appropriate circumstances. In public places we walk without bumping into or touching other people. We maintain appropriate eye contact and distance when conversing with others depending upon who these others are. These norms are learned and education helps in this process. Control mechanisms may be overt and show outward force, as in the case of riot police quelling trouble on the streets. Control may, however, be more covert and subtle when compliance is expected, as in the case of a disparaging look from a teacher when work has not been completed.

Preparing for work: In small-scale and self-sufficient societies children would learn about survival from adults. In these communities adults are multi-skilled and can satisfy most of their wants by using their own abilities. There may be only a few specialist roles such as healer or midwife in such groups. As forms of employment diversified and became specialised, increasingly specific training needed to take place. Payment, in the form of wages, generally reflected the level, scarcity and importance of the skill required. General qualities needed for employment such as those expressed in the transferable skills can be developed at all levels of education. Job-specific training is likely to be workplace based but also to involve further and higher education.

The functions of education may be seen to overlap. The preparation for work involves the developing of minds and learning of important skills. Socialisation is an important part of preparing for adulthood and elements of internalised social control form part of this. Different functions may be to the fore at certain times during a pupil's education. Whereas it may be appropriate to stress the development of the mind and individual freedom to experiment at particular stages, it may be important to stress discipline and the need for self-control at others. Each of these functions can be seen to be appropriate but, taken together, there are potential tensions between them. For example, developing minds involves encouraging a questioning attitude. The image is of a learner exploring and experimenting. However, the need to maintain social order involves pupils showing obedience to authority and 'correct' behaviour. This could be interpreted as the creation of accepting, rather than questioning, individuals.

Pupils may be encouraged to question within the topics chosen by a teacher. Much primary work, for instance, involves investigations by pupils into the world around them. The children may ask questions to do with friction, life cycles, different materials and so on. They carry out investigations designed to find the answers. However, other areas of school life must not be questioned beyond a superficial level: 'Why must we wear this uniform?' 'Will all of this homework help our progress?' 'Why are we studying "this" as opposed to "that"?' Obedience is an important part of any pupil's schooling. When the characteristics of a 'good' school leaver are listed they include independence and initiative, yet prospective employers also look for a willingness to obey instructions and for a neat (in other words conforming) appearance. It seems there is a need for both self-development and self-control. The difficulty is striking a balance. We can see the importance of order, direction, control and discipline but not to the extent that it prevents questioning and individual development. This balance is a judgement which rests upon beliefs about human nature, the working of society and, thus, the purposes of education.

The stress placed upon the different functions of education may be different depending upon the pupil. Some pupils may be pushed academically while others may be prepared for low-level employment. Indeed some functionalists, such as Davis and Moore (1967), saw the sifting of talent and allocating of individuals to appropriate roles in society as an important function of a formal education system. Some pupils may be given freedom to express themselves whereas for others the emphasis may be on modifying their behaviour. Chapters 8–10 examine this potential for treating pupils differently and posit some explanations for it.

The rhetoric of consensus

When considering the functionalist perspective on education we need to ask for whose purposes education exists. One main criticism of functionalist perspectives is the way that they see social structures according to a hidden logic of cause and effect. By saying that education functions for the whole society it is assumed that what is good for the society is good for us all. The implication is that we all have the same needs and wants and also that there is equality of opportunity to benefit from such a system. In short it takes a consensus view of society and ignores the fact that significant differences and conflicts of interest may exist. Inequality, in terms of income or wealth, is actually seen as something which itself performs a function of encouraging us to better ourselves and, in the process, benefits the society as a whole. Vital questions about conflict and difference in societies are explained away by functionalist perspectives.

The rhetoric of consensus also ignores the power differentials between separate sections of society and how these can be used to maintain superior positions. Children from certain groups are significantly more successful in education and it has been posited that this is a reflection of their economic and social background (Bourdieu and Passeron, 1977). Research has also shown that the labelling which attaches to children in lower socio-economic groups serves to further disadvantage them (Hargreaves, 1967). Functionalist theories tend to be 'monologic'. Social phenomena are seen as having single and simple surface causes. Social conflicts are minimised and the normative elements of social life are emphasised.

Functionalists assume that the system must be maintained if the society is to survive. By reinforcing the status quo these functions actually benefit those who are in the best positions. They maintain stability and thus it is easier for those at the top to ensure that their children follow in their footsteps. Those at the bottom are, by and large, kept there. It is pointed out that it is largely their own fault for not taking the opportunities on offer. Thus inequality is perpetuated and regarded as the 'natural' order of things. Education is seen as an important part of the unifying process needed to help maintain a level of consensus within society. Functionalist theories can be valuable in describing how societies and their various elements work together in coherent patterns but are less successful in accounting for change and conflict.

Conflict theories

From our early years we are encouraged to see education positively, as offering benefits to all. But what if, as some social theorists and education researchers have claimed, education is more about promoting dominant ideology and dividing populations into different class and occupational segments? Conflict perspectives propose that schools perform certain social functions but not necessarily to the benefit of all. Some have suggested that they serve the system well but that the system they serve is based on inequalities that schooling or education in general should be challenging. Rather than the consensus envisaged by functionalism, conflict theorists, Marxists for example, see education as reinforcing a class system (see Anyon, 2011, for a detailed analysis of Marxist theories of education).

Marxism perceives a conflict of values in society with those of the capitalist ruling class being dominant. The education system, by operating as an agency of the state, serves to reinforce these values. It helps to keep the working class in their place while preparing middle-class pupils to 'legitimately' take over the powerful positions held by their class. Althusser (1984) formed the concept of ideological state apparatuses (ISAs), a development of the concept of government and class relations. ISAs are significant in terms of maintaining ruling-class ideology and are an important part of the means through which the capitalist state maintains control. Bowles and Gintis (1976) saw a close correspondence between how schools treat pupils and the later experiences they can expect at work. This plays an important part in preparing working-class youth for menial forms of employment. Bourdieu and Passeron (1977) used the concept of cultural capital to explain how the middle classes are able to maintain their position in the process of social reproduction while making this inequality legitimate.

Gramsci (1985; 1991) claimed that ownership of the means of production cannot be enough to guarantee class rule. The ruling class must also work for 'hegemony', a key concept signifying the cultural rule of their dominant ideas and values. The ruling class needs to actively win the support of other members of society and ruling-class concessions have to be made. Gramsci put great emphasis on civil institutions and cultural practices as fields for political action and intervention. This implies a broad idea of the state, political power and authority as being located in everyday practices and ideas. Hegemony is achieved by continual negotiation and has to be constantly worked at. Thus we see the importance of the education system. By claiming to be a meritocracy, in other words where individuals prosper by their own efforts, the education system helps to keep social order and perpetuate the existing inequalities. This is, for the classic Marxist analyst, the purpose of formal education.

Some conflict theorists would consider it possible for subversive elements to work within the system. Gramsci, for instance, suggested that the dominant class can never totally monopolise power as beliefs and ideas are constantly being contested in everyday practices (in schools and universities for example). As a consequence, social change (revolutionary action) can be located in existing institutions and everyday social practices. Others, however, see capitalism as too powerful to be overthrown by individuals. Idealists working within education to change society will, in the long term, become incorporated into the system themselves. In fact, by helping individual working-class pupils to succeed, these teachers may ultimately be perpetuating the myth of a meritocracy. They are in the end legitimating the very education system which is helping to sustain the existing structural inequalities. In the novel *A Kestrel for a Knave* by Barry Hines, an English literature reader for many 14 and 15 year olds in the 1970s and 1980s, the teacher who befriends and guides the poor, badly treated working-class pupil makes no difference to the overall order of things.

Reader Reflection: A view of social disorder

'Riots reflect a broken society'

The explosive manner in which the tensions of London's youth underclass turned into a sustained campaign of violence and looting is a salutary reminder of how easy it is to take normal social order for granted – there or elsewhere. Many parts of the city, one of the world's richest and host to next year's Olympic Games, have been transformed in a few days by arson and theft, with the police left struggling to assert control. (*Irish Times*, 11 August 2011)

The extract above was on the London riots in the summer of 2011. Is it possible to talk of a society being broken? How might a Marxist interpret such riots?

Thus it might be argued that both functionalism and Marxism conceive of the purposes of education as maintaining the current order of society but from very different standpoints.

Sociological perspectives on the process of education

So far we have considered structural theories which place a clear emphasis on how structures relate to the outcomes of education in terms of the reproduction of society's institutions. Now we turn to theorists who approach the effect of education from the perspective of the individual and their interactions within it.

Symbolic interactionism

Social interactionists emphasise the actions of members of society as the source for understanding social phenomena and institutions rather than overarching structures. Max Weber (1864–1920), a prolific German sociologist, produced a hugely influential body of work which has been published and republished several times since his death (1958; 1963; 2002; 2009). Weber was interested in uncovering the meaning behind social actions. The perspective of 'symbolic interactionism' comes out of the development of Weber's thinking and US sociological traditions. George Herbert Mead is often cited as the 'founder' of symbolic interactionism. According to Mead (1934), human beings interact through symbols which define the world and the roles of social actors. (The term, 'actors', is used by symbolic interactionists to refer to people playing their roles in society.) This position emphasises the importance of culture in social formations, institutions and practices such as education.

Culture specifies roles, symbols and interpretations of symbols. Symbols enable the social actors to make sense of their world. While symbols in social interactions must be shared, individuals interpret the actions, meanings and intentions of others. Social life involves an ever active role. Mead emphasises the critical importance of role-taking and interpretation in the development of the 'self'. The idea of the coherent self is learned and cultivated. Social institutions such as schools are composed of many roles. These roles can be chosen to some extent and are interpreted and adapted by the actor, for example parenting can be carried out in many ways. Thus culture is not monolithic and constraining. Subcultures exist and are constantly changing. Cultural meanings often indicate possibilities rather than requirements. Social roles are dynamic and, to some extent, fluid.

While Marxism emphasises *structures* as the dominant forces determining the shape and form of institutions and behaviours, interactionists emphasise *agency* or the freedom and ability of the individual to decide. In more recent times, the sociologist Antony Giddens (1985; Giddens and Sutton 2013) has argued for a theory of social action that sees structure and agency as interdependent: 'structuration' relates structures to action. Giddens writes of the 'duality of structure'; structures do exist but have no existence outside the consciousness of the agents (actors) who act upon them and define them in everyday activity. Language provides Giddens with a model for 'duality of structure'. Language must be rule governed and therefore structural. It depends for its existence on the utterances of individuals who make it happen.

Poststructuralist and postmodern perspectives

Some powerful and influential ideas about culture and society come in the form of theories referred to as 'poststructuralist' and 'postmodernist', though neither of those terms can be used in a completely straightforward sense. The importance of these ideas within education is that they challenge dominant discourses and practices by suggesting that, while these things may be fixed in behaviour and institutions, they are at another level provisional. They also indicate the importance of culture, language and identity – key features of the inequalities that operate through education.

Poststructuralism provides opportunities for rethinking the school as an institution. It considers the nature of knowledge, and how this changes through history and according to culture (see Derrida, 1987; Foucault, 1977; 1988). Poststructuralism is critical of the deep-seated ideas that infuse education systems and traditions. On the whole it is anti-essentialist and anti-traditionalist. It is suspicious of ideas like truth and aware of the historical 'contingency' of ideas and 'systems of thought'. With its emphasis on the importance of language and culture, poststructuralism provides the means for examining all the mundane practices of institutional life and posing questions of them, from what texts are read in English lessons to how discourses of science and knowledge represent gender.

Differing social perspectives, such as those described in this section, are important in the study of education. It is vital to work towards some idea of the relations between the individual, the social structure and the institutions of education. Tracking these relations is complex and problematic but important.

Educational ideologies

Systems of broad beliefs and values about the nature of the world are termed 'ideologies'. Robertson and Hill (2014: 167) define an ideology as 'a more or less coherent set of beliefs and attitudes that is regarded as self evidently true, as "common sense" in opposition to other belief systems'. Ideologies are relevant to all areas of life and are often related. Thus understandings about human nature may be linked to beliefs about law, order, political life, the economic system, the purposes of education and so on. We have explored the purposes of education from a largely sociological perspective. There are, however, other ideologies which analyse both the purposes and nature of education slightly differently. While the education system has a purpose of social reproduction in terms of cultural, economic and political life, it also has a purpose of social transformation. Thus decisions, based upon beliefs about what is important to pass on and what needs transforming, need to be made. In this way ideologies in education are very much linked to views about how society should be organised. Hence there is a strong link between political philosophy and educational theory.

Reader Reflection: The organisation of society

There are many differing positions on the human condition. These lead to alternative visions of what is desirable and what is humanly possible in the organisation of society. These views have tended to be presented as polarised alternatives which offer differing perspectives on the purposes of a formal education system and its concomitant structure.

How do you think society should be organised in a perfect world? How close do you think we can get to your ideal?

Plato and Hobbes

Plato argued that humans are naturally predisposed to perform certain tasks. In the Greek state he identified three levels of society – workers, soldiers and leaders. Society will be 'in balance' when people are performing the tasks for which they have a natural disposition. Thus the purpose of the education system is to prepare different pupils in the most appropriate way for their future roles. This means different teaching methods and content as appropriate. Plato saw traditional, high-status knowledge being appropriate for some people only and practical instruction appropriate for others; everyone 'in their place' doing what they do best leads to a stable society. It is interesting to compare this view of society with the tripartite education system set up in post-war England (see Chapter 4).

In Plato's analysis, to go against this natural order is to threaten the whole existence of society. Encouraging those not suited to rise above their station will cause social unrest, instability, disobedience and civil strife. Ultimately this must be put down by force or it will lead to revolution, anarchy and a total breakdown of the social fabric. In this way everyone in the society will suffer. Thus, for Plato, order was important for the maintenance of society (Curtis, 2011).

In the seventeenth century Hobbes suggested that we all have natural desires which we wish to satisfy. Humans in this respect are no different from other animals. Survival is of the fittest and life can be seen as potentially 'nasty, brutish and short'. We are, ultimately, all on our own trying to satisfy our needs and live in a totally hostile world – a dog-eat-dog existence. Humans do thrive in larger social groups where trade and cooperation can take place. However, the constant pressure to revert back to our natural state needs to be guarded against. Thus for social life to be made possible there need to be rules, laws and sanctions which are rigorously enforced, for example, to take a life or to commit a crime against property leads to severe punishment.

Hobbes explained that parameters of behaviour need to be clear and enforcement strict. Anything less, any sign of weakness, will threaten the superficially stable and secure lives of us all. The line between a well-ordered society and a state of brutal chaos is slim. Respect and fear of the law are what enable a society to exist (see Olssen et al., 2004 for an account of Hobbes and the problem of social order). For Plato and Hobbes the importance of education in maintaining order and thus the existence of society is clear. People need strict guidelines to operate within and discipline needs to be instilled in mind and body. Order is of central importance if society, and the individuals within it, are to have a chance to prosper.

Rousseau

An alternative view of human nature is put forward by the Romantics. In the eighteenth century Rousseau took the view that, far from maintaining society, power in the hands of the few will lead them to reinforce their position which itself results in tyranny. He saw this increasing oppression as leading to violent uprisings from the oppressed in their struggle for freedom. In his view what was needed was to educate all citizens fully. This involved encouraging the development of questioning minds and giving everyone the widest of educational experiences. As our intellects develop we can all contribute to the evolution of society by continuous discussion and reason. Rousseau saw the development of a 'social contract' whereby to maintain their own freedom people respected the rights of others. This would only happen when all felt involved in the society and it would be the height of democratic development. The common good is presented as the 'general will' of the people.

Thus self-discovery and individual development form the basis of education, for Rousseau, leading to a more liberated society (Curtis, 2011). Without this freedom there would always be oppression based on physical force. These freedoms were the very things that Plato saw as dangerous to the fabric of society. On the one hand there is the view that education should be about individual development and fulfilment. All citizens will then be able to play an active part in social life resulting in tolerance of the views of others. This will lead to a 'better' and more just society. On the other, there is the belief that this freedom will lead to instability due to the innate selfishness of human nature. What is needed is social order and a structure which will enable us to lead our lives without fear and within which we can earn our living. A prime purpose of education is to develop individual discipline with a respect for authority and tradition which will ensure this. These opposing views can both be detected when examining political developments in recent education policy.

We can see how our own experiences in schools, colleges and universities mirror one or other of these sets of beliefs. When thinking of our secondary schooling we may recall the ways order was enforced: lining up outside classrooms, detentions, threat of exclusion. Rules were enforced even down to the way work had to be laid out in exercise books. While being critical of the exercise of control over our freedom, we are also aware of what it is like to be pupils in a classroom where order has broken down and the teacher has lost authority. This situation is often regarded by pupils as being fun at first but quickly turns to boredom and frustration at the lack of any constructive activity and direction. A desire grows for a return to an orderly learning environment as pupils themselves begin to complain to wider authorities. The majority of school children, without openly admitting it, welcome the structure and direction a teacher is able to give. Often, however, learning involves both individual choice and external direction and control. Most adults can recall important learning experiences which have affected their personal development, such as a moving poem or story read with feeling by another pupil or a teacher, a word of encouragement from a form tutor, finishing a piece of artwork and taking it home. Such experiences are generated as a result of this complex interaction between self-determination and teacher control.

A typology of ideologies in education

The views of Plato and Rousseau apply to the whole of society and social life. Now let us consider education specifically. Meighan and Harber define ideologies of education as:

> the set of ideas and beliefs held by a group of people about the formal arrangements for education, specifically schooling, and often, by extension or implication, also about informal aspects of education, e.g. learning at home. (2007: 218)

There have been various attempts to classify ideologies in education and Meighan and Harber outline the dichotomous approach which uses polarised types such as teacher-centred versus child-centred, authoritarian versus democratic, and so on. The juxtaposition of only two ideologies may prove rather simplistic, especially when examining long lists of polarised opposites which may or may not be related to other 'pairs' on the list. Meighan and Harber suggest that other more complex typologies attempt to go beyond this.

Lawton (1992), in a seminal account, pointed out that ideologies are used at different levels of generality. There is the broad level which is about the nature and purposes of education within a wider society, as considered, for example, by Plato and Rousseau discussed above. There is the interest group level, which is concerned with how the system should be organised, for instance whether education provision should be a totally free market where schools offer and charge for a service and the customer pays according to what is on offer, or a totally comprehensive state system for all with no choice. Then there is the teaching or pedagogic level which is concerned with the organisation and delivery of the curriculum at classroom level. This involves what should be taught and how it should be taught.

Lawton (1992) suggests that these different levels are very much linked and overlapping. For instance, views on the nature and purposes of education are influential when it comes to considering the organisation of schools, colleges and universities. They will also be significant in deciding what is the most appropriate content and methods of teaching to be applied. How individual teachers view content and teaching methods will, in turn, be linked to how they see the purposes of what they are involved in. For this reason Meighan and Harber (2007) prefer to use the concept of a network of ideologies to show how they operate between, as well as at, these different levels.

Throughout this book there are issues concerning the nature of education, how the system should be organised, what should be taught and how. The relationship and overlap between the three levels of ideology identified by Lawton will be continually stressed. One level cannot be considered without reference to the other two.

Ideologies of education may be categorised into many permutations (see Matheson, 2015; Trowler, 2003). Scrimshaw (1983) suggested organising educational ideologies in terms of their stress upon the individual, knowledge or society as a useful means of categorising such a wide range of ideas. Morrison and Ridley (1989) also used these three headings to neatly summarise clusters of educational ideologies in the following way. Though this typology was developed over 25 years ago, it still provides a useful aid in understanding ideologies of education.

Ideologies which emphasise the individual

Under this heading sit ideologies labelled variously as progressivism, child/student centredness and romanticism. The emphasis is on individual development with the needs and interests of the learner being central. The learning process is seen as vital with discovery and experimentation being at its heart. Learning is held to be rewarding in itself and pupils/students maintain high motivation because of this. The emphasis is on development at different rates with students following their own learning programmes according to their interests. Learning is individualised and lifelong and the concept of failure is not appropriate as it only applies to set courses and fixed parameters of progress. Formative purposes of assessment are favoured over summative ones. Thus student portfolios are regarded as more valid in showing progress than mass exams at the end of the year.

The child-centred approach had made some headway in the 1960s, with the Plowden Report (CACE, 1967) doing much to endorse these ideas, particularly in primary schools. The development of this approach was a reaction partly to the notion which influenced much post-Second World War education policy that intelligence and aptitude were largely innate. There was a growing belief in the significance of environmental influences on the development of the individual.

Various questions and issues are raised concerning the practicalities of this Romantic approach which puts pupils, with their interests, needs and wishes, to the fore. In an age of mass education the development and management of individual programmes becomes difficult if not impossible. There is the issue of the pupil who does not particularly want to progress. For instance, the child in the reception class may be very happy playing and not wish to leave the sandpit. It may be felt that, if the pupil is not to be disadvantaged in later life, the accomplishment of some essential skills should not be left to chance. Can we trust that all children will turn to reading and writing when they are ready or should we give them formal teaching?

This then turns the focus onto the teacher. In a child-centred classroom, to what extent should teachers intervene and how much can be left to the initiative of the pupil? It is difficult for a teacher to allow experimentation in some areas which may not be seen as socially appropriate. As adults we do more than just discourage young people from trying smoking, drinking alcohol and having casual sexual experiences. It is also the case that clear teaching and being 'fed' existing information can save time. The need for every pupil to reinvent the wheel by exploration and experimentation is therefore questionable.

Critics of the 'progressive' approach suggested that the emphasis on individual freedom leads to an increase in permissiveness and a lowering of academic standards. It was suggested (Cox and Dyson, 1969a; 1969b) that this is what happened in the 1960s. A period of full employment and increasing affluence led to the indulgence of the individual and the development of a more 'permissive society', which allowed the social and economic problems of the 1970s to occur. There were similar warnings about progressive teaching from politicians in the early decades of the twenty-first century (see Gove, 2009; 2010). It is worth considering how this relates to the teachings of Plato and the views of Hobbes.

Ideologies which emphasise knowledge

Morrison and Ridley (1989) place ideologies labelled variously as classical humanism, conservatism and traditionalism within their second category. These emphasise the importance of formal knowledge arranged in subjects. In its more classical form there is respect for what is seen as high-status knowledge. Pupils/students need to start by learning basic facts and then progress through increasingly complex levels. This is done through formal, traditional, tried and tested methods. Assessment is also formal, it indicates success and it enables the selection of an elite. These views resonate very much with more recent politicians.

Discipline is an important part of the academic process. The learner is under close supervision in the early stages and only becomes more autonomous when

reaching the higher levels of academic study. Thus in the classroom in early secondary education the whole class is likely to be involved in the same exercises.
Students gain more autonomy as they move from General Certificate of Secondary
Education (GCSE) to more advanced level study. There is even more autonomy
for an undergraduate at university while at the postgraduate level students, as well
as having higher status, are much more in control of their studies. The pinnacle of
independent academic success is found at university professorial level where individual decisions are made about what research to pursue.

The practicality of subjects is less important than high academic achievement
in classical humanism. The public school epitomises the elitism, discipline and
academic standards of this ideology. There is also a strong adherence to the traditional values which have been seen to be those that make a nation great. The
criticisms of the more classical forms of humanism concern its elitism and defence
of privilege. These may be said to maintain inequality and, in Rousseau's view,
would mean the continued use of repressive means to subdue the underprivileged.
The belief in tradition leads to lack of adaptability and innovation which is likely
to result in economic decline when in competition with modern world economies.

The more liberal form of humanism also stresses knowledge but in a less traditional
format. The emphasis is on a core curriculum for all, with elements of choice, as
pupils move through the school system. Providing equality of opportunity is seen as
important, in addition to maintaining academic standards. A tension is felt between
setting by ability to allow the able to progress fully and not appearing to be elitist.

Ideologies which emphasise society

These are again divided into two by Morrison and Ridley (1989). Ideologies including instrumentalism, revisionism and economic renewal form one group. These
ideologies are looking to develop, improve and modernise the economy. The emphasis is on producing workers to enable this to happen. This can mean developing
adaptable, thinking, problem-solving, high-quality individuals as well as placing
value on the traditional worker qualities of reliability and hard work. Education here
has a practical purpose which teaching and assessment should reflect. Competencies
become important and the vocational element is stressed. Individualised programmes associated with vocationalism have shades of the student-centred approach
but with more external direction. This ideology could be seen very much to the fore
in education policy that aimed to prepare people for the 'knowledge-based' and
'learning' society. At that time, individualised and personalised learning (PL), for
example, became increasingly *de rigeur* as access to knowledge expanded via Web
2.0 technology (see McLoughlin et al., 2010).

The second group includes 'democratic socialism' and 'reconstructionism', both of which emphasise the power structures in society. Democratic socialism sees education as important in the creation and protection of equal opportunity for all and the development of all sections of society. The aim is to reform society from within and education must play a significant part in this process. Reconstructionists take this further and point to the possibility of totally reconstructing society through education. Education is seen as a revolutionary force through the enlightenment of the populace and the application of a critical approach to existing structures of social inequality. This is using the education system in the struggle to overthrow existing structures of inequality. Such a revolutionary stance is not generally tolerated by a system it seeks to undermine. The establishment has always been deeply suspicious of teachers who may be seen as potential revolutionaries and in a position to influence the vulnerable young. This ideology was a 'popular' part of the left-wing political movements of the late 1960s and early 1970s and is shown in works such as *Teaching as a Subversive Activity* by Postman and Weingartner (1969).

The value of typologies

Typologies of ideologies can never be more than generalisations, which at times appear very sweeping, of sets of beliefs that are linked together. They are useful in that they help us to understand the actions of groups of individuals but they are never total explanations because of the existence of variations. This can be seen when looking at the ideologies associated with the two major British political parties, Labour and Conservative. There are disagreements between the two and also arguments within each. It should also be noted that at times there is agreement between Labour and Conservatives on certain issues.

Meighan and Harber (2007: 225) outlined 11 significant 'component theories' which, when put together, make up an educational ideology and distinguish it from others. Each ideology possesses a theory of:

- discipline and order
- knowledge, its content and structure
- learning and the learner's role
- teaching and the teacher's role
- resources appropriate for teaching
- organisation of learning situations
- assessment that learning has taken place
- aims, objectives and outcomes

- parents and the parent's role
- locations appropriate for learning
- power and its distribution.

Each ideological grouping outlined above can be analysed according to Meighan and Harber's 'component theories', which reveal how sets of beliefs and values, in the form of ideologies, exist in education. Students take courses, have lessons and are assessed in ways that take a recognisable ideological stance. Different ideologies can coexist within the same institution, even operating alongside each other. Thus schools emphasise the future employment of pupils as well as academic knowledge. Subjects are taught differently and teachers of the same subject may have very different teaching styles. Although often taught in large classes, pupils are treated as individuals by their teachers as well as being classified into sections within the class.

The schooling pupils receive is a result of the decisions and actions of many individuals and groups (Marsh, 2009). These are both professional and lay persons who may be operating at national or local levels as well as within the school. Thus it would be misleading to assume that one dominant ideology has total control. Marsh suggests that it is worth considering the impact of different groups, which he identifies as decision-makers, stakeholders and wider influence groups, upon the classroom. This illustrates the many influences on the actual education received by pupils and also the power possessed by those involved in varying capacities. Even when given a formal national curriculum teachers will decide what each lesson will include. However, they are unlikely to ignore the concerns of stakeholders such as parents, as these are close to their daily activity and can directly affect classroom life. They will also take into account wider influences such as local employers who can offer different kinds of support in lessons and to pupils. Teachers must also pay close attention to school inspections by the Office for Standards in Education (Ofsted) and the increased scrutiny of their work resulting from the publication of league tables of GCSE examination and national curriculum (NC) test results. Thus teachers are very significant in the education process but they are not, and perhaps never have been, totally autonomous.

Kelly (2009) points out that, in examining the development of schooling and the curriculum, one can see the compromise which inevitably results from the constant tensions between competing sets of beliefs:

> which might be broadly polarised as a conflict between the claims of society and those of the individual, the vocational and the liberal, the economic and the humanitarian, a national investment and the right of every child, the instrumental and the intrinsic, what education *is for* and what it *is*, elitism and egalitarianism, and perhaps, in general, between the possible and the desirable, between reality and idealism. (2009: 190)

In considering what knowledge should be included in any curriculum, Young (2013) explains that on the one hand, educators have a responsibility to hand on to the next generation the knowledge discovered by earlier generations, but on the other hand:

> the purpose of the curriculum is to enable the next generation to build on that knowledge and create new knowledge, for that is how human societies progress and how individuals develop. The earliest societies, which did not have schools, remained virtually unchanged for centuries. (2013: 102)

There are, then, various theories concerning human nature and these provide alternative views of how society can be organised and, in turn, of the purposes of education. The education system reflects the differing values of the society in which it exists as well as helping to shape its future. Ideologies are central to the development of education which is not an objective enterprise. Questions concerning its nature and purpose are returned to again and again throughout this book.

Video Discussion

Visit https://study.sagepub.com/bartlettburton4e to watch a video discussion on:

Ideology and education

This video clip discusses issues which are also relevant to Chapters 5, 6 and 11.

Conclusion

Some would argue that too much time is spent looking at questions concerning the nature and purposes of education. There has been a tendency to criticise and decry theorising by academics as being removed from the 'real' issues of education. The recently deceased former Chief Inspector for Education, Chris Woodhead, wrote in his annual report for 1998/99:

> We know what constitutes good teaching and we know what needs to be done to tackle weaknesses: we must strengthen subject knowledge, raise expectations, and hone the pedagogic skills upon which the craft of the classroom depends . . . Why, then, is so much time and energy wasted in research that complicates what ought to be straightforward . . . If standards are to continue to rise we need decisive management action, locally and nationally, that concentrates attention on the two imperatives that really matter: the drive to

improve teaching and strengthen leadership . . . The challenge now is to expose the emptiness of education theorising that obfuscates the classroom realities that really matter. (Ofsted, 2000: 21)

Woodhead's apparent rejection of alternatives could be interpreted as an attempt to close down debate and to silence dissenting viewpoints. In returning to this position statement a number of years on it would be reassuring to find that a new official view had emerged. In essence, however, the establishment view remains largely the same, as the extract below from a speech by Michael Gove (who later became the first Secretary of State for Education in the Coalition government) illustrates.

Reader Reflection: Ideological positions of those who manage the system

The speech entitled 'It's time for modern compassionate Conservative education policy' was made to the Conservative Party Conference in 2007. After suggesting 'setting by ability so that the strongest can be stretched and the weakest given extra help', he spoke of a need for rigour in the curriculum, freedom for good teachers to inspire and liberation from bureaucracy. He suggested that because of bureaucrats who are rooted in discredited 1960s ideology, we have:

five-minute lessons because children are assumed to be incapable of paying attention. Children marking each other's work because that's assumed to be more liberating. And Churchill written out of the curriculum because he's assumed to be yesterday's man. Who do these people think they are – playing games with our children's future and denying them knowledge of our nation's past? . . . Under a Conservative Government we'll have a curriculum that delivers on the basics, equips the next generation for a world of change and gives them back the chance to take pride in our country's history. Anything else would be a betrayal. (http://conservative-speeches.sayit.mysociety.org/speech/599789)

Who do you think the bureaucrats are that Gove is referring to and what is the 1960s ideology they follow?

What key points in the above extract illustrate Gove's ideological position?

To what extent are these views reflected in policies of the current Conservative government?

These views can be seen in a number of the policies and practices systematically pursued by government which, as Chapters 5 and 6 explain, are manifestly the product of a well-developed ideological position. Education, not least because of its ideological basis, will always be important in the political arena and for those who study politics and policy.

Education is a central part of any society. It is to do with helping to shape the future in terms of developing individuals and the promotion of ideas. Politicians, parents, teachers, employers, taxpayers and pupils all have their own views of the purposes of education and what it should involve. The interaction of these sometimes competing interests renders education a fascinating area for study.

Student activities

1. In order of priority compile a list of the ten most important things a school should include in the education of its pupils. Compare your list with those of other students in the group. To what extent are ideologies apparent in these lists?

2. Choose three significant learning experiences that you remember from lessons when you were at school. These may have been isolated incidents or they may have occurred regularly over a period of time. How do these relate to the ideologies of education considered earlier in this chapter? Compare your analysis with others in your group.

Recommended reading

Kelly, A. V. (2009) *The Curriculum: Theory and Practice*, 6th edn. London: SAGE. This is a significant academic analysis of curriculum development and the underpinning ideologies. Suitable for the more advanced student, this is a detailed and challenging volume.

Meighan, R. and Harber, C. (2007) *A Sociology of Educating*, 5th edn. London: Continuum. A good book to read after *Introduction to Education Studies*, this is an interesting account of the different aspects of the educational experience and the sociological perspective on education. An easy-to-follow discussion of ideologies provides an excellent typology to use in analysis. As the title suggests, this book is also useful reading on how social factors influence success in education.

The British Journal of Educational Studies. Oxford: Taylor & Francis. This is an academic journal that is available in printed copy and online having four editions per year. This journal publishes articles which discuss basic principles or topics of importance in the study of education. As such these may be written from a variety of points of view such as educational philosophy, history, psychology, sociology or comparative studies. It is important to refer to such specialist journals that present the most current research and debate.

Access the companion website to this book and find SAGE journal articles exploring this chapter topic in further detail: https://study.sagepub.com/bartlettburton4e.

CHAPTER 3
Researching education

Chapter overview

In this chapter we aim to show the importance of research in developing an understanding of the field of education. The relationship between research paradigms and notions of reality are explored. We discuss how the beliefs inherent in the different paradigms inform the whole research process from the selection of issues regarded as worthy of research, the purposes of the research and questions of validity, to the status of different forms of data and the relevance of different methods of data collection. Qualitative and quantitative methods of data collection are briefly outlined and related to the discussion of paradigms. Research is presented as an integral part of the process of education itself and, as such, is argued to be central to individual and professional development. Action research, educational/school effectiveness research and school improvement research are critiqued in terms of both their methodological features and their contribution to the study of education.

Introduction

Chapters 1 and 2 established that education is a broad area of study involving a number of disciplines. Research from within these disciplines may provide discrete lessons for the student of education or it may overlap and interweave in a complex manner. The questions which interest education researchers often relate to these specific disciplines. For example, some are interested in the individual, how learning takes place and the cognitive processes involved while others may wish to examine social issues such as the ways in which ethnicity, gender and class continue to be significant in terms of 'success' in education. Yet others decide to examine the policies of successive governments and the influence these have had on practice in different sectors of education. The skills to investigate and gather information in the pursuit of these research foci require a working knowledge of the research process. This chapter will consider research in relation to the study of education. It should be read in conjunction with specific methodological texts (for example, Burton and Bartlett, 2009) for practical details of how to construct research projects and devise particular research instruments.

The nature of research

What is research?

Formal research is simply a systematic approach to the data gathering, synthesis and evaluation that we engage in on a daily basis to make sense of the world in which we operate. The 'data collection methods' we typically use include observing situations and events, watching the television, asking questions of other people, increasingly via social media, looking things up in books or, more likely, surfing the web. The goal may be simple and straightforward such as to find out what the weather will be like the next day. It may involve gathering data from several sources, perhaps asking a number of different friends about a controversial occurrence that we missed. We realise, of course, the subtle differences that asking such friends individually, or in certain combinations, would make to the information gleaned.

Local opinion, regional newspapers and international news are all useful but for different interests and purposes. As media channels and web-based information proliferate, in our everyday lives we are required to become more sophisticated and discerning in our judgements about the information presented to us. We are constantly checking, modifying, refining and developing what we know. Thus our skills as researchers directly influence the outcomes of our daily evaluation of information and these skills improve with practice. We become skilled at analysing and evaluating data, making decisions as to its validity or truthfulness. We are aware that information gathered may vary and even conflict and we give more credence to some sources than to others. We expect to hear different accounts of the same issue dependant on the source and we become adept at using all of these accounts to achieve a full understanding of the situation. At a simple level, we all appreciate that reports of the efficiency of the local rail service, for example, will differ according to whether we listen to our neighbours or the service provider.

We evaluate and store or disregard all information presented to us. Different types of research results are presented by the media to help inform our opinions and enable us to make decisions about smoking or not smoking, drug and alcohol use or which trainers to buy. We accept some data more readily than others and though we may enjoy certain noteworthy TV adverts, such as for a particular deodorant, we still remain sceptical of its claims for increasing our sexual magnetism! Presentation impacts differently on people and is a major concern of the advertiser. This is worth remembering when we begin to look at how academic or formal research is presented. This chapter will suggest that we must consider many ways of looking at things and maintain a healthily critical approach to all research findings. No research into aspects of education, no matter how detailed, extensive and apparently objective, can tell the whole story. All research is positioned.

Formal research

The process of academic or formal research has come to be seen as something which others (usually very learned or expertly trained) do. What does the term 'research' mean when used in relation to academic study? Let us begin by considering some definitions of research.

Reader Reflection: Definitions of research

Consider the different aspects of research that these three definitions emphasise:

1. 'Research is a form of disciplined enquiry leading to the generation of knowledge' (Koshy, 2010: 1).
2. 'Research is not just about gathering information, it is also about analysing and *interpreting* that information and using it to make predictions or to build theories about the way the world works – or parts of it at least!' (Evans and King, 2006: 131).
3. 'Social research is the systematic analysis of research questions by using empirical methods (e.g. of asking, observing, analysing data). Its aim is to make empirically grounded statements that can be generalised or to test such statements' (Flick, 2015: 5).

Research has attained a high degree of respectability and educators, politicians, business people and others turn to researchers when seeking information on which to base decisions. Most advanced societies have evolved a research-oriented culture, or are in the process of moving in that direction. Formal research, then, would appear to be the systematic gathering, presenting and analysing of data. Actually, some research methods are more systematic than others. Some research methods are more formalised than others. The process can appear mysterious to 'outsiders', making researchers seem special and somehow different. It is important to 'demystify' the process in the rest of this chapter since we are all players of the research game.

Academic research essentially refines the information-gathering practices of daily living. Watching other people becomes observation, asking questions becomes interviewing. If the questions are written down they are called questionnaires. The difference is that these information-gathering practices are carried out in a more conscious manner. They become more structured, rigorous and deliberate. The findings are recorded systematically and with care. The research methods are formalised for a number of possible motives: to make more 'scientific', to make larger scale, to make more authoritative, to 'prove', to inform action, to take further than individual experiences. Research, however complex or formally presented, is simply a part of the process of finding out and understanding phenomena.

Ontology

Ontology is an understanding of how the world exists. Benton and Craib say that 'an ontology is the answer one would give to the question: what kind of things are there in the world?' (2011: 4). Bryman points out that the basic ontological issues are about 'whether the social world is regarded as something external to social actors or as something that people are in the process of fashioning' (2012: 19). Thus ontology is about how we see the world and our place within it. We may see it as fixed and clear, with social structures to which we all belong in our society, or we may see it as very fluid and something that is different for each of us, existing as separate individuals.

Epistemology

Epistemology is sometimes called 'the theory of knowledge' (Biesta, 2015). It is about how knowledge is created and what is seen to be legitimate knowledge. Bryman (2012) suggests that a basic epistemological issue is whether or not a natural scientific approach is suitable for studying the social world. Some researchers suggest that the social world can be studied according to the same principles and procedures as the natural world. Others would argue that the social world is very different from the natural world and different principles of understanding need to be applied. Thus how we believe the world exists (our ontology) will be closely linked to how we see knowledge being created and suitable means of understanding it (our epistemology). Our epistemology will lead us to the suitable methods used to study it and our understanding of the whole research process.

Research process

Research may be presented in a flow diagram as in Figure 3.1.

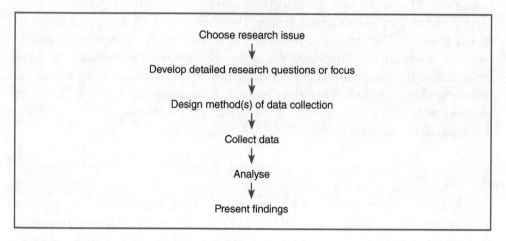

Figure 3.1   **The research process**

Research appears here as far neater, more orderly and more controlled than it actually is. The influence of personal values on the process is also ignored. Every stage in the process can turn out differently if alternative choices are made by the researchers. Just as the whole notion of education is informed by different beliefs and values, so too is the way we study and research it. The education researcher has to make decisions throughout the process which will reflect their ideologies and beliefs concerning both education and research.

Research paradigms

Understandings of how the world exists, what counts as legitimate knowledge and how we research it takes us on to the idea of research paradigms. Paradigms constitute a coherent set of ideas and approaches which are imbued with distinctive sets of values and beliefs. They reflect general agreement on the nature of the world and how to investigate it. Within a paradigm there would be a general consensus on the research methods that are appropriate and acceptable for gathering data and also those that are not, or are at least less, acceptable.

In social sciences research is often divided into two major paradigms, the positivist or quantitative and the interpretivist or qualitative; these are presented as polar opposites (Aliyu et al., 2014). They are perhaps best seen as characteristics clustering into two general groups rather than as clear extremes, as an overly dualist approach doesn't take into account the complex reality of research which often does not fit neatly into a single paradigm.

Positivist paradigm

This paradigm developed in the nineteenth century with the apparent success of the natural, or physical, sciences in advancing human understanding of the world. Scientific advances had led to improvements in many areas of people's lives, notable examples being in the field of health and medicine, and had contributed to increased standards of living.

The scientific approach consists of testing a hypothesis (initial idea, unproved theory) by the experimental method. This often involves having two identical groups. The control group remains untouched – nothing is done to it and all factors which could affect it (variables) are kept constant. The other group, the experimental group, is subject to some change in conditions (certain specific variables are altered in a controlled way). Any resulting change between the experimental and the control group must be due to the change in the variables made by the scientist in the experiment. Experiments are able to establish cause and effect relationships. Altering a particular variable has a particular, measurable effect.

The findings from experiments in the natural sciences are said to be objective, in other words the opinions and hopes of the researcher cannot influence the results of a controlled experiment. The outcome of the experiment, if carried out under the same conditions, will always be consistent. Natural science is systematic, experiments are repeatable, the results are documented and knowledge of the natural world is incremental, being built up over time. Research in the natural sciences thus has high prestige and the findings are treated with respect. Inevitably pure research in the natural sciences, over time, became an area of applied research, which had the potential to inform future policy. Such a status was regarded as desirable by those interested in the social world; consequently interest grew in developing the social sciences.

The positivist belief is that the approach of the natural sciences could be applied to the social world. It assumes that the social world exists in the same way as does the natural world (Bryman, 2012; Punch and Oancea, 2014).

Individual behaviour is continually influenced by various pressures upon us. These may be internal pressures, such as biological and psychological, and/or external pressures, such as the norms and values held by the social groups to which we belong. As a result, regular and predictable patterns of behaviour can be said to be displayed by individuals and groups in society.

Positivists believe that the structures which create the apparent order in social life can be discovered by research. They contend that society can be investigated in the same objective way as the natural world. The approach is empirical in that it shows something exists through observations, that is, data. Going beyond theory and debate, positivist researchers attempt to show that what is being discussed in the theories actually exists because it has the status of the external; it is not just hypothetical. The purpose is to uncover the 'social facts' which make up our world (see Durkheim, 1964; 1970; 2014).

To be objective, the positivist social science researcher would ideally like to conduct experiments in the same way as the natural scientist. Some educational research is able to use this method, for instance certain psychological experiments. However, for much social research it is not possible to create experimental and control groups and to alter variables in a controlled way. People need to be studied in their usual environment if they are to act 'naturally'. Much of the seminal work of the Swiss psychologist, Piaget (1932; 1952) was based on experiments conducted with his own children in 'laboratory' conditions which have since been criticised for their inappropriateness. There are also moral objections to treating people in certain ways, so although it might appear to be interesting to deprive babies of human affection and see how their personalities develop, it would not be allowed in our society.

In order to show relationships between variables researchers frequently use the comparative method. This is where groups are compared and differences are noted. The purpose is to identify significant variables which explain the differences between the groups. The aim ultimately is to show cause and effect relationships. This strategy is felt to be more reliable the greater the numbers used in the comparison. Thus the sample size and its representativeness of the whole population being studied are important factors for the positivist. The findings become more significant when the amount of data collected is larger and can be presented in ways that aid categorisation and comparison. It is important that the researcher maintains an objective standpoint and keeps personal 'contamination' of the data collection process to a minimum. The most effective positivist research is able to be replicated by others, as with experiments in the natural sciences, or at least compared closely with other similar studies. For these reasons positivist research- ers prefer structured methods of data collection which can be carried out on a large scale (macro studies). The favoured data is quantitative, usually presented as statistical tables. This enables others to see how the data has been interpreted and allows for more accurate comparisons. It also attempts to minimise the effect of the particular researcher. The aim is to be able to generalise from the findings.

Certain criticisms have been levelled at the positivist paradigm and the use of statistics in social science research:

- Statistics may show trends but they do not explain why people have done or said certain things. They are unable to yield detailed accounts of people's reasons, thus the meanings obtained from statistical data remain superficial. Statistics of truancy, absence or examination success may show interesting trends but it is the stories behind them that explain these trends. In this way statistics may be seen as impersonal. Positivist methods may ignore the richness of detailed individual accounts.
- Statistical correlations should not be confused with causality. There may be statistical relations between social deprivation and lack of educational success but we need to go further than statistical analysis to see if the link is real and to seek explanations.
- Statistical tables and analysis appear to be objective but the significance of individual researchers in their compilation must not be overlooked. A researcher decides what to look for, designs and asks certain questions yet ignores other possibilities. The statistics have to be collected and the answers interpreted and categorised. It would be dangerous to assume that this whole process is unaffected by human contamination.

See Scott and Usher (2011) for an exposition of strong theoretical grounds for challenging the objectivity and scientific claims of positivist approaches to education research.

Interpretivist paradigm

This is an umbrella term for many social perspectives, notably phenomenology, symbolic interactionism and ethnomethodology (see Denscombe, 2014, and Flick, 2015, for a discussion of these). This paradigm does not hold that society has a fixed structure, hidden or not. The social world is created by the interactions of individuals. There are norms and values but these do not exist as clear-cut entities. They are used and changed by people as part of their daily lives. People, termed actors by some interpretivists, interpret events and act in response. Though there are external pressures upon individuals we are not seen to be controlled by some external system. Weber (see Bruun and Whimster, 2013) maintained that actions must be seen as meaningful at the level of interaction. By this he meant that action is taken to be deliberate and meaningful to those involved and the interpretivist paradigm seeks to understand the meanings behind these actions.

The interpretivist tries to show how choices are made by participants or 'actors' in social situations within the process of interaction. For the interpretivist there is no one objective reality which exists outside of the actor's explanations, just different versions of events. Pupils, the classroom teacher, other teachers at the school, parents, all have a view of 'what goes on' and act according to how they interpret events. The researcher in this paradigm seeks to 'understand' these actions.

Interpretivists prefer more 'naturalistic' forms of data collection, making use of individual accounts and biographies and often including detailed descriptions to give a 'feeling' for the environment. Methods favoured in interpretivist studies are informal interviews and observations which allow the situation to be as 'normal' as possible. These methods are often reliant upon the ability of the researcher to be reflexive in the research process. Interpretivist studies tend to be small in scale (micro), aiming for detail and understanding rather than statistical representativeness. While it is not possible to generalise from such studies, researchers in this paradigm do attempt to be as rigorous as possible.

Woods suggests that qualitative research focuses on natural settings and is 'concerned with life as it is lived, things as they happen, situations as they are constructed in the day-to-day, moment-to-moment course of events' (2006: 2). The researcher seeks to understand and to portray the participants' perceptions and understandings of the particular situation or event. Interaction is ongoing and there is a continuing chain of events which gives insight into how people live and the research emphasises this process.

Woods (2006) also cites the important part played by inductive analysis and grounded theory in qualitative research.

The term 'grounded theory' comes from the work of Glaser and Strauss (1967). Birks and Mills (2015) suggested that in qualitative studies the researchers do not begin hoping to prove or disprove a set hypothesis. They may have ideas on how 'things will go' but the theory comes from the data they have collected after the research has begun. It is 'grounded' in the data and the experiences of the researcher rather than being imposed upon the research before commencement.

In summary, qualitative research seeks in-depth understandings of the meanings individuals and groups ascribe to social events and actions. It seeks to understand the nature and complexity of social interaction. Inevitably there are criticisms of qualitative research; these focus on the small-scale nature of such studies, the relativity of their findings and the inability to quantify or measure their results.

Ethnography

This is a research strategy sometimes adopted by interpretivists which developed from anthropological studies of small-scale societies and social groups (Silverman, 2013). The spread of this approach can be seen as a reaction to the dominance of positivism in social science. Ethnography is characterised by 'thick' descriptive accounts of the activities of particular groups studied. Accounts focus on the micro, spending much time looking at small groups and particular institutions.

For Walford (2009), ethnography takes into account the wider cultural context in which individuals or groups exist and live, as part of seeking to understand their behaviour and values. Fieldwork takes numerous forms and researchers gather data from many sources, with particular reliance on 'naturalistic' interpretive methods, such as participant observation and informal interviews. This is to develop a multidimensional appreciation of these cultures and individuals. The researcher must have a long-term engagement with the situation to observe developments first hand and to experience the culture. Paradoxically the researcher should also attempt to view cultures dispassionately and to step outside their situation at times. This has been termed as viewing situations as 'anthropologically strange' (see Hammersley and Atkinson, 2007). Thus Walford (2009) sees ethnographic researchers developing their theoretical accounts over time as they conduct their ethnography. The aim is to construct an account that gives a deep and rich appreciation of the people who have been studied. Central to the description and analysis in ethnography are the views and perceptions of the actors.

This research strategy, then, studies groups and individuals in their natural settings, considers the perspectives of those involved and the culture they are living in, uses a wide range of methods to develop a deep understanding and produces accounts which both actors and researchers recognise.

Approaches to the research process and the type of data considered acceptable very much depend upon how those carrying out the research see the world. Much falls within the two paradigms of positivism and interpretivism but sometimes this dichotomy proves to be rather too simplistic, ignoring a multitude of variations (see Creswell, 2014, and Pring, 2015). Several proponents of action research suggest that this two-paradigm view of research emanates from a traditional academic approach and they are critical of its application to professionally based research. McNiff and Whitehead (2010; 2011), for instance, suggest critical theoretical and living theory approaches as being more appropriate. Clough and Nutbrown (2012) suggest that research studies often move between these paradigms, selecting the most appropriate for different parts of the study.

Reader Reflection: Research paradigms

Below is a comparison of the positivist and interpretivist paradigms.

Positivist	Interpretivist
Natural science	Naturalistic
Objective	Ethnographic
Macro	Micro
External structure	Created by actors
One reality	Multiple realities
Quantitative data	Qualitative data
Questionnaires and structured methods	Unstructured interviews and observations

How easily do you think research falls into one or the other?

Purposes of research

Clough and Nutbrown (2012) explain that all social research is persuasive, purposive, positional and political and these are the reasons why it is conducted. The need to persuade someone or a group of people about something underlies all research, whether it is persuading customers to buy a particular product or persuading teachers of a particular teaching method. Research is purposive in that it attempts to produce something such as the solution to a problem. Research is positional because it is imbued with the perspective of the researcher and the research funders and is derived from a set of circumstances where a problem was defined necessarily from a particular viewpoint or position. They observe that 'since research is carried out by people, it is inevitable that the standpoint of the researcher is a fundamental platform on which enquiry is developed. All social science research is saturated (however disguised) with positionality' (Clough and Nutbrown, 2012: 10). Finally, research is political because it seeks to make a difference within a policy context. Practitioner researchers, for instance, may seek to change the behaviour policy of a school based on research they have conducted into the efficiency of sanctions.

Positioning of the researcher and critique of research

Our individual position will influence how we approach research. There will be certain issues that will appeal to us more than others and there will be particular types of data that we will find more meaningful. Some researchers believe that their approach is best and will decide to spurn any alternatives. Others, while still preferring their own way, will realise some of the strengths of the alternatives and maintain a more 'tolerant' position of different approaches. Our aim must be to remain as rigorous as possible in our approach, be open to scrutiny at all times and always to act ethically.

Title:	
Author(s):	
Date:	
Aims/abstract and findings: • What are the purposes of the research? • Are they clearly stated? • What are the key research findings? • How do the research/findings add to our knowledge?	
Standpoint: • Is the ontological position taken clear? • Is the epistemological position clear?	
Data collection: • Is sufficient detail given of the methods of data collection used? • Are the methods of data collection appropriate to author's standpoint? • Are they sufficient and ethical? • Are any assertions and conclusions substantiated by the data?	
Worthiness: • Does the article achieve what it set out to do? • Was the research worthwhile?	
References: • Were an appropriate number and variety of references used to support the research? • Are any of these references worth pursuing?	

Figure 3.2   **A framework for the critique of research papers**

It is important to be able to critique research reports and articles when investigating any area of education studies. After all, we can't accept the findings of research reports at face value. Some research projects are very small scale and have been conducted over a comparatively short period of time while others may have enjoyed significant funding. Critique is not about being critical or negative per se but is a process of evaluation of a piece of research in order to assess the significance of its findings. It is about considering the strengths as well as the weaknesses of the research, acknowledging the approach and positioning of the researcher, judging to what extent any findings are supported by the evidence and, ultimately, deciding if the research adds a worthwhile contribution to knowledge and debate in the area. The pro forma shown in Figure 3.2 is a useful aide-memoir to be used in the critique of research reports and articles.

Research methods

There are many ways in which information can be obtained and a list of the most common might include:

- experimental test scores
- interviews
- questionnaires
- observation – structured or ethnographic
- blogs/diaries by researchers
- blogs/diaries by respondents
- personal biographies
- photographs
- video recordings
- content analysis (of student work or texts)
- documents
- official records and statistics
- student examination results.

Each of these can, of course, be subdivided many times as there are so many variations within each category. In deciding which methods to use the researcher will acknowledge the relative data collection time and associated expense of each method. Some methods may not be possible because of the particular circumstances of the study: for instance, the researcher may not be allowed access to observe certain confidential interviews between the head teacher and parents or other members of staff. Researchers are likely to prefer particular forms of data and thus favour certain research methods over others depending on the paradigm they are working within. They may have to make difficult compromises but ultimately will have to decide what is appropriate in terms of the type of research they wish to conduct. It may seem sensible to take an eclectic approach. However, this can only be acceptable up to a point. 'Mixing' data can be useful but it may be inappropriate to use quantitative methods when a qualitative approach is what the researcher favours and vice versa.

Space does not permit a detailed examination of each research method here. Reference to a specialist methodology text is advisable for this. We will now examine briefly three of the more popular methods of gathering data as well as some important research concepts and strategies.

Data gathering methods

Questionnaires

This is a useful method, if carefully planned, for obtaining large numbers of responses relatively quickly and, as such, may be seen as providing quantitative data. It is more difficult to obtain in-depth personal responses by this method and so it is less useful for the qualitative researcher. A questionnaire is simply a list of questions. These can be presented to the respondents in different ways: they may be read out by the researcher who writes down or records the answers electronically. Alternatively, they may be sent by post with a stamped addressed envelope for the reply or they may be given out and collected later by the researcher (Fowler, 2014). Text and email can also be used.

Strengths of questionnaires in data collection

- It is possible to gather large amounts of data relatively quickly.
- The researcher can compare the responses to particular questions by individuals or between different groups of respondents.
- The data can be expressed statistically. It is thus possible to make comparisons with other studies.
- The research may enable overall statements concerning the population to be made, for example the percentage who left school at 18, the percentage who gained certain qualifications, the numbers who felt that they were bullied at school.

(Continued)

(Continued)

Weaknesses of questionnaires in data collection

- Questions about complex issues are difficult to compose.
- Respondents may not find it easy to place their responses into specific categories.
- The short responses required often fail to reflect the varying depth or complexity of people's feelings.
- It is the researcher who sets the agenda of questionnaires not the respondent. The questions may create attitudes by asking the respondents to comment on things which they may not previously have considered. Alternatively the questions may not give enough emphasis to areas which the respondents see as important.
- The researcher may attempt to overcome the above problems by adding open-ended questions. Answers to these will need to be codified by the researcher which can lead to the very subjectivity which the questionnaire may well have been chosen to overcome.

Denscombe (2014) gives useful practical advice on questionnaire design.

Interviews

Interviews may take many different forms. They can vary from being highly structured and very formal to being unstructured and so informal that they appear to be little more than conversations between respondent and researcher (for a detailed overview see Bell, 2014, or Denscombe, 2014).

In the more structured interview the researcher follows a set format with fixed questions. How much they are able to adapt each interview to varying circumstances is decided beforehand but it may be very little. This approach allows for a team of interviewers to interview a large number of respondents and for the results to be standardised. This really is a further development of the questionnaire and is likely to provide quantitative as well as some qualitative data.

Where the researcher prefers the emphasis to be on the respondent's account, a less structured approach is likely to be taken, perhaps relying on a few fixed questions and prompts. The interview may be very informal so it becomes, to all intents and purposes, like a normal conversation. Here the respondents may be very open but the researcher must be careful not to lead them. These less structured interviews are favoured by the qualitative researcher. The most 'natural' interactions between the researcher and the respondent may take place during participant observation or a chance meeting during a case study.

Before carrying out interviews several considerations must be addressed, from the form of the interview and the role of the interviewer to how the data will be recorded and analysed. Crucially the interviewer must determine who to interview. For example, are the views of the head teacher more significant than those of a Year 7 pupil? Certainly the head has more power within the school but it depends upon what is being researched.

Strengths of interviews in data collection

- They can be adaptable to different situations and respondents.
- The interviewer can 'pick up' non-verbal clues which would not be possible from questionnaires, for example annoyance or pleasure shown by the respondent over certain topics.
- The researcher can 'follow hunches' and different unexpected lines of enquiry as they come up during the interview; for example, issues of bullying may become apparent that had not been mentioned or suspected before the start of the study.
- The researcher can obtain detailed qualitative data expressed in the respondent's own words.

Weaknesses of interviews in data collection

- The interviewer may significantly affect the responses. They may influence or lead the respondent.
- Interviews can take a great deal of time and may be difficult to set up. This will restrict the number it is possible to carry out.
- The more unstructured they are the more variation there is between interviews. This makes comparing data more difficult.

Observation

The type of phenomenon to be observed and the perspective of the observer will be key factors in determining the methods of observation selected. The observation may be formal and overt as in many psychological experiments where the researcher notes the reactions of respondents to certain stimulations. Similarly, though separate and at the back of the room, Ofsted inspectors, with their clipboards, are observing the lesson overtly. Observation may also be formal and covert with those being observed unaware of the observer. Here the 'action' may be observed through CCTV cameras, two-way mirrors or the observer may just not be noticed in the crowd. The observer may take part in the proceedings with the subjects of the observation sometimes knowing they are a researcher and sometimes not. Teacher researchers may 'help' in another teacher's classroom while unobtrusively observing.

The techniques employed in the collecting of data are very important in this approach. The observer may be noting events as they occur openly or they may have to remember them to be written up as soon as possible afterwards. The more formal the observation the more detailed a tally chart is devised. The Flanders observation schedule, for instance, is very detailed and will yield quantitative data to be analysed. The schedule proposed by the Quality Assurance Agency to observe teaching in higher education has fixed categories that the observer has to write in. With the more informal observations the schedules become looser in outline until, in full participant observation, the observer is making mental notes under broad headings to write up later.

Thus observation may be formal or informal. It may yield certain amounts of quantitative data or it may concentrate on qualitative descriptions. Much depends upon how the observation is designed by the researcher. Ethically the researcher must be sensitive to the situation. It is less appropriate, for instance, to use overt formal observation methods when researching the counselling of pupils than it is in a formal lesson.

Strengths of observation in data collection

- It is possible to see how people behave in 'natural' situations.
- The researcher can see whether the subjects in the observation act as they say they do.
- An observer can gather large amounts of data in a short time.

Weaknesses of observation in data collection

- Gaining access to situations which would be useful to observe can prove difficult. For example, bullying takes place secretively or only when the observer has 'infiltrated' the group. Outside observers are not normally allowed into confidential discussions such as teacher appraisal interviews.
- It is difficult to observe and record at the same time. For example, Flanders observation analysis used by Ball (1981) in Beachside Comprehensive requires recordings to be taken every three seconds.
- Sometimes it is difficult to categorise behaviour if schedules are being used. It is not always possible to understand actions by observation alone, for example why a teacher treats children differently. A follow-up interview may be needed. This may actually turn a weakness into a strength by providing a fuller analysis.
- The observer may affect the situation. Did we behave as usual when the inspector was in the lesson?
- There are ethical issues of observing people if they do not know that they are being observed. It can be seen as a form of spying.

Any research method can be analysed in similar ways to the three we have out-lined. Fundamentally, research design is a creative activity in which the researcher crafts an approach which is determined by their perspective as well as by the answers to the host of questions raised above. The outcomes of any research are a result of the approach of, and decisions made by, the researcher.

Important research concepts

We now turn to a discussion of the importance of reliability and validity, funda-mental concepts of great significance, in education research. Triangulation is outlined as a significant strategy that can be applied in order to increase the valid-ity of the findings.

Reliability

Reliability describes the extent to which a research instrument or method is repeatable. It is an assessment of the consistency of any method (Punch and Oancea, 2014). Thus the reliability of a measure is the extent to which respond-ents will consistently respond to it in the same way. In other words the more reliable the method of data collection the more likely it is to give similar results in subsequent administrations. An unreliable measure will yield different results every time it is administered.

Positivist researchers who wish to carry out large-scale research are most con-cerned with reliability. The methods need to be capable of being applied to large numbers of respondents in order to generate the data required. To be able to make the desired statistical comparisons the collection of data needs to be consistent, i.e. reliable. In contrast, the interpretivist researcher is likely to be more concerned with the suitability of the methods for eliciting qualitative, accurate and detailed accounts from each respondent. Clearly, then, the emphasis on reliability varies according to the paradigm of the researcher.

It should be noted that a high level of reliability of a data collection instru-ment does not necessarily mean that it is accurate. For instance, if a tutor asks students to evaluate the course by named questionnaire and they are aware that the tutor will shortly be marking their assignments, this is likely to concentrate their minds. Not surprisingly the tutor will have positive student feedback. While this method can be said to be reliable, in that its questions are similarly understood by successive cohorts of students and thus it is always measuring the same thing, its accuracy in terms of the truthfulness of the student responses may be suspect.

Validity

Validity and its measurement plays an important part in determining the appropriate methodology to employ. Validity refers to the 'truthfulness', 'correctness' or accuracy of research data. If results are to be considered accurate the research instrument must measure what we claim it to measure. According to Punch and Oancea (2014: 297): 'An indicator is valid to the extent that it empirically represents the concept it purports to measure'. For instance, tests of mathematical ability might actually be producing results which are indicative of the ability to read the questions rather than mathematical prowess. If the methods are at fault then the findings will be invalid and the research worthless. In aiming to increase validity positivists emphasise the standardisation of data collection while using as large a sample as possible. Thus the piloting of any method for accuracy is very important.

Another approach to validity, more associated with an interpretivist approach, places emphasis on the final account and how the researcher is able to defend the interpretations they make from the data (see Richards, 2015). In other words, the researcher needs to show on what evidence they base their findings. This can be done in a number of ways such as giving full explanations as to how data were gathered, member checks (Creswell, 2014) whereby research participants are asked if their accounts have been recorded accurately, and reducing researcher bias by giving a colleague samples of all data collected to verify the analysis and conclusions drawn by the researcher. In action research the openness of the findings to scrutiny and discussion by fellow practitioners is seen as a significant part of ensuring the validity of what is often small-scale research carried out by researchers who are themselves part of the research project (McNiff, 2013).

Reader Reflection: The use of educational statistics

Educational statistics are social constructs whose collection may be dependent on a number of factors, for example political agendas, practical reasons and specific methodologies. These factors, together with potential omissions, approximations or delusions, should lead users of statistics to question their reliability and validity. (Carpentier, 2008: 704)

Visit the Department for Education (DfE) website. Search for data sets on areas that may interest you such as school league tables of performance, GCSE results or pupil performance in key stage assessments.

Consider the reliability and validity of these in the light of the comments made above by Carpentier.

Triangulation

Triangulation is a navigational term which means to fix one's position from two known bearings. This process is carried out by researchers to increase the validity of their research and it means checking their findings by using several points of reference. In effect, the researcher is approaching the object of the research from as many different angles and perspectives as possible in order to gain a greater understanding (Flick, 2015). Researchers can triangulate by using a number of different fieldworkers in the collection and analysis of data, by seeking the contribution of varied groups of respondents such as pupils, teachers and parents, by using a range of research methods, by considering qualitative and quantitative data and so on. Miles and Huberman pointed to triangulation as a way of life. If findings were consciously checked and double-checked using different sources of evidence then verification would be built in:

> by seeing or hearing multiple instances of it from different sources, by using different methods and by squaring the finding with others it needs to be squared with. (1994: 267)

The positivist would hope to demonstrate congruence of results from triangulation. The interpretivist would use the different sources of data to give greater depth to their analysis, corroborating or leading to discussion of variation in the findings (Creswell, 2014). Thus for Hammersley and Atkinson (2007: 232) triangulation is:

> an attempt to relate different sorts of data in such a way as to counteract various possible threats to the validity of our analysis.

Certainly both paradigms would suggest the use of triangulation to increase the validity of their findings but would use it in slightly different ways. In order to produce a more thorough and rigorous piece of research several research methods are often used in conjunction with one another. The main methods, in fact, often complement each other. For instance, what has been seen during observations can be probed by the researcher in subsequent interviews. This will give an understanding of why something happened as well as a descriptive account. Triangulation is likely to appear as almost a natural process to practitioners who are used to considering different viewpoints and obtaining data from several sources in order to more fully understand particular incidents or aspects of their daily work.

Research strategies

Systematic review and meta-analyses

As the world has become a global village in terms of what is available to us via the internet, and as open access publishing becomes more commonplace, students of education have access to an ever increasing number of studies conducted all over the world. While this can widen our knowledge and enable comparisons across countries, it also makes it even more important to adopt an enquiring, critical stance to the issues we discuss. The sheer volume of studies available and the requirement to discover key findings from the most rigorous and valid studies has led to an interesting development in the form of systematic reviewing, a process which is often funded by research councils or organisations which are trying to determine a specific course of action and want reassurance that a wide range of research backs up their decisions. Systematic reviewers examine studies within a certain field of enquiry and synthesise the key findings that emerge into a meta-analysis. They use a rigorous process of selection and validation of that selection, documenting very precisely their literature search terms and strategies so that their findings are reliable and are valuable to others. Hundreds of relevant studies can be included.

While we can see the value in this approach, sometimes competing meta-analyses are produced for the same research question by researchers from opposing viewpoints. One group might critique the meta-analysis of another research group, claiming they were biased in their selection of studies in order to prove their hypothesis. Nevertheless systematic reviews and meta-analyses are increasingly commissioned and relied upon by policy-makers.

> The extent and scale of research conducted is now so vast that research leaders organise teams to undertake syntheses or meta-analyses *of* the meta-analyses! To give you an idea of scale, John Hattie (2009), an Australian psychologist, produced a synthesis of 800 meta-analyses of studies on student achievement based on 50,000 research studies involving millions of learners which we refer to later in this book.

You can easily search for systematic reviews into educational issues (see for example, Oliver et al.'s (2014) systematic review of interventions targeting youth not in employment, education or training (NEET) populations). Reading such reviews is a useful way of seeking out information for your assignments but, as ever, look critically at these reviews, consider who funded them and why and for whom they were conducted.

Case studies

The case study approach is a research strategy where the researcher aims to study one case in depth. Work in the legal and medical professions is very much based upon case studies (see Thomas, 2015, for a discussion of the use of cases in varying contexts). Here particular cases are examined, usually in order to produce a solution or cure to the issue in question. Each case is unique, which is what makes them so interesting. However, the professionals involved are able to draw upon their knowledge of previous similar cases in order to understand the one currently being examined and to help them decide upon an appropriate ruling or action. For instance, since the law allowed parents to be prosecuted for truancy the first test case which resulted in a mother being imprisoned has provided case law for similar prosecutions to be tested against.

Practitioners in these fields, in developing case studies, draw upon their own experience and documented accounts of previous cases to help them to analyse, explain and where appropriate suggest action. Their own findings can in turn be added to a growing body of case histories. What actually constitutes a case is defined by the researcher and can vary enormously in size. The case could be a local authority (LA), a school, a class or a particular pupil.

By concentrating on a particular case or cases, data is usually collected using several methods. Blaxter et al. (2010) suggest that in this way the case study approach is ideally suited to the needs and resources of a small-scale researcher. Simons (2009), while stressing the qualitative approach to 'understanding' cases, points out that using quantitative data and secondary sources may also be seen as appropriate. As Yin (2014) notes, the forms that the data collected will take essentially depend upon the nature of the particular case to be investigated. In this way triangulation automatically takes place thereby increasing the validity of the study.

A major criticism of case studies is that they lack representativeness of the wider population and thus researchers are unable to make generalisations from their findings. However, proponents claim the importance of the case study approach is the in-depth analysis and the understanding gained. For these researchers, the strength of this research approach lies in the 'relatability' of the findings (Bassey, 1990). By this term Bassey is suggesting that although each case may be unique there are sufficient similarities to make the findings from one study useful when seeking to understand others.

Case studies often provide fascinating reading due to the richness of the data. Examples of the use of case studies in education research include the seminal work of Ball (1981) and Lacey (1970), both of whom explored particular schools, and Willis (1979) who studied a group of teenage boys within a school. Detailed school studies like these are far less likely to be conducted today due to difficulties in obtaining research funding for anything not directly linked to pupil performance. Also, in the current climate of competition between schools, head teachers are less likely to allow researchers into their schools for fear of 'unflattering' findings being made public. Thus research is bounded by what is possible at different periods in time.

Ethical considerations

There are always ethical considerations that must be addressed before embarking upon a research project and also taken into account while the project is ongoing. Researchers may find themselves in a potentially powerful position socially when they have been gathering data in a particular community and care needs to be taken that they do not abuse this privileged position. Researchers should also be aware that the questioning and probing involved in data collection during research can have significant effects on the respondents' daily lives. The British Educational Research Association (BERA, 2011: 4) suggests 'that all educational research should be conducted within an ethic of respect for:

- the person
- knowledge
- democratic values
- the quality of educational research
- academic freedom'.

BERA sets out guidelines concerning the researcher's responsibilities to participants in the research, to sponsors of research, to the wider community of educational researchers and to educational professionals, policy-makers and the general public. Key ethical considerations include:

- securing the consent of those involved
- the openness of the researcher and the research process
- access to the findings by those who have been involved in the research
- the possible effects of the research on participants during the project and in the future
- ensuring the anonymity of those involved.

Those working and researching in fields such as education, social work and medicine are continually presented with ethical dilemmas. For instance, discovering through interviews information concerning the drug use, sexual activity or other deviant behaviour of pupils presents the researcher/teacher with the dilemma of protecting confidential sources or reporting such activity to parents and the 'authorities'. It is important that all researchers take an ethical stance in their research and only act in a way that they can morally justify, even though this may not always be easy (see Maguire et al., 2014, for a discussion of this).

Reader Reflection: Ethical approaches to research

Wiles suggests that 'Ethical behavior in research demands that researchers engage with moral issues of right and wrong' (2013: 12).

Can you think of instances when behaving in ways that are 'right' might prevent you from finding out what you wish to?

Research methodology: some conclusions

- Many research methods can be used to collect data. Even within particular method types there is enormous variation.
- The researcher may use or adapt an existing research instrument. In many cases the researcher designs their own instrument.
- Researchers make decisions concerning the methodology to be used in the light of the type of data they require.
- Practical constraints, such as time, money and the nature of the respondent group, will be significant factors to be taken into account when designing the research.
- The data collected will be a reflection of the decisions made by, and the skills of, the researcher.
- Researchers aim to be as rigorous as possible but inevitably their beliefs and assumptions can affect research.
- Large-scale research projects are not necessarily better than small-scale projects.
- The researcher needs to address ethical issues including the confidentiality of data collected and gaining consent as appropriate.

The design of a piece of research is thus highly significant to the data obtained. Some central influences on this design are the perspective of the researcher, the decisions made due to the nature of the group to be studied, and the resources available to carry out the research. We will now consider, briefly, some recent significant research 'movements' in education.

Education research/educational research

Education, whether in its informal or its more formal institutionalised guises, constitutes a significant part of society and social life so there are many academic subjects interested in it as an area of study and research. For example, historians in their studies of processes over time have looked at developments in and influences of education, sociologists have studied the part that education plays in the structure of society and the power relationships it involves, psychology helps to explain aspects of individual development, and economists have an interest in the development of the workforce and study education as a product to be demanded and supplied as part of market behaviour. These subjects can perhaps be seen as more traditional areas of academic study. They are often loosely termed social sciences, are closely related to each other and overlap. This type of research into education is often termed education research.

Some education researchers are actively involved in the education process itself, e.g. a teacher whose research is often related to teaching and learning and shows a desire to make improvements to existing practice, educational experiences, opportunities and achievement. Such research is frequently termed *educational research*. Elliott (2006) contrasted educational research, which he sees as shaped by a pragmatic theory of knowledge, with *research on education*, which he suggests is shaped by 'spectator' theory. Pring (2015) distinguishes between research that is embedded in the social sciences which may well be relevant to education and that which arises from educational concerns and which draws upon the knowledge that has accumulated within those sciences.

Thus there are different types of research stemming from different traditions and with different purposes that may be termed *education* or *educational* research.

Action research

The development of action research

The development of action research is often attributed to the work of Kurt Lewin (1946) who was seeking ways of increasing productivity in industry by involving a larger proportion of the workforce in decision-making. He also saw action research as a way of tackling many of the post-Second World War social problems.

He developed a spiral of action that involved fact finding, planning and execution. This act of professionals conducting research in order to solve professional problems could be easily applied to many areas, education being a prime example.

The action research 'movement' in education in Britain has been greatly influenced by the work of Lawrence Stenhouse at the Schools Council (1967–72). The Schools Council was the forerunner of various government curriculum agencies but, unlike the subsequent National Curriculum Council (NCC) and the Qualifications and Curriculum Authority (QCA), Schools Council members were drawn from academic educationalists and teachers. Stenhouse felt that teachers needed to be at the centre of curriculum development if it was to be effective. Therefore it was essential that teachers reflected upon practice, shared experiences and evaluated their work if the education of pupils was to improve. For Stenhouse, each classroom could be seen as a laboratory and each teacher a member of a research community.

Stenhouse found the 'objectives model' of curriculum design to be uneducational as it assumed knowledge as a given and discouraged wider questioning and individual development while encouraging passive acceptance of the facts as presented. For teachers to appear authoritative and to present subject content as beyond doubt was a misrepresentation encouraged by many in education. He viewed knowledge and its structure as inherently problematic and contestable. For this reason Stenhouse favoured a process model of curriculum design that was based upon learners questioning and exploring in order to gain their own understanding. Teachers themselves, while having knowledge about what they are teaching, are cast in the role of learners alongside their students. For Stenhouse it was this continual questioning and learning by teachers that gave them more to offer their students. In this way learning itself is a research process and research is seen as the basis for teaching (Stenhouse, 1983).

Stenhouse believed in the professional desire of teachers to improve education for their pupils and so benefit society. For this reason he considered teachers the best judges of teaching. By working in research communities they would be able to reflect upon and then improve their practice. Other interested members of the community, such as parents and employers, would in turn be drawn into this research process. In this way a social democratic ideology ran through the work of the Schools Council. Curriculum reform was visualised as happening at the grassroots level and involving all those with a stake in education. Action resulting from the reflective process was regarded as a means of empowering practitioners and therefore central to the professional development of teachers. It is noteworthy that an abhorrence of the notion of empowering teachers and viewing them as education experts was what led to the eventual demise of the Schools Council under the Conservative government of Margaret Thatcher.

Action research grew in part out of disillusionment with traditional forms of educational research that were conducted by the universities during the 1960s and 1970s. These were felt to adopt an academic approach to research and to be of little practical use to those working in classrooms. They took a disengaged stance and offered no help in terms of the practice of teaching. Also, much influential academic research of the time had promoted a view that either innate factors (Jensen, 1973) or wider social circumstances (Douglas, 1964) largely determined overall educational achievement. It was as though schools did not make a difference to pupil attainment and it was the influence of wider social forces on the pupil or natural ability that were seen as the key factors. If anything, schools only reinforced these existing inequalities, acting as processing agencies in which teachers were unwitting players (Bowles and Gintis, 1976). Such research gave little encouragement to teachers about how to change or improve things.

Though closely linked with higher education institutions which provided mentors who were a valuable source of support, action research was seen as a new approach to research carried out by professionals. It was rooted in practice and moved away from the traditional academic approach based upon the major research paradigms. McNiff (1988) spoke of a wish to create a study of education that was grounded in practice and developed by those involved. Teachers were to develop their research skills to evaluate their practice. The process needed to be rigorous and critical if it was to create effective change. Injunctions to become more critical meant far more than simply evaluating practice for many proponents of action research (Carr and Kemmis, 1986). The development of critical theory was seen as a questioning of the whole purpose and techniques employed by teachers. It involved asking fundamental questions about why things are done in a certain way and why other processes are not used. This would encourage further research, experimentation and, ultimately, change. There would be a linking of theory and practice alongside the development of research for action.

Defining action research

According to Elliott (2003), a lifelong proponent, action research is the study of a social situation in order to improve what happens within it. For Colucci-Gray et al. (2013: 127): 'Action research is traditionally conceived as an activity of knowledge generation for teachers engaging in systematic and critical investigation of their practice'.

Action research often starts with a problem, issue or set of questions arising out of professional concerns. Initial research is carried out to collect data that clarifies the situation. A plan of action is devised in the light of this evidence. This is put into place and the effects carefully monitored. This is likely to lead to further refined questions and so further developments which will, in turn, be implemented and researched. However, what was critical for Elliott (2003) is that the action part of improving practice is an integral part of the teacher's construction of new knowledge and understanding of the problem. The action research process has frequently been shown in diagrammatic form as some form of developmental spiral (see Figure 3.3).

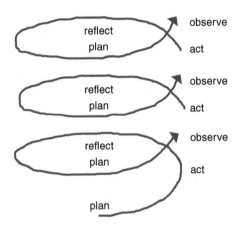

Figure 3.3   McNiff's original model

Source: McNiff, *Action Research Principles and Practice*, 3rd edn., ©2013. Reprinted by permission of Taylor & Francis

Action research is curriculum development at the classroom level. It is concerned with how to improve education practice and it is practitioners themselves who carry out the research in examining and developing their teaching. The nature of this form of practitioner research means that it is carried out in the teacher's own place of work and so the case study approach is the most common. Ideally, an eclectic view of data collection is taken with the researcher using a variety of methods to examine the particular issue. The process whereby researchers are able to use their own understandings to interpret the situations they are investigating is termed *reflexivity*. This is an important aspect of action research and it is expected that the reflexivity of the researchers will be heightened as they develop their research skills.

Increased validity is aimed at through a rigorous approach to the research coupled with triangulation and openness at all stages of the process. Validity is also strengthened as communities of researchers in schools examine and discuss each other's findings, an activity described by Elliott (1993) as 'discursive consciousness'. This process would involve others and develop a

wider understanding of the nature of education as part of the social democratic process. Kemmis and Wilkinson (1998) also stressed the participatory
nature of action research. They saw action research itself as a social and educational process that is part of the development of a professional community.

Criticisms of action research

The use of diagrams showing action research as a continuous process of development has been criticised as inadvertently promoting a rigid approach to research.
Dadds, for instance, realised that 'the tidy action research cycle was never that
tidy in the practices of research' (Dadds and Hart, 2001: 7). Diagrams that indicate stages in a research cycle may encourage the view that these are the
'correct' order in which to conduct action research. This may create problems
when any new researcher finds that they are deviating from these prescribed
stages. The diagrams themselves may appear daunting and even confusing to the
novice. In fairness, many of those who designed action research diagrams, such
as Elliott (1991), only intended them to be used as guides. More recently McNiff
(2013) has developed her original model, which she accepts could be seen as
rather prescriptive, to show how the action research process can take many turns
(see Figure 3.4). This model is seen to represent a 'generative transformational
evolutionary process' (2013: 66).

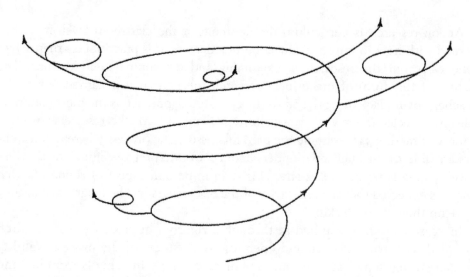

Figure 3.4   McNiff's new model

Source: McNiff, *Action Research Principles and Practice*, 3rd edn., ©2013. Reprinted by permission of Taylor & Francis

Action research for the twenty-first century

There have always been different interpretations of what action research actually involves. For many of the proponents of the late 1970s and early 1980s it provided a whole philosophy of the future development and control of education linked to the social democratic movement in the wider society. An evangelical approach to action research that sees it as a quest for personal and professional fulfilment can still be seen in the work of many educationalists (see McNiff, 2013; McNiff and Whitehead, 2010; 2011). However, for others it remained at the level of problem-solving for teachers. They were not concerned with developing a new educational science, nor did they take a critical stance on the basic values and actions in their practice. This second, rather narrow approach to teachers as researchers may be seen in the utilitarian approach taken by many politicians and managers. It fits the more recent development of what is termed practitioner research which describes the process whereby professionals, such as teachers, conduct research into their own practice (Bartlett and Burton, 2006b; Burton and Bartlett, 2005).

Educational effectiveness research

The adoption and development of managerialist strategies in the 1980s with their aim of increasing efficiency by improving results and reducing costs led to a growth of research in what became known as school effectiveness, later educational effectiveness. As its title implies, this approach sought, by using quantitative analysis, to identify what led to the creation of effective schools.

Perhaps the first significant study in Britain using this approach that caught the public imagination was *Fifteen Thousand Hours* by Rutter et al. (1979). Using statistical techniques comparisons of schools were made that identified the factors that set more successful schools apart from the less successful. Over the years these factors have been added to and refined by a number of studies (see Kelly, 2012; Kyriakides et al., 2010; Sammons et al., 1995; Teddlie and Reynolds, 2000; Townsend, 2007; Tymms et al., 2015).

Lists of school effectiveness characteristics were an apparent panacea for policy-makers but all the lists tended to be very similar, usually citing strong and effective leadership, high expectations of pupil achievement and behaviour, an orderly atmosphere with an emphasis on learning, monitoring of pupil progress and clearly enforced discipline with positive reinforcement of success.

Various criticisms have been levelled at educational (school) effectiveness research (see Creemers and Kyriakides, 2012; Elliott, 1998; Gorard, 2010; 2011; Skourdoumbis and Gale, 2013). The data collected was statistical and there were issues concerning the accuracy of its measurement. Indeed it was questionable as to whether an agreed definition could even be arrived at for many of the factors, such as 'an orderly atmosphere' or 'effective leadership'. The term 'effective' is itself a value-laden term when applied to education. There are different opinions as to what constitutes an effective school or effective teaching. Many felt that this research considered effectiveness from a managerial perspective only. It became tied to measurable outcomes within education. Thus exam results and truancy figures could be used to judge effectiveness but not the happiness of pupils or the job satisfaction of the teachers. For most teachers, the factors identified by such research described common-sense approaches which they were already pursuing. The difficulty they had was in implementing them in adverse circumstances but the research offered no help with that. Essentially, as this research was carried out by 'outside' researchers rather than teachers, the findings often appeared to be another presentation of management ideology being passed down from above. The result was that they were often treated with cynicism by those working in schools.

School improvement research

The disillusionment with the positivist approach of educational (school) effectiveness research and its associated ideology was countered by the development of the 'school improvement movement'. This has the individual school at its centre and through a research approach seeks to develop and implement strategies that will lead to improvement. It encourages a more eclectic approach to data collection and can therefore take a less restricted view of what is meant by school improvement. School improvement research sees the school as a community and recognises the importance of those with a 'stake' in the findings being involved in the research. Hopkins et al. (2014) identify five phases involved in conducting system and school improvement approaches. These phases evolve and overlap. They involve:

Phase 1 – understanding the organisational culture of the school;

Phase 2 – action research and research initiatives at the school level;

Phase 3 – managing change and comprehensive approaches to school reform;

Phase 4 – building capacity for student learning at the local level and the continuing emphasis on leadership;

Phase 5 – towards systemic improvement. (Hopkins et al., 2014: 257)

Thrupp and Lupton (2006) suggest that, while school improvement research does acknowledge that schools operate in different environments, it still needs to give more prominence to their particular contextual circumstances in order to avoid drawing misplaced generalised conclusions. This would allow the impact of local factors such as the nature of housing, employment opportunities and cultural diversity to be taken into account. This is more the approach taken by Harris (2009). Taking the school improvement approach she promotes local activism and action as the key to combating social inequality and suggests that educational leadership should be primarily concerned with helping to build a strong community.

Video Discussion

Visit https://study.sagepub.com/bartlettburton4e to watch a video discussion on:

Education research: its nature and purposes?

This video clip discusses issues which are also relevant to all chapters as they all use data to support positions.

Conclusion

The research process is complex yet is often presented as falling readily within two paradigms: positivism and interpretivism. The positivist believes in the need for scientific research, the purpose being to uncover facts to permit an explanation of reality. The focus is on large-scale, quantitative methods, carried out in an objective manner. The interpretivist, on the other hand, sees multiple realities which are created by the actors themselves. Interpretivists prefer small-scale, qualitative methods involving 'rich' accounts and description to the impersonal statistics of the positivists.

The ideological underpinning of data collection becomes apparent when particular groups of researchers, or 'schools of research', are analysed. Ideologies of education link in a complex way with the types of research carried out. Thus action research, developed by practitioners, emphasises qualitative methodologies, seeking to understand what is happening in order to change and improve it. Education is characterised as a constantly developing process.

Educational or school effectiveness research is also concerned with improving education but takes a much more positivist approach. The aim is to collect quantitative data in an objective manner so that comparisons can be made using large numbers of statistics. By using various statistical techniques factors which influence outcomes can be isolated and measured. Findings can be used to alter the practice of teachers. The emphasis on objectivity fits with a view of education as a product which can be measured. The school improvement approach takes a more qualitative view of school development and a more eclectic approach to data collection.

An analysis of these examples of educational research has clearly illustrated the ways in which beliefs and values both predicate and are a part of the research process.

Student activities

1. Design a small-scale research project using the following headings:

    - Issue or area to be researched
    - Research questions
    - Data collection methods

2. Choose a piece of published research and critique it using the pro forma given earlier in this chapter. Make particular reference to:

    - the paradigm of the research
    - methods of data collection used – appropriateness, strengths, weaknesses
    - validity and reliability
    - relationship of findings to the data
    - presentation of findings.

Recommended reading

Every degree course has some form of methodology section concerning the particular area of study. Education and the social sciences are no exception and as a result there are a multitude of high-quality texts available.

Birks, M. and Mills, J. (2015) *Grounded Theory: A Practical Guide*, 2nd edn. London: SAGE. There has been an upsurge of interest in grounded theory among education studies students in recent years for whom this book provides a valuable introduction. It outlines the fundamental concepts of grounded theory and describes the strategies and techniques employed by researchers using this approach.

Burton, D. and Bartlett, S. (2009) *Key Issues for Education Researchers*. London: SAGE. This is a companion text for *Introduction to Education Studies*. Being written especially for education studies students this book guides and supports students through their own research projects. It also outlines philosophical approaches underpinning research together with the key concepts and current debates in education research.

Flick, U. (2015) *Introducing Research Methodology*, 2nd edn. London: SAGE. This book gives an outline of different research paradigms and underpinning philosophies of research. It then presents a clear account of different research methods and is thus a very useful aid for students and early researchers embarking on initial research projects.

Punch, K. and Oancea, A. (2014) *Introduction to Research Methods in Education*, 2nd edn. London: SAGE. As the title suggests this book introduces the reader to conducting research in the field of education. It considers all aspects of the process from designing research questions to writing up results and is aimed specifically at the student and novice researcher. As such it is a very useful initial research text.

Access the companion website to this book and find SAGE journal articles exploring this chapter topic in further detail: https://study.sagepub.com/bartlettburton4e.

PART 2

POLITICAL AND HISTORICAL DIMENSIONS OF EDUCATION

CHAPTER 4
A modern history of schooling

Chapter overview

The study of education systems, structures and processes cannot be complete without an understanding of their histories. Understanding how schools and schooling developed and what motivated both individuals and various authorities to develop education establishments and systems helps us understand the current state of play in education.

This chapter will explore briefly the period leading up to the introduction of state education as we know it and will chart developments since the Second World War including the establishment of comprehensive schooling, finishing at the inception of a national curriculum (the story of which will be picked up in Chapter 5).

Introduction

The history of modern education has been dominated by the period from 1870 since this was a symbolic 'moment' of huge transition, leading to the present order of things. We begin our overview in the period prior to 1870 when the foundations of the state education system were being laid. The history of this modern period in education can be divided roughly into the following phases:

- 1800–70: towards state education
- 1870–1902: the first stages of elementary schooling
- 1902–44: establishment of secondary schools and local education authorities

- 1944–65: universal secondary education
- 1965–1970s: comprehensive schooling
- 1970s–1988: education policy discord and the Education Reform Act 1988.

Each of these phases represents a significant stage in the development of education, though as we know, events rarely fit into a neat chronology as developments often have various stages and are progressively refined. There is overlap and discontinuity between these stages, as well as progression of linked events. The phase belonging to the comprehensive school does not, for instance, represent the unequivocal triumph of comprehensive schooling.

Considerations when studying the history of education

Already, then, we can see that it is important to consider how we approach an examination of the history of education and to be clear about the pitfalls. We have already discussed in an earlier chapter the need for education researchers to take care to approach sources critically rather than at face value. This is particularly important with historical sources which are by their nature context bound and at a distance and therefore more difficult to expose to the regular queries we might pose about provenance of the source, validity of data, sample size, etc. We need, therefore, to be fairly provisional when drawing conclusions from any historical studies and try to triangulate our sources and our methodological approaches as fully as possible.

Some historians would argue that too much emphasis is put upon education policy developments to the exclusion of individual or localised struggles and achievements. Often these developments are assessed via access to official government reports and quantitative data but Carpentier (2008) reminds us that this raises questions about whether indicators measure the same thing over time. Conventions may change in relation to the statistical categories or methodologies employed but there could also be real changes on the ground in the activities they are supposed to measure. So historians of education must consult these statistics with a clear view of what the categories meant at the time. If we are to meaningfully compare historical data from different time periods we must consider them within the context of their production. 'For example, it is necessary to keep in mind the differences between elementary and primary levels of education, the moving borders between further and higher education as well as the distinctions between the institutions of higher education (universities, colleges, polytechnics etc.). Such caution is also crucial for transnational analyses' (Carpentier, 2008: 706).

The use of quantitative resources such as population growth statistics, economic data on employment, the labour market, prices and interest rates, household finance, etc. is important though as it enables us to contextualise the historical development of education. For instance, it is easy to demonstrate that both contemporary and historical analyses have created justifications for education policy developments using data on immigration, poverty, health and social class. Clearly, then, engagement with political, social, economic and demographic issues is both inevitable and desirable within any history of education. Our understanding of education reform is greatly enhanced by an examination of how social change, economic pressures and political drivers impact upon the funding of education, its expansion and changing structure, curriculum and pedagogic approaches. Historians should take care, however, not to limit their study by over-relying on empirical data and to avoid using historical data to inform or confirm theories and models which may have been taken out of their historical context. In any research there is a danger when analysing information that we may try to shape it to the theory or idea we have already formulated by over- or underestimating certain evidence or even ignoring it altogether. While theoretical findings and conclusions might offer more sophisticated interpretations of historical events, we cannot get carried away in applying a new theoretical model and end up attempting to rewrite history! Similarly we mustn't forget that historical interpretations that have been in the literature for some considerable time are themselves not completely objective and independent of theories that existed during their construction.

Reader Reflection: Analysing the significance of education events

Consider a significant educational development, event or initiative from the past 200 years and apply some or all of the following questions to it:

Did the event occur during a period of economic prosperity or recession?

Was there any impact on demographic growth or decline at the time?

Was the reform contingent upon any significant political development such as the extension of voting rights?

Was there any relationship between the initiative and the level of unemployment?

Now draw up a list of other questions you might apply in any such analysis.

Carpentier (2008) argues for a combination of quantitative and qualitative approaches in order to help us understand the structures and processes behind comparative statistics to inform our historical interpretations. Exploring classroom practices, reading teacher diaries, perusal of lesson plans and conducting interviews with former pupils and teachers would help us understand the impact of changes in legislation and in the formal arrangements of schooling on the daily lives of pupils and teachers. Historical biographical accounts can generate very rich, new perspectives on the factual information available via an examination of major legislative changes. See, for example, Jane Martin's account which uses the auto/ biographical practices of a married couple who taught in state schools

> as a lens through which to explore the larger questions of the intersection of biography and history, the distinction between lived experience and historical experience, the link between generation and social change (2007: 515).

With these cautionary notes in mind we now proceed to an examination of what are considered by most education historians to be the key stages in the development of education and its inexorable reforms.

1800–70: towards state education

Since the Middle Ages the Church had provided some form of rudimentary education to many poor children within charity schools and orphanages as well as more formal education within monasteries and public schools for a small, relatively privileged section of the population. During the early years of the nineteenth century large numbers of children in the new urban centres were working in factories while those remaining in rural areas worked in agriculture or cottage industries of various kinds. The early 'poor' schools of the 1800s were voluntary and funded by philanthropists and religious groups. They were designed principally to train large numbers of urban working-class children.

A monitorial schooling system managed these large numbers via a rank-and-file ordering of all pupils in a single space, using predominantly rote learning. These schools could teach large numbers of pupils with the presence of a single instructor by organising them by ability and breaking down the learning into small elements to be learned by repetition. The teacher selected a number of the most able pupils as monitors who instructed small groups of children while the teacher disciplined them and examined their work before they could progress to the next element. The problem with this system was that it concentrated on the learning of facts rather than problem-solving or creative activities and made no allowance for the different rates at which children worked and the different ways in which they learned.

Legislation appeared during the nineteenth century to control the employment of children and to protect them from sexual abuse and from exploitation as cheap labour. This was a period of rapid industrialisation, technological evolution and population growth so the changes in legislation on both schooling and child labour are inextricably linked with economic and labour conditions. This has been described as the invention of childhood because, before this, children were generally considered (and dressed) as smaller versions of adults. As such, their characteristics and needs were not generally considered as distinct from those of adults. Hopkins (1994: 6) argued that

> the transformation of working class childhood during the 19th century was not the consequence of any profound change in attitudes to children. It was rather the product of philanthropic and compassionate motives together with a concern of social control at a time of unprecedented change: a swelling population, industrialization, urbanization.

The monitorial system thus fell into decline in the second half of the nineteenth century as the government began to grant-fund voluntary schools, which were almost exclusively run by the Church, from 1833. The *ragged schools* established by John Pounds to educate destitute children free of charge were supported and extended by Lord Shaftesbury since there was a need to civilise the masses. Shaftesbury was concerned about girls in mining districts who drank, swore and fought and he felt that education was the way to deal with such behaviour. In order that parents could go to work in the increasingly labour-intensive city factories some form of social control and respectable values had to be instilled in children. Ragged schools were governed by elected boards of prominent citizens and this formed the governance model for the elementary schools that were to follow. It is worth noting, however, that Dick (2008) has argued that while several historians have linked the education of the poor with messages promoted by industrialists and industrialisation, training in literacy was not extensive in late eighteenth- and early nineteenth-century England compared with many other countries and education for the masses in the late eighteenth and early nineteenth centuries was based on patriarchal social models rather than capitalist ones.

As elementary schooling began to gain pace for five to ten year olds and the hours of attendance were extended, pressure grew on the authorities of education to ensure that schooling was achieving what the various interest groups expected.

To address this, the Revised Code of 1862 laid down conditions for school managers to claim grants for children attending. To be eligible for these grants children had to attain one of six standards in reading, writing and arithmetic. Each standard in each subject was stated in terms of a precisely defined skill to be demonstrated, rather like contemporary national curriculum attainment targets. This imposed a concentration on the basics and became known as 'payment by results' (Martin, 2008). Thus, even before universal elementary education was legislated for, its foundations were well established.

Reader Reflection: Data sources for education reforms

Quantitative sources allow historians of education to identify trends and patterns and can complement the traditional approach to the history of education that is based on institutional and legislative landmarks. 'Payment by results' data is a good case in point.

Consider how comparing and contrasting qualitative and quantitative sources may allow you to refine your analysis of the formation and implementation of educational policies.

Carpentier (2008) suggests we consider the impact on the ground of any given piece of legislation. For instance, through records, statistics and qualitative accounts we could explore whether the implementation of payment by results following the 1862 Revised Code led to cuts in funding or the impact of the Forster Act on enrolment and budgets after 1870.

Choose an education reform and list at least three different sources of data you think would help provide as full a picture as possible of its impact educationally, socially, politically or economically.

1870–1902: the first stages of elementary schooling

Modern education systems across Europe evolved out of various needs that came together through the large transformations of society that took place during the eighteenth and nineteenth centuries. Industrial development and increasing urban populations drove the development of schooling (Menter et al., 2015). Within a more industrialised society the factories needed literate and numerate workers, especially as Britain's economic position in the world began to be challenged by Germany and the USA. Key political changes had led to most working-class men being granted the right to vote in 1867 so it was important to ensure that their education enabled them to understand what they were voting for.

Education Reform Act 1870

The Education Reform Act of 1870 was designed to legislate for subsidised elementary education for all up to the age of 13. Education reform had been on the agenda since the government started to provide grants to schools in the 1830s. However, opposition from a number of different interest groups delayed it. The establishment of elementary schooling was fraught with contentious issues. Firstly, there were the widespread concerns among the upper and middle classes about the possible consequences of educating large numbers of people, their worries being that an educated population would not obey its 'superiors' and that workers would leave their menial jobs. There was also a deep-seated resistance among laissez-faire liberals, conservatives and working-class activists to the idea of state-funded compulsory education. They were suspicious of the state's efforts to control education on different grounds. Those who believed in laissez-faire values argued that state intervention and funding in education would endanger freedom of thought, reduce personal initiative and, if it involved no cost to people, would be perceived as having no value.

A further set of concerns and political lobbying came from the very powerful voice of the Church, which had dominated schooling for centuries with most education for children delivered through Church of England schools. The importance of educating the masses in Christianity could not be underestimated since it came with a clear message about the lower classes' place in society and a fear of what would happen in the afterlife if good behaviour within that place was not maintained. The Church had the physical and financial means to deliver schooling because those in whose interests it was to educate people in this way, landed gentry and important industrialists for example, supported it. There was also reluctance on the part of government to spend money on education.

Various religious conflicts arose about education. The Church of England wanted to maintain control of its schools so refused to cooperate with government inspectors. Catholics and others wanted single denomination schools. Radicals and non-conformists wanted secular education. These conflicts continued from the 1840s through to the 1860s and delayed agreement on the provisions in the Act. Eventually, as its power declined, the Church of England's ability to influence the education agenda diminished, leading to a universal agreement that public funds would be required if large-scale education was to be developed. This in turn had ramifications for the curriculum because if public rates and taxes were to pay for part of the education a partial withdrawal from religious instruction was possible.

Forster Elementary Education Act 1870

The Forster Elementary Education Act of 1870 required partially state-funded board schools to be set up to provide primary (elementary) education in areas where existing provision was inadequate. Board schools were managed by elected school boards. Children still had to pay a small fee to attend. Though the 1870 Act did not make education compulsory to begin with, by 1880 all children between the ages of five and ten were required to attend school (Martin, 2008). In 1891 the Free Education Act provided for the state payment of school fees up to ten shillings per week so by the end of the century most children were attending schools and were in some form of full-time education for a significant segment of their early lives. The school leaving age was increased to 11 in 1893 and 12 in 1899. The emergence of state education with the rapid development of the school as a central institution of civil society represented a massive change in social order.

Early urban state schools can be seen to have this socially symbolic function in their dramatic and often cathedral-like architecture. The powerful, conservative nineteenth-century idea that education for the working classes was potentially dangerous and might give the proletariat ideas above their station was evident in the limitations of the early elementary school curriculum. Early state educators believed that education was necessarily about making the nation cohesive, fostering and cultivating national identity. There was little embarrassment about the political function of that ideological effort.

Thus the elementary school emerged in the nineteenth century as a new form of institution with a newly formulated social mission. The school as we know it is closely related to this recent ancestor. These 'new' elementary schools that appeared like 'beacons of the future' over the urban landscapes of the industrialised nation were quite different from the 'monitorial' schools that had successfully drilled working-class children in the basics of literacy and numeracy. They were often constructed using a grand architectural design, which strongly resembled the nineteenth-century factory buildings dominating the post-Industrial Revolution skylines of urban industrial centres. Their purpose was to educate and control these newly urbanised and industrialised societies. The schools were designed to represent a new form of aspiration for mass urban populations; their grandiose and imposing architecture was designed to reflect their grand purpose of governing and transforming populations.

They also operated a more subtle pastoral and disciplinary regime than the monitorial system with its huge drill rooms. In the elementary school the teacher was brought closer to the pupils in smaller classrooms and the culture of the children met with the supervisory gaze of the teacher in the playground. The large space in the hall could be utilised for the promotion of collective identity and moral guidance. Elementary schooling was to be the basis for the development of an entirely new kind of 'human technology' capable of producing responsible and self-governing citizens. This self-governing aspect of the school's characteristic way of working remains very powerful. It is deeply embedded in the work ethic that prevails in schools and in the contemporary drive to develop a self-managing, self-governing citizenry through state-funded education.

Reader Reflection: Ideological basis of curriculum

In the early phase of the elementary schools (1870–1900) the curriculum was largely concerned with the teaching of values, virtues, literacy, numeracy, personal hygiene, physical maintenance, domestic skills and rudimentary knowledge about the world and the nation's considerable influence within it. The pioneers of state education had seen the emergent school as the potential instrument of moral transformation, especially important in relation to urban populations that were deemed to be threateningly amoral and disorganised. The school could be a key instrument in the training of populations and in the construction of the idea of community.

What are the ideological underpinnings of this early curriculum?

The development of the school as a key component of civic life, particularly in urban centres, transformed the nature of society and the individual's role within it. In its early phases (from 1870) the school was primarily designed to produce a new form of citizen who was basically literate, was trained how to behave and had learned some rudimentary facts about the world. At the same time the new urban centres in Britain became governed and organised locally. Amenities and systems for cleanliness and health were provided, for example public baths, drainage systems, new technologies of hygiene and waste disposal. It is possible to see the school as one very important manifestation of this civic concern while also recognising the extent to which it represented a vast extension of government influence on social control and social improvement. The early education system was thus concerned with the moral, physical and spiritual condition of the population. Domestic economy and the civic virtues of cleanliness and personal self-management could be taught and some of the negative effects of urban poverty could be dealt with by health care and large-scale feeding programmes managed through schools.

1902–44: establishment of secondary schools and local education authorities

When, in 1897, voting rights were extended to every male householder living in a borough constituency and those earning over £10 in lodgings, the need to educate for democracy was further strengthened, leading to expansion of the school system.

Pre-First World War legislation

With society having become more accepting of state intervention the Balfour Education Act of 1902 legislated for the development of grammar and secondary schools and developed the free place system, which provided funded scholarships for a few able but poor children to attend grammar school. Despite this, only 10 per cent of children had secondary school places by 1944. Secondary schools were for the fee-paying middle classes. For the remaining 90 per cent elementary schools up to the age of 14 were all that was available.

The 1902 Act also replaced the school boards of the 1870 Act with local education authorities (LEAs). The government's Board of Education would now only deal with 318 LEAs instead of 2,500 school boards and over 14,000 voluntary schools. The act was particularly significant because it legislated for all schools, including denominational schools, to be funded through rates.

In 1904, two years after the 1902 Education Act had laid the basis of the compulsory education system, the Board of Education published an *Elementary Code* and regulations for secondary schools. This continued the tradition of the elementary school stressing conduct and discipline with minor emphasis on subject knowledge. The Act itself spoke strongly in terms of 'self-sacrifice', 'respect for duty', 'respect for others', 'instinct for fair play', 'loyalty to one another' and other qualities that emphasised the personal, moral dimension of the curriculum. More secondary schools emerged after 1904. They mostly tended to borrow the academic curriculum of the private schools, which had modified classical curricula. The Act specified: English language and literature, at least one language other than English, geography, history, mathematics, science and physical exercises. It added the proviso that girls' schools should include 'housewifery'.

Post-First World War development

After the First World War, state-funded education in Britain was regarded as important in improving the quality of life of the oppressed classes. Social reformers and revolutionaries saw it as a mechanism for enabling class inequalities to be challenged and swept aside. A number of forces and factors combined to pressure for the idea of a type of schooling different from the well-established elementary school system. The war exposed the deficiencies in British scientific and technical education so the Fisher Education Act of 1918 made secondary education compulsory up to the age of 14 and gave responsibility for secondary schools to the state. Under the Act, many higher elementary schools and endowed grammar schools sought to become state-funded central schools or secondary schools. However, most children attended primary (elementary) school up until age 14, rather than going to a separate school for secondary education.

Early primary schooling developed in a learner-centred direction. The Hadow Report of 1926 was an influential document recommending a free two-stage education system to meet post-war demands for more education for older learners. It gave guidelines on primary schooling for the general direction of the curriculum which focused on the need to prepare to live a civilised life.

At this stage access to proper secondary education for working-class children was strictly limited. The vast majority of children finished their education at 13 or 14. It was only exceptionally that successful working-class children could gain access to full secondary schooling and higher education. As the urban populations threatened to become self-organised and a force for radical political change, governments became increasingly concerned to counter political ideals with social values and new opportunities realised through the school. Public debates about the need to change education often took the form of a tension or conflict between ideas about the health and wealth of the nation – education as a means towards economic growth, stability and improvement – and education as a social right. Clearly a major shift in the public idea of education was taking place during this period. At the same time, thought was being given to the kind of curricula that were suited to different groups within the population. Sir Cyril Norwood had read Classics at Oxford and had been Head of Bristol, Marlborough and Harrow public schools. He believed the world was divided into 'men who know . . . and men who don't know' (Carr and Hartnett, 1996). The Norwood Report of 1943 identified three types of curriculum:

- The first type of curriculum is academic in orientation and pursues knowledge for its own sake having an indirect relation to 'considerations of occupation'.
- The second type of curriculum is directed to 'the special data and skills associated with a particular kind of occupation'. This curriculum would always have a limited horizon and would be closely related to industry, trade and commerce 'in all their diversity'.

- The third type of curriculum balances training of mind and body and teaches the humanities, natural science and the arts to a degree which enables pupils to 'take up the work of life'. While practical in orientation it would appeal to the 'interests' of pupils and would not have as its immediate aim the preparation for particular types of work.

The Second World War seriously disrupted educational services and developments. The evacuation of children from the cities to the rural areas led to school closures and discontinuity of experience for pupils. It was recognised that families who had suffered through the war deserved a better future (Menter et al., 2015). There was concern to encourage the 'spiritual, mental and physical' well-being of the community.

1944–65: universal secondary education – the tripartite system

In 1944 the Butler Education Act established a Ministry of Education with the power to influence LEAs and created a universal system of secondary education for the first time. The Act defined the modern split between primary and secondary education at age 11 and created the opportunity for a *tripartite* hierarchical system of grammar, technical and secondary modern schools as proposed by the Norwood Committee in 1943. The Norwood Committee had recommended that consideration be given to general needs that would pertain to all, arguing that despite differences all pupils have common needs and a common destiny, so physical, spiritual and moral ideals are of vital concern to all. Explicitly different types of education were deemed to be relevant for these pupils. The civil servants who had forged this new version of the education system drew their authority from the division of humanity expressed in Plato's ancient work, *Republic*:

> You are all of you in this land brothers. But when god fashioned you, he added gold in the composition of those who are qualified to be rulers; he put silver in the auxiliaries and iron and bronze in the farmers and the rest.

Apart from making religious education compulsory, the 1944 Education Act made no stipulations concerning the curriculum. This whole area was left to the discretion of the teachers and the individual schools. It was seen as inappropriate in this period, as fascism was being defeated, that politicians should 'dictate' any curriculum. Leaving such decisions to professionals operating locally was regarded as a democratic safeguard.

A national system locally administered

The 1944 Education Act is often represented as *the* defining moment in the history of modern education. Chitty (2014: 18) suggests that the Act 'owed much to a growing appreciation among policy-makers, administrators and teachers of the importance of state education to economic advance and social welfare'. Secondary education was to be provided for all according to the age, aptitude and ability of each pupil. This was to be a right for all pupils, rather than being based on ability to pay, as had largely been the case before the Second World War. The Act established a nationally funded education system, which was overseen by the Ministry and administered by LEAs. As politicians in the depths of the Second World War considered the peace to come, the vision was to create a prosperous, thriving society. How to do this and what it would look like were seen differently by politicians of the left and the right (McKenzie, 2001). Whatever the political perspective, education was to play an important part in realising the dream. In terms of the division of responsibility for the new national education system which the Act created there was a 'balance of control' (Porter, 2009) between central government, local government and the schools. This system of checks and balances has been portrayed as a period of consensus or, alternatively, a triangle of tension between state, LEAs and teachers, which ensured that no one group obtained too much power in the running of the education system. For Pring (2012: 30):

> It was a partnership between Local Education Authorities, locally elected, which maintained the schools, the teachers who were responsible for what went on inside them, the government which provided a large part (but by no means all) of the funding and the Churches in that they owned historically many of the schools.

Labour won the post-war election promising a new welfare state. In a radical agenda of social transformation, nationalisation accompanied a fresh vision for social welfare and social mobility. Thus it was a Labour administration that encouraged the creation of the tripartite system under legislation passed by the previous Coalition government. Labour ministers denounced those who took issue with them for promulgating a social philosophy based on three types of schools. They claimed that by abolishing fees in maintained schools they had ensured that entry to the various types of schools would be on the basis of merit. Education was made compulsory up to age 15 in 1947. The number of young people attending universities was also expanded and there was the expectation that working-class children would have access to education of the most 'complete' kind as well as of the highest quality. This advance was seen as essential as much on the grounds of realising the nation's economic and industrial potential as on grounds of social justice. A new vision of the nation as cohesive and purposeful with common goals seemed to be on the verge of realisation.

Influenced by thinking at the time that intelligence was relatively fixed and could be measured and having been given the legal responsibility to provide a suitable education, the LEAs developed the tripartite system of education in many areas. In this system pupils went to a primary school until the age of 11 where they were inducted into the school system and began learning the basic skills of the three 'Rs'. This was seen as an important time when the intelligence and aptitude of the child began to develop. In their final year of primary school, pupils took the 11-plus, an intelligence test designed to show both their ability and aptitude. Based upon the results pupils were sent to one of three types of secondary school.

1. *Secondary grammar schools* were for the 'more intelligent' pupils with an academic aptitude. The emphasis was on traditional subjects and knowledge. It was expected that these pupils would be suitable for a university education in the future or would take a career in the minor professions or the white-collar sector.
2. *Secondary technical schools* were for pupils with a practical aptitude. Their curriculum would be based on craft and technical skills. It was envisaged that these pupils would be suited to future careers as skilled workers and engineers in industry after taking apprenticeships.
3. *Secondary modern schools* were for pupils who did not fit either of the above categories and were suited to a more general education to prepare them for their future lives as citizens and (largely unskilled) workers.

Growing criticism of the tripartite system

Throughout the 1940s and 1950s the Labour Party continued to defend the tripartite system but the system gradually lost credibility. Concerns were raised about the validity of 11-plus tests, especially since sociological studies revealed that social factors played a powerful role in determining which type of secondary school pupils went to. The new education system was fraught with problems. While it certainly did have the effect of enabling more working-class young people to gain access to an expanded higher education system, it remained shot through with inequalities. Statistics produced by large-scale studies of social differences in educational attainment grimly revealed that significant numbers of working-class children were failing to succeed, either by not passing the 11-plus examination which determined whether they went to secondary modern or grammar school, or by being unable to capitalise on opportunities that were on offer if they were given a place in a grammar school through a lack of financial and cultural resources (Halsey et al., 1980). The capacity for working-class children to take advantage of the opportunities that were apparently being placed freely before them became the crux of big debates about the state of education. Questions centred on where failure was to be located: the children themselves, the parents and their lack of educational nous, the school system or the whole of working-class culture which became increasingly significant in the discussion (see, for example, Douglas's 1964 study). There were at the same time large-scale popular 'parental' concerns over inequalities in the tripartite system that the comprehensive school was at least partly designed to confront (see Jackson and Marsden's seminal 1962 study).

Criticisms of the tripartite system began to emerge and pressure to change the system grew throughout the 1960s. Though the three types of school set up in most LEAs were supposed to have 'parity of esteem' this was not the case in practice (Jones, 2016). Grammar schools were academic and therefore seen as superior. Certainly parents who had career aspirations for their children needed them to take the General Certificate of Education (GCE) O level examinations, an examination in each subject at 16 which preceded the GCSE. It was designed for the top 40 per cent of pupils and led on to A levels taken in school sixth forms which only the grammar schools offered. Increasing parental pressure was put on pupils, especially middle-class pupils, to gain a place at grammar school. Children were coached for the 11-plus and it was soon realised that this was not an accurate measure of innate ability as had at first been supposed. The whole notion of intelligence being fixed and pupils falling into one of three types became highly questionable. Academically able pupils were often also very practical and technically minded. Likewise lack of academic ability was not necessarily made up for in practical aptitude. The pressure to obtain a grammar school place affected the primary school curriculum, which was increasingly based on preparation for the 11-plus.

Very few technical schools were built. Those that were came to be seen as for those too bright for secondary modern school but not good enough for grammar school. Secondary modern pupils often felt labelled as failures at 11 as they had, from the time of selection, effectively been rejected as lacking in intelligence. These schools became regarded as 'sink' schools with pupils often seeing little reason to work hard. Some secondary modern schools began to copy the grammar school curriculum by developing examination streams to enable some of their pupils to take GCE O levels. The argument that separate schools were required to provide different curricula for different abilities began to be seriously undermined. There appeared to be a great wastage of talent caused by the poor development of pupils placed in secondary modern schools. This feeling was reflected in the growing unease concerning the validity of the increasingly discredited selection procedure. The argument for abolishing the 11-plus grew. This was especially strong among middle-class parents becoming anxious at their children's chances of entering grammar schools. The more radical versions of this view were expressed by left-wing demands for the eradication of public schools in England and Wales and for the institution of a new 'comprehensive' school system (CCCS, 1991).

Walford (2006) suggested that, as a result of the problems generated by the tripartite system, the pressure for the development of comprehensive education came from a range of groups with different interests and ideologies. By 1965 the idea of the comprehensive school was well established in the public consciousness.

The growth of comprehensive schooling (1960s and 1970s)

After the Second World War education was increasingly seen, in advanced industrial societies, as a key investment in the promotion of both economic wealth and social justice. This was a period of growth after the destruction of the war with full employment and a steady rise in living standards. According to Chitty (2014) both major political parties were committed to the principles of the welfare state, along with full employment and a mixed economy. In education throughout the 1950s and into the 1960s the emphasis was on expansion. The economy was changing to processes of mass production and the growth in white-collar and professional employment meant that these new workers needed to have completed more education. Education became increasingly seen as an economic investment. A link was perceived to exist between an educated workforce and an expanding economy. The future labour force was regarded as human capital and as such it needed to be developed.

The swinging 60s

The 1960s was a time of rising standards of living. It could be summed up by the election slogan of Conservative Prime Minister Harold Macmillan that: 'You've never had it so good'. Many factory workers were now earning high wages, and could be seen to be living a 'new lifestyle' (see Goldthorpe et al.'s 1968 thesis of the affluent worker). The structure of society was altering and more people were becoming middle class due to increasing affluence. Certainly the majority were materially much better off and with these improved living and working conditions came raised expectations for the future. Thus the argument for increasing public expenditure on education became irresistible. The comprehensive school movement was born from an alliance of three groups:

1. leading sections of the Labour Party keen to promote social reform through education
2. the organised sectors of the teaching profession who favoured a more egalitarian system
3. some key intellectuals in the new education-related academic disciplines able to exert some influence on government thinking.

Comprehensive schooling was successfully sold to the electorate as an opportunity for making what was seen as valuable in grammar school education available to everyone. It was also presented as being essential for the needs of industrial modernisation which would enhance the wealth of all. In this it was related to Labour Prime Minister Harold Wilson's rhetoric of a 'technological revolution' (CCCS, 1981). This revolution would involve the reshaping of the social infrastructure of the country accompanying industrial expansion. Schools and the new universities would be egalitarian powerhouses to effect this dual transformation – a powerful vision. The detail of how investment in education would be transformed into specific economic benefits was never actually clarified and the concept of human capital always remained at a general level of application.

The comprehensive revolution

According to Chitty (2014), Labour was able to put what were seen as the sound economic arguments of developing human capital alongside desires for social reform as justification for the comprehensivisation of state education. Anthony Crosland, the Labour Secretary of State for Education, issued Circular 10/65 and then 10/66 which put pressure on LEAs to reorganise on comprehensive lines (see Lawton, 2005, for an outline of the arguments put forward by Crosland for this reorganisation). Halsey et al. (1997) suggested that the focus on the link between education and social democracy at the time can be seen in the increasing movement for reorganisation of secondary education. It was felt that in these comprehensive schools pupils from varied social backgrounds would mix and tolerance and respect towards each other would be created. Comprehensives would provide greater opportunity as pupils would be allowed to develop rather than being separated out and discriminated against. This in turn would allow the development of social democracy:

From the democratic-socialist perspective of the time it could be seen and still can be defended as a major advance in breaking down the barriers of class, gender, and ethnicity. (Halsey et al., 1997: 5)

The move towards the comprehensive school was designed to heal the divisions of the tripartite system; it was an attempt to provide a form of education that would cater for all. It was conceived of as a major political breakthrough in the development of the principle of equality of opportunity. In comprehensive schools entrance is not by ability as pupils are accepted across the whole range. In the first instance these secondary schools were often neighbourhood schools, taking all pupils from a particular geographical area in which they were situated. The 11-plus was abolished in those areas which introduced comprehensive education. This immediately reduced the pressure on pupils in their final year of primary school and also on their parents. Primary schools were now more able to follow the progressive recommendations of the *Plowden Report* (CACE, 1967). Pupils were no longer clearly stigmatised as failures at 11. They were not divided up into separate schools according to ability and they could not be identified in the street by a secondary modern or grammar school uniform.

Some of these schools were new and were built to cope with expanding numbers of pupils now entering secondary education. They were large and able to offer economies of scale. The raising of the school leaving age to 16 in 1970 meant that the curriculum had to be rethought to be more inclusive. This led to increased choice and diversity in the curriculum with more extra-curricular facilities available. A generation of 'ROSLA' (raising of the school leaving age) children caused significant pedagogic issues for teachers who suddenly had to devise educationally justifiable but life-relevant experiences for young people who in many cases wanted to be at work. Schools developed a vocational curriculum for such pupils offering courses in car maintenance, keeping allotments, child care and hair and beauty. There were also differing ways of organising the teaching in these schools. Some used setting, some streaming and, increasingly, in the 1970s, classes were of mixed ability. It is interesting to note that primary schools had always been comprehensive schools in the way this term was now being applied to secondary schools. Pupils in primary schools too had usually been taught in mixed-ability classes.

Although it was never the case that there existed a single and unitary form of the comprehensive school curriculum, there were a number of tendencies that appeared to make the curriculum more relevant to the newly extended school population. This sometimes meant the inclusion of vocational areas of study for the non-academic, but it also meant that subject boundaries began to be less rigidly adhered to. Integrated humanities and integrated science courses appeared, for example. New, open forms of assessment came into being through the Certificate of Secondary Education (CSE) examination and began to infiltrate the socially and academically prestigious GCE. In 1985 these two different systems were unified into the GCSE and forms of assessment became much more liberal, flexible and open. Continuous assessment through coursework and module tests came to have equal status with end-of-course examinations.

'Comprehensivisation' was not to make a dramatic break with the thinking and practice of the time. Although mixed-ability teaching did develop in a number of comprehensive schools, the majority were still to be streamed according to 'ability' (DES, 1965), albeit the divisions between differently labelled pupils would be more fluid and open to movement. It would appear that, while the goal of social mobility dominated, the desire to relinquish ability-based organisational structures was more muted. The comprehensive school was, however, intended to enable greater flexibility and opportunity to those whose fate had hitherto been determined at the moment of the 11-plus examination. The trend with new schools was to make them community schools so that there would be joint use of facilities. This was both a more efficient use of resources and helped promote the social democratic ideals of the Labour Party. In some LEAs the reorganisation of the tripartite system into comprehensive schools did cause problems with amalgamations between traditional grammar and non-academic secondary modern schools. There were issues of split sites and clashes of school cultures. For many, comprehensivisation did not have the successful start that had been hoped for.

The project of comprehensive education, involving a break-up and reformation of the previous tripartite system, was never in fact complete. Comprehensive schools were not universal, though in some areas they became the dominant form of state provision.

Reader Reflection: Selective or comprehensive schooling?

Jones (2016) points out that during the period 1965–88, selective grammar schools remained powerful magnets in many areas and the private/public school system was largely untouched by developments in the state sector, leaving the question about inequality and an elite system open and unanswered.

There is continuing debate as to whether selective or comprehensive schooling is the most effective form of secondary education. In considering the arguments put forward for each assess the dominant underpinning ideologies.

Where do you stand on this issue?

The history of special educational needs: the categorisation of pupils

It is worth taking a sideways step at this point to chart the development of a system of education for pupils who were considered as needing special, often separate, education provision. As with any historical analysis, the development of special educational needs (SEN) is better understood if we first consider its ideological frame of reference. Several key ideological perspectives can be identified in the field of special and inclusive education.

Models of disability

Medical models of disability focus upon diagnosing the 'problem' and providing appropriate 'treatment', cures or strategies of action for individuals. Disability is regarded as a tragedy which unfortunately some people have to live with. While the focus on treatment is viewed as beneficial, individuals may feel that they are only perceived as cases, patients or clients rather than people. They become labelled and are treated entirely in terms of this label. They and their families may feel powerless to make decisions concerning their lives being under the controlling influence of a range of professionals. The medical and scientific evidence behind the professional practice may be generally sound but some aspects of the 'treatment' and the methods used have evolved as bureaucratic and convenient ways of managing groups of people or may even be the result of ad hoc decisions taken by different 'experts'.

Social models of disability switch the focus from the individual to society. This model suggests that we should be questioning, examining and changing society itself. The whole concept of disability and special educational needs is seen as the result of social processes whereby certain individuals and minority groups are identified, labelled and then marginalised. It is the wider society that segregates and encourages the practices of discrimination. Advocates of the social model support moves towards greater integration and inclusion, perhaps where special schools no longer exist, where schools and public places are designed with all people in mind in terms of mobility and access, where teaching and the curriculum is adapted to suit all pupil needs and students are educated together. It is assumed that these integrative processes would ultimately lead to a more open, just and tolerant society. Critics of this model see it as being naive and ignoring the reality of disability. By not taking individual impairment into account all of those with disabilities may become perceived as a uniform group.

Hodkinson (2016) identifies disability movement perspectives such as the affirmative model of disability and the rights-based model of disability that can be seen as extensions of the social model. The affirmative model is built upon the premise that disabled people, not medical or educational professionals, should have control of their lives. The model is based upon firstly identifying and challenging how society excludes people and, secondly, seeking to develop a positive self and public image of disabled people. The rights-based model is a more radical approach that promotes positive legal and political action by those with disability to confront social prejudices and to demand their human rights.

The development of special education

In pre-industrial Britain people with widely differing physical and mental abilities were able to live and work together within the same communities though their contributions may have varied and allowances made for individuals with any extra individual care provided within the family and close group.

The onset of industrialisation and the development of factory working led to radical changes in lifestyles. Work became something that, for many, was done in specific locations away from the home over set hours and consisted of a limited or specialised range of tasks, perhaps part of the overall production of particular goods. Society became increasingly urbanised in the transition from largely rural, self-sufficient, subsistence communities to a cash-based economy. This transition required changes in the workforce. Output needed to be consistent, workers had to be able to follow direct instructions to complete specific tasks. Over time certain levels of literacy and numeracy were increasingly required at work and in daily life; a mass, low skilled, compliant workforce was needed and to provide this a universal system of education was required. As looked at previously the Forster Act (1870) heralded the creation of such a system in England.

From this time all children were supposed to be educated and schools found that some, due to physical or mental differences, were difficult to teach and were not making the expected progress. This became an increasing problem when payment to schools was based on results. Some pupils came to be seen as uneducable and, due to the extra resources they used, as adversely affecting the progress of their peers. The question was what to do with these pupils.

While certain physical handicaps, blindness for example, had led to the creation of a number of residential schools over previous years, they were philanthropic institutions and certainly not designed for the issues being created by this newly evolving education system. A number of committees and acts (the Egerton

Commission, 1889; the 1893 Education Act; the Sharpe Commission, 1898; the 1899 Education Act) now looked into the education of these 'different' children and proposed separate special schools to be set up and run by the local boards that had been created under the Forster Act. So over a comparatively short period of time a process of categorisation was devised whereby children were now separated out into a range of institutions.

What is interesting, and perhaps shocking, is the terminology used to identify these 'different' children and how they have remained in use over the years as forms of insult and abuse. For instance the Egerton commission recommended that each school board should appoint a medical officer to distinguish between children who were 'feeble-minded, imbeciles or idiots'. The 1921 Education Act identified five categories of children with disabilities which included mentally defective and physically defective clearly using a medical deficit model.

The years 1902 to 1944 are a period that Hodkinson (2016) calls the 'zenith of categorisation'. If some pupils were to receive a different/special education, which was more expensive for the school boards to provide, it became important that they could be identified or 'diagnosed' effectively and in the early 1900s medical and psychometric methods were being developed by psychologists such as Burt (1935) and Schonell (1924) which could do this. Forms of intelligence quotient (IQ) tests were used to measure the intelligence of children so that those who could not be educated in normal schools were identified and then sent to special schools. Making such diagnoses using these new scientific methodologies appeared unquestionably sensible to policy-makers of the day.

The 1944 Education Act stated that education should be provided to all pupils based upon their age, aptitude and ability. As we have already noted, aptitude and ability were assumed at this time to be relatively fixed largely as a result of the development of the psychometric movement. LEAs, which had replaced the local school boards, were now to be responsible for ensuring there was local provision for all pupils including those deemed to suffer from any disability of mind or body that would involve the provision of special schools or specialist teachers. The Act established 11 categories of handicap: blind, partially sighted, deaf, partially deaf, delicate, diabetic, educationally sub-normal, epileptic, maladjusted, physically handicapped, and children with speech defects. Clearly the medical model with its deficit view of the individual was, once again, pre-eminent at this time. Children were to be placed in mainstream education or special schools catering for different forms of handicap. Those classed as 'severely sub-normal' and regarded as uneducable were sent to National Health Service training centres. The 1944 Act thereby created a hierarchy of schools from grammar schools down and, with it, a corresponding hierarchy of pupils into which all children fitted somewhere.

A move away from testing and segregation

By the 1960s, as noted earlier public attitudes had begun to change regarding the classification and dividing up of pupils within the education system which was increasingly seen as unfair. There was growing scepticism of psychometric testing and the belief that intelligence was fixed was shown to be incorrect. In a similar way to which parents were increasingly unhappy if their children went to a secondary modern as opposed to a grammar school, parents with children in special schools were critical of the restrictions, segregation and labelling they were subjected to. It was increasingly felt that many pupils in special schools would be better off in mainstream education. They would not be separated from their wider peer group and the education of pupils already in mainstream would not suffer if teachers and schools were prepared to accommodate a more diverse range of pupils.

A number of years after changes had been taking place in 'mainstream' education, with the large-scale abandoning of the 11-plus and the development of comprehensive schools in the 1960s and early 1970s, the Warnock committee was set up to look into special education, reporting in 1978. The report's findings and the resulting 1981 Education Act will be picked up in Chapter 6.

Major education policy discord of the 1970s – the 1988 Education Reform Act

The post-war consensus has perhaps tended to be overstated. Though there was a move towards comprehensive education this was still not universally accepted. There was some opposition to these new forms of secondary school, particularly within the Conservative Party, where many saw a need to re-establish a Tory identity. Many Conservatives felt that they had gone along with the consensus for long enough and that it was damaging both to the electoral prospects of the party and to the country. They pointed to an insidious move to the left, which had gone largely unnoticed, under the auspices of a national consensus. Britain was felt to be in decline, both morally and economically, by many Conservative politicians from the mid-1960s onwards (see Tomlinson, 2005).

Economic crisis

There was little concern among the general public with problems in education so long as there remained full employment. This appeared to be the case in the 'swinging 60s' with the increasing affluence, a football World Cup win and hope for even more prosperity in the future. Rising standards of living for all sectors of society, while not reducing inequality, created at least a semblance of unity, according to Chitty. Economic crisis, when it came in the 1970s, had a significant effect and 'fundamentally altered the map of British politics' (Chitty, 2014: 32). Education had been linked with the rebuilding of society after the Second World War, with secure employment, better living standards and the eradication of poverty. When there was recession, however, questions began to be asked about how effective education had been and the value gained from money previously invested. The whole of compulsory education came under scrutiny. Economic pressure to reduce spending focused attention back onto fundamental questions concerning the purposes of education.

Public outcry

Throughout the 1970s there was growing public concern regarding education, which was actively fuelled by the media, the press in particular. There was a public perception, whether based on fact or not, that education was in crisis. Standards were felt to be falling. There are ideological issues here about standards of 'what' and how they are being measured (see Kelly, 2009, for a discussion of the use and meaning of the term 'standards').

'Progressive' and 'child-centred' approaches adopted in primary schools, which had been promoted particularly in the light of the Plowden Report and much sociological and psychological research of the 1960s, were now questioned. It was felt that these approaches had led to indiscipline, lack of direction in pupils' learning and a resulting lack of knowledge acquisition. Pupils were no longer being taught the basic skills of reading, writing and arithmetic in any systematic way. Classrooms were portrayed as chaotic with little learning taking place.

These public concerns were highlighted by the William Tyndale Primary School case, which made the headlines in 1976 as being overly progressive and indisciplined. Here, despite the worries expressed by parents, the head teacher of William Tyndale claimed the professional expertise to continue with progressive teaching methods. The Auld Report (1976), which was set up to investigate the case, found many faults with how the school was being run. This instance, by the media attention it drew, strengthened the public mistrust of teachers, teaching methods and teachers' control over the curriculum. In secondary schools, in particular, the curriculum was felt to be too academic for many young people. It was not practical and not relevant to their future and appeared to be out of touch with modern life. This was held to account for much pupil unrest, which was perceived to be part of a growing discipline problem within schools that was spilling over into the wider society.

These new comprehensive schools now came under increasing criticism and teachers and teaching methods were seen as the prime cause.

Mixed ability

Mixed-ability teaching practices in secondary education had expanded throughout the late 1960s and early 1970s. Informed by child-centred ideologies which aimed to motivate pupils and encourage an individual approach to pupils' learning, they were increasingly criticised by traditionalists. Having to cope with such a wide range of ability in each class put a great deal of strain on many teachers, whole-class teaching being inappropriate. Pupils still often felt labelled within their classes and disruption was made worse as the able were often not challenged while the less able could feel left behind. The perception was that comprehensives were producing mediocrity by teaching to the 'middle', with ability and potential being wasted as it had been in the tripartite system. Thus, as well as the secondary curriculum not being relevant, academic standards were felt to be falling. By emphasising individual development and equality, it was felt that comprehensives and primary schools were discouraging the very competitive spirit that was needed to improve the economy. Comprehensives were at a further disadvantage in that they were often compared to, and in fact in some areas were in competition with, grammar schools that only taught able pupils.

The curriculum

The curriculum had changed in many comprehensive schools. Critics saw the traditional subjects and their content being diluted into themes or topics. History, geography and religious education were now often combined with aspects of sociology to form 'social studies' or 'integrated humanities'. Some felt this led to important traditional knowledge not being taught and being replaced by the transmission of what were portrayed as left-wing egalitarian beliefs. Teachers were not felt to be upholding traditional stable values and were stereotyped as 'lefty', indoctrinating, long-haired and lazy. Schools and teachers were apparently to blame for many of the country's problems. In a seminal article in the *Times Educational Supplement* (Weinstock, 1976: 2) entitled 'I blame the teachers', key industrialist Arnold Weinstock blamed them for the economic and social problems of the time. These criticisms were cited and much of the growing unrest captured in a series of Black Papers written by a group of right-wing politicians and thinkers published between 1969 and 1977 (Cox and Boyson, 1975; 1977; Cox and Dyson, 1969a; 1969b; 1970). They 'provided a hostile critique of comprehensive

trends in Britain' (Pring, 2012: 34). They criticised falling standards and an associated moral decline and put both down to progressive teaching methods encouraged
in the Plowden Report (CACE, 1967). The Black Papers claimed this ideology led
to sloppiness, lack of rigour, decline in discipline and disruption in the education
of all pupils.

The 'great debate'

The Black Papers critique can be seen as a humanist backlash against the prevailing progressive and social democratic ideologies of the time which had also been
linked to the reconstructionists. The solution suggested in the later of the papers
was to take control of the curriculum and the running of education away from the
teachers and the educationalists and place them in the hands of the parents and
employers. Thus a policy of market forces was proposed, where the power of the
consumer, not the producer, determined the 'product'. These criticisms of the
education system and those who had been running it reflected the growing importance of what became known as the 'New Right' within the Conservative Party.
They raised questions about the purpose of education in society including issues
of what and how pupils should be taught. As value for money came to be seen as
increasingly important in the growing recession, these questions were also asked
by the Labour Prime Minister of the time, James Callaghan.

Under increasing economic pressure and with growing public concern being
expressed over education, a speech made by Callaghan at Ruskin College in 1976
marked a significant point in the history of recent education policy. Callaghan's
intentions for the speech are still debated (see Ball, 2013, and Lawton, 2005). It
could be taken as a critique of a system in crisis or it could be interpreted as a
desire to move to a more radical agenda. He did not openly condemn education;
in fact he noted achievements, though this was done with faint praise.

Callaghan spoke of issues that caused him concern and that needed attention.
He felt that the curriculum was not appropriate for the needs of a modern economy and that many of the brightest pupils were not being encouraged and were
even being discouraged from taking up courses relevant to careers in industry. He
noted the great strides in social aspects of education but was also worried that a
number of pupils were not acquiring the basic academic skills needed in later life.
Though teachers were professionally involved in the curriculum, he felt it should
not just be left to them – others in society needed to be involved. To this end
Callaghan proposed a 'great debate' concerning the curriculum. Certainly this can
be seen as the first significant occasion since the 1944 Act on which teacher
autonomy in curriculum matters was questioned by the government in power.

What this speech signified was the growing public feeling stoked by politicians and the media that the education system needed to be more accountable. It was felt that teachers and LEAs needed to be responsive to the wider society which was, after all, paying for education. In ideological terms the focus was shifting away from the individual pupil and more towards society and the importance of traditional knowledge.

When Labour lost the general election of 1979 there followed a substantial period of Conservative government up until 1997. The early Thatcher years were a time of economic and social upheaval. There was a change in emphasis from the social democratic policies of the consensus politicians to the rigours of monetarism and the free market. This was reflected throughout government policy and so too in education. Education had come to be seen as part of the national problem and it provided a convenient scapegoat for intractable economic and social issues. Education could also, while undergoing a process of reform, be seen as a future solution to many of the economic difficulties of the time. It could prepare suitable workers and instil social responsibility and respect for authority among the young. What had previously been an education programme for a new affluent society had come to be seen as politically biased and damaging to the nation's development. It was claimed there was a need to get back to basics, to eliminate political meddling in education, to return to traditional values and at the same time modernise education for the needs of a changing economy. There was an ideological shift taking place in public life from progressivism to (classical) humanism alongside instrumentalism and economic revisionism.

The post-1944 period began with what has been portrayed as a general consensus in terms of the desirability of development and expansion in education. There was hope for the future and for the development of a better society. By the early 1970s there had been rapid curriculum development, an increase in the 'pupil-centred approach' to learning and the implementation of the first wave of comprehensive schools. By the mid-1970s there was an economic downturn and education increasingly became a focus of national concern through the 'great debate' on education. In some quarters it was felt there had been a fall in academic standards and that teachers, with their progressive teaching methods, had played a major part in the nation's moral decline. The stage was now set for the demise of the comprehensive school system and the increasing importance of the market in secondary education.

Following the 1979 general election, when the Conservative Party regained power, they implemented two key policy changes. New vocationalism was expanded. Labour had made some efforts beforehand, but the Conservatives expanded it considerably through initiatives such as the Technical, Vocational and

Educational Initiative (TVEI), which existed to advise schools on relevant curriculum changes. There was scepticism that the true reason for this scheme was one of a series of attempts to reduce the power of LEAs, which the Conservative government felt had too much control at a local level (Phillips, 2001). Initiatives such as Youth Training Schemes were devised ostensibly to improve the vocational training of 16 year olds but additionally, of course, to reduce the high youth unemployment, which was regarded as one of the causes of city riots in the late 1970s. The Conservatives also introduced the assisted places scheme in 1980 which allowed 'gifted' children who could not afford to go to fee-paying schools to have free places if they passed the school entrance exam.

By the 1980s the political ideology that drove the Conservative government, that is, competition through market forces, alongside a desire to return to traditional values began to spawn a series of policies which were to dramatically change the face of modern education in Britain. These became manifest mostly through the 1988 Education Reform Act (DES, 1988) which introduced both structural and curricular changes. These were aimed at creating a 'market' whereby schools competed with each other for 'customers' (pupils) and ensured a traditional subject-based curriculum for all pupils. The (rather crude) theory was that, in exposing the achievements of schools through close inspection of a tightly controlled national curriculum and league tables of examination results, weaker schools would lose pupils to the good schools and would be forced to improve or close.

At this point we leave our historical overview and pick up the story of ideologically driven competition and diversity in Chapter 6 because the policy initiatives that have shaped English education since the 1988 Reform Act need careful and thorough examination within prevailing political and socio-economic influences. Meanwhile, we pause to examine notions of curriculum with a particular emphasis on the English national curriculum as a case study.

Reader Reflection: The history of English education – a sad story?

In the conclusion to his book, Gillard (2011) assesses the history of English education as a long struggle to create an education system which values all and says it has, in many ways, been a sad story. He goes on to explain:

> In the 19th century there was hostility to the very idea of mass education and, when that argument was eventually won, the system which evolved was based on the entrenched class divisions of English society.

In the first half of the 20th century the divisions continued, only now they were presented as being based on theories of intelligence rather than on social class.

By the middle of the century these theories had been shown to be spurious, and for a brief spell – in the 1960s and early 1970s – it looked as though, finally, England might get a truly comprehensive public education service.

But since 1976 (when Callaghan gave his Ruskin College speech and started the 'Great Debate') the trend has been back to division and elitism.

Prime ministers from Thatcher onwards have sought to replace public service with market forces.

To what extent do you agree with Gillard's assessment?

Conclusion

This historical appraisal has revealed huge ideological shifts and conflicts that can still be felt in contemporary values and ideas about education. We have seen how nineteenth-century concerns about education for the working classes being dangerous have given way to powerful, often socialist, pressures to make education accessible to the people and to reconstruct the curriculum along more inclusive and liberal lines. The seminal 1944 Act seems to have instigated many of the themes that still haunt debates about education. A central issue remains the provision of differentiated schooling. While liberally providing education for all, the Act ensured that differentiation of provision would be structurally established, a legacy that remains powerful. The contemporary curriculum, with its tensions between academic knowledge and life skills, liberal conceptions of learning and vocational training, bears something of the unresolved tensions of that history (CCCS, 1981).

We might conclude that, since the Second World War, industrial societies have seen the development of education systems in terms of the social democratic ideals of social equality. Schools and the processes of schooling are viewed as instruments of social advancement. Expansions of the higher education system during the late 1940s, the 1960s and the 1990s represent significant phases in the development of this ideal. During these periods the school was increasingly seen as a route towards the social advancement that higher education appeared to offer. This represents a very significant change from the situation before the Second World War under the elementary school system. The transition to the tripartite system and later to comprehensive schooling was designed to enable greater numbers of working-class children to make progress through the school to higher education and thereby to social advancement. The education system, at least in the state sector, was being redefined in this process as ostensibly merito-cratic. Reay (2013) has argued that this meritocracy was never realised and remains a powerful myth that helps hold the social hierarchy in place – little change then from the power that church schooling exerted to keep the working classes in their place 100 years earlier.

In this chapter we have taken a fairly standard chronological approach in which we have looked at the large-scale legal and societal changes that have impacted on the school system. There are, of course, other ways of viewing this history. Important areas of educational history have been opened up by a cul-tural studies oriented approach where questions might be asked about specific histories in the field of education. For example, the study of the role of women in the management of early board schools would help uncover the unwritten gender politics of a small but significant segment of the history of education. Exploring the practices of schooling after the First World War in the cultivation and promotion of ideas of the nation and empire, for example, might necessi-tate doing some archaeological or genealogical research into textbooks, recorded events, ethnographic work with the elderly and so on. Recent historical studies include accounts of the education experiences of traveller and refugee popula-tions in England and Wales, studies conducted of teachers' roles in resistance in Europe during the Second World War, analyses of early school photographs, and studies of the cultural and social implications of school architecture. Thus dif-ferent historical studies provide different perspectives on the complex interactions of policy, institutions, practices, individuals and social groups within the field of education. Overarching histories of education may still pro-vide useful accounts of larger movements, surface trends and changing legislative frameworks for education.

It seems self-evident, perhaps, that the study of history should be central to education studies. It is necessary to understand the ideological context and politi-cal motivations for education reform and the changing social and economic conditions which helped shape them. This helps us make sense of the various educational processes, pressures, events and developmental stages that have given rise to the contemporary education scene. Studying even what may appear now as remote examples may provide useful points of reference to review and rethink contemporary dominant practices.

Student activity

It is interesting to research the history of schooling through individual case studies. Find out what you can about the history of one particular school. Evidence consisting of statistics, written accounts and pictures can be found in local and national archives, newspaper records, public libraries and perhaps from the school itself. Relate any data you find to broader social and economic events of the time and also to the history of the education system.

Recommended reading

Chitty, C. (2014) *Education Policy in Britain*, 3rd edn. Basingstoke: Palgrave Macmillan. In this very useful book for the education studies student Chitty considers the nature of education before giving a historical overview of education policy from the 1944 Education Act onwards. He then looks at developments in certain key areas such as the compulsory school curriculum, pre-school provision, higher education and citizenship.

Gillard, D. (2011) *Education in England: A Brief History*, www.educationengland.org.uk/history. This is an excellent online text which, remarkably, charts the history of education from 600 AD to the present day. It is full of helpful facts, detail about all the education acts and includes some commentary. It has a very helpful timeline which includes the key events, acts and individuals within the story of English education.

Jones, K. (2016) *Education in Britain: 1944 to the Present*, 2nd edn. Oxford: Polity Press. In the decades after 1944 the four nations of Britain shared a common educational programme. By 2015, this programme had fragmented: the patterns of schooling and higher education in Wales, Scotland, Northern Ireland and England resembled each other less and less. This new edition traces and explains this process of divergence, as well as the arguments and conflicts that have accompanied it.

Access the companion website to this book and find SAGE journal articles exploring this chapter topic in further detail: **https://study.sagepub.com/bartlettburton4e.**

CHAPTER 5
Curriculum

Chapter overview

This chapter considers the meaning of the term curriculum. There follows an epistemological analysis that considers differing views of the nature and organisation of knowledge. These views are significant in that they are closely linked to perceptions of the world. Thus understandings of knowledge, education and the processes of research are closely related. The chapter goes on to examine curriculum frameworks that involve an analysis of aims, content, pedagogy and assessment. The significance of beliefs about the purposes and nature of education in the creation and development of any curriculum is then illustrated with reference to the English national curriculum.

Introduction

The notion of curriculum, its purpose, features and functions tend to be taken for granted. One of the functions of a study of education is to open up these central, and apparently given, ideas to probe them more critically. The curriculum of educational establishments such as schools, colleges and universities has a powerful legal basis and represents an important social requirement, which is regulated and kept under strict control by various institutions. Changing the curriculum can be a difficult, long-winded and bureaucratic process. All of this indicates that the curriculum and the view of knowledge and learning it embodies are regarded as important matters for governments and for the processes of governance that occur in the various institutions of education – schools, colleges and universities.

The regular and regulated curriculum that we are familiar with embodies a set of ideas and practices that have evolved. Different subjects on the curriculum have their own different histories, the traces of which can be seen in their present forms. Subjects have a 'life of their own' that is expressed in textbooks and in traditions of practice and is written into the very language of professional discourses (Ball, 1993). Subjects are 'authorised' and gain legitimacy, so they accrue institutions and embedded practices around themselves. Examination authorities such as the (English) Office of Qualifications and Examinations Regulation (Ofqual) significantly influence the form and shape of curriculum subjects and the subject practices of teachers.

Teachers interpret the curriculum within the context of their own situation, their subject and general professional practices, the culture of the department and the general ethos of the school. This represents a significant measure of control by teachers but at the same time they are constrained by their role in the school and are required to behave in certain ways and to subscribe to certain values. There is always a tension between a teacher's capacity to act on their individual judgement and to conform to external constraints. As Reay (2006: 292) points out:

> Teachers do not simply deliver the national curriculum and enact a positive discipline policy, they also confront contextual circumstances such as dilemmas over levels and distribution of resources, acts of violence and aggression, complex patterns of interpersonal and group relationships, power struggles for control and dominance, disputes over achievement, and issues about what constitutes 'really useful knowledge' for different groups of students. All these multi-faceted dilemmas facing teachers are imbued with gender, ethnicity and social class.

The nature of the curriculum

'Curriculum' is a term frequently used in a variety of ways by those involved in education and its meaning is often taken for granted. Hayes suggests that it is in fact difficult to find agreement on this apart from perhaps 'the sum total of what pupils need to learn' (2006: 57). However, even here it is unlikely that a consensus can be reached over what pupils do actually *need* to learn. Sometimes the term 'curriculum' is used to refer to the content taught on a course. However, this is more properly called a syllabus. A curriculum is more than this. Over 35 years ago Jenkins and Shipman (1976: 26) defined it thus:

A curriculum is the formation and implementation of an educational proposal to be taught and learned within the school or other institution and for which that institution accepts responsibility at three levels: its rationale, its actual implementation and its effects.

Lawrence Stenhouse (1975: 53), a key educational developer of these times, expressed his idea of curriculum differently, as:

An attempt to communicate the essential principles and features of an educational proposal in such a form that it is open to critical scrutiny and capable of effective translation into practice.

The curriculum is often referred to as though it were a collection of subjects that appear on the timetable of education institutions such as schools. Kelly (2009) suggests that this is very limiting and that a broader way of looking at the curriculum is in terms of all the experiences that the school provides.

Reader Reflection: What does a curriculum include?

How well do you think the following definition of the curriculum offered by HMI in 1985 encapsulates school life?

A school's curriculum consists of all those activities designed or encouraged within its organizational framework to promote the intellectual, personal, social and physical development of its pupils. It includes not only the formal programme of lessons, but also the 'informal' programme of so-called extracurricular activities as well as all those features which produce the school's 'ethos', such as the quality of relationships, the concern for equality of opportunity, the values exemplified in the way the school sets about its task and the way it is organized and managed. Teaching and learning styles strongly influence the curriculum and in practice they cannot be separated from it. (DES, 1985a: 11)

A whole curriculum will be a particular way of organising these different elements. What is taught, how it is put into a particular arrangement of learning experiences, the kind of teaching methods used to 'deliver' the curriculum and how the learning of pupils is assessed: all these things are factors in what the curriculum is. This means that the curriculum is a complex and multi-faceted 'entity' rather than just a collection of different subjects. Subjects may be important but they make up just part of the whole curriculum. Understanding the curriculum involves exploring what is taught, why it is taught and how it is taught (Husbands, 2012).

Kelly suggests that there needs to be awareness of the differences between the planned curriculum, what is intended, and the 'received' curriculum, what is actually experienced and happens. He also refers to the formal curriculum, what is timetabled, and the informal curriculum, what happens outside of the timetable and could be called 'extracurricular activities' (2009: 12). The informal curriculum should not be confused with what has been termed the 'hidden curriculum'. The hidden curriculum refers to the messages implied by school rituals: learning how to be obedient, how to cope with long periods of boredom and inactivity, and learning to remain silent in certain formal social contexts (see the seminal work of Bowles and Gintis, 1976; Willis, 1979). The hidden curriculum includes all the 'unofficial' learning that happens, for example the social and emotional exchanges between pupils, which for adolescents often constitute powerful motivation for school attendance with the formal curriculum at times simply being background noise. Thus it is essential that a study of the curriculum looks at the unintended experiences as well as those that are official and planned. (The significance of the hidden curriculum is looked at in more detail in Chapter 10.)

The curriculum is not a given but is a selection from a range of possible choices and it will therefore always represent a particular view of knowledge and learning and define for a particular education system or setting what is important in terms of knowledge and learning. Moreover, the curriculum is made. It is a social construction that sits at the very heart of the education system and gives shape and form to much of what happens in schools. Decisions based upon ideological beliefs are made at every stage in the development and delivery of any curriculum and determine what kind of knowledge is contained within it, how it is delivered, assessed and so on.

In modern state education systems, the curriculum is likely to derive from a complex amalgam of different ideologies rather than from one completely consistent, clearly defined paradigm. The official curriculum can also be considered a public statement about what is significant knowledge. Knowledge included in the curriculum has an authority and is vested with considerable legal, social and moral force. Curriculum knowledge has been chosen to be there and is therefore the knowledge that really matters, and its determination involves policy-makers far beyond educational settings. To control the curriculum is to exert considerable power so governments regularly intervene in the nature of the school curriculum.

When considering English schools, for example, a number of stakeholders can be identified who all have varying influence on the official and delivered curriculum.

- Civil servants drew up and politicians voted upon the legal framework of the curriculum and this remains at the centre of political debate and policy.
- Ofsted inspectors influence how the curriculum is taught because inspection grades affect public league table positions which in turn impact on parents' choice of school.
- Employers are involved with schools through governance, attendance agreements, work placements and so on, passing opinions on to head teachers, governors, and local and national politicians.
- Local authorities (previously local education authorities) support schools in their authority, offering professional development courses for teachers and other school personnel as well as support services for pupils with a range of needs.
- Parents have a vested interest in the school and the quality of the learning experiences for their children.
- Teachers deliver the curriculum and pupils will respond to this in different ways.

Thus there are many different groups that can influence how the curriculum is made manifest and how it evolves.

The structure of knowledge

Epistemology

Epistemology (theory of knowledge) is concerned with questions of knowledge, how we know what we know and how we may orient ourselves to what we don't know. Epistemologists may ask questions of knowledge, its sources, its history, its 'provenance', its claims to authority and where these derive from. Issues about the relations between the knower and the known, between teaching and learning, between individuals and institutions would also concern them. Enlightenment or modernist epistemology can be characterised by a certain kind of faith in progress. It is associated with the rise of scientific knowledge. Descartes (1596–1650) is most frequently cited as the first thinker of the modern period to confront the question of knowledge and consciousness, responding to the question: How can I be sure that I know what I know?

Descartes could only be certain of anything because he could be certain of himself as a thinking subject. For Descartes it is self-consciousness that guarantees knowledge. Immanuel Kant (1724–1804) was fascinated by the critique of knowledge proffered by the sceptics of the eighteenth century who pursued a line of thinking that meant that certainty about anything could not be guaranteed. His philosophy is an elaborate attempt to confront that uncertainty and scepticism with a thoroughly logical account of human understanding and knowledge.

Kant's ideas, though radical at the time of their introduction into European thought, are now so deeply embedded that they can be said to be fundamental to Western thinking. Rationality was seen as the very stuff of thought and, through conflicts between different ideas, new knowledge and ideas come into existence which are themselves transformed and surpassed by others (Hegel, 1770–1831). This rationalism came to dominate thinking, for example Darwin detected progress in the order of beings in nature through his law of natural selection.

We are born into a world of knowledge and meaning that pre-exists the individual. We don't each of us have to find out everything for the first time. We draw on existing and established forms of knowledge held by others and this raises the question of authority and power in the process of knowledge acquisition. Children may be encouraged to explore the world around them for themselves. Some models of education emphasise the investigative nature of learning but children must also acquire established skills and knowledge, like reading, for example, which they cannot make up for themselves. This always requires the submission to a prior authority, an order that precedes the individual. Our knowledge of the world is the product of a complex network of factors: family background, formative experiences, cultural identity, social class, gender and language are all contributory to our sense of who we are but also our sense of what the world is like and what constitutes significant knowledge. Different ways of life and belief systems will inevitably produce different knowledge and different orientations towards it.

Knowledge comes not just as a body of 'facts' about the world; it comes packaged in a certain style. Official knowledge as expressed, for example, in the school curriculum may clash with alternative forms of knowledge that may belong to the lifestyles and belief systems of different cultural groups (Eagleton, 2000). In recent times awareness of cultural difference and its impact on schooling has increased, and there have been attempts to address potential exclusions of certain cultural groupings through a variety of policy measures in the US and the UK.

Reader Reflection: Is your version of knowledge the same as mine?

It is often difficult to argue that knowledge is anything other than an unassailable set of facts because those that we deal in every day seem to be just that. For example, who could argue that water is not wet or that 2 + 2 add up to 4? However, we may debate what wetness is – does it feel different to you and to me? We might also argue about whether 4 is the right answer. Perhaps the things we are adding together include sub-components or are of different sizes so is '4ness' always the same? Complicated isn't it? Or are we just asking too many questions?! Then again, for many years people were convinced that the world was flat.

Knowledge – absolute or provisional?

It is the case, then, that knowledge, no matter how well established scientifically, cannot be totally fixed and absolute. Knowledge is always, in some way, relative and contingent, even though for the practical purposes of living we must behave as if certain knowledge is simply true and reliable.

Clearly there are degrees of provisionality here. We would be deeply unhappy if we thought, for example, that the science of aerodynamics relating to flight engine technology was a kind of open-ended affair dependent upon opinion and belief. But even this kind of hard scientific technical knowledge rests on premises about matter, about physics and so on, that are changing all the time. Thankfully the form of practical knowledge that enables aeroplanes to be effectively managed through take-off, flight and landing is secure (although conditions do change above the speed of sound). Aerophysics is changing constantly and revisions are being made to knowledge in this area, hence new technologies of flight have come into being over the past 100 years. We may, for good reasons, think of medicine as a well-established field of contemporary research and knowledge. We are aware, however, of the developmental nature of medical knowledge and that new discoveries and technologies of treatment are emerging all the time. Scientists frequently argue about the precise nature of the tiniest particles of matter and whether they are particles or waves of energy, just as historians argue about the precise methods for the dating of archaeological evidence. Thus scientific, medical truth is not absolute at any time, but it is often represented as such or at least as unquestionably authoritative.

Organising knowledge as subjects

In the Middle Ages mental knowledge was classified in universities into the trivium and the quadrivium. The trivium was concerned with logic, grammar and rhetoric; the quadrivium with astronomy, music, geometry and arithmetic. The trivium was studied first and the quadrivium followed. The quadrivium could not be studied without the trivium. This classification was overtaken by others in the nineteenth and the twentieth centuries as interest grew in education for the masses. Singular forms of knowledge such as physics, chemistry, sociology and psychology emerged. New formations also developed including architecture, engineering, information science and education. Different subjects could come together to produce quite new forms and orders of knowledge.

The idea of the curriculum as the organisation of knowledge into separate subject areas developed powerfully through state education systems (Bourdieu and Passeron, 1977; Bowles and Gintis, 1976) but it was Paul Hirst, in the 1970s, who argued that the curriculum could be related to universal 'forms of knowledge', distinct areas that have their own concepts. These had to be testable against experience and they each had particular criteria for establishing this relation with reality. Hirst (1975) divided knowledge into the following seven forms: mathematics, physical sciences, human sciences, history, religion, literature and the fine arts, philosophy and moral knowledge. In order to be fully educated we need to study all of these forms. It is this view of knowledge which structures the present-day curriculum in schools and which still exerts powerful influence over subject divisions in other academic institutions like sixth-form colleges and universities, for instance. Fields of knowledge exist which cut across these forms. These are created by borrowing from several forms. Examples of fields would be business studies or geography. Knowledge is deemed to inhere in specific subjects that fit within a particular form. They may relate to one another but also have their own discrete and different sets of ideas, practices and contents. These are not just collections of facts; they include ways of looking at things and modes of understanding. Each subject follows its own rules and practices with its own discourse.

Counter to the idea that knowledge is fixed, complete and knowable is the idea of knowledge as constructed through social activity. Different social practices, engaged in by different groups of people, will necessarily give rise to different types of knowledge and different ways of knowing. Foucault (1977) saw knowledge systems as shifting according to the dominant 'episteme' or regime of knowledge. These systems are not progressive and may differ radically from one historical period to another. Young's (1971) work was influential in considering how knowledge can be organised through the curriculum and teaching groups to exercise control over pupils. He was interested in the way that only some pupils are given access to high status knowledge, i.e. those in the top sets who are seen as the most able. Those in the lower sets are given watered down versions of subject knowledge. They are often channelled into low-status subjects with a vocational emphasis. Thus teachers are 'gatekeepers' to knowledge, allowing or denying access to pupils. These issues are dealt with in more depth in Chapter 10.

Postmodern perspectives on knowledge

Postmodern views of the curriculum characterise it much more as a provisional social construct rather than as the expression of functional and intrinsically important knowledge. In the postmodern world, knowledge is at the centre and controlling it is a means to exercise power. Knowledge in this view is always contested and what we take for progress, the steady march of science, for instance, towards more inclusive and more powerful explanations of the world, is really the victory of one set of ideas and one kind of knowledge over others (Lyotard, 1986).

Education institutions are endowed with the power to grant social status to individuals, to award them credentials, and to authorise ideas and practices with the status of socially significant knowledge. Individuals receive status through accreditation systems that validate their knowledge at different levels, thereby producing a knowledge hierarchy.

In contemporary global conditions, knowledge is rapidly changing shape and form, largely under the influence of new, electronic means of storage and distribution. Some knowledge becomes commercially very significant and its circulation increases via new technologies. Knowledge becomes more fragmented and more specialised. Hybrid forms of knowledge are produced (as with cultural studies, for instance). The conventional institutions of knowledge – schools, colleges, universities – become subject to the logic of performativity, required to be more cost-effective and more productive and measured against performative criteria (Lyotard, 1986; Lumby, 2009). The contriving of league tables to measure schools' and colleges' success at GCSE and A level is a powerful example of this.

In summary, this brief look at knowledge has indicated that some thinkers within the functionalist tradition have espoused the singular view that the conventional curriculum of schooling (as in the case of the national curriculum in England and Wales, Australia, New Zealand and South Africa) follows the shape and logic of knowledge itself. Against this position is the idea that the curriculum is actually shaped by a number of forces, many of them having little or nothing to do with education or knowledge. It has been claimed that the curriculum embodies what has been set as knowledge by powerful groups in society. It has also been argued that knowledge is actually always a contested field, that the value of what is learned is of less importance than the social authority that learning in institutions carries with it. It has been suggested that discourses of knowledge are historically 'contingent', that they appear and hold authority according to the political, economic and social conditions that give them legitimacy rather than according to their 'scientific' truth.

Reader Reflection: Disciplinary tribalism 'is stifling creativity'

In a *Times Higher Education* article, Matthew Reisz (2011) explores a potential weakness of organising knowledge into subject disciplines. Reisz reported on a conference presentation delivered by an education professor, Gill Nicholls, in which she argued that 'although the division of knowledge into discrete, and often tightly policed, disciplinary blocks may be effective in creating "academic tribes and territories", it often fails to serve the needs of students and society'. Discussing 'the changing nature of disciplines and scholarship', she explained that 'the very notion of a discipline implies "both a domain to be investigated and the methods used in that domain . . . emphasising characteristics that separate discrete units of knowledge as opposed to those that might relate them"'. But 'many practical problems require a variety of complementary perspectives', she said. 'To create the best prosthetics, for example, experts in computer engineering, health services and material science need to come together, and routes to promotion and prestige should aid, not prevent, such collaborations' (Reisz, 2011: 16).

Think of some other examples of when subject boundaries are not allowed to artificially constrain development and solutions.

Having considered the nature of knowledge, how it is organised and how certain forms of it gain ascendancy through ideological positioning, we can now examine the structure of curricula.

Curriculum frameworks

Marsh (2009) suggests the use of frameworks – a list of significant headings – to help design and also to analyse existing curricula. When analysing a curriculum, or even a part of a curriculum, it is useful to consider it under headings such as: aims and purposes, content, teaching and learning principles (pedagogy) and assessment of learning.

Aims and purposes

There are many forms curricula can take and these reflect the different aims they were designed to achieve. The current curriculum in English schools, for example, aims to provide a broad and balanced education for all pupils in state schools between the ages of 5 and 16. This involves promoting their spiritual, moral, cultural, mental and physical developments and preparing them for adult life. The effectiveness of the curriculum can thus be judged in terms of how well it does these things.

Other curricula may be much more specific in their aims. Much vocational training, for instance, has a clearly defined set of practical skills and knowledge in which trainees are expected to demonstrate competence to successfully complete the programme. It is very important to consider aims and purposes as we would expect these to greatly influence the content, methods of teaching and learning, and forms of assessment that make up a curriculum.

Content

Many considerations govern the content of a curriculum and these stem from its overall aim or purposes. What kinds of knowledge should be taught? What values do they represent? How useful are they? How relevant is this knowledge? Practical relevance, of course, is not the only criterion for establishing the value of knowledge. There may be powerful cultural reasons for learning certain things. Subjects like French and German provide good mental exercise and require the application of discipline in learning and applying rules so it is unimportant whether or not the subject content is pertinent to the needs and demands of modern life. The training involved in conjugating French verbs is transferable to any kind of learning whether academic or worldly. It could be said to be about training in the acceptance of authority and as such is a way of averting more creative kinds of learning. Others might say that the kind of learning embodied in the declining of Latin nouns or reading Shakespearean texts is actually about joining a learned caste, becoming a member of an elite social group who may recognise and relate to one another through their common heritage of 'useless' but socially powerful knowledge.

The characteristic content of the school curriculum is defined in terms of subject knowledge but also in terms of the kinds of thinking and related skills – literacy and numeracy, for example – that might be deemed to be appropriate for learning. Subject organisation implies different and discrete areas of knowledge. The national curriculum for England and Wales had ten specified subjects when it was first introduced. It named three core subjects (English, mathematics and science) and seven foundation subjects (history, geography, technology, music, art, physical education (PE) and, at secondary level, a modern foreign language). This selection of subjects indicates a particular view of knowledge and learning. The terms 'core' and 'foundation' suggest a hierarchy of knowledge with implications for status relations between subjects. One of the issues with basing a curriculum around subjects is that a significant decision has to be made by someone about which subjects to include and which to leave out. Even when a subject has been included it should not be assumed that the content within it is in any way a given. At first sight, deciding what to teach in mathematics and science may appear unproblematic. In reality, however, what is included in these subjects and how the material is taught and learned are hotly contested issues (see Harlen and Qualter, 2014, and Haylock, 2014, for a discussion of maths and science curricula). Such struggles over prioritisation of content take place in all subjects. What aspects of history, for example, should be taught? History looks very different when presented from different perspectives. The Scots, English and French do not necessarily interpret British and European history in the same way. How we teach about the slave trade or the rise and fall of the British Empire can be very contentious. When teaching geography what regions do we give preference to? Do we consider our own part of the world to be more relevant or important than other regions? Such decisions about content and its presentation relate to all subjects to a greater or lesser degree.

There are various ways of organising curriculum content. These may not be subject based but instead organised around key experiences. Several commentators on the modern school curriculum have looked at the idea of moving away from strict subject boundaries and have advocated that learning, teaching and assessment be structured around critical themes where a number of different conventional subject areas can meet. Lawrence Stenhouse (1975), for instance, working for the Schools' Curriculum Council in the 1960s, advocated a more integrated approach to curriculum design that centred on themes or issues rather than separate subjects. He developed the Integrated Humanities Project that aimed to make the content more relevant to the learners. He felt that subjects created artificial boundaries that made understanding more difficult. In an integrated curriculum when learning about their local environment, for example, a pupil would look at aspects of history, geography, and social and moral education. Pupils would collect information, measure, count, present results and produce written accounts. They would be 'doing' different subjects simultaneously and learning the appropriate skills in an applied way. While these applied methods of empirical work endure in the way pupils are taught today, Stenhouse's ideological position on curriculum organisation conflicted with the more traditional view of subjects held by those who drew up the national curriculum in the 1980s.

This discussion has centred on the school curriculum and we must remember that this is just one area of education. In vocational learning the organisation of knowledge is often more clearly combined with the development of practical skills. Consider, for instance, how curriculum content and knowledge can be organised very differently in apprenticeships, nursing courses and teacher education.

Reader Reflection: What did you study at school?

Map out the curriculum you studied in primary school, lower secondary, Years 10 and 11 and sixth form. Consider the similarities and differences.

Why did you choose these subjects?

Were some options not available to you?

Did this impoverish your experience?

Pedagogy

Pedagogy, or the science of teaching, is concerned with the methods of teaching and learning. It involves structural features such as the learning environment, the classroom and a mode of practice, for example a teacher giving instructions or asking questions. Pedagogical ideas are in part developed from theories about how people learn. Different and contradictory accounts of how learning takes place exist and conflict with one another. (See Chapters 8, 9 and 11 for more detailed discussion of psychological theories of learning and for further information on pedagogical trends.)

There are many different traditions of learning. In Europe, for example, there is much more emphasis on pedagogy as a distinctive branch of educational knowledge. Pestalozzi, Montessori and Frenais have been associated with different versions of pedagogy. The challenge to institutions of learning to construct an effective and inclusive pedagogy was made by J. S. Bruner in 1972 when he claimed that any aspect of any subject could be made accessible and taught to anybody at any age. In the UK the influential Plowden Report (CACE, 1967) stimulated an emphasis on child-centred learning. This stressed creativity, spontaneity and individuality in an effort to draw out what was there already in the child. More recently, interest among theorists of pedagogy has turned to socio-cultural activity, using social constructivist theory that derives from Vygotsky (Engestrom, 1993). These theorists see learning as social and cultural and emphasise the role of language in mental development. This implies a different way of organising the experiences of learning from that of child-centred approaches. The emphasis on subject knowledge in the national curriculum lent itself to more traditional methods of whole-class teaching and formal classroom settings but the pedagogic approaches of social constructivism have become very influential in UK schools. (See Chapter 9 for an elaboration of Vygotsky's ideas.)

Methods of teaching and learning give rise to questions about autonomy and authority. We might consider what are the 'best', most productive, most relevant and most socially desirable forms of practice. How much should teaching and learning within a curriculum be concerned to cultivate the development of autonomy, initiative, critical awareness and other qualities that might be thought of as central aspects of citizenship? How much should it be about developing discipline of thought and acquiring important formal knowledge? Once again the answer depends upon the particular curriculum but also on how we perceive the nature and purposes of education.

Teaching and learning can take many forms. The emphasis may be on practical applications, experimentation, didactic teaching or open learning. Even within a particular course the teaching methods can vary greatly. For instance, students learning a modern foreign language (MFL) may have a very different experience from peers taking the same subject in the next room. One teacher may emphasise an interactive, oral approach to language development whereas another may stress writing and rote learning as ways of extending the students' vocabularies.

The following learning situations are commonly experienced by students:

- mass lectures
- whole-class work
- small group investigation and discussion
- individual learning
- e-learning.

Learning activities can include making notes, use of stimulus material presented by the teacher/lecturer, investigation in learning centres and libraries, searching through electronic sources, group discussion, practical activity such as experiments, web development or making artefacts, problem-solving individually or in groups. There are many possibilities and combinations (Capel et al., 2016; Petty, 2014; and Pollard et al., 2014 outline a range of these).

The form teaching and learning takes depends upon the particular curriculum, the nature of the knowledge and the preferences of the teachers and, sometimes, of the learners. Consider, for instance, how you might organise a learning programme for a foreign language or the history of England. Promoting learning within these programmes would be approached very differently because of the nature of the subject content in each. Furthermore, the teacher's preferred method may be experiential, active learning involving the pupils in investigative tasks. Alternatively, the teacher may have a didactic style where the students are told what to do and are given a large amount of written dictation. The methods and activities employed in learning experiences that we undertake in our daily lives will be very different again. Learning to drive a car, for example, is likely to involve practical driving activity and didactic instruction, though even here the 'style' of individual instructors can vary enormously.

In summary, then, decisions on appropriate pedagogy depend upon the purposes of the learning, the type of material to be taught and the ideological views of the 'best' methods held by those 'delivering' the curriculum.

Reader Reflection: 'Almost everything taught to children is forgotten'

Gillard (2011) cites a damning indictment of curriculum planning and review by Simon Jenkins, a *Guardian* newspaper columnist:

> The truth is that the entire curriculum is juju. Nobody knows its purpose. It is a miasma of archaism, bogus assumption, bland assertion and inertia. Nobody assesses what is a sensible way of spending a day, week or term. Nobody thrashes out the appropriate balance of vocational and educational, preferring to leave politicians to decide on the basis of 'what was good enough for me'. Almost everything taught to children is forgotten. The waste of money, time and talent must be stupendous. Yet we sail happily on, gazing over the stern and marvelling at the wake trailing behind. (Jenkins, 2010)

Do you agree with Jenkins' strident position? Do children forget most things they are taught? Does that matter if other skills are developed along the way?

Assessment

There are many ways in which educational progress and achievement may be judged (assessed). These vary from the formal to the very informal and each provides different kinds of information from statistical results to verbal feedback.

Purposes of assessment

Assessment is conducted for a variety of reasons.

1. *To monitor progress.* Here assessment will indicate how the student is progressing. This is often referred to as formative assessment or assessment for learning (see Assessment Reform Group, 2002, or Harlen, 2008, for an outline of the principles of assessment for learning). Formative assessment may be ongoing, for example regular feedback on coursework, or it may be periodic as with regular tests. It can form part of a diagnostic process providing a basis for decisions on future learning and for developing a record of progress. Assessment is seen here as an integral part of the learning process rather than as something that just happens at the end (Hargreaves et al., 2014).

2. *To indicate a final level of achievement.* After completing a course a final grade or level is often awarded as part of the certification. This is referred to as summative assessment or assessment of learning and is done by judging practical, oral, written or graphic coursework and examinations either against a set of specified criteria (criterion-referenced assessment) or in relation to the achievements of a group of people (norm-referenced assessment). (See Harlen,

2008 for an outline of the principles of assessment of learning.) It is a final assessment and judgement about individuals' achievements in relation to established standards and norms. These assessments can of course be very significant in gaining entry into other educational institutions such as sixth-form colleges and universities or for employment purposes.

3. *To evaluate the teaching and learning process.* Through assessment teachers can determine which aspects of the learning students find most difficult and also the effectiveness of different pedagogical approaches. This can be done while the curriculum is being taught using the results from formative assessments. An end-of-course evaluation can be conducted that also uses the summative assessment results.

4. *To enable comparisons of achievement by external agencies.* External agents such as local authorities, Ofsted, politicians and parents are able to use the results of national assessments, such as GCSE results and national curriculum scores, to compare education institutions. This is particularly the case when league tables are compiled with this purpose in mind.

Types of assessment

Reader Reflection: Your assessment experiences

Consider your experiences and feelings towards the following types of assessment:

- formal exams
- written essays and dissertations
- presentations
- practicals
- vivas
- classwork
- peer marking (learners judging each other's work)
- video-recorded debates or performances
- e-tasks
- questions of the whole class
- individual pupil questions.

The type of assessment used will depend upon the reasons for the assessment, the nature of the learning and also the ideological beliefs underpinning the curriculum. The list above moves from more formal to informal modes of assessment or from 'harder' to 'softer' forms. Formal mechanisms tend to elicit more quantitative data on performance, allow easy comparison between individuals and whole cohorts of pupils/ students and may appear more objective. Those forms of assessment that provide 'hard' data may be more valued. However, while appearing more accurate, their validity may actually be open to question. Often the most difficult and complex issues cannot be answered through simple multiple-choice type questions and so longer accounts have to be given that must be interpreted when marked. This leads to human error. It may also be open to question as to how much understanding and ability an examination is actually able to measure. The softer, more informal modes of assessment, such as dis- cussing work with a student, may reveal the full extent to which an individual learner understands. However, making comparisons of large numbers of students is impossible by such a method. Thus different forms of assessment each have their strengths and weaknesses and are compatible with different purposes.

Assessment issues in relation to the curriculum are many, complex and varied. Assessment has important public functions and can dominate curriculum pro- cesses and practices. The curriculum may be assessment-driven and risk losing sight of its broader objectives. Hall and Sheehy (2014) suggest that assessing learn- ing is not a neutral or value-free activity – it is always bound up with the attitudes, values, beliefs and sometimes the prejudices of those carrying out the assessment and those being assessed. The purposes of the assessment will have a significant effect upon how both the assessors and the assessed perceive the process. For instance, formative assessment can be done in a relaxed manner that is open and honest. Both assessor and assessed may feel it to be a positive process. However, a final summative assessment, when results are to be used as part of an accountabil- ity process, is likely to be a much more anxious process for those being assessed. Because of these potential conflicts the purposes of assessment need to be clear from the outset. It is difficult, if not impossible, to devise one form of assessment that is able to fulfil all of the possible assessment functions.

It is appropriate now to consider how the elements that comprise a curriculum become manifest in practice.

The national curriculum: a case study

Background to the English national curriculum

Since the Second World War, and before the 1988 Education Reform Act, central government had no direct hand in controlling or defining the curriculum of schools. In the 1944 Education Act only religious education was specified as a compulsory subject and even in that case parents had the right to opt out on behalf of their children. Otherwise the curriculum was left to the control of local authorities and schools (in association with governing bodies after the 1986 Education Act). Of course this does not mean that the school curriculum was a free for all before the 1988 Act. In reality it was subject to many constraints and shaping factors that tended to ensure a degree of uniformity across schools and across the country, including external examinations such as GCE Ordinary (O) and Advanced (A) levels, school culture and well-established professional habits.

Prior to comprehensivisation, secondary modern schools had a practical and vocational orientation while grammar schools had a more academic curriculum, dominated by a conventional array of subjects up to 16-plus including English, mathematics, modern foreign languages, the sciences and the humanities. Comprehensive reorganisation led largely to the emulation of this grammar school curriculum throughout secondary schools. During the 1980s the secondary school curriculum in England and Wales had been broadly divided up into English (13 per cent), maths (13 per cent), science (16 per cent), design and technology (4 per cent), foreign language (5 per cent), history and geography (10 per cent), art, music, drama and design (7 per cent) and PE (8 per cent), with the remaining 10 per cent taken up by other subjects (DES, 1987). Talk of the 'entitlement curriculum' (HMI, 1994), which would provide a broad and balanced diet for all pupils, had existed since the emergence of *Curriculum 11–16* (HMI, 1977). In primary schools, where there was little concern with external examinations, the curriculum was more open and could be quite varied from school to school in terms of both content and style.

We will now analyse the national curriculum using a curriculum framework of purposes, structure and content, teaching and learning, and assessment to help us to understand its implementation and development.

Purposes of the national curriculum

The national curriculum was introduced by the Conservative government of Margaret Thatcher in the Education Reform Act of 1988 after a period of criticism of educational standards in schools (see Chapter 6 for an account of the build up to the 1988 Reform Act). The dominant political ideology of the government, termed the 'new right', comprised a combination of traditionalism and belief in the importance of market forces. This was reflected in the development of a national curriculum that emphasised a traditional approach to education and, when coupled with other Tory education reforms, promoted competition between schools. The aim of the school curriculum as stated in the first section of the Act and quoted in the implementation document *From Policy to Practice* (DES, 1989a) should be to provide a curriculum that is balanced and broadly based and which:

a. promotes the spiritual, moral, cultural, mental and physical development of pupils at the school and of society; and

b. prepares such pupils for the opportunities, responsibilities and experiences of adult life. (Education Reform Act 1988, quoted in DES, 1989a: 2)

These aims were restated in the 1996 Education Act (section 351) and are currently the values underpinning the school curriculum (see www.gov.uk/government/collections/national-curriculum). They are very broad, as is appropriate to a curriculum that was designed for all pupils in compulsory state education from the ages of 5 to 16. They are able to encompass all ideologies of education, as outlined in Chapter 2, since they are concerned with the individual, knowledge and preparation for a role in society. It is in the actual structure and implementation of the curriculum that the traditional (classical) humanist influence becomes increasingly apparent.

Deriving from these aims the original four purposes of the national curriculum were:

1. to establish an entitlement for all pupils
2. to establish standards that can be used to set targets and measure performance
3. to promote continuity and coherence
4. to promote public understanding of and confidence in the work of schools.

Structure and content of the national curriculum

The curriculum was introduced as a legal entitlement (requirement) for all pupils in state education from the ages of 5 to 16. The teaching and assessment of the national curriculum was divided into four key stages as follows:

- Key Stage 1 – up to age 7 (Years 1 and 2)
- Key Stage 2 – up to age 11 (Years 3–6)
- Key Stage 3 – up to age 14 (Years 7–9)
- Key Stage 4 – up to age 16 (Years 10 and 11)

The national curriculum in England was divided into the following subjects for the first two key stages, with the first three designated as 'core' and the rest as foundation subjects: English, mathematics, science, information technology, design and technology, history, geography, music, art, physical education. At Key Stages 3 and 4, these subjects were supplemented by a modern foreign language. By 1991 at Key Stage 4, music, art and PE had ceased to be compulsory but still had to be available for pupils to choose as part of their entitlement and *either* history or geography or a combination of the two could be taken. All subjects had to be taught according to their programmes of study laid out in the national curriculum documents. The specific requirements concerning each subject varied according to the age of the pupils.

A series of changes to subjects included as compulsory at Key Stages 3 and 4 have been made since the inception of the national curriculum with modern foreign languages, for example, dropped at Key Stage 4 in 2004 and citizenship added as a compulsory subject from 2002. Religious education has had to be provided throughout all the key stages along with sex education and careers education at Key Stages 3 and 4 and work-related learning at Key Stage 4. Schools also had a requirement to cater for the personal and social education (PSE) of their pupils.

Reader Reflection: Does the curriculum never change?

It is interesting to compare national curriculum subjects with the subject regulations for 1904 and 1935 (Chitty, 2008):

1904	1935
English language	English language
English literature	English literature
One language	One language
Geography	Geography
History	History
Mathematics	Mathematics
Science	Science
Drawing	Drawing
Due provision for manual work and physical exercise	Physical exercises and organised games
(Housewifery in girls' schools)	Singing
	(Manual instruction for boys, domestic subjects for girls)

How might we account for the consistency of curriculum offering for over a century of education?

The national curriculum was not intended to take up all of the time pupils are in schools but there are no statutory regulations about how schools should divide up their time. A few years after its inception a review commissioned by the government made some recommendations indicating that English should occupy 14 per cent, maths 12 per cent, science 13 per cent, technology and foreign languages, religious education and PE 5 per cent each, and that the remaining 43 per cent should be discretionary but should include a balance of other specified subjects (Dearing, 1994).

Teaching and learning in the national curriculum

Decisions about how to teach the curriculum were originally left to the teachers. However, the content that was prescribed in detail for all subjects when the curriculum was first introduced had to be taught to all pupils. All pupils were to be assessed, as described in the next section, and the results made public in the form of performance tables for each school. The 1993 Education Act saw the creation of the Office for Standards in Education (Ofsted) which was to inspect every school at least once every four years. These factors put great pressure on teachers to ensure that they covered all aspects of the curriculum and left them little time to deviate from it. Effectively they had to 'teach to the test' in order to ensure the highest possible pupil scores in the assessments. Clearly this pressure led to a narrowing of the range of pedagogic methods teachers could employ and to some extent stifled the creativity of both teachers and pupils. Later we will see how the Labour government took far greater control over teaching and learning via the introduction of national strategies at Key Stages 1–3.

Assessment in the national curriculum

It was the assessment framework that gave shape to the national curriculum, drawing criticism that the assessment tail was wagging the curriculum dog (Gipps and Stobart, 1993; Stobart, 2008). The framework was established by the report of the Task Group on Assessment and Testing led by Paul Black (DES, 1989b). It represented a major break with the school-based assessment traditions of the past as it established national, externally marked tests at ages 7, 11 and 14. This was later amended to assessment at 7 and 14 being internally marked by teachers due to the severe pressures caused by the assessment regime. The programmes of study for each subject were set out in booklets published by the Department for Education and Employment and the Welsh Office (some together and some separately). Each subject was divided into different attainment targets, as illustrated in Table 5.1 for the core subjects of English, mathematics and science. By late 1991 the original excessively high number of attainment targets in maths and science had been reduced from 14 and 17 respectively.

Table 5.1 Attainment targets for English, mathematics and science

English	Mathematics	Science
En1 Speaking and listening	Ma1 Using and applying mathematics	Sc1 Scientific enquiry
En2 Reading	Ma2 Number and algebra	Sc2 Life processes and living things
En3 Writing	Ma3 Shape, space and measures	Sc3 Materials and their properties
	Ma4 Handling data (Key Stages 2–4)	Sc4 Physical processes

For each attainment target in most subjects nine successive levels of attainment were identified. Each of these had level descriptions. In effect this meant that the national curriculum set out how pupils should make progress in each subject area from the very beginning of their studies at age five to the end of Key Stage 3 at age 14. These levels did not coincide directly with key stages as there was recognition that children may differ in their rates of progress. However, it was specified that by the end of each key stage, the vast majority of pupils should have levels of attainment within the following ranges:

- end of Key Stage 1 – levels 1–3
- end of Key Stage 2 – levels 2–5
- end of Key Stage 3 – levels 3–7.

There was also a level 8 for 'very able' pupils and a ninth unnumbered level for 'exceptional performance' at Key Stage 3. These levels of achievement did not apply to Key Stage 4 when pupils would be taking GCSEs. Originally national curriculum assessment was intended for all of the subjects but due to the pressures this created for teachers and pupils it was limited from 1994 to the core subjects.

Reader Reflection: Academic versus creative and physical achievement

It is notable that the emphasis within the curriculum and its assessment is on traditionally academic rather than creative or physical achievement. For the core subjects (maths, English and science) pupils are expected to achieve a certain level of competence. Publicly available league tables are compiled on the basis of pupil and school achievement in

(Continued)

(Continued)

these subjects, elevating their importance within the curriculum and the community. There is no similar official requirement for pupil achievement in any of the other subjects nor are they reported on within league tables.

Consider the status relations of these subjects.

Is it appropriate?

Should we value the ability to add up more than the ability to draw or play the violin?

In a society that is worried about the increasing obesity of its population would it be sensible to require all pupils to attain a certain level of competence in PE before they could progress further?

Why do we not value physical achievement equally with academic achievement?

Do these questions depend on your perspective? A PE teacher may take a very different view from an English teacher.

Or does it depend more on the cultural norms that our education system exists within?

Criticisms of the national curriculum

So it was that the national curriculum, a historical milestone in the history of education in England and Wales, came into being after 1988. It was attacked in many ways and on many grounds at the time (Bash and Coulby, 1989; Lawton and Chitty, 1988; Pring, 1989). In the years following, the national curriculum continued to receive critical treatment from educationalists, many of whom agreed with the principle of a national curriculum but deplored the process of its implementation and development, lamenting the unimaginative form it had taken (Lawton, 1999) and its shape and size (Conway, 2010; Lawton, 2008). Complaints included the absence of a clear educational purpose, its disregard of recent debates about curriculum and the failure to engage in detailed and sustained consultation with teachers and other education professionals. There was early pressure to reconsider the curriculum as originally established.

The original national curriculum was critiqued on the following grounds (Gipps, 1993):

- It was too bureaucratic.
- It centralised control of education.
- Private schools were exempt.

- The curriculum was felt to be too traditionalist and too conventionally academic in orientation.
- There was an enormous amount of content to be covered that left little time for exploration outside of the formal curriculum.
- Testing at 7 and 11 was felt to be dangerous in terms of labelling.
- The theoretical ideas underpinning the notion of cumulative achievement within all subjects were challenged.

The testing regime put great pressure on pupils and teachers alike. It was felt that the national curriculum worked against the spirit of comprehensive reform that had envisaged the development of a school curriculum based on the idea of a common culture (Lawton, 1975). Whetton (2009) has argued that national curriculum assessment evolved from a criterion-referenced system based on tasks marked by teachers through to an externally marked examination system. This creates huge pressure on pupils, given that the results are widely used by the public and successive governments, which have been unable to identify a better system of accountability. Studies have shown that the results of NC testing are not fully reliable year on year (Newton, 2009). Concerns about validity arise from the results being used for too many purposes, with high-stakes accountability purposes distorting teaching and learning by encouraging narrow teaching to the tests (Stobart, 2009). Wyse and Torrance (2009) found that while primary pupils made initial gains in achievement following the introduction of the NC testing arrangements, these plateaued after the year 2000 and even led to negative effects on pupil achievement.

Some critics (Ball, 2003) claimed that the national curriculum favoured certain (middle) class groups above others. It has also been accused of working against the cultural orientations of ethnic minority groups in its historical, cultural and linguistic biases (Gillborn, 2001). Thus the history syllabus was primarily British (English) history that stopped at the end of the Second World War. It took no account of more recent world conflicts such as the Middle East crisis, the Cold War and the decline of the British Empire. In English the literature studied was British and all pupils had to study Shakespeare. The emphasis given by the national curriculum to Christian religious traditions was also noted as symptomatic of cultural bias (Troyna and Carrington, 1990).

It was in the introduction of national standards that the national curriculum was felt by some commentators to be most likely to accentuate class differences. The introduction of standardised age-related testing meant that children could be ranked and ordered as never before with their value to the school, in the labour market and in the sphere of education varying accordingly. For some this meant that the national curriculum was a massive machine for differentiating children against fixed norms – a very powerful, pervasive form of control. The decision to publish test results exacerbated these fears at a school level on the grounds that it could further disadvantage schools operating in deprived areas. In some schools these league tables of results led to the organisation of pupils on ability grounds, a policy later encouraged by the Labour government (see DfES, 2005a). Even at primary level this is now commonplace. Known as setting, this approach has been criticised on grounds of equality of opportunity but sits well within a differenti-ated school system with grammar schools, city technology colleges and later specialist schools, academies and free schools.

By 1993 increasing pressure from teachers and parents provoked Dearing's review of the national curriculum and testing arrangements. This made relatively small changes to the structure but could not achieve the radical rethink that some called for. Nor could it provide the kind of ideological rationale and professional support for the curriculum that it had lacked from the outset (Chitty and Dunford, 1999).

In the main, subsequent changes have been in the form of cutting subject con-tent requirements, making some subjects optional thereby allowing increasing specialisation at Key Stage 4, and limiting national assessment to the three core subjects. Critics pointed to the potential for incoherence created by offering increased choices within what was originally planned to be a common entitle-ment curriculum, e.g. Millar (2011) highlighted the difficulties in teaching physics to post-16 students who had specialised in three separate sciences at GCSE alongside those with a GCSE joint award (with 33 per cent less physics). Swarbrick (2011) pointed to the problems facing MFL teachers working with Year 7 students – some of whom received several years' specialist teaching in primary school, while others had either no experience or studied a different lan-guage. Pupils' experience of history was equally fragmented and, as Counsell (2011) explains, the goal of providing all young people with a usable 'big picture' of the past was scotched because some abandoned their study of the subject at the age of 14 (or even 13) but others continued for another two years.

From national curriculum to national strategies

When New Labour came to power in 1997, it decided to give priority in the primary school curriculum to literacy and numeracy, with the aesthetic and creative areas of the curriculum being downgraded and marginalised (Chitty, 2008). Chitty argued that there was a marked deterioration in the overall quality of primary education because of the narrowing of the curriculum and the intensity of test preparation.

Following increasing curriculum prescription which radically altered the ownership that teachers had over what they taught, the Labour government then launched an unprecedented interest (interference?) in the *way* the curriculum was taught. From 1998 a number of 'national strategies' were introduced by the government which advised on the 'best' means of teaching and learning. The primary curriculum was 'supplemented' by the literacy and numeracy strategies outlined in the non-statutory documents covering literacy (DfEE, 1998a) and numeracy (DfEE, 1999). Though not a legal requirement these strategies prescribed both content and methods of teaching for English and maths in the primary school and the majority of primary schools followed them, sometimes with their own modifications, as school inspections focused particularly on pupils' achievements in literacy and numeracy. In 2000 the Key Stage 3 strategy was developed which again focused on teaching and learning strategies but included all three core subjects – English, maths and science. It became known as the Secondary National Strategy from 2001. In 2003, the Primary National Strategy was set out in *Excellence and Enjoyment: A Strategy for Primary Schools* (DfES, 2003b). This extended the remit of the strategy but still focused on core subjects primarily.

In its annual plan for the national strategies, DCSF (2008) explained that the aim was to raise achievement and progression in all phases and settings through personalised learning and high-quality, well-planned teaching which addresses individual needs. There was to be a particular focus on the core subjects and early years and targets were set for standards and progress, with key performance indicators, to be achieved by 2011. Ofsted conducted a large-scale impact study on the 2008–9 national strategies implementation, reporting mixed outcomes:

> The National Strategies have contributed to a national focus on standards and have helped to focus teachers and others on discussing and improving teaching and learning. The National Strategies' initiatives have yielded successes with individual teachers, departments, groups of pupils and schools. When viewed against the nationally agreed targets for 2011, however, the overall improvements in standards and progress over the last four years have been too slow. (Ofsted, 2010: 4)

In 2009 the Labour Education Secretary, Ed Balls, had already become aware of these failings via a major review of primary education, the Cambridge Review (Alexander, 2009), and had decided to withdraw the primary literacy and numeracy strategies from 2011 while insisting that daily literacy and numeracy hours (prescriptive hour-long lessons) remained. On the one hand this can be seen to reduce the controlling hand of government but on the other it presents a huge change for schools, particularly at primary level, to react to. For over a decade primary teachers had been used to following externally produced guidance for much of their teaching strategy; now they would have to go back to relying on their own professional judgement. A whole generation of teachers trained over this period had known nothing other than the national strategies so, while they may have relished their new-found pedagogic freedom, they may also have struggled with it.

Reader Reflection: Key findings and recommendations from Ofsted's (2010: 5–6) impact report on the National Strategies between 2008 and 2009

- The National Strategies have contributed to a productive and professional debate around pedagogy. Almost all the schools visited considered that the National Strategies had contributed to improving the quality of teaching and learning and the use of assessment.
- However, in over half the secondary schools and a third of the primary schools visited, despite their engagement with the National Strategies, the survey found weaknesses in basic teaching skills. Responsibility for eradicating these weaknesses lies with the schools' leadership.
- In nine of the local authorities visited, a considerable emphasis by the National Strategies on monitoring was at the expense of helping to develop expertise and capacity.
- Evaluation of the impact of the National Strategies' many programmes was a serious weakness at national and local level. It was often difficult for the schools and local authorities visited to assess which initiatives worked and which did not.
- The frequent introduction of new initiatives, materials and guidance led to overload and diminished the potential effectiveness of each individual initiative. Local authorities were learning how to manage this by tailoring the National Strategies to the requirements of individual schools.
- Taken together, national agencies, including the National Strategies, provided a very considerable number of diverse, changing and sometimes overlapping programmes. Systems for communicating with schools and local authorities did not help them to have a good understanding of the coherence of different initiatives.

What causes would you attribute to the failures within this government-sponsored national initiative? Think about political motivations (at many levels), the effect of monitoring on individual teacher performance and self-esteem, etc.

Labour's proposed new primary curriculum

In 2008 the Labour government launched a major review of the primary curriculum led by Sir Jim Rose, a prominent primary education expert. Their proposals centred on a reorganisation of the subject areas into six major groupings 'to make it easier for teachers to organise lessons spanning more than one subject and to place an even stronger focus on English, maths and ICT' (DCSF, 2009a: 8). The six areas of learning were intended to support not replace subjects:

1. Mathematical understanding
2. Historical, geographical and social understanding
3. Understanding English, communication and languages
4. Scientific and technological understanding
5. Understanding the arts
6. Understanding physical development, health and well-being.

Teachers would still teach separate subjects such as maths, music and history alongside more 'cross-curricular' work – lessons and projects that combine more than one subject or skill – as this was felt to make lessons more interesting for children and help them use their knowledge in different situations. Interestingly, this seemed to have resonances with the primary curriculum of the 1960s and 1970s during which time 'topic' work and themes were used to study subjects in an interdisciplinary way. Labour claimed the new curriculum would also give teachers more freedom to teach knowledge and skills in different ways, using their own professional judgement. This is paradoxical given the extent to which the New Labour government had for ten years sought to micro-manage the curriculum and the way it was taught. Many felt the plans were sound and the new curriculum, which had been subject to much expensive fact-finding, research and debate, was due to be taught in schools from September 2011 but it did not get through parliament before the general election and new Coalition ministers quickly confirmed that they would not proceed with it.

The Coalition's national curriculum review

The Coalition of Conservatives and Liberal Democrats entered government with a commitment to giving schools greater freedom over the curriculum and quickly instituted a comprehensive review of the national curriculum in England for 5 to 16 year olds. As a means of demonstrating its power as a new government administration and securing nationwide impact, a curriculum review can be a very effective exercise. In announcing this new review the Education Secretary Michael Gove said:

> We have sunk in international league tables and the national curriculum is substandard. Meanwhile the pace of economic and technological change is accelerating and our children are being left behind. The previous curriculum failed to prepare us for the future. We must change course. Our review will

examine the best school systems in the world and give us a world-class curriculum that will help teachers, parents and children know what children should learn at what age. (DfE, 2011)

The official announcement of the review clearly stated that it would:

- replace the current substandard curriculum with one based on the best school systems in the world, providing a world-class resource for teachers and children
- consider what subjects should be compulsory at what age
- consider what children should be taught in the main subjects at what age. (DfE, 2011)

An expert panel was commissioned under the chairmanship of Tim Oates that after a certain amount of internal disagreement reported in December 2011. Following a period of consultation, the government produced the new curriculum in 2013 for implementation in stages in September 2014 and 2015. This is the version of the national curriculum currently being delivered (see DfE, 2014a on DfE website for full details).

Reader Reflection: The aims of the national curriculum

The National Curriculum in England: Framework Document (DfE, 2013a) cites the aims of 1988 as continuing to relate to the overall curriculum for all state funded schools. However, it now gives a more specific aim for the national curriculum itself.

> The national curriculum provides pupils with an introduction to the essential knowledge that they need to be educated citizens. It introduces pupils to the best that has been thought and said; and helps engender an appreciation of human creativity and achievement. (DfE, 2013a, Para 3.1)

From these aims what do you perceive to be the key aspects of this curriculum?

Content changes

The review declares that schools are free to organise their day as long as the content of the national curriculum programmes of study is taught to all pupils (DfE, 2013a). The rewritten curriculum is slimmer in terms of overall content but intended to be more challenging by focusing on core subject knowledge with a stronger emphasis on skills such as essay writing and problem-solving.

The maths curriculum, for instance, expects pupils to be able to do more at an earlier age. In science there is a shift towards hard facts and 'scientific knowledge' with new additional content in the primary key stages. At Key Stage 3 the separate subjects of physics, biology and chemistry have a clearer identity. In the English curriculum Shakespeare becomes even more prominent, with pupils between the ages of 11 and 14 expected to have studied two of his plays. History remains largely British-based including European and world events from 1901. The 'new' subject of computing replaces ICT across all key stages and is counted as a science for English Baccalaureate (EBacc) purposes (see the EBacc section later in this chapter). This subject switch signifies a radical shift from focusing on the handling of data and operating programmes to programming itself, an aspect not previously widely studied by pupils as it was considered too specialised. Learning a foreign language now becomes compulsory in primary school at Key Stage 2.

Changes to assessment

In line with the curriculum changes, the assessment of the curriculum has also been radically overhauled. The individual attainment targets are no longer so prominent. In the maths and also the science sections of the curriculum framework, for example, it states that 'By the end of each key stage, pupils are expected to know, apply and understand the matters, skills and processes specified in the relevant programmes of study' (DfE, 2013a: 89 and 137). The assessment process is significantly changed with levels of attainment being abolished and from 2016 the outcomes are to be reported for each pupil as a scaled score for each core subject. Individual pupil progress will be determined in relation to average pupil progress on the same baseline.

The current structure of the national curriculum, in terms of which subjects are compulsory at each key stage, is set out in Table 5.2 below (DfE, 2014a). All schools are also required to teach religious education at all key stages. Secondary schools must provide sex and relationship education.

Criticism of the changes

It is early days in the implementation of the revised curriculum but there has already been criticism that the new primary curriculum requires children to cover some topics, particularly in maths and science, far earlier than previously. It is feared that this may cause difficulties with conceptual understanding and lead to pupils becoming confused and disillusioned from an early age. The history curriculum has also prompted debate with some claiming it is too narrowly British based.

Table 5.2   Structure of the national curriculum

	Key Stage 1	Key Stage 2	Key Stage 3	Key Stage 4
Age	5–7	7–11	11–14	14–16
Year groups	1–2	3–6	7–9	10–11
Core subjects				
English	✓	✓	✓	✓
Mathematics	✓	✓	✓	✓
Science	✓	✓	✓	✓
Foundation subjects				
Art and design	✓	✓	✓	
Citizenship			✓	✓
Computing	✓	✓	✓	✓
Design and technology	✓	✓	✓	
Languages		✓	✓	
Geography	✓	✓	✓	
History	✓	✓	✓	
Music	✓	✓	✓	
Physical education	✓	✓	✓	✓

Note: At Key Stage 2 the subject title for languages is 'foreign language'; at Key Stage 3 it is 'modern foreign language'

In announcing the curriculum review the language of the Secretary of State openly disparaged the existing curriculum blaming the previous Labour administration. It also assumed a strong link between educational achievement and economic performance. The Coalition government thus presented itself as the saviour of the education system while simultaneously dealing with one of the supposed causes of a failing economy: education. International comparisons were made uncritically, indicating that schooling in England was falling behind global competitors. There was no recognition of the limitations of these comparative statistics or of choosing data that conveniently fit their own political agenda (see Chapter 7 for a discussion of the uses and abuses of international league tables). Once again curriculum reforms were presented as something clearly needed in order to raise standards and make the country more competitive economically.

The prevailing Coalition narrative of traditionalism, with its strong Tory influence, ensured that the freshly reviewed national curriculum closely resembles that studied by Coalition ministers in their own school days! It is important to note that the national curriculum is not compulsory for academies and free schools (see Chapter 6) which now make up a majority of England's secondary and an increasing number of its primary schools. This constitutes a fundamental structural weakness in the provision of a nationally coherent curriculum.

Reader Reflection: Curriculum criticism in Australia

The following two extracts are taken from a newspaper article concerning the newly elected Conservative Australian government setting up a review of the national curriculum even before changes from the previous review by the outgoing administration have been fully implemented. When reading it consider how the criticisms raised mirror recent controversies over the National Curriculum in England.

1. The Abbott government's rapid-fire review of the national curriculum has been labelled as premature by parents and teachers, given the new content has not been fully rolled out in schools.

   The education minister, Christopher Pyne, announced on Friday the appointment of the conservative education commentator Kevin Donnelly and the public administration academic Ken Wiltshire to lead the Coalition's promised review of the national curriculum. Setting a deadline of May or June, Pyne said the 'consultative' review would look at complaints the curriculum was overcrowded, heavily prescriptive and rigid. The minister also raised concerns the curriculum downplayed Western civilisation, the Anzac story and the role of conservative prime ministers while placing excessive focus on unions and the Labor party.

2. The criticism of 'constant' changes comes as the lead writer of the history curriculum, Professor Stuart Macintyre, rejects claims the material contains left-wing bias, saying it was refined through an 'exhaustingly consultative' process that included a wide range of education experts [...] lots of people had opinions about what children need to learn but they failed to appreciate the demands placed on teachers, who may variously be teaching a group of mainly Indigenous students in Alice Springs, a multicultural classroom in western Sydney, and a group on the outskirts of Melbourne. (Daniel Hurst, Guardian, 130114) www.theguardian.com/world/2014/jan/13/national-curriculum-review-premature-say-parents-and-teachers

Is it inevitable that reviews of the national curriculum in any country will be politically based?

Final observations on the national curriculum

There were significant problems initially in terms of the sheer volume of content, assessment and bureaucracy associated with the national curriculum. Some might say these have been steadily ironed out over time; others would claim teachers have simply given in or become 'acclimatised' to them. Having been in place for over 25 years the national curriculum is all that current pupils and a substantial proportion of teachers have known, so the subject content, pedagogic guidance and assessment regimes are all regarded as 'normal'. When first introduced, the curriculum was very traditional and as such only reflected the beliefs of a small ideological base. To some extent it broadened under pressure from different stakeholders with the introduction of more vocational learning and the creation of subject options, particularly in older year groups. More recent governments, however, with very different ideological leanings appear to have turned the national curriculum back towards being even more traditional. What we need to remember is that this curriculum is just one possible structure. It reflects the dominant ideologies that introduced it and the political power of the different groups who have helped to shape it.

Reader Reflection: 'Back to the 19th century with Michael Gove's education bill' (Ball, 2011)

The following extract is from an editorial piece by the academic Stephen Ball providing a commentary on a key reform of the Coalition government. When reading it consider how Ball uses historical references to make his points.

> Michael Gove's education bill ... offers another set of small moves and incursions that are moving English education further away from a common, comprehensive system and gradually closer to a patchwork of diverse provisions and providers. In fact, the system is beginning to look more and more like it did prior to 1870.
>
> [...]
>
> Just like under Margaret Thatcher, education is to be subject to a two-pronged process of change. On the one hand is the free-market economics of choice, competition and contestability, opening up new routes of entry and exit into school provision. On the other, the authoritarian, elite, nostalgic Conservatism that is founded on a 'curriculum of the dead' and the minute correctness of school uniforms. There are two political fantasies here. One is a fantasy market of perfect choice and perfect competition. The other is a fantasy curriculum based on Boy's Own comics and a vision of England rooted in the one-nation Toryism of Disraeli, Baldwin and Butler.

Ball's piece is a very good example of how his own ideology influences his analysis of government actions in relation to our education system and its curriculum.

Do you agree with Ball's analysis?

Can you present a different analysis (even if you don't agree with it)?

Early years' curriculum: foundation stage

From the 1990s there has been increasing demand for, and concomitant expansion of, early years' education. This has been largely driven by parents' desire to secure quality and affordable childcare for their pre-school aged children as increasingly couples and also single parents with young children are in employment. This growth in demand has fuelled the expansion of provision and, with a growing public awareness of the safety and care of young children, greater regulation and monitoring. There remain sharp differences in opinion as to the purposes of this comparatively new sector of education and how it should develop. Is it an 'early start' to schooling in a world where a child's performance at school and the associated league tables take centre stage or is it a place of play, exploration and informal learning during a period of early child development? Also, is it possible, and if so to what extent, to be both of these things?

The Education Act 2002 included the foundation stage as part of the national curriculum. This made the following six areas of learning in the foundation stage the statutory curriculum for children aged three to five:

1. Personal, social and emotional development
2. Language and literacy
3. Mathematical development
4. Knowledge and understanding of the world
5. Physical development
6. Creative development.

These early learning goals had first been introduced in 2000 (DfEE/QCA, 2000) to replace the previous curriculum guidelines for this phase (known as the desirable learning outcomes) and became a statutory requirement for those providers receiving government funding. While many early years' teachers welcomed the recognition that the foundation stage brought to this phase of education, criticism was levelled at the subjecting of very young children to an increasingly formalised curriculum at the expense of exploration and play. It was felt that this may actually hinder their intellectual and emotional development (Moylett, 2003). These views appeared to have little impact, however, as the early learning goals and the foundation stage were both replaced in 2008 by the Early Years Foundation Stage (EYFS) framework (DCSF, 2007). This framework included 69 statements within the six areas of the learning goals, which established expectations for children to reach by the end of the stage (aged five). Although it was perhaps not originally intended that each of these statements should be assessed, the prevailing obsession with testing children led to just that in many early years' settings, which created great dissatisfaction among teachers and parents.

The Coalition government introduced a revised EYFS (DfE, 2012) which came into force on 1 September 2012. It introduced a new slimmed down curriculum for nought to five year olds and reduced the paperwork for teachers involved in its delivery. A further updated EYFS (DfE, 2014b) came into effect on 1 September 2014 which made amendments to the safeguarding and welfare requirements. In the new EYFS framework seven areas of learning were identified along with 17 early learning goals. These included prime and specific areas of learning:

- *Prime areas of learning*

  - communication and language
  - physical development
  - personal, social and emotional development

- *Specific areas of learning* (which feed into the prime areas)

  - literacy
  - mathematics
  - understanding the world
  - expressive arts and design.

The curriculum will be delivered mostly through games and play. Assessment is formative, ongoing and is primarily observational and should not disrupt normal learning activities. Children's progress is reviewed at two key points. When they are between age two and three a short written summary is provided to parents outlining their child's development in the areas of learning. The summary will identify strengths and any areas where a child's progress is less than expected. Areas of concern must also be raised. The summary should identify activities and strategies a provider intends to use to address issues or concerns (DfE, 2014b). At the end of the EYFS in the final term of the school year when they turn five, which for most children is the reception year in primary school, an EYFS profile report must be completed for each child. In the profile, development is assessed against the 17 early learning goals with a short commentary on each child's learning characteristics. Year 1 teachers are given a copy of the profile report for when the child begins school and the LA also has access to it if required. Note that the need to assess is still very much in policy-makers' minds even if the points of assessment and the volume of goals or statements are reduced.

In September 2010 all three and four year olds became entitled to 15 hours a week of state-funded early education. This resulted in 96 per cent of three and four year olds receiving state-funded education. From September 2013 the entitlement was extended to 15 hours of free education per week for all looked-after two year olds and two year olds from families who met the criteria for free school meals (FSM). From September 2014 the number of early learning places was extended to around 40 per cent of all two year olds. More schools now offer nursery provision and the times available extend from 8am to 6pm with increasing availability of after-school and holiday care. To help parents further the Coalition government introduced a new tax-free childcare scheme to support working families from autumn 2015, worth up to £2,000 per child each year. There was the introduction of an early year's pupil premium (see Chapter 6 for an explanation of the pupil premium) in 2015 and increased support for lower income families via universal credit. Thus more and more children from earlier ages are spending increasing amounts of time in early years' settings. The sector has expanded accordingly to take account of this increase in numbers and this rapid recent development is a good example of the ideological nature of curriculum development. Important decisions have been made concerning appropriate content, assessment and reporting. The nature of this curriculum will have a significant impact upon young children and their early development. It will have an influence on how they see themselves and how they are seen by others beginning from a very young age.

14–19 education

Much attention has been given in the past two decades to the curriculum offered to young people across the 14–19 age range and is of particular significance now that all English pupils are required to stay in education or training until their eighteenth birthday. This phase of education overlaps with the national curriculum's Key Stage 4.

The 14–19 Curriculum: an academic–vocational divide

Following much hand-wringing about the stasis of the GCSE and A level qualifications structure and the increasing irrelevance of testing pupils at age 16 when many did not leave school to embark on a working career until 18, the Labour government commissioned the Tomlinson Report (Tomlinson, 2004). There had been concerns for some considerable time about the retention of the A level as the 'gold standard' for high quality, post-16 education and many arguments had been posited in favour of replacing this narrow, traditionalist A level study and examination with a broader diet of relevant learning in the form of some kind of international baccalaureate.

Thus, Tomlinson's review was vested with a great deal of both political and educational expectation and, had his far-reaching proposals been accepted, they would have radically changed the face of 14–19 curricula and qualifications. Tomlinson's main proposal was to replace GCSEs, A levels and vocational qualifications with a single diploma over a ten-year period of reform. The diploma would have functioned at four levels: entry (equivalent to pre-GCSEs), foundation (GCSEs at grade D–G), intermediate (GCSE A*–C) and advanced (A level). Students would have been able to progress at their own rate resulting in mixed-aged classes. Advanced-level students would have taken more challenging questions to get even higher marks than were available under the A level system. The diploma would have been made up of modules adapted from the existing A level and GCSE modules. Students would have chosen their own combination (open diploma) or opted for one of the 20 pre-designed combinations (specialised diploma). This would have strengthened vocational qualifications as so-called 'academic' modules could have been studied alongside more 'vocational' ones. All pupils would have also studied 'functional' mathematics, ICT and communication skills and submitted an extended essay, as well as undertaking 'wider activities' in the form of work experience, paid jobs, voluntary work and family responsibilities.

To the dismay and annoyance of many educators and policy-makers, Tomlinson's Report was caught up in political manoeuvring and, even after the recommendations were watered down, the report was quietly shelved as Labour headed into the general election of 2005 and wanted to avoid upsetting middle England by rocking the A level boat. It was left to the Coalition government elected in 2010 to commission the Wolf Report of 2011 into vocational education. Its findings were damning as to the state of much vocational education for 16–19 year olds. Too many young people were doing low level vocational qualifications in further education (FE) with little benefit for their career prospects. Wolf suggested that the apprentice system be strengthened to provide meaningful vocational training.

Students who had not obtained good GCSE grades in Maths and English on leaving school should continue to study these subjects during their vocational programmes to improve their literacy and numeracy. In schools pupils between 14 and 16 should concentrate on their academic core rather than vocational courses. In response to the Wolf Report, in order to strengthen vocational qualifications and give them parity with academic programmes, the technical baccalaureate has been developed in three areas of vocational education for 16 to 18 year olds. Having begun in September 2014 it is to be reported in league tables from 2017 onwards.

The three elements of the technical baccalaureate are:

1. a high-quality level 3 vocational qualification – only the best courses, recognised by employers, will continue to count in league tables
2. a level 3 'core maths' qualification, including AS level maths
3. the extended project, which will develop and test students' skills in extended writing, communication, research, and self-discipline and self-motivation. (DfE, 2013b)

Over the same period the Coalition government called for GCSEs and A levels to be made more rigorous with coursework being replaced with exams and the ending of modular structures that enabled assessments to be retaken several times during a course to improve the final grade. A* grades were created to denote excellence.

Reader Reflection: curriculum mediators

McCormick and Burn (2011) highlight the distinction between curriculum specification at a national level and its interpretation and enactment by teachers in schools. They note that a number of other powerful mediators of the curriculum in recent years – the Qualifications and Curriculum Authority and the National Strategies for Literacy, Numeracy and Key Stages – have now been abolished.

But several others – most notably the examination boards and the publishers – remain, with the two sometimes very closely intertwined. Both have exercised considerable influence and there are questions over the nature of the relationship between the new curriculum (and its assessment structures) and the examination specifications developed to meet GCSE and A level national criteria.

All three public examination boards in England – AQA, OCR and Edexcel – now endorse textbooks designed specifically for their GCSE and A level specifications. Edexcel is also directly owned by the publishing company Pearson.

Consider the issues of ownership and control within curriculum and assessment raised by such a close relationship between organs of the state and commercial businesses.

The English Baccalaureate (EBacc)

Soon after coming into government, in 2010, it was announced rather peremptorily that schools' success would only be measured by the EBacc. The EBacc is not an actual qualification but the achievement of A*–C in each of a specific group of subjects at GCSE. The subjects are English, mathematics, two sciences, a language and a humanity. While it turned out not to be the case that EBacc immediately became the only measure of achievement in five GCSEs A*–C and other subjects were still reported in league tables, the number of pupils achieving EBacc is an increasingly significant indicator.

The EBacc 'combination' was announced without consultation and the choice of certain subjects to be included at the expense of others without debate caused consternation. Adams (2013), for instance, found the omission of arts education an indication of 'the new philistinism' that has overtaken the English education system. Pring (2013: 139) points out that without the inclusion of the arts or design and technology the 'dualism between the "academic" and the "practical" ("knowing that" and "knowing how") is reinforced'. In a very short time this return to a very traditional curriculum mix has had a huge impact on curriculum planning, with vocational subjects quickly dispatched from core curricula because of the power of league table comparisons of schools' results. Essentially, school leaders have responded to the enormous pressure that changing the market value of certain subjects has put on schools.

This refuelled, virtually overnight, the academic/vocational divide that policymakers and teachers had been trying for over a decade to expunge. Successful partnerships between schools and FE colleges through which pupils in Key Stage 4 could spend half their week studying vocational subjects such as BTECs, NVQs and Vocational Diplomas in engineering, sport, the service professions or social care came to an abrupt end with no thought for the educational needs of the pupils for whom such subjects had proved beneficial. Schools once again required the majority of pupils to spend more time in the classroom rather than the workshop in order to study the core subjects deemed by the Secretary of State alone to be worthy of study. The years of arguments about parity of status between academic and vocational subjects were swept away at a stroke, driven by the view that traditional academic subjects were far more worthy than vocational subjects. There was not even the pretence at consultation on this issue and no engagement at all with the argument that vocational subjects may be equally valuable forms of study within a balanced curriculum for 14–16 year olds.

The creation of the EBacc thus significantly influenced the 14–16 curriculum, reinforcing an academic focus. Curriculum coherence at the 14–19 stage has clearly proved elusive and the policies of the Coalition and subsequent

Conservative government have sought to preserve the divide between academic and vocational learning. The move towards the traditional EBacc combination was further promoted, with the newly elected Conservative government announcing in June 2015 an intention to ensure that in future all pupils will take the EBacc combination to GCSE level (DfE, 2015a).

Reader Reflection: 'Gove's on the Bac foot with a white paper stuck in 1868'

John White, a long-established academic within education studies and Emeritus Professor of the Philosophy of Education, Institute of Education, London University, wrote in the *TES* on 21 January 2011 that:

> Michael Gove has outstripped Kenneth Baker in backwardness. Baker's 1988 national curriculum matched almost point for point the curriculum for the new state secondary schools of 1904. Gove has surpassed him by nearly 40 years.

> His new English Baccalaureate is virtually a carbon copy of the 1868 Taunton report's curriculum for most 'middle class schools', as they were then called.

> The new award will be given to all 16 year olds who have good exam grades in 'English, mathematics, the sciences, a modern or ancient foreign language and a humanity such as history or geography'. Taunton's list is identical, except that it makes both history and geography compulsory.

> How is it that a curriculum designed for clerks and shopkeepers in Dickens' England is at the cutting edge in 2010? Gove's White Paper does not say. It talks of giving pupils a 'properly rounded academic education' via 'a wide range of traditional subjects'. It also strongly hints that a reformed national curriculum will be cut down to these 'core' subjects. But it gives no reason why.

> [...]

> No reason given why school education should be built around a totality of knowledge, rather than some other aim – equipping children for a flourishing life, for instance, or for civic responsibility. No reason why, even within its own terms, science, maths, history, geography, mother tongue and another language complete the circle of knowledge. What about economics, political science, psychology, sociology, religious knowledge, philosophy, self-knowledge . . .?

White's piece is strongly worded and clearly written from his own ideological perspective.

What would you say White's ideological influences are?

Do you agree/disagree with him? In part or in whole?

Does his analysis help you make sense of the issues?

> **Video Discussion**
>
> Visit https://study.sagepub.com/bartlettburton4e to watch a video discussion on:
>
> *Education systems and the curriculum: who decides what we should know, how we should know it and why?*
>
> This video clip discusses issues which are also relevant to Chapters 4 and 6.

Conclusion

The impact of different ideologies and beliefs on the creation, positioning and structure of a curriculum has been illustrated. We have seen that the nature of knowledge and views on what it is important to 'know' play a central part in the design of any curriculum. Knowledge can be structured and presented in different ways. In the context of modern schooling, traditional subject knowledge may be seen as important or knowledge may be presented thematically. Teaching and learning can take many different forms depending upon the purpose of the curriculum and the beliefs of the teachers. Assessment is a fundamental element of the curriculum and can also take many forms. These will reflect what the designers and deliverers of the curriculum see as important in terms of student outcomes. They are tied very much to the purposes of the curriculum and beliefs concerning the nature of education.

The structural features of the curriculum are thus influenced by the purposes and beliefs of the teachers, course designers, examination boards, government ministers and established discourses. The final delivered curriculum is often the result of a complex interaction and power struggle between the various interested parties.

> **Student activities**
>
> 1. Look at the government website at www.gov.uk/government/collections/national-curriculum to view the DfE national curriculum. Choose either the primary or secondary curriculum and read the section entitled 'Aims'. Identify the key words. To what extent do these concepts inform the subjects that make up the curriculum that is available on the same web pages?
>
> 2. Look again at the national curriculum, click on 'Curriculum assessment' then 'Assessment principles: school curriculum'. Comment on these principles, considering why they are included and defining your own thoughts and reactions to them.

3. Some critics have suggested that the curriculum should be rethought and that the traditional subject-based curriculum is moribund and anachronistic. What might be included in a radical rethink of the curriculum in terms of contents, experiences, teaching and learning, and assessment? Is it possible to define a new programme for learning? What would be the basis for this new curriculum and how would it meet the needs of contemporary conditions and people?

Recommended reading

DfE (2013) *The National Curriculum.* Accessed at www.gov.uk/government/collections/national-curriculum. This document is the legal framework for the national curriculum in England. It is an interesting document to use when analysing curriculum requirements.

Harlen, W. (ed.) (2008) *Student Assessment and Testing*, 4 vols. London: SAGE. This set brings together key articles providing theoretical discussion and reporting research in student assessment throughout the range, from pre-school to post-school education. The range of purposes, procedures, policies and properties of assessment are covered in the four volumes. You may find these easier to locate in your university's library.

- *Volume 1: Assessment Roles and Purposes* – focuses on the role that assessment and testing can take in education.
- *Volume 2: Methods and Technical Issues in Assessment* – brings together studies of different ways of conducting assessment going beyond testing, and some that are designed to assess a range of competencies such as problem-solving, learning dispositions and critical thinking.
- *Volume 3: National and International Assessment* – includes articles on the methods, design and use of findings of national surveys, such as the National Assessment of Educational Progress (NAEP) and the Assessment of Performance Unit (APU), and international surveys of the Institute of Economic Affairs (IEA) and the Organisation for Economic Cooperation and Development (OECD).
- *Volume 4: Assessment Policies and Systems* – considers how assessment and testing for a particular purpose impacts on students, teachers and on other parts of an assessment system.

Marsh, C. J. (2009) *Key Concepts for Understanding Curriculum*, 4th edn. London: Routledge. As the title suggests this is a basic text on curriculum. It covers all areas of curriculum development including defining, planning, assessing and managing as well as discussing significant ideological issues. This is a very useful book for education studies undergraduates.

 Access the companion website to this book and find SAGE journal articles exploring this chapter topic in further detail: https://study.sagepub.com/bartlettburton4e.

CHAPTER 6
Politics and policy in education

Chapter overview

In Chapter 4 we gave a historical outline of the development of the modern
English education system. Inevitably such developments are influenced by
their political, social and economic context so it is important to examine the
relationship between policy and political ideologies in education. In this chapter we discuss the meaning of the phrase 'education policy' and provide
guidance in constructing a policy critique. We then consider the nature of
political ideology and an overview and commentary follows on the development of the state education system in England from the coming to power of
the Thatcher Conservative government in 1979 to the present. This period
sees a prolonged shift from a comprehensive to a market forces approach to
education policy.

Introduction

Previous chapters have indicated that the development and organisation of systems of education is not a straightforward matter. Education is not a neutral
concept. We may wish for the development of 'the good society' but what this
actually looks like and how we get there can be viewed very differently. A 'good
society' may be based on the discipline and order shown by citizens, it may be
a result of the freedom of all to develop themselves, or more likely it will be a
combination and balance of both of these things. Consider how often pupils are
subjected to punishments and controls to make them comply yet are also

encouraged to question and explore. The purposes of education may be broadly agreed as developing minds, imparting significant knowledge, ensuring the continuation of social order and preparing young people for future employment. However, constructing the detail of an educational experience is a highly problematised, political activity.

Chapter 5 has shown how educators must grapple with issues of curriculum content and pedagogy: what must be taught and also, perhaps, what is best avoided. For instance, what do we tell young people about drugs and sex? Do we allow wide-ranging discussion on such topics in our schools? Which teaching styles and techniques are most effective? Should the emphasis be on disciplined learning or freedom to explore? Drawing back from the detail, it is also necessary to engage with issues about the universal nature of education. What aspects should be for all citizens? Will they be compulsory? If so, for how many years shall people be expected to study? Is the education provided different for different sections of the population? If so, in what ways and how is the populace to be divided? Is it to be paid for by the state or the individual? The answer to this may depend upon whether society or the individual is deemed to be the beneficiary. The circumstances an individual is born into are clearly very important in determining subsequent educational experience.

Kelly (2009) suggests that education is a political activity whereby society prepares its young for adult life. Education and politics are 'inextricably interwoven' and it is not possible to discuss education without considering the political environment:

> The political context, then, is a major element in any scheme or system of education, and one without reference to which such a scheme or system cannot be properly understood. (2009: 187)

The history of the development of any education system illustrates competing views as to the purposes of education and how these are best met. These views are very much linked to how individuals would like to see their society develop (see Chapter 2 for a discussion of ideology in education). As education has to be paid for and may affect the quality of a future workforce, any system also has to be seen in relation to the economy.

We will now look at what political policy is and how education policy derives from this. We will then consider political ideologies and how these link to beliefs about education. This will help frame our analysis of the substantive part of the chapter – the development of the modern education system from Thatcherite government through to the current Conservative administration of today.

Analysing education policy

Political policy

In any society and within political life more broadly we can see that groups of like-minded people come together to form their own policy based upon their ideological beliefs about how society should be developing. These groups may become formalised into political parties or pressure groups. Their policies will be developed and refined through argument and debate within the group. If they come to power they will begin to implement their policy. Ball (2013: 8) suggests using a common-sense view of policy as:

> something constructed within government (in the broadest sense) – what we might call big-P policy that is 'formal' and usually legislated policy . . . But we need to remain aware that policies are made and remade in many sites, and there are many little-p policies that are formed and enacted within localities and institutions.

Education policy

Bates et al. (2011: 54) define education policy as: 'The raft of laws and initiatives that determine the shape and functioning of educational systems at both national and local level'. As education is so important in any society, it will form a major part of any government's plans. If we accept the premise above that educational aims have an ideological basis then education policy is the plan or blueprint by which these aims are put into practice. It is likely that due to changes in social and economic circumstances these policies will be amended and adapted. For instance, introducing school or university reform during times of economic restraint can significantly affect what any government is able to do. It is also likely that policy will be challenged by those with opposing ideologies. A change of government is likely to lead to an ideological shift, thus aspects of the education system are in a continual state of being 'reformed'. Successive governments, for instance, have altered the content and assessment of the school curriculum and also the structure of secondary schooling. Of course politicians also have to respond to external events and so changes introduced may be reactive rather than proactive, for example, corporal punishment was finally abolished in schools due to a European ruling on human rights rather than the beliefs of the sitting Conservative English government.

As the importance of formal education has grown significantly over the last 200 years, so has the role of the state – and in turn the government that happens to be in power – in shaping educational developments. The study of education policy to a very large extent involves examining the intent and actions of governments, their ability to implement their particular policies and the effects of that implementation. As each new government assumes that its approach to education will change things for the better, all policy changes are presented as 'reforms'. We have discussed education ideologies in Chapter 2; it is important that we also consider broader political ideologies when looking at education policy as it is these wider beliefs about society from which the education ideologies spring.

Political ideologies and their relationship to education

In an earlier chapter we discussed the creation of 'the good society' and how there are varying perceptions of what this consisted of and how it is achieved. These value positions are termed political ideologies. Political parties and some pressure groups are groups of people of similar ideological belief who come together to promote their views, to gain political power themselves or to influence government in order to change society in some way.

Political ideologies can be classified in many different ways. We will briefly consider these before looking specifically at some of the key beliefs that have shaped education policy in Britain since the Second World War. Political ideologies are often placed, for the convenience of a quick categorisation, somewhere along a left–right spectrum. This is actually a very simplistic binary divide and should only ever be used as a rough indicator. Where exactly groups or individuals are placed on this spectrum will fluctuate over time and in different circumstances. For example, the Conservative party is assumed to be on the right side of the spectrum but in some periods the party may be considered to be more to the right while in others it is seen as more to the centre. The same can be said for individual party members, some of whom may be classed as extreme right-wingers while others may be seen as more towards the centre-right. There can also be great differences between extremists and moderates on the same side of the spectrum as well as similarities between groups that one would expect to be 'poles' apart. For instance, historians often point to the similarities in methods of governing employed by both fascist and communist governments even though their ideological beliefs may differ.

Accepting the tenuous nature of using the left–right spectrum, some political parties associated with the right are Fascist, National Socialist, Christian Democrat, and Conservative while Labour, Social Democratic, Socialist and Communist would be placed on the left. Again, in very general terms and with varying levels of extremity, values associated with the left include social equality and social justice involving the redistribution of wealth, economic intervention with state ownership of key industries and state provision of a range of services. Those associated with the right include the defence of individual rights, private property, capitalism and the free market, social stability as achieved through the promotion of traditional values, strong leadership and the reduction of state bureaucracy. While the left accuses the right of supporting the upper classes and privilege, the right accuses the left of collectivism at the expense of the freedom of the individual. Of course, as implied previously, there is division within these different groupings and also overlap between them. Hence, at times when internal division is great, parties may split apart, new ones are born and sometimes coalitions and alliances are formed in a compromise to guard against what is seen as a greater enemy.

Key questions to ask when analysing education policy

In order to analyse policy it is possible to break down the political process into different stages or phases. When examining these it is useful to consider a number of questions for each stage. These questions can form the basic starting point for your critique and answers to each are likely to lead to further questioning and so to a deeper analysis. This form of typology can be used to analyse one policy initiative or a whole policy approach.

Reader Reflection: A typology for analysing policy

- *Development of policy:* the macro analysis

  - What changes are being proposed?
  - Who is proposing the changes/reforms?
  - Why are they being proposed? (This includes justifications for, or the values that underpin, these changes.)
  - Who will be affected and in what ways?
  - How do the proposals link to other proposed changes in education and also to wider social policy initiatives?

- *Implementation of policy:* the micro analysis

  - What are the detailed proposals?
  - How have things changed as the policy is introduced?

- *Effects of policy*: analysis over time (this could be macro and/or micro)

  - To what extent were the original proposals implemented?
  - Which stakeholders have been affected and in what way?
  - To what extent have the original aims been met?
  - What future developments are likely to result from this policy?

  An example of a policy area you may wish to consider analysing is that of the 14–19 curriculum.

The linking of education policy to wider political ideologies

The rest of this chapter will examine the development of education policy from the coming to power of the Conservative government of Margaret Thatcher in 1979 up to the present. The key changes can be seen to be resulting from changes in the dominant or ruling ideologies. The typology in Table 6.1 attempts to identify the major ideologies with some key features. These will be explained in more detail as we move through the analysis.

Ideologies are useful tools to help us analyse political beliefs. They provide a means to compare and understand change over time. They should not be over-reified into a rigid set of principles set in stone (Buckler and Dolowitz, 2009).

Table 6.1 A typology of recent significant political ideologies

Right Wing			Left Wing	
Conservative			Labour	
Ideology	Neo-Conservative	Neo-Liberal	Social Democrat	Socialist
Key beliefs	Traditional values leading to a healthier, more stable society.	Market forces and individual freedom leading to greater economic efficiency.	Opportunity for all and responsibility for all.	Social equality for all. State ownership of major utilities and industries.
Education policy	Discipline, school uniform, 'proper subjects', traditional assessment.	Parental choice leading to competition between providers. League tables.	Choice and variety of schools within a strong state framework.	Free education provision. Abolition of public schools. A comprehensive education system for all.

Source: adapted from earlier models by Trowler (2003) and Bates et al. (2011)

During our consideration in previous chapters of the education system in England we were able to see the effects of differing ideological beliefs and the pressure these bring to bear on the political process. It is worth remembering, however, that any particular 'slant' that we, as authors, have placed on the telling of these developments will itself be invested with our own ideologies and backgrounds. We made decisions based on wider academic reading about what to include and therefore what to leave out. It is important to keep this in mind during your reading of the next section which now moves to an analysis of the 'education market'.

Reader reflection: The left/right spectrum

Fascist ——————————— versus ——————————— Communist

Where on the left–right spectrum would you place the following?

- the Conservative Party
- the Labour Party
- the Liberal Democrats
- UKIP
- the SNP
- the current Secretary of State for Education
- the current president of the United States.

Developing the education market: Conservative, Labour, Coalition and Conservative administrations

We now chart the development of a policy of market forces and, paradoxically, the increasing control of central government during the Conservative administrations of the 1980s and the first half of the 1990s. This contrasts with the development of 'third way' politics by Labour from the second half of the 1990s and into the twenty-first century. We then discuss the education policy of the Conservative–Liberal Democrat Coalition administration that came to power in 2010 and finally the re-election of a Conservative government from 2015, which returns our focus to the development of the market and increasing central control. The influence of political ideologies on education is well illustrated through this analysis and, having charted the historical progress of educational reform of both the English education system and its curriculum in the previous chapters, it is interesting to note the ideological movement from approaches that emphasised a comprehensive system for all to those that emphasise market forces, choice and competition.

After the defeat of the Conservatives in 1974 a movement for reform had arisen within the party. It was felt that for many years the two main parties, Labour and Conservative, had been similar in their 'centralist' approaches to government. The rhetoric of consensus which resulted had hidden a steady drift to the left which was illustrated by policies such as the comprehensivisation of education (Chitty, 2014). Certain right-wing thinkers, such as the Black Paper authors, felt that it was this drift which had led to the decline in fortunes not only of the Conservative Party but also of the country. They argued that socialist policies had ignored traditional values and stifled the important characteristics of individual achievement and entrepreneurship. The stress on equality of opportunity had been at the expense of competitiveness and the developing welfare state had created a culture of dependency and conformity. These policies were considered inevitably to lead to a steady economic and moral decline.

Conservative policy: the rise of the New Right

The Conservative policy became influenced by groups within the party identified by the term the 'New Right'. This was not a coherent force but what Trowler (2003) labelled an amalgam of ideologies and associated groups. Their point of unity was a common enemy in socialism. The potential internal conflicts of the New Right were overcome and factions within the party were held together by the strong leadership of Margaret Thatcher. The origins of the New Right can be seen in traditional strands of Tory thought stemming from the nineteenth century. These are a combination of a desire for order and stability in society along with the importance of individual freedom and enterprise. Both of these were seen as necessary to the creation of a thriving economy (see Ball, 2013; Bates et al., 2011; Tomlinson, 2005). These two positions can be described as neo-conservative and neo-liberal.

Neo-liberalism (market forces)

Neo-liberals attest to the importance of a free-market economy which involves freedom of choice for consumers and producers with minimum state interference (see Ball, 2013). These ideas stem from the economic model of perfect competition. This assumes that in the running of an economy there are certain factors of production, these being labour, land and

(Continued)

(Continued)

capital, which are pulled together by entrepreneurs. These factors will be used most effectively when supplying the goods which consumers demand. Producers will endeavour to provide what consumers want, to sell their products and make their profit. This profit enables them to expand and to be even more successful in the future. Those producers who do not make what the public want, or who cannot produce it as efficiently (cheaply) as competitors, will go out of business while those who meet demand and are the most efficient will survive. The factors of production used by those who go out of business are released to be used by more efficient producers in this or other industries. Thus competition leads to the most effective use of resources which will ultimately benefit the whole society.

The neo-liberals advocate minimum interference by government in the market. They suggest that this only benefits the less efficient producers and allows the production of goods which the market has not demanded. Protected industries, like those which are nationalised, will never become truly efficient and will always need to be supported by taxpayers' money. This protectionism means we all pay more for our goods and leads to a weak economy that will ultimately fail in world markets. Free competition benefits us all by creating efficiency of production and a strong economy.

It has been suggested that education can be seen as another product. Competition will, as in other industries, lead to more efficient use of resources while satisfying consumer demand. This will put a stop to the educational establishment forcing its own view of what should be supplied as education on everyone. This competition will in turn make the system more cost-effective and be part of economic regeneration.

Neo-conservatism (traditional values)

Neo-conservatives believe in the importance of upholding standards and traditional values. This ideology stresses the importance of authority, a national identity and high standards (Robertson and Hill, 2014). Economic decline can be traced to moral decline of which the education system is a major cause. The neo-conservatives feel that this is largely due to progressive teaching which lacks an important stress on values and discipline. There needs to be greater supervision over the work of teachers and LEAs alongside reform of the curriculum seeing a return to traditional subjects and teaching methods. In contrast to neo-liberals who tend to talk about choice, competition and the market in education, the neo-conservatives are more likely to advocate traditional values and traditional subjects.

New Right education policy

Though different, both of these ideological standpoints revealed dissatisfaction with the educational developments of the 1960s and 1970s. One ideology emphasised freedom of choice and markets, the other the need for control and a return to tried and tested methods. There was clearly potential conflict between these groups but they shared the view that things needed to change. In spite of their differences neo-conservatives and neo-liberals both had a mistrust of state professionals who prevented the development of a free market and efficiency and were also seen as subversive. A policy developed which reflected both ideologies – stressing one and then the other at different times. The policy was not totally contradictory. Indeed it has been suggested (see Bates et al., 2011; Robertson and Hill, 2014) that it was necessary for central government to take control of the curriculum to allow the market to develop, thus preventing the producers, i.e. the teachers and LEAs, from stifling the development of competition by their control.

The government's mistrust of teachers and suspicions as to their subversive motives was brought to a head in 1986 and 1987 in a prolonged industrial dispute over pay and conditions. This resulted in severe disruption in schools. By their actions the teachers lost much public support and the government became even more determined to reform schooling and to alter the balance of power in education. The policies of many LEAs on equal opportunities, anti-racism and so on began to be seen as 'loony leftism' by the Conservative government. Increasingly it was felt that the producer control of the education system needed to be broken. The Conservative government introduced some changes in the early 1980s with major reforms in education occurring from the 1988 Education Reform Act onwards. Perhaps the most significant of these early changes was the setting up of the assisted places scheme, whereby able pupils from state schools were offered places at public school, with the state assisting the parents with the payment of fees. This can be said to show a mistrust of the state system and a belief that the private sector was superior. It also diverted public funds from the state to the private sector. The Education Reform Act of 1988 which followed was arguably the most significant piece of legislation since the 1944 Act but was only one of a series of Conservative acts that led to significant changes to the education system.

Conservative policy: implementation 1979–97

Conservative reforms should be seen in terms of how they were designed to create the market of the neo-liberals, to reinforce a more traditional morality of the neo-conservatives or in some cases achieve both of these potentially contradictory goals. They were to tip the balance of power away from the teachers and LEAs, sometimes towards the centre, at other times towards parents thereby giving choice to consumers.

Allowing parental choice of school

Prior to the 1980s pupils were allocated to a school by their LEA and the number of pupils on each school roll was also decided by the LEA. This enabled them to plan for the education of all pupils within their authority. It also meant that they could control intake for each school and thus balance the size of schools in the authority. Parents had comparatively little say in the schools their children were sent to by the LEA and it was usual for pupils to be allocated places at their local primary or secondary school.

Under the 1980 Education Act parents were able to express a preference for the school they wanted their children to attend and to appeal against the LEA's decision if they were unsuccessful. This meant that schools now had to start attracting parents and marketing themselves if they were to maintain a sufficiently high intake of pupils. This was particularly important in the secondary sector as parents were able to consider schools over a wider travelling distance for their children. The impact of this change was increased after the 1986 Education Act reduced the powers of LEAs and increased that of parents on school governing bodies and required LEAs to provide financial and other information to parents and school governors. But the biggest boost to parents exercising their right to choose came when the LEA was no longer able to protect undersubscribed schools by giving them extra funding to cushion the fall in pupil numbers due to the introduction of 'local management of schools'.

Creating increasing autonomy of schools (local management of schools)

For half a century each LEA had been in control of the budgets for all maintained schools in its area and it allocated funds according to its own policy. Some schools may have been given more funds by the authority than others for a variety of reasons. In this way the LEA could protect schools from falling rolls and they could be given extra support if they were having particular problems. In effect this meant that some schools were subsidising others. From the point of view of the neo-liberals this meant that the efficient were paying for the inefficient and there was no financial incentive for schools to become more effective or to make an effort to be more attractive to parents and pupils.

The 1988 Education Reform Act gave head teachers more control over their own budgets and forced LEAs to pass on to schools a high percentage of the money allocated to them by central government. The money was to be allocated on the basis of the number of pupils on roll. Successful schools would grow as more parents opted for them, so would receive more money enabling them to further build on their success. Those who were unable to attract pupils and were suffering from falling rolls would need to act quickly if they were to survive. Thus the consumer would reign supreme in the market and schools would need to offer the sort of education which attracted parents. The LEAs were no longer able to interfere as they had lost much of their financial power.

The creation of city technology colleges, grant-maintained schools and specialist schools

For parents to be able to exercise choice there needed to be different types of school available. Greater diversity would stimulate competition and force existing state schools to change more quickly so from the late 1980s a new type of school, the city technology college (CTC), was to be jointly funded by the government and industry. They were to be technology and industry oriented for pupils of secondary school age. This epitomised the link between education and economic development. They were designed to offer opportunities to pupils from inner-city areas who were oriented towards technology. It was expected that these schools would provide models of good practice that other schools in the area would have to follow.

Schools that wanted the freedom to develop in their own way and to sever links with the bureaucratic LEAs could become grant maintained. This meant that they were funded directly from central government and were in total control of the whole of their budget. Increasing diversity among schools was encouraged to further stimulate the market. Later the CTC concept was modified and widened, enabling more schools to join the City Technology Trust scheme, provided they were able to attract matching funding from industry. Towards the end of the Conservatives' third term of office the specialist secondary schools initiative was launched whereby secondary schools could apply to become specialist schools in a particular area of the curriculum – science, music, technology, modern foreign languages or sport. Once again the schools needed to attract sufficient private funding to support their application.

Though the Conservative government expected that the majority of schools would welcome the option to become grant maintained, they did not, and this category of school was later abolished by the Labour government. However, the concept of CTCs and specialist schools, though initially slow to 'take off' was later embraced by Labour in its desire to raise standards.

Introduction of the national curriculum

Politicians in the mid-twentieth century had not dared to prescribe the curriculum for fear of appearing similar to fascist or communist dictators and thus undemocratic. This fear had passed into history with the world wars now so distant. With the increasing public concern over education, a national curriculum was now seen as a way of ensuring an appropriate schooling for all pupils. For the New Right it was a way of breaking the subversive control that teachers exerted over the curriculum. The national curriculum was to be compulsory for all pupils aged 5 to 16. It was to be assessed and it was envisaged that test results at the end of the four key stages would be made public in the form of league tables. The results would show how pupils were progressing, how schools were achieving, and how standards were being raised.

The subjects and their content were traditional, clearly reflecting the influence of the neo-conservatives. The neo-liberal element of the party perhaps did not favour this traditional approach since it had no element of choice for the consumer. However, they did go along with it in that future changes in content could be made and it would certainly encourage competition with the publication of national curriculum test results. These would provide large amounts of information about the 'output' of each school for the consumer.

Regular inspections of schools

In 1993 a rigorous inspection service was set up under the newly created Office for Standards in Education (Ofsted). As well as checking on the running of each school, inspection reports were made public giving the consumer information on which to make informed choices. Schools deemed to be 'failing' would have to improve rapidly or be severely dealt with.

The introduction of league tables of schools

League tables of school performance were developed in the first instance to show GCSE results. These would provide consumer information and encourage competition among producers. The aim was to expand the tables to include end-of-key-stage results.

The concept of an education system driven by market forces was becoming more and more influential towards the end of the Conservative administration in all sectors of education and it was proposed to extend this further had they won the 1997 general election. There was also, paradoxically, a move to allow schools greater powers to select pupils. This was part of the neo-conservative ideal of schools for an academic elite as had existed before comprehensivisation. The high-status selective schools would perhaps naturally be formed from those that were already oversubscribed.

Reader Reflection: Analysis of Conservative policy

The Conservative reforms were designed to create the market of the neo-liberals, to reinforce a more traditional morality of the neo-conservatives or in some cases achieve both of these potentially contradictory goals.

How did each of the policies implemented by the Conservatives over this period (out-lined above) actually work towards these different goals?

Special educational needs: The Warnock Report

The developments in special education during the 1980s and 1990s are very significant and are at first appearance separate from the wider neo-liberal and neo-conservative education policy. The Warnock committee, set up to look into special education, reported in 1978 with its findings incorporated in the 1981 Education Act. The terminology of handicap was abolished to be replaced by the concept of special educational needs. These needs were to be determined on an individual child basis by a combination of education and medical practitioners. The specific requirements of each pupil were to be outlined in a statement of special educational needs. This would be reviewed annually and become a document of entitlement.

The Warnock Report estimated that approximately 2 per cent of pupils would fall into the category of having severe enough SEN to require a formal statement with up to 20 per cent experiencing some special educational needs not requiring a formal statement during their school life. Significantly Warnock stated that where practical and possible these special educational needs should be met in mainstream education thus reducing the segregation of pupils into special schools. The recommended approach for the majority of pupils was one of integration. As funding would follow the individual statement, mainstream schools could set resources aside for pupils requiring them. It was expected that teachers would develop their teaching to cater for a greater diversity of pupil rather than expecting pupils to be separated out into narrow groupings. This shows a desire to move away from the segregation and labelling of the past. However, significantly, the report said that for this integration to be possible it had to be in accordance with the parents' wishes and it had to be possible for the child's educational needs to be met in the 'mainstream' school while maintaining efficient use of resources and not adversely affecting the education of the other children in the class.

The Act proposed integration where it was possible but there was no statutory requirement to move pupils from special to mainstream schools. Any potential adverse effects and inefficient use of resources were open to professional interpretation and while some LEAs embraced the principle of integration and encouraged the teaching of pupils with SEN in mainstream schools, others did very little. Ultimately parents of children with special needs still had very little say in where they were educated and the placement decisions were largely in the hands of the LEAs. As Hodkinson (2016) notes, the 1981 Education Act may be observed as having been highly significant for the development of educational provision for children with SEN but it failed to bring about the end of the Victorian principles which still maintained segregated educational practice.

A further criticism of Warnock was that, while abolishing the previous terminology applied to pupils, it merely replaced one set of labels with another. 'Educationally subnormal' and 'maladjusted' were replaced with the generic label, SEN, and linked to individual children by professionals with their acronyms such as an SLD (severe learning difficulty) or EBD (emotional and behavioural disorder). Warnock did, however, by introducing the notion of integration, sow the seed for a further stage of public awareness development towards the notion of 'inclusion'.

Conservative policy: a critique

It was not all plain sailing for the Conservative government and its education policy. The national curriculum encountered a number of problems during its introduction. Large amounts of prescribed content implemented over a very short timescale, coupled with the fear of untried assessment methods, placed great strain on teachers and schools. This was exacerbated by government reforms on school management being introduced simultaneously.

This caused confrontation between teachers and the government and resulted in the boycotting of the early end-of-key-stage tests. In response to increasing public disquiet the government set up the Dearing Commission to look into the curriculum. While its brief was to make a complex system more 'workable', the ideological basis of the curriculum was not open to question. The Dearing Report, published in January 1994, did recognise the unwieldy nature of the curriculum.

There was far too much content and the assessment was very complex and time-consuming. It proposed a streamlining of the curriculum which would give greater flexibility to the individual schools and teachers in their planning. This allowed more time to be spent on mathematics and English in the early years and the possibility of subject choice and vocational options in the later years. The subjects were to be reviewed for September 1995 with a promise of no further changes for five years. Only the core subjects of English, mathematics and science were to be nationally tested though teachers were expected to monitor pupil progress in the other subjects in relation to the national curriculum levels.

By the end of the Conservative period in office the balance of power had changed with LEAs having lost much of their power to central government and individual schools. Control of the curriculum was still an area of contention but certainly it was no longer solely the preserve of teachers. It was now quality-controlled and monitored by government agencies. A market had developed with the introduction of greater parental choice and financial control delegated to schools. This had a great effect on how schools were run with an increasing emphasis on management training, cost-effectiveness and efficiency. Schools now operated much more on the lines of individual businesses. The producers, in this case the head teachers running the schools, were able to respond to the wishes of the consumers, that is the parents.

However, only a handful of CTCs had been created due partly to the difficulty in attracting funding from industry and partly to strong local opposition in some areas from parents and politicians. Similarly, nowhere near as many schools had opted for grant maintained status as the government had hoped. Allowing parental choice also caused problems for many parents. In each LEA certain schools, usually with good examination results and in the more affluent areas, became oversubscribed. As pupil places were limited in oversubscribed schools the choice again became that of the school (the producer). This was often based on set catchment-area criteria and neither the school nor consumer had a free choice in reality. Finally, the status of teaching had changed. Teachers had suffered criticism for many years, had come under scrutiny from Ofsted and retained little professional control over the curriculum. Many education theorists of the time talked of the proletarianisation and deprofessionalisation of teachers (see Apple, 1988; Bartlett and Burton, 2003; Furlong, 2005; McCulloch, 2001; Ozga, 1995).

When the Conservatives came to office in 1979 there were mounting problems with an economy that was undergoing a major restructuring in terms of employment and production. Under their stewardship education policy shifted towards stressing traditional forms of knowledge, the needs of the workplace and the promotion of enterprise through competition. This was reflected in the policy of the

New Right which was a combination of neo-conservatism and neo-liberalism. Towards the end of their term of office public opinion began to swing against the tyrannies of tradition and a free market in favour of modernism and governmental restraint of market excesses. Thus there was a move back towards liberal humanism and social democracy. However, this was not to alter the long-term shift away from a comprehensive system of education controlled by local authorities towards a differentiated school system, driven by market forces.

New Labour policy: ideology and perspectives on education

Two ideological standpoints that form the historical basis of Labour ideology are outlined below. It is useful to have these in mind when considering the development of Labour policy.

Socialism

There are many different views on what socialism is and the various forms it can take. Socialists emphasise social equality and fair distribution of wealth. Private ownership of land is illegal or frowned upon and economic production is owned and often controlled by the state. Individual needs, such as housing, education, health care, wages, food and clothing, are provided by the state.

Socialism is considered a working-class intellectual movement involving the overcoming of oppression and exploitation by the ruling capitalist class. This is usually seen as occurring through some form of revolution or uprising. This struggle leads to social equality and no ruling class where production is controlled by the people, i.e. the state.

Many small-scale communities are run on socialist lines of equality, sharing and cooperation with decisions made through whole-community or elders' meetings. Examples of such groups would be hunting and gathering communities such as Kalahari bushmen or the Kibbutzim in Israel. Many governments have claimed to be socialist such as Communist China, the Soviet Union and Cuba but how they operate often appears to be similar to traditional dictatorships.

In the UK the Labour movement developed through the formation of worker trade unions. The Labour Party was created to enable this working-class movement to gain political power in Parliament. This collective movement had socialist principles at its heart and fought for the development of a welfare state where all would be secure. They also opposed the inequalities of the class system in the UK that had created and maintained such inequalities and unfairness. Those who formed and joined the early Labour movement and Labour Party believed that changes towards a socialist society could come through peaceful political reform from within the system. This was the Fabian socialist approach to a more fair and equal society involving incremental change (see McKernan, 2013). The Bevanites of the Labour Party in the 1960s most epitomise this view with their pressure for nationalisation of industry and the development of social welfare systems. Others believed that this could not be done against the forces of capitalism and so formed their own more extreme groups outside of the Labour Party and Parliament advocating revolution.

Opponents argue that socialism is based upon a utopian image of society that ignores the selfishness of human nature. There is little incentive to work hard to better oneself when all are paid the same or similar wages and a welfare system supports the unemployed. Innovation, entrepreneurship and competition are not encouraged in such a system and this will lead to a stagnant economy. Inefficient production results in the rationing of essential goods and the unavailability of luxury items which in turn creates black markets and corruption.

Socialist regimes are criticised for being autocratic with the rise of a bureaucratic elite that effectively become a ruling class with privileges for themselves and their families, as parodied in George Orwell's novel *Animal Farm*. In the end, critics argue, socialism constrains the freedom and creativity of the individual.

Social democracy

Again, there are many interpretations of social democracy. Social democrats believe in many socialist ideals such as individual freedom, fairness, opportunity for all, welfare systems that provide support to those in need, the reduction in extremes of both wealth and poverty. The free market is seen as important but in need of constraints. The state needs to regulate and even own certain key industries and services to ensure supply is available to all; this will also benefit private industry and ultimately the economy as a whole. For example, supplying education and health care to all benefits the whole population and secures a higher quality labour force for industry. If the state maintains the roads and transport infrastructure then the population benefits from being mobile and industry is able to move products and raw materials more effectively. Thus a mix of state intervention and private enterprise is encouraged that will ultimately benefit all.

Social democrats advocate opportunity for all and also care for all who need it, such as those with disabilities, the old, the ill, and the poor (Robertson and Hill, 2014). This requires state provision of quality key services. These are paid for out of wealth generated by the economy, i.e. taxes. It is emphasised that this state support requires responsibility from the people to play their part. In other words, everyone has a duty to work if possible, care for their children and be good citizens. Social democracy can be seen to be a mix of socialism with a free market, the aim being to obtain the benefits of each while preventing the potential misuses. This clearly moves towards the centre ground and begins to resemble Conservative centralists who favour free markets but see the need for this to be combined with a 'social conscience'. The 'revisionists' in the Labour Party in the 1960s led by Gaitskell and Crosland advocated this approach but were defeated by the Bevanites (Beech, 2006). However, it remained a powerful ideology within the Labour Party and became stronger from the 1990s onwards.

After the defeat of the Callaghan administration in 1979 and in their first years out of office Labour moved to the left with the growing influence of the Militant Tendency within the party. It was presented in the media as a party of extremists and the Conservatives were able to portray Labour as unelectable. During the next 20 years the 'modernisers' set about altering the image and policies of the party. These efforts finally bore fruit with the victory in the 1997 general election. Lawton (2005) outlined the mixed ideological origins of the Labour Party having been formed from a combination of socialist groups and the declining Liberal Party. Many people considered the Labour Party's prime task as representing the working classes on issues of employment, housing and social conditions but there was little discussion of a socialist view of education. The party had usually merely suggested minor amendments to the existing system in order to make it fairer for working-class children.

Labour had supported the development of the tripartite system, believing that the 11-plus would provide equal chances to all children of obtaining a grammar-school education. Grammar schools were seen as a route whereby working-class children could improve their futures. Labour politicians did not acknowledge the inequalities of the selection process and its effects on maintaining social disadvantage at this time (see Chapter 10 on how social factors can influence achievement in education). In the 1960s the Labour policy on comprehensive education was never made compulsory. Many LEAs ignored their instructions and maintained the tripartite system. Though wishing to use education for the benefit of all sections of society, Labour had no real image of how comprehensive schools should operate and no view on the curriculum. These important areas were left to educationalists to decide. The feeling, as expressed by Harold Wilson when Prime Minister, was that comprehensive schools should aim to provide a grammar-school education for all.

Labour ideology under Tony Blair rested on the social democratic principles of ensuring equality of opportunity and individual freedom within a strong state framework. The state protects us, and in so doing, allows us to become free. This is freedom with responsibility involving fellowship and cooperation. Under New Labour this is expressed as a partnership between individuals and the state. Both are seen as having duties and responsibilities to each other if, ultimately, we are all to benefit from economic and social development. According to Tony Blair (Wintour, 1994: 8) New Labour was not so much

> a set of rigid economic ideological attitudes, but a set of values and principles. The simple case for democratic socialism rests on the belief that individuals prosper best within a strong, active society whose members acknowledge they owe duties to each other as well as to themselves, and in part at least depend upon each other to succeed.

New Labour saw a need to modernise Britain even if this meant questioning traditional Labour beliefs. The 'modernisation project' was how Prime Minister Blair was able to embrace the wider electorate. It was by calling for a pragmatic approach to the solving of Britain's problems rather than so-called dogma that New Labour appealed to the 'middle ground'. It was this 'common'-sense attitude, and not being tied by traditional allegiances of left and right, that Labour presented as the 'third way'. This was seen to be for the benefit of the whole country and thus the Tories and anyone else who disagreed with the government were now presented as the intolerant extremists.

The third way

The increasing impact of globalisation and the profound social changes that have accompanied it, as outlined in Chapter 7, led many social commentators, such as Giddens (1998 and 2000), to suggest that the policies of the traditional left with their emphasis on state control were no longer feasible. However, although there appeared little doubt as to the power of the global market and the inability of governments to maintain total control over their own economies, Giddens made the point that we should not assume that governments now have nothing to offer against the forces of globalisation. He suggested that there is a complex two-way interaction between the global and the local. While global forces influence nations, governments can operate to promote, protect and support where appropriate. Rather than withering away under the growth of the global market, governments can play an active part in helping their people respond. Thus Giddens suggested a third way that lay between the old forms of state socialism and the tyranny of totally free markets. It involved the state promoting competitiveness and efficiency while encouraging inclusion by ensuring the provision of services such as education, health and social security. These structures would provide individuals with the support they needed to operate freely in the global 'knowledge' economy. Governments also had an important part to play in the development of the civil society that gives individuals identity, security and belonging in an increasingly uncertain world.

There was a strong emphasis on social justice and the rights and responsibilities of each citizen (Buckler and Dolowitz, 2009). The language of partnership was used to describe the relationship between government and citizen. It is this third way ideology that influenced the thinking of a number of world governments at the beginning of the new millennium. Defined by Lund (2008: 44) as a 'blend of Margaret Thatcher's market orientation and "Old" Labour's commitment to state-sponsored social justice', the third way involved the adoption of neo-liberal principles combined with a strongly stated commitment to 'fairness and justice within strong communities'.

(Continued)

(Continued)

It has been suggested that the third way, despite its strong social democratic base, went further towards the acceptance and promotion of free-market principles than Labour had done previously. The Labour party under the revisionists was portrayed as socialism with a free market; in developing the 'third way', it can be suggested that Blair altered the balance towards a free market with socialism (see Ball, 2013, for a discussion of Labour's position).

New Labour policy: implementation 1997–2010

New Labour and social inclusion

For the Labour government this third way ideology manifested itself in the desire to provide vital services such as health and education for every individual and the creation of opportunity for all to succeed in life while at the same time stressing the duty of everyone to play their part in society. Gibson (2014) identifies inclusion as a political movement emerging from the disability rights pressure groups of the 1980s. It demanded civil rights and equal opportunities that could only be brought about through social change. The Labour government of Tony Blair embraced the notion of inclusion. Inclusion calls for the involvement and participation of all and so resonates with any group excluded from society on economic, social or physical grounds. This was an appealing policy that could be used to heal the rifts opened up during the Thatcher era of rapid economic and social changes.

One of the perceived dangers of the modern global economy was that while many of us benefit from the advanced technology, some sections of society, through a combination of factors such as unemployment, poverty, lack of education and skills, become excluded. They remain at the 'margins', unable and powerless to take part. Though socially unjust, the existence of such alienated groups may also be perceived as potentially dangerous to the stability of society as a whole. They are more likely to be involved in crime, drugs, social disorder and potential unrest. Such groups needed to be included within society by gaining employment and feeling that they had a future and something to contribute. Key areas of policy through which this could be achieved were health, employment, social services and, most importantly, education. Thus the whole notion of inclusion was widened.

Defining inclusive education is as fraught with difficulties as is its implementation. Exclusion can be based upon a range of factors such as ethnicity, gender, income and age as well as ability. In its broadest sense inclusive education is about the opportunity for all and involves removing barriers whenever possible. Armstrong (2015) suggested that the term had been used differently and, while some proponents took a broad approach, official documents primarily used the term inclusion in education to refer to policies involving pupils with SEN. She suggests that inclusive education concerned all learners and not just those deemed to be vulnerable or as having special needs.

Thus, inclusive policies involve opening up opportunities for all and a consideration of the rights of all children. In this sense the policy can be closely aligned to concerns about ethnicity, gender and poverty as well as SEN. This broad view of inclusion and social justice became an important part of Labour's ideology of the third way.

Special educational needs and inclusion

When applied to the area of SEN using the disabled rights approach, inclusion signified moving forward from segregation to integration to active participation in society. A key aim of full inclusion is that pupils with special educational needs should be educated in schools equally alongside their peer group. While encouraging the development of inclusion in education, Labour's policies were never compulsory (see DfEE, 1997). In reality this meant that decisions concerning provision of care and education remained largely in the professional domain. During the Labour administration there was some movement of resources from special schools into mainstream schools as previously this varied across LAs. Also the parallel development of a measurement by results culture across education did not encourage schools to accept pupils who were likely to affect league table scores. Thus inclusion worked better for some pupils, such as those with less severe physical disabilities, than others, those with learning and behavioural problems for example.

There was also criticism that even when pupils were taught in the same school how they were treated could be very different as could the attitudes of others towards them. Webster and Blatchford (2015) explain the subtle and explicit forms of separation which pupils with SEN experienced daily in mainstream schools. They were frequently found to work in separate work stations/places from their peers, be supported by teaching assistants for the majority of their time and so have less interaction with the class teacher; as a result their pedagogical diet was impoverished compared to their peers. Pupils with SEN may be in the school but were not necessarily included and involved. According to Hodkinson (2016), although the language of inclusion had been introduced, in reality, practices largely remained similar to those of integration or even separate provision.

Activists called for full inclusion, i.e. the same provision for all, but critics considered this too simplistic an approach. They maintained that separate provision may be important for some in order to ensure they received the relevant specialist support, which could be diluted or missed altogether in a mainstream situation. From this perspective the approach of allowing but not promoting full inclusion can be seen as a means of preserving choice for those with special needs. Labour seemed to be following the approach begun by Warnock of encouraging the teaching of pupils with SEN in mainstream schools while also maintaining special schools. The issue that bedevilled policy intentions was finding an agreed vision of inclusion. Did it involve all being educated and living in the same environment or was it possible to have different but equal provision based upon need while ensuring equal rights and involvement in society? How did people who had been categorised by social processes, wrest the ability and freedom to choose how they were educated and how would others in society respond to this?

Warnock made several controversial interventions in the early 2000s that heightened arguments both for and against inclusion. In 2003 she said there were far more statemented children than had ever been envisaged and that the process had ceased to be about what the child needs and had become a battle for resources (Shaw, 2003). In 2005 she claimed that the policies of inclusion and statementing were not working and called for a new commission to look at the whole area of special needs provision. She also suggested that small special schools were the best way forward (Warnock, 2005).

New Labour and lifelong learning

The Fryer Report (NAGCELL, 1997), building on discussions provoked by Beck and Giddens, agreed that the UK was going through a period of profound social change that characterised it as a risk society. It noted changes in employment through the introduction of new work practices, the application of new technologies, the production and delivery of new products and services, and the reduced size of workplaces (NAGCELL, 1997: 11). The type of worker required in the future would be very different, with diminishing opportunities for unskilled and semi-skilled employment and those with only 'one-industry' or task-specific skills increasingly at risk. We were thus seen to be in the midst of changes in the time, location and forms that work takes.

Arnove (2013) suggested that the development of a global economy and the increasing inter-connectedness of societies posed common problems for education systems around the world. The Labour government placed education as a central plank in its policy agenda of modernisation, with the concept of lifelong learning as an important element within that policy. Taylor felt that 'New Labour's policy on lifelong learning could be divorced neither from its general education policy nor from its broader human capital approach to education, within an ideology of "marketised welfarism"' (2005: 101). Labour felt a need to build on existing strengths of the education system but also to overcome the spiral of disadvantage whereby 'alienation from, or failure within, the education system is passed on from generation to generation' (DfEE, 1997: 3). Thus the importance of education, both in the compulsory years and throughout life, was stressed. The theme that ran through this government policy was once again the development of human capital in order to compete in the knowledge economy.

The learning age

The Labour government published its green paper *The Learning Age: A Renaissance for a New Britain* (DfEE, 1998b) in response to the Fryer Report. It saw the greatest challenge for the country as the need to equip ourselves with new skills, knowledge and understanding. To remain competitive in this new world required the modernisation and reform of many of our traditional social and economic institutions. Labour politicians spoke of the need for a 'can do' culture which was central to the modernisation project. To succeed they needed

> the commitment, imagination and drive of all those working in our schools and colleges, if we are to set aside the doubts of the cynics and the corrosion of the perpetual sceptics. We must replace the culture of complacency with commitment to success. (DfEE, 1997: 3)

They wished to heal the atmosphere of hostility created by the Conservative years of confrontation and the mistrust of government that had developed among those working in education.

> Education is the key to creating a society which is dynamic and productive, offering opportunity and fairness to all. It is the Government's top priority. We will work in partnership with all those who share our passion and sense of urgency for higher standards. (DfEE, 1997: 9)

Education, lifelong learning and the creation of a learning culture were seen in Labour policy (DfEE, 1998b) as a key part of the wider process whereby individuals work together, with the help of government, in forging a better and more inclusive society. Thus education and lifelong learning were important on two levels. On the individual level, if people were not to be excluded from society they would need to be educated to obtain employment in the modern economy. Those in work would need to continually upskill to maintain their employability. At a national level, if our economy was to compete in the new global market we needed to develop a 'flexible' labour force that was adaptable and able to respond immediately (Bartlett and Burton, 2009). Continuous learning was portrayed as of central importance in the context of a transformed, globalised economy (Taylor, 2005: 103). With this emphasis came a greater interest in and scrutiny of educational standards.

Excellence in Schools

The White Paper *Excellence in Schools* (DfEE, 1997) outlined Labour's six policy principles for raising standards:

Education will be at the heart of government.

Policies will be designed to benefit the many, not just the few.

Standards matter more than structures.

Intervention will be in inverse proportion to success.

There will be zero tolerance of underperformance.

Government will work in partnership with all those committed to raising standards. (DfEE, 1997: 5)

The main objectives of Labour's education policy were both social and economic. They sought to improve educational experiences and to raise the educational standards of all learners to create a high-quality, flexible labour force able to compete in the global knowledge economy. Those sections of society that had traditionally been excluded needed to be involved to ensure that no group was left behind in the social changes taking place. Thus Labour espoused a belief in social justice and opportunity for all, together with an individual responsibility to play one's part. To achieve this inclusive and prosperous society New Labour pursued their ideology of the third way that involved traditional Labour policies of state support and social welfare combined with the benefits of individualism and the market.

The Labour administration spanned three terms and Hatcher (2008) notes that the policy emphasis did alter over this time. The first half of the Blair government focused upon the 'standards agenda' within schools and involved developing teaching, concentrating upon the areas of literacy and numeracy and improving pupil performance. This was to be monitored through a number of key targets. Moving into their third term, when it appeared that the drive to increase pupil performance by emphasising teaching and processes within schools had stalled, the focus shifted towards the structure of schools, involving employers and industrialists more in the education system.

In July 2004 Labour published its five-year strategy (DfES, 2004b). Acknowledging the overall improvement in standards of teaching and pupil performance, the need to go even further was identified. Significantly it was noted that:

> We have opened up opportunity at every stage of life. But we have not yet broken the link between social class and achievement. No society can afford to waste the talent of its children and citizens. So major challenges at each key phase of life remain. (DfES, 2004b: 4)

Despite the reforms aimed at raising educational achievement in Labour's first two terms of office, those in lower socio-economic groups continued to perform less well and the differences in performance between the lower and higher socio-economic groups widened as pupils got older. The links between poor health, disadvantage and low educational outcomes were seen as remaining 'stark' (DfES, 2004b: 12). It was also noted that, in terms of attainment, there was a large 'middle group' of pupils who were not being challenged and whose performance also needed to be improved. This was seen as the time to modernise the traditional comprehensive system of state education in order to meet these further challenges. A monolithic state system of standardised comprehensive schools was no longer regarded as appropriate to meeting modern needs. Different groups apart from the state, such as businesses, voluntary bodies and religious groups, also needed to be involved in the running of schools where appropriate. On the basis of the experience of their two previous terms in office Labour identified five key principles of reform underpinning the drive for a step change in children's services, education and training.

Reader Reflection: Labour's key reform principles

- Greater personalisation and choice, with the wishes and needs of children, parents and learners centre-stage.
- Opening up services to new and different providers and ways of delivering services.
- Freedom and independence for frontline head teachers, governors and managers with clear, simple accountabilities and more secure, streamlined funding arrangements.

(Continued)

(Continued)

- A major commitment to staff development with high-quality support and training to improve assessment, care and teaching.
- Partnerships with parents, employers, volunteers and voluntary organisations to maximise the life chances of children, young people and adults. (DfES, 2004b: 5)

What do you think each of the five key principles of reform mean in practice?

These five key principles fitted the multi-professional approach which involved health, education and social services professionals with the child at the centre. The emphasis on personalised learning allowed schools and education professionals to concentrate much more on the needs of individual pupils and how to improve their learning. It was expected that this would help to reduce the disaffection felt by many pupils through the standard curriculum. Within this strategy Labour also took the opportunity to expand the specialist schools programme and to promise the introduction of 200 independently managed academies. These moves amount to a significant distancing from the existing comprehensive system of secondary education.

Curriculum reform

- The national curriculum was reformed to become more flexible and relevant to vocational needs.
- In primary education there was a drive to reduce class sizes for the youngest children and an emphasis on essential skills for the whole learning process, hence the development of literacy and numeracy strategies and greater emphasis on ICT.
- At Key Stage 3 greater emphasis was placed on literacy, numeracy and ICT skills and the development of personalised learning.
- The teaching of citizenship was introduced to help address rapid social change and the potential fragmentation of established communities.
- Post-16 education saw a dramatic increase in the number of pupils who stayed on in education after 16. A levels were modernised becoming modular in nature and assessment. Specialised vocational diplomas for 14–19s were introduced from 2008, combining general education and applied vocational learning. Schools and FE colleges worked together in innovative ways on the educational provision for 14–16 year olds.
- Existing quality assurance measures were further developed: inspections became 'lighter touch' for institutions performing well but those deemed

unsatisfactory needed to improve rapidly or risk being closed down, taken over or reopened as an academy.

Many of Labour's policies did not just involve the domain of education and training. They were part of wider social policies that were aimed at inclusion with overlap between social, economic and education policy in what supporters of the third way would portray as 'joined-up government'. Strategies were developed that took a broader approach to child and family welfare aimed at improving the future chances of children and their parents by involving health, social and education agencies. A key development was the Sure Start programme for nursery age children and their families.

Sure Start

Sure Start Local Programmes (SSLPs) were launched in 2001 to combat child poverty and exclusion. They targeted children under four and their families in areas of high deprivation. By providing improved services in education, health and child care the aim was to improve the life chances of these children. They were to provide integrated support tailored according to local need that included:

> supporting children's personal, social and emotional development, improving parenting aspirations and skills, providing benefits and housing advice, helping families back into employment, providing access to good early education, and addressing family health and life chances. (Hall et al., 2015: 90)

These Sure Start programmes developed children's centres which provided integrated support in child care, health and parenting from a range of professionals. The first National Evaluation of Sure Start (NESS) in 2005 reported that the programme had made little impact but a second evaluation in 2008 found positive changes in children living in SSLP areas when compared with those not living in such areas (NESS, 2008).

Every Child Matters

During the 1990s and early 2000s a number of child abuse cases had caused public concern. Investigation into the death of a young girl, Victoria Climbié, led to the setting up of the Laming Inquiry. The Laming Report (2003) found that key services responsible for the welfare of children and young people were operating separately with no coordination between them. It was this lack of a cohesive approach that had prevented the sharing of significant information and decisive action being taken that could have prevented the death of this child. The resulting Children Act of 2004 and the publication of *Every Child Matters: Change for Children* (DfES, 2004c) had a significant impact on services working with children. From this time the child was to be put at the centre and services built around their needs rather than the other way around. This can be seen as very much a continuation of the Sure Start approach.

The 'remodelling' of the teaching profession during this period meant that teachers were expected to liaise more with other professionals working with children. Other adults apart from teachers were now employed in the classroom, such as teaching assistants and learning mentors, as part of improving the teaching and learning process. There was also a rapid expansion of nursery and early years' provision at this time based upon the presupposition that a good start is more likely to lead to a positive view of learning throughout the compulsory phases of education and beyond.

Every Child Matters (ECM) recognised that education initiatives alone could not solve social inequalities. In each authority, local education and social services were now combined into an integrated children's services approach under a Director of Children's Services. This enabled the creation of multi-agency teams bringing together school nurses, social workers, educational psychologists and the police. Education, social and healthcare services would be provided on the same site in children's centres and extended schools thus making them the centre of local communities. This policy was very much of the view that schools could compensate for society and was similar to earlier initiatives such as the Education Priority Areas of the 1970s, the Education Action Zones of the 1990s and the Head Start programme that ran in the US.

Reader Reflection: The five common outcomes for children under ECM

1. Being healthy
2. Staying safe
3. Enjoying and achieving
4. Making a positive contribution
5. Achieving economic well-being.

What do you think of each the above outcomes? Do they promote particular views about society and the future roles children are expected to play?

If you had to choose five goals for the raising of children what would they be?

Even though the rhetoric of ECM and Sure Start is about involving parents, the underpinning assumption is that structures are needed as well as support from professionals. A deficit model of the family is the starting point for both of these initiatives and many parents from the deprived areas in which they were set up were suspicious of the middle-class notion of a functional family being promoted by the (external) support agencies.

Reader Reflection: ECM

Do you think that Sure Start and ECM structures can compensate for society?

How can the effects of a deprived social and family background be compensated for?

Specialist schools and academies

> From 1997 onwards a current of opinion within New Labour wanted to provide alternatives to traditional comprehensive schools. (Ward and Eden, 2009: 51)

On coming to office Labour proceeded with the specialist schools programme initiated by the previous Conservative administration. Secondary schools were allowed to specialise in particular curriculum areas but they needed to secure sponsorship from business, charities or other private sponsors. This was seen as a way of bringing increased financial support and expertise from industry into education, the ultimate aim being to raise standards in schools. The programme grew and more schools opted for specialist status as the amount of sponsorship required was reduced. One of the concerns about this increasing differentiation of provision was that specialist schools would be more successful in middle-class areas and with middle-class parents generally and so lead to increasing social segregation. The GCSE results of these schools was improving overall but this is more likely to have been due to the changing background of the pupils in them over time than the specialist curriculum or the teaching itself (Ward and Eden, 2009). The government's response to claims that specialist schools would increase division was to argue for more schools to become specialist and so increase the numbers of students benefiting.

As Goodman and Burton (2012) explain, a further attempt by Labour to address underachievement in schools in England and Wales came with the introduction of City Academies. These were a new type of secondary school designed to replace failing comprehensive schools in urban areas. Emulating the

US Charter School initiative, the rationale was that they would raise education standards across the country by broadening diversity and choice of schools by promoting competition among providers. With their greater intake of 'free school meals' pupils than state comprehensives they would shed the culture of low educational aspirations often held by deprived communities, replacing this with a motivated, 'can do' attitude. Independent from local authorities but still funded by the state, academies were to be founded and governed by sponsors including businesses, faiths, charities and universities. A defining characteristic of academies was that, due to their independence from LAs, they were not to be bound by the constraints of the national curriculum.

The attempt to simultaneously endorse the free market *and* social justice was characteristic of the third way ethos underlying Labour's policies under Tony Blair. By jointly prioritising equality and marketisation, Labour positioned itself away from the traditional neo-liberalism of the Conservatives. Academies could be seen as a way of adhering to both market forces and social justice, increasing school choice and hence competition between schools while jointly addressing the link between deprivation and poor educational attainment.

The initial requirement for academy sponsors to cover 10 per cent of the capital costs for a new building, capped at £2 million, was terminated in 2009 in an attempt to entice more sponsors. Instead, skills and leadership and the organisa-tion's educational track record and its commitment to working with local parents, teachers and pupils were identified as the criteria by which potential sponsors would be evaluated (DCSF, 2009c). While there was early criticism as to how far these initial academies did go towards breaking the cycle of underachievement (Gorard, 2009; PricewaterhouseCoopers, 2008) for Ward and Eden (2009) the fundamental issues were that academies were independent from the local author-ities and the external sponsors remained outside the democratic process, not accountable to the community.

As we shall see, the policy of creating academies was to gather further momen-tum after the defeat of the Labour government with the incoming Coalition administration.

Reader Reflection: Sponsorship of schools

What do you think the benefits and issues would be of a big company such as Ford Motors, McDonald's or Manchester United sponsoring several academies across the country?

Think of the effects upon individual schools and pupils and also the system generally.

Building Schools for the Future programme

As part of a commitment to improving the quality of education in 2005 the Labour government embarked on a significant programme of rebuilding and refurbishing secondary schools under the Building Schools for the Future (BSF) programme. This was to take place over a 15-year period with LAs being asked to take part in waves. Most of the new builds in the BSF programme were funded through the Private Finance Initiatives (PFI) to encourage outside contractors to pay for them. Promoted as an investment in public services, this was effectively moving the control and future maintenance of school buildings out of the hands of the LAs. There were also criticisms about the cost of some of the buildings, their design and whether they would make any significant difference to educational standards.

The expansion of higher education

Higher education became an increasingly significant issue towards the end of the millennium and continues to be so. In the early 1990s the system was in a funding crisis. Since the 1950s student fees had been paid by the state and the students were able to apply for a means-tested maintenance grant that was also state funded through the LEAs. This system worked well when the numbers of students entering HE was small. However, as the percentage of students entering HE had dramatically increased over a 20-year period the costs of support to the taxpayer had soared. It was increasingly felt that students should bear more of the burden of cost rather than just the taxpayer. Between 1990 and 1999 the maintenance grants were reduced and were steadily replaced by student loans. However, there was still the issue of tuition fees and the Dearing Commission was set up to look into the paying of these. Due to the sensitive nature of this issue it was side-lined by both the Conservative government and the Labour Party in the run up to the general election of 1997.

The Dearing Report was published after the election (NCIHE, 1997) won by Labour. Its proposals resulted in the Teaching and Higher Education Act of 1998 that abolished the student maintenance grants and improved the student loan system that was to replace it. These loans were not to be paid back until the graduate was in full-time employment and earning £10,000 per year. The act also introduced student contributions to university fees. These were to be paid up front and amounted to £1,075 per year (index-linked). Now that the principles of students funding their own living while at university and also paying towards the fees had been established rather than these being a cost to the state, it could only be a matter of time before they began to bear more and eventually all of the costs

(Ward and Eden, 2009). Fears developed that debt from the loans and fee contributions would deter potential students from poorer backgrounds from entering HE.

After a further White Paper and arguments concerning funding, the Higher Education Act of 2004 allowed universities to charge students 'top-up' fees of £3,000 on top of the government payment to the university per student. This was to help universities meet their increasing running costs. However, these fees were no longer to be paid up front by students and, along with the loans, were only to be repaid when the graduate was in work and earning at least £15,000 per year. A system of grants was to be introduced for the poorest students. It was hoped these measures would prevent students from poorer backgrounds being discouraged by the threat of fees while at the same time ensuring greater security within the HE funding system. By placing payment upon the consumer it was envisaged that the universities would now become part of a true market and so have to 'give value for money'.

However, the funding – or rather the underfunding – of HE remained an issue that became more urgent as the election of 2010 approached. Vice-chancellors from both the traditional research universities and the new post-1992 universities (polytechnics before 1992) complained that they had been cutting costs and making efficiency savings since the 1980s. They had also expanded in terms of student numbers yet their income per student had fallen significantly due to the reduction of core government funding. They argued that what was regarded as a world-class system was in danger of falling apart if funding was not improved. Members of the powerful Russell Group of Universities argued the need to raise their own fees if they were to maintain standards compared with the best universities internationally. The two main political parties realised that something needed to be done and that whatever was decided would not be popular. As they could see little gain in raising this as an election issue both parties shelved it until after the impending general election. Only the Liberal Democrats made HE an election issue by promising to abolish student fees in their manifesto.

Support for 16–18 year olds

Labour introduced a range of measures to improve education and training opportunities in the workplace. These included programmes to develop the basic literacy, numeracy and ICT skills of those in low-paid jobs, the long-term unemployed and young offenders. The need to update older workers in ICT skills and other new forms of working was also recognised. Those on welfare benefits were provided with suitable skills training after an assessment of their needs. Financial support was also available for the low paid. In 2004 the Education Maintenance

Allowance (EMA) of up to £30 per week was introduced for 16–19 year olds whose family incomes were low. This was designed to enable these students to continue into further education rather than leave due to financial pressures.

New Labour policy: a critique

Lawton (2005) suggested that while Labour introduced many policies aimed at monitoring and raising standards in schools, it dispensed with very little of what the Conservatives initiated. As Reay (2008: 640) put it: 'In many ways Blair has trod a well-worn path, following the steps of Old Tory policies, as much as he has forged a "new" Third Way in educational policy'. She also said that 'Blair and his educational policies can be seen as a bridge between the past and the future, in which he has acted as a conduit for very old inequalities of social class to be reinvented in new, thriving forms; a very "New Labour" perpetuation of educational inequalities' (2008: 647).

Walford (2005) pointed to contradictions with policy initiatives that, on the one hand, were aimed at reducing inequality and providing better opportunities for the disadvantaged and, on the other, at encouraging diversity and the development of markets. Labour politicians wished to improve standards but there was no questioning of the nature of these standards which were taken as read. The term 'modernisation' was used but it was modernisation based on old images of what was important.

The government's school improvement policy emphasised performativity and was 'founded upon the twin pillars of accountability (inspection, test scores, league tables) and standards (target setting, monitoring, raising achievement plans)' (Harris and Ranson, 2005: 573). This assumed that the causes for low performance lay essentially within the school and resulted from poor leadership or ineffective teaching and that these faults could be rectified. This was not necessarily the case because many poorly performing schools in deprived areas had great difficulty in raising their performance for perfectly legitimate reasons beyond their control.

This obsession with targets became less pronounced in the final Labour term of office as policy moved towards modernising schools themselves. Though equality of opportunity remained part of the Labour rhetoric, the policies that encouraged differentiation and specialisation did not match this. Labour abolished grant-maintained schools and the assisted places scheme but there was no proposal to do away with grammar schools. Labour oversaw the rapid expansion of the specialist schools programme and the development of new city academies and trust schools, arguing that these developments were needed to improve the quality of secondary education and offer parental choice. However, such choice tended to reinforce the very social inequalities that Labour was trying to eliminate (Ball, 2013).

Middle-class parents were more able to operate the system to their advantage to ensure that their children received the 'best' from the system (Ball, 2013; Reay, 2013; Tomlinson, 2005). Schools in the areas chosen by large numbers of middle-class parents tended to perform well and were oversubscribed. Those who could not make the choices that help them to escape the poorer, more deprived geographical areas remained in the schools deserted by the middle class. These were likely to become sink schools, less likely to attract extra resources and teachers. They remained underperforming and less able to rise from this position. These high-poverty contexts exerted downward pressures on quality that were very difficult to overcome (Lupton, 2005).

In these ways the development of an education market helps to reproduce social inequalities (Ball, 2013). In promoting different forms of school that were run by external partner bodies and thereby providing choice to parents, the effect was to further emphasise social differences in achievement rather than to resolve them (Harris and Ranson, 2005; Taylor et al., 2005). Such measures increase rather than diminish social segregation, leaving working-class students stranded in predominantly working-class schools (Reay, 2006; 2008).

It may be that the existence of a risk society and the need to develop an adaptable workforce have been greatly exaggerated and are really little more than social myths. The political rhetoric of lifelong learning involving individuality, adaptability and operating in the 'knowledge economy' may have drawn attention away from real structural inequalities in society by emphasising the importance of individual action.

New Labour to new politics: Conservative-LibDem Coalition government 2010-15

The 2010 general election came at a time of global financial insecurity following the failure of international banks, deepening economic recession and public disillusion with politicians after an expenses scandal that had dogged the last few months of the Labour administration. It resulted in a coalition government formed through an alliance between the Conservative and Liberal Democrat parties. There was pressure on all government departments to make rapid spending cuts and a number were announced almost immediately in education. In July 2010 the new Secretary of State for Education, Michael Gove, announced that the BSF programme was to be scrapped with only those projects currently underway to be completed. This led to public outcry in those LAs that had not yet had any schools rebuilt and were left with pupils being educated in buildings of very poor quality. In October 2010 the government cancelled the EMA scheme as part of its budget cuts. They argued that much of the money previously spent on EMA was not targeted correctly and many students were receiving funding who did not need it. It was replaced by a bursary that could be applied for through FE colleges of up to £1,200 per student per year. This was to cost the government £180 million per year as opposed to the £560 million per year spent on EMA. Central government was also no longer to fund Sure Start projects which now had to rely solely on individual local authorities for support. Thus, during the Coalition years these projects were significantly scaled down and many closed altogether due to the cuts and savings local authorities had to make.

In the run up to the election Michael Gove (2009) had said that: 'Schools should be engines of social mobility. They should enable children to overcome disadvantage and deprivation so they can fulfil their innate talents and take control of their own destiny'. The new administration brought with it the promise of an education revolution. Cameron and Clegg, Prime Minister and Deputy Prime Minister, in their preface to the White Paper *The Importance of Teaching* (DfE, 2010a: 4) proclaimed that:

> No country that wishes to be considered world class can afford to allow children from poorer families to fail as a matter of course. For far too long we have tolerated the moral outrage of an accepted correlation between wealth and achievement at school, the soft bigotry of low expectations . . . Of course schools are not solely responsible for this problem. In far too many communities there is a deeply embedded culture of low aspiration that is strongly tied to long-term unemployment. The Coalition Government's Work Programme and welfare reforms will help to tackle these issues. But schools do have a crucial role to play.

Gove went even further in the White Paper, stating that:

> Our schools should be engines of social mobility, helping children to overcome the accidents of birth and background to achieve much more than they may ever have imagined. But, at the moment, our schools system does not close gaps, it widens them . . . This injustice has inspired a grim fatalism in some, who believe that deprivation must be destiny. But for this Government the scale of this tragedy demands action. Urgent, focused, radical action. (DfE, 2010a: 6)

Such rhetoric places the 'blame' squarely on previous Labour administrations, parents, communities and schools with the Coalition government playing the role of saviour!

The reforms of the Coalition

The fairness premium

As part of their mission to reduce inequality and narrow the achievement gap between rich and poor the Coalition government introduced the 'fairness premium' (Goodman and Burton, 2012). According to Deputy Prime Minister Nick Clegg, every child should have the chance to get ahead and there needed to be greater emphasis on fairness in terms of social mobility and life chances. Over the next four years this fairness premium would be used to fund disadvantaged children and young people from age 2 to 20. Two initiatives identified to receive funds from the premium were additional pre-school education and the 'pupil premium'.

The additional pre-school education funds entitled the most disadvantaged two year olds to 15 hours a week of pre-school education. This was in addition to the 15 hours already available to those aged three and four. The scheme was an extension of a pilot put in place by Labour, the aim of which was to improve social and cognitive outcomes for those children and increase the take-up of part-time early years' education offers for three to four year olds (DCSF, 2008). Consistent with the aims of previous initiatives such as Sure Start, this early intervention aimed to benefit disadvantaged children by providing intervention before gaps in development had time to become established and increase the likelihood that those children from disadvantaged backgrounds would be at a baseline stage of cognitive development similar to their less disadvantaged peers when they began formal schooling. Taken together with the cuts in Sure Start funding, however, this initiative did not represent the progress it at first appeared to.

The pupil premium was introduced in April 2011 and was designed to close the attainment gap between disadvantaged pupils and their peers by raising the achievement of disadvantaged pupils from reception to Year 11. The pupil premium is extra funding paid to schools per pupil for those eligible for FSM or who have been looked after for six months or longer. The funding was to be monitored by schools providing data on how they used the pupil premium, Ofsted school inspections reporting on the spending of the premium and performance tables that tracked the attainment of pupils. In 2015 the pupil premium was extended to encompass children in the EYFS. However, by the end of the Coalition administration the pupil premium seemed to have had little impact on pupil achievement in secondary schools (Cocco, 2015) and the DfE admitted that children from disadvantaged backgrounds continued to be far less likely to get good GCSE results (DfE, 2015a).

Curriculum reform

As discussed in detail in Chapter 5 the Coalition made significant reforms in several key areas of the curriculum. On coming to power they abandoned the newly completed Labour review of the primary national curriculum in favour of their own whole curriculum review. Their aim was to replace what was termed by Gove, 'a substandard curriculum' with one that prepared children more effectively for the future. The final new curriculum framework was published in 2014. The reforms concentrated upon the content of the curriculum which was made slimmer overall, more challenging and focused on core subject knowledge with a stronger emphasis on key skills. The whole assessment process of the national curriculum was overhauled with the scrapping of the old levels of attainment. The Early Years Foundation Stage was also reviewed and slimmed down. With no consultation the EBacc became a significant part of the league tables for schools, significantly omitting any arts or technical subjects in its composition. The GCSE and A level exam system was also reformed with the replacing of coursework elements with exams and a more rigorous grading system. In the vocational sector the technical baccalaureate was introduced in 2014 in order to strengthen vocational qualifications for 16 to 18 year olds. The rhetoric across all of these reforms was, as with previous governments, of raising standards, but with the emphasis firmly on traditional subjects, knowledge and forms of assessment.

The Coalition's academies

Central to the 2010 Conservative Party manifesto and thus the education policies of the Conservative–Liberal Democrat Coalition, was a mass expansion of the academies programme (Goodman and Burton, 2012). These academies lay at the heart of the new Secretary of State's 'education revolution'. Like Labour previously, the Coalition identified narrowing the achievement gap and raising standards for all as the primary motivations for academies (DfE, 2010b). The aim was for academy status to be the norm for all state schools (DfE, 2010b). Academies are characterised by autonomy from local authority control, the freedom to set their own staff pay and conditions and liberation from the national curriculum, though they do have to teach English, mathematics and science.

It is these freedoms that, according to the government, would allow academies to drive up standards. There were, however, a number of key differences between Labour's academies and the academies programme put forward by the Coalition. For Labour, academies were only located in deprived areas or built to replace failing schools. Under the Conservative-led Coalition, however, schools did not need to be underperforming in order to gain academy status. On the contrary, although all schools were able to apply for academy status, initially only those schools that performed best were, under the Academies Act 2010, automatically eligible for conversion to academy status and could be fast-tracked. In 2011 the eligibility for conversion to academy status was extended to all schools performing well. Originally the decision to fast-track outstanding schools was defended on the grounds that they would work in partnership with a weaker school in order to help that school improve. It was a DfE requirement that fast-tracked schools support at least one weaker school and that this support was focused on having a measurable impact on standards. Failing schools could still be shut down and reopened as a sponsored academy, the sponsor often being another already outstanding academy. Other schools, not yet classed as performing well, could join 'chains' or groups of schools some of which were already successful academies as part of their own application towards academy status.

New academies, converted from former local authority state schools under the 2010 Academies Act, like all previous academies, are effectively independent schools, each run individually or as part of a chain, by an academy trust (a private company) with charitable status. These converter academies are largely publicly financed with a funding agreement between the academy trust and the Secretary of State for education. Thus any financial administration is removed from the LA to central government. This significantly increases the importance of the Secretary of State to individual schools at the expense of LAs. From the 2010 Academies Act onwards all newly built schools were to be academies or free schools, so LAs could no longer create local authority run schools, though they still had a responsibility to ensure there were adequate numbers of school places locally.

The growth in the number of academies was extremely rapid under the Coalition. In the ten years following their introduction in 2000 under Labour, 203 academies had opened in England. In the Coalition's first nine months in power, this figure had more than doubled with 442 academies open. In January 2012 there were 1,000 secondary academies (a third of all secondary schools) by July this was 41 per cent of all secondary schools. By the general election in 2015 over half of secondary schools were academies.

This rapid increase can be attributed to a number of factors. Along with the new streamlined application procedure, converter academies received their per capita funding direct from the DfE and this also included their share of the LA allocation for services provided for schools. This gave them more money to spend in spite of having to pay for services previously provided by the LA. In times of increasing austerity this was felt to be more attractive to the management of many schools. There was also extra funding available to make the conversion to academy status. Pring (2012) points to the considerable financial benefits to convert at this time as being an important factor in a school's decision to apply for academy status. West and Bailey (2013) suggest that while Labour saw academies as solving an issue of failing schools the Coalition has used them more broadly to effect system-wide change.

Free schools

The expansion of the academies programme also involved the introduction of a new branch of academies known as 'free schools'. Based on the Swedish model, if teachers, parents and other groups such as religious organisations were not satisfied with the education providers available in their area they could apply to set up a free school. If successful, the parents, teachers or others who proposed the new school would have some (but not total) control over the appointment of school staff and the setting of the school ethos. Often the group setting up the school used a company or specialised organisation to run the school on a daily basis. As with all academies, the admission arrangements must be fair and transparent with entry open to pupils of all abilities from the area. They could not be academically selective. Though they got off to a rather uncertain start, by the end of the Coalition government 254 free schools had been opened. For Walford (2014) these new free schools were another major step forward in the diversification of the educational system while simultaneously reducing the involvement of local government in education.

In pursuing the academies and free schools programme, the Coalition government perpetuated previous neo-liberal beliefs that independence from LAs and competition between providers would lead to a raising of standards. It was a mistrust of local authority controlled education that drove this policy. As Higham (2014: 124) puts it: 'Many of the initial motives for these moves remain central to contemporary policy, including the promotion of choice, diversity and competition. The related mistrust of local authorities ... [is] also palpable'. Page (2014) suggests that the development of free schools along with the wider academy programme sound the death knell for the egalitarian comprehensive system pioneered by the social democrats of Labour in the 1960s and 1970s.

Reform of higher education funding

As a result of the 2010 Browne Report of Higher Education and Student Finance the new Conservative and Liberal Democrat Coalition government made significant changes to the funding of HE to come into effect from 2012. The funding per student that was paid to universities by the government was to be abolished apart from some funding for students taking STEM subjects (science, technology, engineering and mathematics). Universities were to obtain their teaching income from student fees. They were to be allowed to raise fees up to £9,000 per year. However, it was expected that the majority would not raise them this high and those that did would have to justify it in terms of what they provided. The loan system was to be modified to pay for the higher fees and student loans. Graduates were not to begin paying back until they were earning £21,000 per year. In the short and medium term the government would still have to effectively fund HE until returns from the loans began coming in via the income tax system. This would take many years but the basis on which the system was funded was now fundamentally changed. It was clearly the consumer, i.e. the student, who would pay rather than the state (West et al., 2015).

These changes, as politicians from all parties had expected, caused great public outcry. The Liberal Democrats were embarrassed, so soon after the election, to appear to be reneging on their pre-election promises to abolish tuition fees. It was feared by some that the higher fee would put off students, especially from poorer backgrounds, from entering HE. The Coalition government pointed out that no one would begin to pay back until they earned above a certain income so it was not like a 'normal' debt.

Another fear was that this market would lead to an increasing divide between the traditional Russell Group universities and the newer post-1992 universities who relied upon teaching as their main source of income. The Russell Group would still obtain money from research, they were wealthier to start with, they taught STEM subjects so would benefit from continued government funding in this area and, being high-status institutions, they could expect continued applications from students. The post-1992 universities were in a less favourable position having fewer resources apart from their teaching income that was now threatened by a free and unpredictable market. Nearly all universities did in fact charge the full £9,000 fee, which brought into even sharper relief the increasing emphasis on public accountability of the quality of the student experience, the perceived 'currency' of degrees from different institutions and universities' relative student employment rates. Increasingly students were perceived as consumers to be wooed. This raises an interesting paradox in the context of a university's control of the teaching and assessment of degrees. Even if the pursuit of a university education is considered to be a partnership between teacher and taught rather than a product to be bought, it is clear who has the upper hand in that partnership given the university's ownership and control of the means by which (assessment) the consumers (students) purchase (study for) its key commodity (degree qualifications).

Considerable concern developed about whether these new funding arrangements would lead to rapid change and 'rationalisation' in the HE sector with some institutions facing financial problems and possible merger or even closure. There was potential for the early parts of degree courses to be offered more cheaply in FE colleges and for greater franchising of courses to private companies who could offer degrees in competition with universities. The Coalition also proposed that more teacher training would take place in school rather than in university institutions which would have the greatest detrimental funding impact on post-1992 universities. Although, by 2015, recruitment to HE had not been significantly reduced by the funding reforms, many of the other concerns had materialised, with the increasing diversification and creeping privatisation of the HE sector.

Special educational needs: Coalition approaches

In a document released by the cabinet office outlining the proposed policy of the new Coalition government, David Cameron is quoted as saying:

> We believe the most vulnerable children deserve the very highest quality of care. We will improve diagnostic assessment for school children, prevent the unnecessary closure of special schools, and remove the bias towards inclusion. (Cabinet Office, 2010)

The Coalition introduced the Children and Families Act (DfE, 2014c), a wide ranging piece of legislation, part 3 of which dealt with children with special needs and disabilities. An important intention of the Act was to give parents and the young people themselves as much say in the choice of provision as possible. The LA became responsible for conducting an educational, health and care (EHC) assessment and forming an EHC plan if required. These plans replaced the previous SEN statements. The LA must produce 'a local offer' (information about education, health and social services it provides for disabled children, young people and those with SEN) designed to help those making the choices.

It is unclear at present whether increasing parental choice will move SEN provision towards inclusion in the mainstream or to the strengthening of special schools. Certainly the aim of the legislation was to weaken and undermine the control of the LA in determining provision. What remains ongoing is the debate concerning the nature, meaning and potential impact of inclusion.

Coalition policy: a critique

With their having come to power as an alliance of two independent political parties in 2010, one may be forgiven for thinking it would be difficult to 'pin' down the political and educational ideologies that drove policy in the new Coalition administration. However, even during a period beset with economic problems, certain ideological themes can be detected. Cuts due to financial constraints affected all areas of education but Sure Start, EMA and BSF suffered in particular. Along with the introduction of students paying more for their higher education these policies constituted a move away from state support for some aspects of education. The drive towards market forces was clear in the Coalition's promotion of academies and free schools, its rhetoric about reducing the bureaucratic control of administrators and giving head teachers the power to make decisions (DfE, 2010a). Walford (2014: 265) suggests that:

> The rapid expansion of Academies and Free Schools marks a dramatic change in the way that schooling is provided in England. The local authority system of provision, funding and management of local schools, whereby democratically elected bodies plan appropriate provision for the whole local population, is being dismantled. It is being replaced by a greater diversity of provision, more competition between schools, and increased involvement of non-elected individuals and groups in the nature of local schooling.

As with Thatcher's Conservative government of the 1980s and 1990s a neo-liberal approach had a strong neo-conservative theme running alongside it. Consecutive Secretaries of State spoke of a return to traditional educational values, the importance of blazers and ties as part of school uniform, setting pupils by ability, the need for pupils to study more 'rigorous' subjects, the importance of exams, a knowledge-based curriculum and British values (BBC, 2010; DfE, 2010a; Gove, 2007; Morgan, 2015a). In earlier chapters we have mentioned the Coalition's review of the national curriculum with its emphasis on traditional subject areas. Young (2011: 277) stated that along with cuts in resources to schools 'the Coalition government's "return to subjects" policy would in all probability lead to new inequalities'. By the DfE's own admission, the Coalition's initial aim to make schools into the 'engines of social mobility' seems to have had little impact on the continuing underachievement of children from disadvantaged backgrounds (DfE, 2015b).

Reader Reflection: Comparing policy

Exley and Ball (2011) suggest common themes within Conservative education policy since the Thatcher era:

On the one hand . . . belief in markets and a minimal state, basic beliefs of neo-liberalism, have meant a push for privatisation, the 'liberation' of schools to innovate and diversify and an enhanced role for parents as consumers in an educational marketplace. On the other, strong distrust of a 'left wing' teaching profession coupled with firm conservative beliefs in 'real' subjects and that 'the old methods are the best' when it comes to teaching discipline and the curriculum.

It is interesting to compare the policy of the Labour government, the Coalition government and the current Conservative government in the light of these common themes.

A return to single party government: the Conservative administration from 2015

The general election of May 2015 saw the return to power of the Conservatives with an (unexpected) majority of MPs resulting in a mandate to govern without the support of any other party. This has effectively led to the continuation of the dominant Conservative elements of policy from the previous Coalition administration. In areas of the curriculum the Conservatives have continued to roll out the changes to the content and assessment of the national curriculum announced during the previous Coalition administration. The government intends that in future the EBacc will be followed by all pupils up to the age of 16 and the new Technical Baccalaureate (TechBacc) is continuing in post 18 vocational education. In school governance the emphasis on expanding the number of academies and in particular free schools has been stepped up further. Immediately after the election victory the Secretary of State for Education, Nicky Morgan, echoed the words of her predecessor in seeing free schools as the 'modern engines of social justice' (DfE, 2015c).

Free schools are at the heart of the government's commitment to deliver real social justice by ensuring all pupils have access to a world class education. This is at the core of our commitment to govern as one nation – creating a country where everyone, regardless of background, can achieve their high aspirations. (Morgan, 2015b)

With this in mind, the government has pledged to open 500 new free schools during the life of this parliament. The ability to appeal against the conversion of a failing school into an academy by the LA or parents, for example, has also been removed in the Education and Adoption Act of 2015. This will speed up the process of compulsory conversion of such schools into academies while simultaneously silencing any objections. This would seem to reinforce the view of Gunter and McGinity (2014) that academies are being forced onto local communities.

This policy of converting schools from LA control into academies may, however, not be as automatically successful in raising standards as the Conservative government claims. Stewart (2015) suggests that the evidence does not support the Secretary of State's claim about the superior performance of academies. In fact his figures show that when schools are converted to academies their improvement in GCSE results is no better than similar LA schools. Similarly, Gorard (2014) found no convincing evidence to show that academies are any more effective than schools they have replaced or are in competition with.

Conclusion

With the election of the Conservatives in 1979 education policy was strongly influenced by the New Right. This was a mixture of neo-liberalism, which proposed the creation of the free market involving consumer choice and competition to raise standards, and neo-conservatism, which advocated a return to the traditional values that had allegedly made Britain successful in the past. Disillusionment with this combination of traditionalism and a free market lacking in adequate constraints led to a step back towards the centre in terms of ideologies with the development of Labour's third way. With their 'modernised' form of social democracy Labour seemed to be attempting to combine the benefits of a free market while ensuring the exercise of social constraint and state support.

In education Labour's aim was to open access and raise standards for all sections of society by emphasising partnership and the involvement of all concerned. This involved recognising the professionalism of teachers and increasing public spending on education. Conversely it also meant the setting of targets and emphasising the accountability of those working in education. At the same time the competition between schools, the traditionalist curriculum and the diversity of provision to maintain consumer choice remained.

Third way politics can be characterised as a mixture of ideologies and an attempt at compromise, which was able to flourish, some would argue, because of the desire for conciliation following the confrontational approach of the Conservative years in government. However, many would claim that this eclectic approach to education policy is not very significantly modified Thatcherism and likely to fracture when put under pressure. There was clearly a dichotomy, for instance, between the rhetoric of professional recognition for teachers and greater accountability and control through performance management systems that emphasised targets. There was also a contradiction between policies that promote market forces and a desire to develop social justice for all. It was the steady and continued move during the Labour years towards the market and the encouragement of private business and industry to become involved that led many critics to accuse Labour of continuing the approach of the previous Conservative government.

The Coalition administration appeared once again to be promoting the neo-liberal and neo-conservative ideologies of individual choice and markets combined with traditional schooling methods and curricula. It is clear that this is also the direction to be followed during the Conservative government elected in 2015. The rhetoric of raising standards and promoting opportunity and social mobility remains. As successive government policies since the Second World War appear to have had little impact on social inequalities in educational achievement it will be interesting to see if the actions of the current Conservative government will make any difference. What is clear is that since the mid-1970s there has been a steady drift away from a vision of a monolithic state comprehensive system of secondary education towards one in which schools are more autonomous, differentiated and market driven. West and Bailey (2013) see this as policy layering and revision over successive administrations. Pring (2012) notes how we have moved over a period of 30 years from a system in which power in education was spread, creating a democratic balance between the local and the national, to a system where, in spite of the rhetoric of choice and competition, increasingly, the power over schools and the curriculum is centrally placed in the hands of the Secretary of State.

This brief analysis has considered important developments in education since the Second World War. Brevity can breed oversimplification and the emphasis of some points at the expense of others. Nevertheless, we have at least highlighted how beliefs about the nature of education, the possession of political power, and economic and social circumstances all help to shape policy and lead to change in the education system. It is important to realise that there is no one objective, unchanging vision of how education should be that is superior to all others. What should be taught, how it should be taught and issues of measurement and standards remain, as ever, dependent upon ideological belief. Successive governments develop their views of education in relation to their vision of society. To those in power, therefore, their proposals are generally not seen as contentious since they are for the good of society. Governments do find it difficult, at times, to do all they would wish because of opposition from those with alternative standpoints. This continuous political process leads to the evolution of the education system. Public opinion about the type of education that is desirable also changes with time and circumstances so the resulting development of education is a product of the struggle between competing ideologies.

Student activities

1. Visit the Department for Education website (www.education.gov.uk). Look up current publications on educational developments. Read through several of these and try to identify the key parts of current education policy. How do these key parts relate to the ideologies discussed in Chapters 2 and 6?

2. Obtain the education policies of several political parties. Try to differentiate between the policies and identify the ideological basis for them.

3. Visit the Eurydice website (http://eacea.ec.europa.eu/). This site is run by the European Commission and provides information on the organisation of the education systems and current policy developments of member states. Compare the current reforms and priorities in education for several different countries in Europe. Try to account for similarities and differences between them. Draw on information you compiled when doing question 3 in Chapter 1.

Recommended reading

Ball, S. (2013) *The Education Debate*. 2nd edn. Bristol: Policy Press. This is an advanced text but is well worth reading. Ball introduces key concepts in education policy, examines the recent history of education policy and outlines current models of policy and current key issues. Stephen Ball is one of the most significant academic writers in this area.

Bochel, H. (ed.) (2011) *The Conservative Party and Social Policy*. Bristol: Policy Press. This edited book examines the development of the Conservative's approach to social policy up to, and including, their coalition with the Liberal Democrats. It provides a range of interpretations of the different areas of social policy and so enables an understanding of how education is one part of this.

Hodkinson, A. (2016) *Key Issues in Special Educational Needs and Inclusion*. 2nd edn. London: SAGE. This book explores the field of special education needs and inclusion. It examines the ideological and political debates that have shaped its historical development. This is a very accessible account having been written especially for education studies students.

Ward, S. and Eden, C. (2009) *Key Issues in Education Policy*. London: SAGE. This book has been written specifically for education studies students. The authors explain fundamental concepts required to analyse education policy and go on to examine government policy in a number of key areas such as the curriculum, market forces and social inequality. This is a very useful introductory text on educational policy.

Access the companion website to this book and find SAGE journal articles exploring this chapter topic in further detail: https://study.sagepub.com/bartlettburton4e.

CHAPTER 7
Globalisation and comparative education

Chapter overview

Globalisation is a process that has generated increasing interest for politicians, educationalists and industrialists alike in terms of its impact across the world. In this chapter we look at the meaning of globalisation and different perspectives on its effects. We then go on to consider comparative education. This is a specific area of education studies that uses the comparative methodology to give insights into whole education systems or their components. We point out the strengths and dangers of using data gained via this approach.

Introduction

Marshall (2014) points to three main theorist groups in the globalisation debate. The first, the hyperglobalists, sees globalisation as a phenomenon that is making traditional social and economic configurations of nation states and economies increasingly irrelevant and powerless as the world becomes more the 'same'. A second group, the sceptics, suggest that things are much as they always have been with a number of economically and politically powerful nations controlling much of what happens globally. Thus much of the discussion concerning globalisation is merely political rhetoric and scaremongering. Finally, the transformationalists consider how the traditional balance of power between different parts of the world changes as some countries are integrated into the world economy while others are not. It questions how power bases crumble and new ones arise. For instance,

Europe, having had a very powerful colonial past, has become less significant in the world and the influence of the former Communist Eastern bloc has withered away while India and, perhaps more significantly, China, are rapidly becoming increasingly important on a world stage. In both cases their increased significance derives from the acceleration of their economies. Africa, however, while having large reserves of natural resources and economic potential, due to its history of repression and lack of infrastructure, remains largely a poor and exploited continent.

Definition and development of globalisation

There is no singly agreed definition of globalisation. As with much terminology, globalisation has a range of meanings. Harber (2014: 19) suggests that it may be more accurate to 'speak of globalisations in that globalisation has many strands'. If by globalisation one means movement of people, ideas and products around the world then it has always existed. From the earliest of times there have always been migrations of people. There have been voyages of exploration, wars of conquest and the development of trade over land and by sea. What has changed is the speed and ease with which labour and goods can now be transported in response to fluctuations in supply and demand around the world. Thus markets have been able to expand until we have what can be termed a global economy. While there are many benefits that can derive from globalisation, such as greater choice of goods at lower prices resulting from market forces, there are also potential problems.

Competition may benefit the wealthier parts of the globe but those who are poor and forced to sell their labour and economic assets cheaply remain disadvantaged. There is the distinct possibility that the market will result in the dominance of the culture of the rich at the expense of the rest, i.e. the 'McDonaldisation' of the world as Western, predominantly American, tastes spread and the demand for their products increases globally while smaller cultures and languages are lost (Ritzer, 2001). A number of international companies now exist that reach across national and continental boundaries and so are able to circumvent individual government threats of control and taxes. As shown in the banking crisis of 2008, if one or two of these global companies get into difficulty the knock-on effect is quickly felt worldwide.

Technological and social change

There is no doubt that since the middle of the twentieth century, there has been rapid and continuous change in our society affecting all areas of our lives.

Though we have been focusing here on our own and similar developed societies, many of these changes are also happening in all societies, to different extents, across the globe. Patterns of employment, housing conditions, health care, leisure activities, individual mobility and forms of transport have all changed. If we consider forms of ICT used in the home we can see the extent of these changes. Sixty years ago few households had a television; home cinema and live streaming is now commonplace. Twenty-five years ago very few households had a personal computer (PC) and these were large and very slow. Fifteen years ago few houses had internet access. If they did it was often through a shared telephone landline and certainly wasn't wireless; broadband did not then exist. Today not only do we mostly connect to the internet wirelessly at home but increasingly this is over mobile networks. Video recorders will have appeared in most homes and disappeared again over a 25 period. These advances and developments are taking place in all areas of our lives. Consider the history of music storage and playing media, from vinyl records, through tapes, CDs and DVDs to iPods, mobile phones and 'smart' watches. As we look through multinational chain stores and retail outlets we can see how commodities that service all parts of our lives are continually being updated or replaced as being redundant. Even the stores them-selves are now threatened by online shopping.

This rapid and accelerating pace of change can be seen as a result of a combina-tion of developments in economic production, ICT and globalisation. These are very much interlinked forces.

Development of economic production

Methods of production have changed rapidly over a comparatively short time from labour intensive to mass production to automation requiring few people, if any, in the actual manufacturing process. Goods can be produced more quickly and cheaply than previously. A greater variety of products are made in larger num-bers than ever before and consequently the standard of living for the majority of people has risen.

Development of ICT

While the development of factories that employed early mass production tech-niques of machines linked by conveyor belt revolutionised industry, the development of modern computer and robotic driven systems has produced a further revolutionary leap forward. IT now plays an important part in all areas of our lives. This has meant that new skills and knowledge are required by us all, both in our daily lives and at work. At the same time many of the old working skills have become rarer and even obsolete, as they are no longer in demand as part of the production process. Older trades disappeared years ago but now even skills that were developed and prized in the past 50 years have already become redundant. Many tasks that required engineering skills, for instance, are now done by machines and much of the manual and mental dexterity required by some jobs is no longer needed. For example, typewriting was superseded by word processing but even this skill is becoming redundant as voice recognition software enables information to be dictated.

The technology is advancing so quickly that it becomes very difficult to keep up and the need for workers to be able to update becomes more important than the skills they currently possess. One of the key factors in creating such rapid change is the revolution in communications that has taken place. It is now possible to access information and communicate instantly and at any time across the globe via the internet and the World Wide Web. It is as though the earth has shrunk and time has been compressed into smaller units (Edwards and Usher, 2000). This is clearly a fundamental element of the globalisation process. Rapid developments in telephonic technology now mean that visual communications can be sent immediately around the world as evidenced in numerous recent conflicts and insurrections such as those in Afghanistan, Syria, Iraq and the Ukraine.

The risk society

Beck (1992) saw these forces of the market, modern technology and globalisation as creating changes in the very nature of society, an evolution from modernity to reflexive modernity. This reflexive modernity is characterised by an increased lack of certainty in our lives and consequently individuals have to make constant decisions about how they act in their daily lives. Their choices concern how they work, what they spend their money on, and personal relationships with family, friends and others. We will benefit or not according to the decisions we make and so each choice involves an element of risk. Beck said we are now living in a 'risk society' where, due to the rapidly changing social environment, we can no longer be sure of our social structures, such as the family, work or even the government itself, as they are in a state of constant flux. Market forces, which are beyond individual or state control, are seen to have increasing power; in tandem with this is the stronger emphasis on individualisation. Beck notes a growing variation in the ability of individuals to manage their positions in this risk society. Some sections of the population benefit from greater choice, wealthier lifestyles and the latest technology. For others – those who do not have the marketable skills required for regular employment – this increasing choice brings the risk of them losing out even more, resulting in widening social division. These divisions occur within countries but can also be seen as happening globally with great differences between the wealthy and poor areas of the world. Thus it is not only the 'modern', 'advanced' societies that are changing according to this thesis, but the poorer, 'underdeveloped' rural communities are also being affected. There are large migrations of people across the world as those from poor areas move to seek even subsistence employment in the richer countries. As these are the younger, stronger and more qualified members of the population this in turn makes the country they have left even weaker.

Reader Reflection: Education as economic investment

When he was Prime Minister, Tony Blair referred to education as 'the best economic policy we have'.

Why do you think that education is seen as so important in the context of such rapid change?

Arguments that counter the risk society

The idea of the risk society and the 'onslaught' of globalisation presents a rather stark picture for those that are in danger of being left behind or excluded. However, this assumes the earlier view of globalisation as an unstoppable movement and that individuals, groups and governments are powerless in its path. Ball (2013) says that such a deterministic approach to globalisation can be used to explain almost anything and sees the development of a more reasoned and relational stance as being more realistic. He suggests that globalisation does not affect all nation states equally and at the same time. Some states are able to mediate or deflect global policy trends while others are not.

Thus in analysing any society and, more specifically, its education system we are likely to see a mixture of the global and the local and this mixture will vary from place to place. From this viewpoint the state and individuals are not powerless. They actively create their own cultures through an interaction between local, national and global influences, some of which are more powerful than others. Ball explains the influence of globalisation on individual national policies in the following way:

In each of its main dimensions – economic, political and cultural – it is possible to see globalisation as reducing the autonomy and specificity of the national and the local, while at the same time policy ideas are received and interpreted differently within different political architectures, national infrastructures, national ideologies and business cultures. (2013: 35)

Having looked at views on globalisation we now turn our attention to the study of comparative education.

Comparative education

Reader Reflection: Why compare education?

The academic study of comparative education has grown enormously since the middle of the twentieth century reflecting the increasing interest in education in many parts of the world. Think about what the reason for this might be.
   Reasons for this growth of interest include, for example:

- post-industrial nations wanting to improve their existing systems in order to remain competitive
- impetus for newly emerging European Union states to modernise quickly
- developing countries wishing to overcome disease and poverty.

Education is of central concern in all of these examples so comparing and learning from others facilitates better understanding and further improvement.

Comparative education means comparing aspects of education, looking for reasons that may account for any similarities and differences. It is usually applied to the broader comparisons of one nation's education (or aspects of this) with those of another. Arnove (2013: 9) sees three dimensions within comparative education.

1. The *scientific dimension* (called by some the academic approach) is about theory building and understanding about the working of education systems and how they interact within different societies.
2. The *pragmatic dimension* is about studying other systems in order to discover what can be used to contribute to improved policy and practice at 'home'.

The pragmatic dimension is sometimes referred to as education 'lending' or 'borrowing'. The pragmatic dimension can lead to adapting what others do or even to straight copying.

3. International education is the *global dimension*. Arnove sees this dimension as contributing to international understanding and peace. Comparative education will become more important 'as processes of globalisation increasingly require people to recognise how forces from areas of the world previously considered distant and remote impinge upon their daily lives'.

These three dimensions can be seen as separate but overlapping reasons for the study of comparative education. For Clarkson (2009) the consideration and study of other education systems is a way of breaking with our prejudices and developing a deeper understanding of others, something she sees as vitally important in the context of globalisation.

Problematising comparative education

While clear advantages exist for studying comparative education there are also significant pitfalls of which students need to be aware when comparisons are made between education systems from different countries.

There are dangers arising from adopting an attitude of cultural superiority, the assumption that education in developed (our) countries is superior to foreign practices which may be seen as backward. When developed countries become involved in the economy and education systems of the 'underdeveloped' they are open to accusations of cultural imperialism. Wright (2003) looked at how colonial regimes imposed their education systems and euro-centric definitions of knowledge, even when their emerging colonies were gaining independence, as part of aid packages. This enabled the colonial powers to maintain some level of influence over weak and emerging post-colonial states. Wright did note, however, that over time the post-colonial states began to adapt and subvert the colonial curricula. Similarly Kowalski (2014) examined international practices supporting social and economic development. He shows the sometimes unexpected effects of support and aid from the 'developed' to the 'undeveloped' world resulting in those 'developing' becoming increasingly dependent upon the donor. Nguyen et al. (2006) refer to the need for *culturally appropriate pedagogy*, a pedagogy that focuses on educational competence in a global context and which addresses the cultural context of learners and teachers. Their study in Confucian Heritage Culture (CHC) countries such as China, Vietnam, Japan, Korea, Singapore, Taiwan, Hong Kong and Malaysia found that Western-style group learning is not always as appropriate as earlier research studies had suggested since traditional CHC lecture-based education often generates higher achievement. Thus Nguyen et al. counsel that it is vital to conduct research on how culturally appropriate methodologies can be implemented instead of relying on imports that ignore the complexities of cultural learning environments.

Reader Reflection: 'Educational borrowing'

'Britain should be wary of borrowing education ideas from abroad', by Pasi Sahlberg (2015)

The following extract comes from an article by Finnish educator and scholar Pasi Sahlberg critiquing policy initiatives that draw from selective interpretation of international findings. When reading it consider how he uses comparative points to underpin his argument.

> The argument for more traditional schooling to raise test scores ignores a growing pool of internationally comparable data and academic research on good pedagogy and school improvement. The Organisation for Economic Cooperation and Development, which sponsors the influential Pisa study, makes this clear. In its most recent reports on the 2012 Pisa study, the OECD lists four suggestions for improving overall performance of education systems. It says that school choice and competition are not related to improved performance; autonomy over the curriculum and assessment appears to improve performance; the percentage of students enrolled in private schools is not related to a system's overall success; and the highest performing education systems are those that combine excellence with equity.

> This evidence from across OECD countries indicates that market-based education policies are not the best way to improve a country's educational performance. Similar conclusions are drawn in research on some states in the US, Chile and Sweden, where market solutions have been experimented with in school reforms.

> Why, then, are market-based education policies so persistent in today's education world? One reason is that, with the expanding pool of data and studies funded by various interest groups, it is easy to cherry-pick evidence that supports any chosen policy direction. By selecting information carefully, any education analyst can claim his or her findings as 'evidence-based' and justify favourable ideas.

> *How does current policy in England to raise educational standards relate to the recommendations of OECD cited above?*

> *In the light of this how might English policy be criticised and also how might the OECD recommendations be criticised?*

Cross-national comparisons of pupil performance are now central to educational policy debates and politicians may use comparisons as a means of justifying ideologically based policy and education reform (Auld and Morris, 2014). Often these comparisons are only partial, are quickly conducted and their validity is highly suspect. There is a rather dangerous assumption that education directly influences economic performance and so improving education is likely to increase efficiency and hence lead to greater competitiveness. When an economy begins to have problems it is easy to blame the education system.

This same assumption suggests that if you wish to improve economic production you should look at other countries and find out why their education systems are producing more effective employees. This approach is facilitated by the availability of comparative assessment data.

Comparative testing

A number of organisations conduct international tests to compare student achievement in different countries. The Trends in International Mathematics and Science Study (TIMSS) compares data on the mathematics and science achievement of US students with that of students in other countries (http://nces.ed.gov/timss). TIMSS data have been collected every four years since 1995, with the latest in 2015.

The Progress in International Reading Literacy Study (PIRLS) is a large international comparative study of the reading literacy of young students. PIRLS 2001 was the first in a planned five-year cycle of international trend studies in reading literacy coordinated by the International Association for the Evaluation of Educational Achievement (IEA). The latest took place in 2011 and involved over 50 countries. The PIRLS study focuses on the achievement and reading experiences of children in grades equivalent to fourth grade in the USA (Year 5 students in England). The study includes a written test of reading comprehension and a series of questionnaires focusing on the factors associated with the development of reading literacy (http://nces.ed.gov/surveys/pirls). The next round of PIRLS will take place in 2016.

The OECD funds the Programme for International Student Assessment (PISA). This is a three-yearly cycle of assessment across a number of countries (71 countries took part in the 2015 round) focusing on reading, maths, science and problem-solving (www.pisa.oecd.org). We are able to compare educational achievement in different countries over time using data from these tests. The results are frequently used by politicians to show the benefits or failings of recent policy depending upon their positioning.

Examples of politicians using the data from the international tests

In the most recent OECD PISA survey . . . we fell from 4th in the world in the 2000 survey to 14th in science, 7th to 17th in literacy, and 8th to 24th in mathematics. The only way we can catch up, and have the world-class schools our children deserve, is by learning the lessons of other countries' success. (From the Foreword to *The Importance of Teaching* White Paper (DfE, 2010a) by the Prime Minister and Deputy Prime Minister)

Since the 1990s our performance in these [PISA] league tables has been at best, stagnant, at worst declining. In the latest results we are 21st amongst 65 participants in the world for science, 23rd for reading and 26th for mathematics.

For all the well-intentioned efforts of past governments we are still falling further behind the best-performing school systems in the world. In Shanghai and Singapore, South Korea and Hong Kong – indeed even in Taiwan and Vietnam – children are learning more and performing better with every year that passes – leaving our children behind in the global race.

That matters because business is more mobile than ever, and employers are more determined than ever to seek out the best-qualified workers. Global economic pressures, far from leading to a race to the bottom, are driving all nations to pursue educational excellence more energetically than ever before.

And today's league tables show that nations which have had the courage radically to reform their education systems – like Germany and Poland – have significantly improved their performance and their children's opportunities. (Gove's statement in the House on the publication of the OECD's 2012 PISA results)

So, what was our response to PISA? Well, since coming to power in 2010, this government has implemented the most significant reform plan for a generation – and learning from the most successful education systems around the world has been central to that plan.

Three key principles which draw on the best international evidence have consistently guided our approach:

- increased autonomy for schools, coupled with
- strong accountability, all underpinned by a
- rigorous academic curriculum

This plan is working. Today, a million more pupils are in good or outstanding schools, as judged by Ofsted – England's schools inspectorate. (Nick Gibb, School Minister Speech to the OECD, 'Reforming education through international evidence', 22 January 2015)

(Continued)

(Continued)

These comments from politicians at different stages in the life of the same government use test results from international comparative studies to justify their reforms. The data show the changes in student scores and in league table rankings over time but not the reasons for them. The data does not take account of wider cultural, economic and social influences upon the scores so it could be misleading to assume that any differences in scores are due to the education system alone or even in large part.

However, as Smith (2012) points out, international tests are complex to design and administer with high potential for error and so great care needs to be taken when interpreting the results. She goes on to say that education systems, local policy and the social and economic contexts in which education operates are changing within different countries all the time. Such factors need to be taken into account when examining the relative performance of students within their countries and internationally (see also Cowen, 2014).

A comparative study might look at pupil performance, teaching methods and assessment in, for example, maths and language. Once the successful formula has been identified, it can be copied or at least adapted for use in other countries. This approach has led to overseas visits and surveys being conducted by British politicians and school inspectors (HMI and Ofsted). Many changes in pedagogy and curricula have been justified by such international comparisons. Evidence to support politicians' opinions is often cited whereas alternative examples can be ignored or explained away. Britain, for example, has increasingly developed structured pre-school education and assessment but this would not appear to be based on comparisons with other countries since it is not the practice in many economically and educationally successful countries. Conversely, a concern for the reading development of primary age children led the Labour government to import the Reading Recovery scheme from New Zealand (www.readingrecovery.ac.nz). One-to-one teaching by a specially trained teacher for children making the slowest progress in literacy after a year at school is supplementary to classroom instruction. Reading Recovery was widely implemented in English speaking countries throughout the world. However, the process of identification of successful practices from other education systems, their introduction into a 'home' system and their acceptance or assimilation is very complex and presents many problems (Phillips and Schweisfurth, 2007). The reading recovery scheme proved to be very expensive and difficult to maintain in times of increased austerity.

There are, of course, flaws in adopting an overly simplistic comparative approach. Only parts of the systems are examined rather than the whole picture and these are usually seen in isolation. Wider social and cultural influences are not taken into account. We will see in different sections of this book just how important such contextual parameters are in explaining how each education system develops. Ignoring these renders it difficult to claim clear cause-and-effect relationships for educational initiatives.

Comparisons of educational systems and practices can be useful but only if they are made within the broad context of understanding whole cultures. This takes a great deal of time and care when conducting such research. This is illustrated in a study by Chikoko et al. (2011) involving researchers from both South Africa and England working together. The study examined the approaches to teaching controversial issues in schools used by trainee teachers in both countries. The careful analysis had to take into account the vast differences both between and within these societies and could only be conducted with a detailed understanding of each. Similarly, Oates (2011), in comparing national curricula from a number of countries, argues against simple 'policy borrowing' from other nations. He suggests that great care needs to be taken when examining the success of others but that a sophisticated analysis will 'enable us to usefully put up a mirror to our own system' (2011: 137). Attempts to find 'quick fixes' become even more attractive in our current context of technology-enabled, instantaneous communication but developing an awareness of how systems work and interact with society is essential.

Conclusion

In this chapter we have examined globalisation and theories about how it affects society and education in particular. Comparative education has been introduced as a distinct area of study. And we have shown how the findings of such studies, as with all aspects of education, are inextricably linked to their socio-economic and political context.

Student activities

1. Visit the TIMSS website (http://nces.ed.gov/timss) or the PIRLS website (http://nces.ed.gov/surveys/pirls). Describe what the charts on international comparisons of achievement show. What different explanations can be given for these results? Search through past editions of the education and popular press from the time of the first publication of these statistics. In what different ways have they been presented and interpreted?

(Continued)

(Continued)

2. Visit the PISA website (www.pisa.oecd.org). Read about the methods of assessment and then complete an online assessment.

3. Visit the Eurydice website (http://eacea.ec.europa.eu/). This site is run by the European Commission and provides information on the organisation of the education systems and current policy developments of member states. Compare the structure of the education systems of several different countries in Europe. Note the similarities and variations in how these countries choose to educate their citizens. Note, particularly, differences in when children start their formal education, how young children are educated, the structure of compulsory education and the provision for vocational education. This is also a useful task for Chapters 5 and 10.

Recommended reading

Bartram, B. (2010) *Attitudes to Modern Foreign Language Learning: Insights from Comparative Education.* London: Continuum Press. This publication is a very good example of comparative education in practice. In drawing on the results of a tri-national comparative survey of secondary school pupils' attitudes towards MFL learning Bartram shows how to conduct in-depth comparative analysis.

Harber, C. (2014) *Education and International Development: Theory, Practice and Issues.* Oxford: Symposium Books. This is a comprehensive introductory text for those interested in the complex relationship between education and international development. It provides a critical overview and analysis of the key theories, ideologies and issues of education in developing countries.

Marshall, J. (2014) *Introduction to Comparative and International Education.* London: SAGE. This book provides an accessible introduction to comparative and international education. It examines the major themes and theories in the field. It looks at how education takes place in different social, political and economic contexts and explores how globalisation may influence practice.

 Access the companion website to this book and find SAGE journal articles exploring this chapter topic in further detail: https://study.sagepub.com/bartlettburton4e.

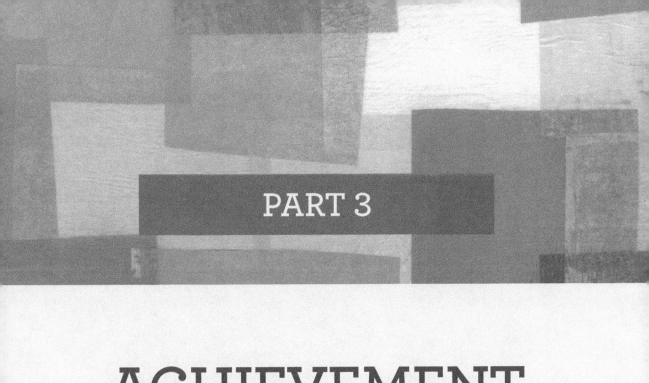

PART 3

ACHIEVEMENT IN EDUCATION

CHAPTER 8

Individual achievement: major psychological theories

Chapter overview

Chapter 8 focuses on the individual and achievement from a psychological perspective. It examines briefly the influence of philosophy on ideas about how the mind works and explores the concepts of self, intelligence, cognition, personality, creativity, motivation and metacognition. The major perspectives on learning are outlined including behaviourism, Gestalt theory, Piaget's cognitive-developmental theory and the information-processing approach.

Introduction

A focus on the individual points us in the direction of psychological research since it is concerned with individual *cognition*, which covers knowing, understanding, remembering and problem-solving. It is also able to illuminate our understanding of human behaviour, motivation, achievement, personality and self-esteem. Throughout this book we maintain that our positioning influences the explanations we develop for phenomena. Psychology is no different so it is important to briefly chart the most significant influences from within philosophy from which different views about the way mental processes work have been derived. We will also give an overview of the seminal work of the earliest psychologists and of classic twentieth-century psychological research which is relevant to education.

Leaving a long-established legacy are:

- the debates of seventeenth- and eighteenth-century philosophers about rationalist and empiricist explanations of human understanding
- the earliest psychological investigative approaches of introspection and functionalism
- behaviourist learning theory with its emphasis on external stimuli for learning
- gestalt theory which developed principles of perception grounded in the brain's search for 'wholeness'
- personality theories: psychoanalytic, psychometric and humanist explanations
- motivation theories: instinct, drive/need and cognitive explanations
- creativity and intelligence theory: the impact and controversy of IQ testing
- cognitive-developmental theory: Piaget's maturational explanation of human development and learning
- cognitive psychology: schemata and concepts, information-processing theory – processes of attention, perception and memory.

The influence of philosophy

The French philosopher Descartes' seventeenth-century notion of the *dualism* of mind and body still prevails as a common-sense explanation of the mechanistic, material body existing in parallel with something quite non-material, the mind.

Reader Reflection: 'In my mind's eye'

The work of neuroscientists shows us, of course, that the mind is just as material as the body because the brain is an organ in the same way as the liver is, but to think of it so mechanistically can be difficult to comprehend as we know that other organs such as the liver or the kidney do not 'think' like the brain does!

Think, for example, how easily we use expressions like 'in my mind's eye'.

Effectively here we are ascribing the brain a human form of its own, a kind of 'mini-me'. This is a good example of how the brain needs to work with concrete images or examples to understand abstract concepts. We will learn more of this later.

Similarly, the seventeenth- and eighteenth-century argument about whether knowledge exists outside of human reasoning and experience is still played out today. *Rationalists*, like Descartes, believed that there is knowledge beyond experience, the existence of God for example, or of abstract ideas like 'triangle'. *Empiricists*, on the other hand, maintained that all knowledge derives from experience. Thus Locke, a late seventeenth-century English philosopher, believed children were born with a blank slate for a mind on which all learning and experience is imprinted. He advocated individualised instruction and control of self through reward and punishment. In contrast, in the eighteenth century the Swiss Romantic Rousseau believed that talent and genius were inborn along with an innate sense of right and wrong. He advocated a free, unrestrained environment which the child would explore, learning at their own pace. These ideas could be found over a century later within the progressive movement of Montessori education for example.

What follows from these differing perspectives are very different accounts of the way the mind works. Thus empiricists see the mind as an information-processing device which applies processes of attention, sensation, perception and memory to each new stimuli (experience). Conversely, rationalists, and a subsequent related group of thinkers, *nativists*, governed by their belief that some ideas are innate, maintain that the mind is similarly pre-programmed with an inherent structure of concept development and language acquisition. Researchers within these opposing traditions necessarily take different approaches to psychological study, with the starting point of empiricists being objective, experimentally acquired data on human behaviour from which theories about mental processes are developed. Rationalists and nativists will start from their theories of a priori knowledge and innateness of mental structures and explore how these are manifest within human behaviour. Three centuries on, the nature/nurture debate is still alive and well with much research data now available to support both sides of the argument.

Immanuel Kant, the eighteenth-century philosopher, is often considered to be the most influential figure of pre-twentieth-century cognitive thinking. A rationalist for most of his life, he was strongly influenced by David Hume, the British empiricist who distinguished between ideas and impressions and gave an early account of concept formation. Kant theorised that mental representation requires concepts *and* sensations. In other words, we need information about which to make judgements but we also need to be able to discriminate (Brook, 2001: 427). *Representationalism* held that thoughts are intermediaries between the physical objects or abstract ideas we experience and the internal mental structures of our minds.

If you think about 'kindness' you are representing a socialised act that you have experienced using the mental structures of concept formation and discrimination.

In the 1970s a parallel theory was developed by Fodor (1975). Fodor espoused a Language of Thought, a mental language through which we are able to think and reason. Kant was the first theorist of the modern era to suggest that the mind was a system of functions, a position which continues to spawn much research.

Early psychological ideas

The earliest psychologists did not emerge until the late nineteenth century. Darwin's (1859) work on the origins of species was influential in establishing child psychology as a scientific discipline. Preyer, a German researcher interested in ontogenesis (the origin and development of individual beings), is sometimes said to be the father of modern psychology. The earliest psychologists used methods of *introspection* – reporting on one's own feelings and thoughts – to find out how minds worked. Wilhelm Wundt established the first psychological experimental laboratory in Leipzig in 1879 where he studied behaviour through experimentation and systematic self-observation methods. He believed that ultimately the only way to systematically study the differences in societies' beliefs, language, personality and social cognition was to detail everything about those societies.

Around the same time William James was working in the USA, on the first modern psychology textbook (James, 1890). He was very interested in states of consciousness and took a phenomenological approach to their analysis. (In psychology *phenomenology* holds that each person's perception of events or experiences is unique and determines how the person will react, therefore the study of psychology should concern these individual perceptions.) Like John Dewey, James developed a *pragmatic* or *functionalist* explanation for phenomena – that words and thoughts are only meaningful in relation to the purpose to which they are put.

Thus a school is not defined conceptually in terms of its physical properties as a building but in relation to its purpose as a community of learning.

Similarly, mental processes were seen as adapting to the function in hand and, as such, functionalists stressed the need to examine mental phenomena within natural contexts. Influenced by Darwin's new theory of adaptive evolution, they also believed that mental processes transcend species such that, for example, the processes involved in moving from one place to another would be fundamentally the same whether within human or animal because their function or goal is identical. This signalled a move away from introspective methods which could not be used to examine the behaviour of other species.

In contrast to functionalism, other early psychologists were interested in the structure rather than the function of mental activity. Ebbinghaus (1964 [1885]) used introspective methods to study memory systematically; he memorised hundreds of nonsense syllables and then studied the rate of memory loss at recall. He established the importance of *associations* in learning, that is, adding to what is already known. The modern-day version of this is *connectionism*, in which a cognitive architecture of ever-increasing neural connections is proposed as an explanation for thinking and understanding.

Behaviourist theory

Introspection had obvious drawbacks in terms of reliability because of its first person perspective; nevertheless, the contribution of these early psychologists was fundamental to the discipline's development. Approaches concentrating exclusively on observable behaviours emerged in the early part of the twentieth century through the work of the Russian physiologist, Pavlov (1927), and of Thorndike (1911) in the USA. Pavlov trained dogs to salivate through the association of external stimuli (a buzzer) with food and Thorndike measured how long it took cats to escape from puzzle boxes outside of which their food lay. This behaviourist school of psychology was developed further by two US psychologists, Watson (1913) and Skinner (1957), who revealed laws of stimulus–response, conditioning and reinforcement. Watson famously claimed that he could teach a child anything. These psychologists realised that *classical conditioning*, where new signals are acquired for existing responses, could be contrived to create associations or 'learning'. An example of this can be presented as follows. You will probably be able to recall situations in which your behaviour has been classically conditioned. For people of the authors' ages, for example, the sight of a dentist's chair can evoke fretful behaviour! Sometimes unpleasant experiences become irrationally associated with particular places, colours, odours or even people. A teacher who is constantly carping at pupils while teaching them mathematics might condition pupils to dislike the subject.

Reader Reflection: Classical conditioning

Unconditioned stimulus	Unconditioned response
Teacher instructs pupils to work quietly	Pupils work quietly on tasks
Conditioned stimulus with additional stimulus	**Unconditioned response**
Teacher instructs pupils to work quietly while putting her fingers to her lips	Pupils work quietly on tasks
Conditioned stimulus	**Conditioned response**
Teacher puts her fingers to her lips	Pupils work quietly on tasks

Now generate some examples of conditioned stimulus–response situations for yourself.

Operant conditioning is often deployed when rewards and punishments are administered in education settings. It differs from classical conditioning because an unconditioned stimulus is not required. Reinforcement of a required behaviour is given by the teacher to encourage children to behave in a way that optimises their learning. Buckler and Castle (2014) give the example of ignoring children who shout out in class but listening to those who put their hand up when they wish to speak. Deployed consistently, this can be effective in encouraging the required behaviour of all the children in the class. In operant conditioning it isn't necessary to administer a reward or punishment in response to each behaviour; as long as the response is administered intermittently the behaviour change will persist.

Instructional programmes and schemes designed to help learners with special educational needs use a simple, incremental design wherein a small step in learning, for example forming a letter of the alphabet or adding a simple sum, is followed by the positive reinforcement of being correct. Primary schools have for many years adopted the use of stickers, smiley faces and merit stars to reinforce pupil learning. Positive teaching schemes which train teachers to use praise, ignore poor learning behaviour and reward good learning behaviour were developed in the 1980s by Birmingham psychologists Wheldall and Merrett (1985) (see also Beaman and Wheldall, 2010; Merrett, 1998; Wheldall, 2006). Schemes of assertive discipline (Canter, 2009; Canter and Canter, 1977; Kavanagh, 2000), direct instruction (Liem and Martin, 2013) and precision teaching (Kubina and Yurich, 2009; Meacham and Allen, 1969; Roberts and Norwich, 2010) also became very popular in schools in many countries during the 1990s. Since then such systems have become more sophisticated with a greater emphasis on the social aspects of behavioural improvements. Nevertheless, all such schemes are external to the learner, encouraging and reinforcing learning behaviour, so they do not reveal knowledge of the learner's cognition. Boghossian (2006) explained that in the behaviourist approach information is received from external sources, and what is true and what is false is determined by the teacher. Although achieving results in the short term, teachers will be mindful that external reinforcers have a limited life expectancy, for example, with a recalcitrant, self-conscious 14 year old or a nine year old who has received her fiftieth smiley face. There are also concerns about whether it is ethical to concentrate so narrowly on performance behaviours in the interests of raising academic achievement (Moran, 2008). Wentzel and Brophy (2014) discuss these issues in detail, having consulted a large number of research studies.

The challenge in education is to harness the external reinforcer to an intrinsic desire to learn through a sense of personal achievement. Albert Bandura (1977) who developed social learning theory thought that reinforcers were not always necessary because children learn from watching or listening to others – *observational learning*. Society encourages parents and teachers to model good behaviour, attitudes and values for children to learn from. Boyd and Bee (2014) explain that Bandura's work increasingly emphasised the impact of observational learning on cognition, whereby children extract abstract rules from observing behaviour without such rules being explicitly stated, for example, if a child observes her parents regularly depositing bottles into bottle banks she might learn a rule about environmental friendliness being important without actually being told this. Boyd and Bee (2014) consider Bandura's theory highly influential as it goes a considerable way to bridging the large gap between behaviourist learning theory and cognitive-developmental theory, even changing its name to social cognitive theory (Bandura, 2008).

The strength of observational learning between peers has been noted for some time with concern that it isn't necessarily a good thing, for example, the 'laddish' ethos that can be generated through peer modelling among boys has encouraged some to feel that working hard in school is not 'cool' or masculine. Behaviourist approaches have been deployed particularly in relation to improving the social behaviours of unruly or challenging youngsters. Simonsen and Sugai (2013) have done a great deal of applied research in the area and are strong advocates of positive behavioural interventions and supports (PBIS) models when there is a need to manage high risk youth behaviour, arguing for their efficacy in both mainstream and alternative education settings. These models include the design of individual student behaviour support plans but have, as a primary goal, the implementation of prevention practices that target the entire school population.

Behaviourist learning theory or stimulus–response theory was predicated on a very simplistic form of *associationism* wherein each response becomes the stimulus for the next, thus forming an associative chain. Although attractive, this explanation does not account for the creativity which individuals bring to their thinking.

> If somebody says the word 'egg' to you, multiple chaining is possible because you might associate egg with omelettes but also with ornithology or Easter.

Wilson (1999) contended that the external processes of behaviourism must have corresponding internal processes which generate them and vice versa. In other words, we are not reinforced in a way of behaving unless we have reasoned, even at some basic level, about the consequences of consistently performing that action. In its most extreme form, behaviourism seems not to concern itself with these internal cognitive processes. Noam Chomsky (1965) criticised the principles of behaviourism for their failure to explain complex human behaviour such as language and communication. Chomsky argued that there are pre-existing mental structures including an innate language structure that has a latent grammatical structure which develops as an individual matures. Behaviourism dominated psychology during the first half of the twentieth century and, as we have seen, its influence is still felt. Its separation from cognition may seem strange to us now but it was not until the 1960s and 1970s that the focus on mental processes begun in the nineteenth century was revived. We will look at these mental processes later because, as Buckler and Castle (2014) note, the cognitive perspective places the functions of the brain at the centre of human behaviour.

Gestalt psychology

An alternative view to behaviourism, 'gestalt' psychology, was developed simultaneously in Germany by Wertheimer (1923), Koffka (1935) and Kohler (1940). They were disdainful of behaviourism and associationism for their treatment of sensory experiences as independent segments of experience. Gestalt psychologists maintained that animals and humans perceive things and events in their most simple, unified form as a coherent whole, that the whole is greater than the sum of its parts. They used perceptual experiments which indicated that people tend to reorganise information to impose order on it, for example by extracting an image from its background (figure/ground principle), by grouping things together if they are in close proximity (principle of proximity) or by completing missing lines to create a whole picture where, for instance, a triangle shape is drawn with a break on one side (principle of closure) (Hayes, 2010).

> Think about what happens when look at a sentence that has one word missing – you perceive the word to be there in order to allow you to make sense of the sentence. Now read that sentence again!
> *Have you spotted the missing word that you inserted?*

These principles can guide teachers towards appropriate ways of presenting information to pupils to aid their understanding. Whereas behaviourists explained that trial and error led to the solving of problems through the development of associations, gestalt psychologists believed that animals and humans developed insight in order to determine the solution. These views were influential within research into the perceptual processes of cognition but have been criticised for *describing* rather than *explaining* perceptual activity.

Social psychologists emphasise the importance of seeing cognition embedded in its context – personal, social and environmental. Personality development, social cognition and motivation have all to be understood if an individual's education is to be maximised.

Personality theory

There are a number of distinct approaches to personality; we will deal with the main three – psychoanalysis, psychometrics and humanism. Looking back briefly to how the Greek physician Galen explained personality differences by reference to bodily fluids or humours, gives some idea of the diversity of views in this field. Galen associated:

- a *melancholic* personality – pessimistic, suspicious, depressed – with black bile
- a *sanguine* personality – optimistic, sociable, easygoing – with blood
- a *phlegmatic* personality – calm, controlled, lethargic – with phlegm
- a *choleric* personality – active, irritable, egocentric – with yellow bile. (Child, 2007)

While the association with bodily fluids might be hard for us to accept, we will all recognise the personality descriptors used. Buckler and Castle (2014) note that Galen unwittingly established a list of personality types with Rudolf Steiner (2008) adopting them to differentiate the needs of learners.

Psychoanalytic theory

Freud's (1901) psychoanalytic theory has influenced psychological study because of his ideas about the unconscious processing of information. Freud denied the supremacy of a single governing self-will and, like early cognitive psychologists, contended that behaviour derives from the interaction of complex internal systems. He proposed that personality development depended on stages of psychosexual development. While many of Freud's ideas have been opposed, the notion of stages of development governing personality was pursued further by Erikson (1980) who proposed eight stages of conflict resolution which people go through during a lifetime. Boyd and Bee (2014) note that in both Freud's and Erikson's theories the success an individual has in negotiating these various stages depends heavily on the interactions they have with people and objects. The centrality of this interactive element is key to both Freud's and all subsequent psychoanalytic theories because if a stage is not successfully resolved old behaviour patterns emerge holding the individual back. For instance, a child who does not receive unconditional love in its early years may find it very difficult to make relationships in later life.

Erikson's stages of psychosocial development explain the way in which an individual's self-concept develops. For instance, adolescents go through a role identity conflict which must be resolved in order to progress healthily to young adulthood. Thus, in schools teachers often encounter, and try to deal sensitively with, the identity confusions young people experience.

Psychoanalytic explanations of personality development are known as *idiographic* because they are concerned with how the features of individuals contrive to shape personality behaviour.

Psychometric approaches to personality

In contrast, others, most notably H. J. Eysenck and R. B. Cattell, were interested in *nomothetic* explanations – the comparison of individual features with those of the averages or norms of the rest of the population. This approach had already been used within the psychometric method of intelligence testing. The emphasis of behaviourist approaches on the search for objective evidence also impacted upon the development of personality theories. Thus Eysenck (1947) developed self-report measures which sampled an individual's responses to situations which were said to reveal underlying personality traits. Through factor analysis Eysenck revealed two independent dimensions of personality: extraversion–introversion and neuroticism–stability. In 1976 he added a third dimension: psychoticism–normality. Since these qualities were thought to be normally distributed throughout a population, the average person would score at the midpoint of each dimension. Only exceptionally would an individual be found to be extremely introverted or neurotic and so on, but variations would be found along the three dimensions. Behaviour traits were said to be associated with certain personality types, for example the more extraverted person would present as outgoing, lively and gregarious. It is interesting to note the similarity between Eysenck's personality types and those outlined by the Greeks; notice the compatibility between the description of a stable extravert, for example, with the description of a sanguine personality.

The criticisms of Eysenck's approach are, first, that in isolating just three personality dimensions there is an oversimplification of a complex phenomenon and, second, that self-report measures are unreliable in that they are affected by mood and context at the time of completion. Eysenck (1967) postulated that the inheritance of features of the nervous system could account for basic personality type differences. In 1908 Yerkes and Dodson had demonstrated that a certain amount of cortical arousal is necessary for people to engage in activity but that too much can lead to a fall-off in performance. Thus imaginative, lively teaching can increase pupil interest and attainment but too much stimulus from the teacher may over-excite learners and lead to off-task behaviour. The 'Yerkes-Dodson law' also explains how different types of task are affected by arousal. Tasks which pupils are used to are less affected than those that are new and so higher levels of arousal may be necessary to promote the most effective learning. The level of arousal is also affected by a learner's state of anxiety so the more anxious they are the less able they may be to perform well (Long et al., 2011). Eysenck related this to personality types, positing that an extravert's cortical arousal system required different levels of stimulus from that of an introvert. Similarly, he thought that people who inherited a strong automatic nervous system – the part which deals with stress – were likely to react more to emotional situations, in other words to exhibit more neurotic behaviour.

Reader Reflection: Cortical arousal

Considering the biological basis of personality in this way can be helpful to teachers in understanding something of why pupils behave or present as they do. Eysenck developed questionnaires for use with adults and separate ones for children.

(Continued)

(Continued)

If too much stimulus is known to be counterproductive for introverts or too little stress affects neurotics adversely, teachers can try to create different conditions according to individual personality traits.

Obviously this cannot be achieved individually for each person in a class of 30 but the teacher can be sensitive about expecting introverts to thrive on a lot of noise or neurotics to fare well without a certain amount of drama in their lives.

How much cortical arousal do you need to stay on task? How does this vary in relation to the type of task?

Do you notice differences in this regard between yourself and others in your peer or study group?

Do the different levels seem to fit the personality types of yourself and your peers as Eysenck suggested?

Personality measures

Raymond Cattell (1970) also developed a trait theory of personality, using factor analysis of questionnaires to determine 16 source traits of personality. He developed a test known as the 16PF which is widely used, especially in the selection of people for certain jobs (see Cattell and Mead, 2008, for further description). Often head teachers and others in education management are given the 16PF at interview to examine whether they are suited to the post. The test provides a profile of an individual's personality across the 16 dimensions. These include, for example, expedient–conscientious, timid–venturesome, relaxed–tense. Cattell's theory has been criticised for oversimplification and for ascribing too rigid a set of characteristics which does not fully capture the range of human personality behaviour. It is also weakened by the fact that the theory has never been entirely successfully replicated. Boyle and Helmes (2009) caution that users of such instruments should always investigate the methods by which a scale was developed and the reported psychometric properties of personality measures before using them,

One personality assessment instrument that retains favour in both education and work settings is the Myers-Briggs Type Indicator (MBTI) (Myers Briggs et al., 1998). The MBTI is a self-report questionnaire based on Carl Jung's personality types. The MBTI assesses people across four scales: sensing–intuition, extraversion–introversion, thinking–feeling and judging–perceiving. Fallan (2006) used this instrument with business studies students in Norway, concluding that the student's personality type affects both the most effective mode of learning and even the student's selection of major areas of study. He found the most dominant personality type among business students is the sensing and judging (SJ) student. SJ students select subjects where facts, procedures and sequential learning are the usual mode of learning. Ayoubi and Ustwani (2014) conducted a study in Syria with 89 students, finding correlations between their choice of faculty and their MBTI personality type. There were some significant findings, for instance, students in the faculties of both education and of sciences were found to be significantly more judging than perceiving and more sensing than intuitive; these were both the other way around in the faculty of fine arts. There were also significantly more thinking than feeling students in the faculties of education and of economics.

A large number of such studies continue to be conducted, producing often quite convoluted interactions between phenomena such as subject choice or student satisfaction and the personality dimensions in question, but shedding little light on how these affect student learning and achievement. With all self-report instruments, the issue of whether people give what they feel to be socially acceptable responses and whether a different situation or frame of mind would spawn different answers has to be considered when using the test. It is probably safest to take the view that these tests may provide a skeletal guide to personality types but that only a deeper knowledge of the individual concerned will flesh out the story.

Humanist theories of personality

It is helpful to briefly examine studies from social psychology which elaborate the influence of social interaction on personality and behaviour. In 1902 Cooley wrote about the 'looking-glass self' in describing the socially interactive nature of self-perception. The critical role of significant others in this analysis was also a feature of Carl Rogers' (1983) view of personality which was grounded in the notion of the developing self-concept. Rogers believed that every individual has an inbuilt need to reach their potential, that is, to *self-actualise*, and an equally important need for approval from others (Hayes, 2010). The centrality of this led Rogers to argue that the personality could not be perceived as separate traits as the psychometric approaches proposed but as a coherent whole. In order for self-actualisation to be successful the individual has to have experienced unconditional approval, usually from parents, in order not to worry about how their views and talents will be regarded and therefore be free to pursue and develop them. Where children have been granted approval which is always conditional on good behaviour, they tend constantly to seek approval from others. This can sometimes manifest as deviant school behaviour as they strive for approval from their peers. It can also appear as setting very high standards for themselves that they almost always cannot reach. The healthy development of the self-concept is therefore fundamentally important and teachers are now taught to appreciate this in their dealings with young people (Lawrence, 2006). A scheme popular in English primary schools that harnesses the power of peer approval is known as Circle Time (Bliss et al., 1995), in which pupils give positive feedback to one another. Studies have found that this raises the self-esteem of participant pupils (Miller and Moran, 2007).

We also know that students' self-concepts are positively affected when they enjoy teacher support, interest, encouragement and high expectations. The relative significance of teachers is dependent less on their perceived status as authority figures than on the organic nature of their relationship with individual pupils. Lawrence (2006) suggested that teaching is more effective where the teacher is able to establish a close relationship with pupils. A differentiated classroom, where a choice of tasks increases the pupils' ownership and direction of the learning, may enable the pupil to define the parameters of teacher and peer involvement. The extent to which a teacher or peer is significant to the pupil will be a factor in this definition. In a more tightly structured, 'closed' classroom environment which relies on greater teacher input and direction, the pupil's control over who shares in the learning process is restricted. Thus a pupil for whom the teacher is not significant may have little commitment to either the task or the guidance. If significant others affect an individual's learning, framing a context where the pupil can control this would suggest a greater potential for learning. For instance, the organisation of group work could, on at least some occasions, pay heed to pupil friendship groups.

Pinxten et al.'s work (2015) looks more specifically at how pupils' individual academic self-concepts (ASCs) (i.e. how one perceives oneself in an academic context) are formed. They explain that learners form their ASCs by comparing themselves with others and by comparing their own performance in different academic domains. 'While general ASC reflects an individual's evaluation of his or her academic abilities across subjects ("I am good at most school subjects"), domain-specific ASCs reflect an individual's impression of his or her ability in a specific academic domain, such as mathematics ("I am good at mathematics")' (Pinxten et al., 2015: 124). ASC and achievement are mutually reinforcing so for equally achieving students the one with the higher ASC is more likely to achieve better over time. It is thus important to foster high ASCs by allowing pupils to make perceptible gains in their learning. For some learners in some subjects small steps will lead incrementally to a better domain-specific ASC, while for others greater challenge will be required. Again, we see the importance of teachers knowing their pupils as individuals.

Personal construct theory

George Kelly's personal construct theory (Kelly, 1955) does not fit into any of the three traditions described above. His is a phenomenological approach which explains the uniqueness of personality development and learning behaviour by reference to the personal constructs which people use to make sense of new situations, information and so on. Kelly believed that we react not to a stimulus but to what we interpret the stimulus to be (Child, 2007). He developed a technique known as the *repertory grid method* which reveals bipolar constructs held by individuals in relation to significant others. Thus an individual may hold a construct such as sensitivity–brashness; another person might see sensitivity juxtaposed with strength (for a full description of the technique and its applications see Fransella, 2005). Winter (2013) describes a wide range of applications of personal construct theory, concluding that it remains a radical approach over half a century after Kelly published it.

Differences in pupils' behaviour and responses would be deemed a product of the various theories they have to explain events, which are in turn a product of their previous experience and analysis of it. Theories or *constructs* are progressively refined as more interactions occur. Sets of constructs held by pupils about learning in a particular subject will therefore differ, as will the teacher's. If the teacher holds a construct which defines reticence of oral response as lack of understanding rather than as uncertainty of the context or shyness, they might adapt their instruction in a way which is inappropriate to the learner's needs. The pupil's construct of oral response may include a perception that the ownership of the vocabulary lies with the teacher, or it may be shaped by cultural and ethnic reference points at variance with those of the teacher.

Henderson-King and Smith (2006) researched the meanings that undergraduate students ascribe to their education and how these meanings relate to their understanding of the constructs of academic motivation and values. Ten meanings emerged including career preparation, independence, making social connections, changing the world, stress and escape. It would be interesting to conduct this same research with their tutors to explore the extent to which their meanings converged with those of the students. Svennberg et al. (2015) did explore teachers' constructs in a Swedish study that examined what PE teachers consider important when grading students. They were particularly interested in why teachers tend to use internalised criteria for their assessment (including curriculum-irrelevant criteria) and in teachers' inability to predict some constructs' relevance to the grades:

> Sometimes constructs that a teacher considers as being most important for the grades, like dancing, have little relevance to the grades awarded to the students. On other occasions, constructs that a teacher does not think should influence the grade, like having experience of club sport, have great relevance to the grade awarded. This indicates that the teachers are only aware of part of their grading practice, while some of the grading is tacit and influences the grading taking place in the realisation arena. (Svennberg et al., 2015: 211)

Given that there is a limit to which teachers and learners can clarify their constructs within their interactions, it would seem best to foster a learning situation in which the individual constructs of each participant can be accommodated. Such a situation would involve pupil-centred learning, peer interaction, individualised learning and self-monitoring. Opportunities for testing and extending these constructs, in other words opportunities for learning, might thus be liberated from the framing effect of the teacher's constructs so that pupils, with access to resources and support, could interpret the task and develop their learning according to their own frames of reference. In so doing, they might construe the situation more inventively such that the constructs are altered through what Kelly calls 'constructive alternativism'.

Motivation

Healthy self-esteem is fundamental both to learners' academic performance and to their emotional well-being since it affects motivation. Studies of motivation have revealed the relationship with a range of cognitive-based processes such as children's attributions for their successes and failures, perceptions of control over their own learning processes, metacognitive processes, self-perceptions of ability and beliefs about the utility of effort (see Wentzel and Wigfield's 2009 handbook on motivation at school for an extensive range of perspectives and research in this field).

Motivation and competition

Reviewing studies into motivation, Leo and Galloway (1996) warned 20 years ago about the potentially debilitating cognitions that may develop within primary children as a result of the national curriculum and resultant pedagogic practices that emphasise between-pupil ability comparisons rather than individual task-related or mastery goals.

We have seen in Chapter 5 that this warning has become a reality with a culture of teaching to the test developing as a consequence of league table comparisons of schools which in turn derive their data from the individual test scores of pupils. Frick's (2013) review of several research studies into the effects of such high stakes testing confirmed it has created performance oriented classroom atmospheres worldwide and, notwithstanding cultural differences, this has had a detrimental effect on intrinsic motivation and pupil creativity. Motivating pupils in this competitive context where the pressure is felt at many levels – school, teacher and pupil – is a very different matter from motivating learners where the goal is for an individual to exceed their previous 'personal best'.

Within education it has traditionally been thought that a certain amount of competition between individuals increases motivation. The dangers in such an approach are, however, clear. Inevitably, differences in ability impact on the outcomes of a competitive learning situation and, in order for some to win the competition, others have to lose. Covington (1998) exposed the detrimental effects of competition on motivation, pointing to the tendency of learners to avoid the risk of failure by not attempting things and to the demise of learner integrity which is encouraged by competitive practices. Neither can a competitive approach to learning be reconciled with some of the current influences on education. The collaborative approaches suggested by social constructivists, for example, would be antithetical to a competitive learning environment because they rely on working together. High levels of motivation to learn among students must be the holy grail as far as teachers are concerned. The differences between teaching a self-motivated adult and a recalcitrant 15 year old are well known and theories of motivation are helpful in explaining these differences.

Motivation theories

Child (2007) provides a useful examination of motivation theory, noting the early twentieth-century instinct theories derivative of Darwin and Freud, the drive and need theories of the 1930s and 1940s, and the cognitive theories of the 1950s and 1960s. To these might be added behaviourist theories since Skinner's ideas about reinforcement of behaviour highlight the effect of praise and punishment on motivation to learn. Instinct theories emphasised the animal urges and instincts humans are born with, for example instinctive fight and flight responses. Drive and need theories differentiate between the basic survival needs of hunger, thirst and warmth, and the secondary or social needs such as the need to achieve, to dominate, to affiliate with others and so on.

Maslow's hierarchy of needs

A very well-known drive or need theory is Maslow's (1954) hierarchy of needs which explains that basic needs must be satisfied before the drive for the higher-level needs of love and belonging, high self-esteem and, finally, *self-actualisation* or the achievement of one's full potential can be aspired to.

In some cases pupils come to school with some of their basic needs not met as they arrive hungry or poorly clothed. Others may feel unloved.

If Maslow is accurate in saying that these needs must be attended to first before the child can begin to be interested in any form of self-actualisation through learning, teachers need to be very sensitive to individual differences.

Given that these needs *are* met, teachers have an important role to play in creating the circumstances which will facilitate self-actualisation. Pupils need to feel safe and valued in class, they need to be listened to and empowered to make decisions about their learning.

Cognitive theories give weight to the role of thinking within motivation, which it is contended plays a greater part than instinct and need/drive theories allow. They also point to the effect of an imbalance or cognitive dissonance between normal performance and unexpected performance (Festinger, 1957). For example, if a pupil normally passes tests quite easily but one day fails, this could either motivate them to try harder to redress the failure or it could lead to avoidance of that particular subject. An example of a cognitive theory is Rotter's (1966) *locus of control* theory in which those with strong internal control believe that it is by their own efforts and talents that they will succeed and those with strong external control believe that any success or progress they make is down to luck or other external factors such as task difficulty. This was developed further by Weiner (1972) into *attribution theory*. As well as attributing their successes and failures to internal or external factors, Weiner argued that learners attribute them to stable causes like ability or unstable causes such as effort. This attribution affects how future tasks are then approached; for example, if a pupil attributes failure to unstable causes or internal locus of control they are more likely to persist in the face of failure (Child, 2007). Conversely, attribution to stable causes and external locus of control will lead to minimal effort because responsibility for the failure is being attributed outside of the learner. Covington claimed that many minority pupils 'exhibit an external locus of control. They feel like pawns of fate, buffeted by forces beyond their control' (1998: 63).

Most of our readers, as adult self-determining learners, will of course attribute their success or failure within education studies to unstable, internal causes such as effort levels! It can be a major challenge, however, to encourage adolescents to take responsibility for their own learning. Child points out the link to McClelland's (1955) theory of *achievement motivation*. Pupils with a high need to achieve usually attribute any failure to internal causes of lack of effort while low-need achievers attribute their failure to external factors. McClelland's work was developed further by Atkinson (1964) who reasoned that a person's behaviour in relation to a particular task or activity resulted from a combination of their motivation towards success and the avoidance of failure, their subjective judgement about how successful they might be, and an incentive value they would place on success, in other words how much pride they would take in the achievement. His work indicates the complexity of the dynamic between success, failure and motivation. Long et al. (2011) suggest this model allows us to characterise learners in terms of their level of motivation to attempt tasks or to avoid failure. Repeated failure, unsurprisingly, does not motivate learners to achieve but a mixture of success and failure may be productive; fear of failure is usually destructive because it leads to safer, lower-order tasks being chosen.

Reader Reflection: Motivation and personality

It is not so much the failure itself that impacts on academic achievement as the meaning ascribed to the failure. Therefore teachers need to help pupils to reflect on their feelings about the failure so they can separate the meaning they ascribe to it from the actual task they failed at. This should ensure further learning in that area is not inhibited by fear of failure.

Think about you and your motivational levels. How well motivated are you to succeed within different modules? What does this depend on? Does your view of the lecturer play a part in how well you want to do? Have you noticed differences between yourself and your fellow students in this regard?

You can think of many more questions along these lines and perhaps develop a mini-research study from them.

Gervis and Capel (2016) provide a useful chart comparing the theories since the 1950s which we have looked at above. They also include McGregor's (1960) *theory x, theory y* ideas about managers. This is relevant because teachers manage learning and learners. Theory x managers assume the average worker is lazy, lacks ambition, is resistant to change, is self-centred and is not very bright, while theory y managers assume the worker is motivated, wants to take responsibility, has potential and works for the corporate good of the institution (Gervis and Capel, 2016). Relating this to teachers, they explain that a theory x teacher externally motivates pupils with controlling actions while theory y teachers encourage intrinsic motivation through self-development.

Intrinsic and extrinsic motivation

It can be argued that intrinsic motivation in learners is more productive than extrinsic motivation, not least because it does not require reinforcement through external rewards and punishments. Sometimes, however, teachers will provide these external reinforcers initially with the aim of encouraging task success in learners which will in turn create intrinsic motivation as a product of the pleasure derived from that success. This behaviourist approach to motivating learners could be seen in Wheldall and Merrett's (1985) positive teaching programmes in the 1980s (discussed earlier) which advocated positive teacher reinforcement for good learning behaviour.

There are opposing perspectives on the relationship between extrinsic and intrinsic motivation. Wentzel and Brophy (2014) juxtaposed a number of meta-analyses in which researchers reviewed large numbers of studies to explore whether extrinsic motivation undermines intrinsic motivation. They write that the behaviourists' review (Eisenberger and Cameron, 1996) seemed to support their argument that giving external rewards does not undermine intrinsic motivation but the opposing school of thought (Deci et al., 1999) claimed the behaviourists' review to be overly selective of studies that supported their position. In contrast, the Deci et al. review (1999) found that studies indicated a clear detrimental effect of external reward-giving on subsequent intrinsic motivation and that this detriment increased if rewards were contingent upon task completion and performance levels.

Reader Reflection: Using meta-analyses of psychological research

You may recall we outlined the increasing use of meta-analyses as a research strategy in Chapter 3.

Look back at that now so that you are aware of the strengths and weaknesses of this approach.

How might these affect your view of the research outlined above?

Motivation is a very complex area of study because it involves personality factors, social and environmental factors, previous experience, the developing self-concept, physical well-being and so on. For instance, in a study of the relationship between academic self-concept, intrinsic motivation, test anxiety and academic achievement among 170 nursing students, Khalaila (2015) found that for students with high intrinsic motivation, a greater level of test anxiety did not decrease their achievement. It is clear, then, that the interplay of these influences on human behaviour results in a very individualised picture of learner motivation.

Intelligence and creativity

Individual differences in human competence and performance have always provided a rich research ground for psychologists, the fruits of which are invariably controversial. Francis Galton (1869), a British psychologist of the second half of the nineteenth century, was interested in the hereditariness of genius, advocating the need to measure individual differences. His work laid the foundations of what has developed into probably the most contentious explanation of individual differences, intelligence testing theory, or psychometrics, which seeks to measure the ultimate intellectual power an individual has.

Intelligence testing

The first test was devised for the French government by Alfred Binet and Theodore Simon in 1905. It is important to note that right from these early beginnings the intelligence test was devised for the practical purpose of determining how well a child might do in school. Not surprisingly, then, the test contained items which resembled school tasks, such as comprehension of facts and relationships, vocabulary measures, and mathematical and verbal reasoning (Boyd and Bee, 2014). Soon afterwards Lewis Terman of Stanford University modified and extended the test, developing the Stanford-Binet which has tests for each age of child and can be used from around age three. Terman (1924) derived the child's 'intelligence quotient' by dividing the mental age the child had achieved in the test by its chronological age and multiplying this by 100. Nowadays an individual's score is compared with the scores of a huge standardised sample of children of the same age. The average score is 100 with the majority of children scoring between 85 and 115. The very few who achieve very high scores of above 145 are said to be 'gifted' and those with scores below around 55 are said to have moderate to profound 'retardation' (Boyd and Bee,

2014: 212). A score of 115 was said to be the threshold for passing the 11-plus examination to attend grammar school (Child, 2007).

At the heart of the controversy over IQ testing is the question of whether it tests some innate, immutable ability. Hebb (1949) distinguished between Intelligence A – innate potential entirely dependent on neurological facilities – and Intelligence B – interaction of Intelligence A with the environmental influences upon an individual. In this analysis Intelligence B can vary while Intelligence A cannot (see Child, 2007). Child notes that neither is directly testable and that the best we can manage is indirect sampling of some aspects of intelligent behaviour using standardised tests.

Reader Reflection: The Flynn effect

IQ tests have to be re-standardised over time because scores have been rising steadily over the past half century.

Children across the world can solve harder problems than children of yesteryear so the average score would now be 115 if the tests had not been adjusted.

This is known as a secular trend or the Flynn effect after James Flynn, the psychologist who discovered it (Flynn, 2007, cited in Boyd and Bee, 2014).

Sigal and McKelvie (2012) point out that most researchers agree with Flynn himself that the secular trend is due to environmental rather than genetic factors.

Have scores been rising as a consequence of better nutrition, greater access to education or is there a flaw in the tests because of their resemblance to school-based tasks which breeds familiarity and therefore improves test competence?

What are the implications of this for our reliance on such tests?

Intelligence and achievement

To at least some extent, then, an IQ test is a test of achievement. Boyd and Bee (2014) cite research which indicates that IQ tests can demonstrate good but by no means unassailable levels of both 'reliability', as individuals' scores are fairly stable over time, and 'validity', in that there is a reasonably strong correlation between IQ score and school achievement grades. Both stability of score and predictor of school achievement are stronger in older children. In terms of stability of test results, Bee et al. (1982) found that a typical correlation between a Bayley mental test score of a 12 month old and the score of the same child at age four on the Binet test was only 0.20 or 0.30. Citing Birney and Sternberg (2011),

Boyd and Bee (2014: 216) explain this stability is more demonstrable from about age three when 'consistency in performance on IQ tests such as the Stanford Binet or the WISC-IV increases markedly'. Fluctuations do occur, of course, especially when huge life events occur for individual pupils, for example the birth of a sibling or violence in the home, which would inevitably impact on test concentration and therefore reduce performance.

Intelligence theories

A number of intelligence theories were developed during the twentieth century.

General and specific ability (Spearman)

Charles Spearman (1927) believed two types of intelligence could be identified by IQ tests – g factor (general ability) and s factors (various mental abilities detected in different degrees by different tests). Cyril Burt's Hierarchical Group-Factor Theory proposed group factors of intelligence as well as g and s factors because many tests involved a number of skills at the same time, for example verbal ability together with a specific ability (Child, 2007). General ability was thought to govern a series of abilities such as verbal, spatial, practical and numerical skills, which themselves interacted with specific abilities measured by each test item. Thurstone (1938), a US psychologist of the 1930s, felt that g and s abilities should be compounded to give a range of factors known as primary mental abilities which provided a broad profile of abilities rather than an overall measure. These included verbal comprehension, number ability, word fluency, perceptual flexibility and speed, inductive reasoning, rote memory and deductive reasoning.

Creative intelligence: convergent and divergent thinking (Guilford)

Guilford (1950) proposed a model of the intellect which had 120 mental factors derived from three independent aspects of intelligent acts. The individual carries out operations, such as remembering or thinking, using content like symbols or figures, in order to produce outcomes, for example relations or implications. Albert and Runco (1999) point out that Guilford's seminal work on creativity challenged the simplicity of intelligence testing which sought to locate people along a single dimension. Guilford (1967) suggested that measuring intelligence and creativity was far more complex than this. He posited two forms of thinking: convergent, wherein a single correct answer is sought, and divergent, which produces a whole range of possible answers.

Fluid and crystallised intelligence (Cattell)

Cattell (1963) defined two types of intelligence. Fluid intelligence includes reasoning and memory processes and spatial performance; Cattell thought this to be hereditary and measures of it vary according to the individual's processing speed at the time of measurement. Crystallised intelligence reflects the accumulated products of processing carried out in the past and can be tested by general knowledge and vocabulary questions; Cattell maintained that it is influenced by environment and is therefore likely to increase with education and experience (Salthouse, 2001).

Intelligence: nature or nurture

In 1955 Cyril Burt, the British psychologist, claimed to have found high correlations between the IQ scores of 53 sets of identical twins who had been brought up in different environments. These findings were very influential because they seemed to indicate the relative lack of importance of environmental factors to intelligence. The English education system paid great attention to Burt's conclusion that there should be different types of education depending on innate intelligence. His argument supported the separation of children into grammar and secondary modern schools. In 1976, however, Burt's findings were exposed as fraudulent. The importance of this case cannot be overstated because it shows how ready people were to believe that IQ is inherited. Burt's figures were also used as the basis of further studies, for example Jensen's (1969) controversial race studies. Jensen argued that intelligence was 80 per cent inherited and 20 per cent environmental. However, as Chapter 10 explains, Labov's (1973, 1997) work on linguistic/cultural differences in relation to educational achievement debunked the myth of black unintelligence.

Reporting on research studies which throw light on the relative influence of hereditariness and environment, Bee and Boyd (2010: 185) cite Bouchard and McGue's (1981) studies of the few pairs of identical twins reared apart which found a strong correlation of between 0.60 and 0.70 in their IQ scores. However, more detailed analysis of the cases revealed that the less similar the environmental circumstances the less correspondence is found between twins' IQ scores. The nature/nurture argument is more productively approached, then, by examining the interaction of heredity with environment. Weinberg (1989) proposed that genes establish a *reaction range* for IQ which can vary as much as 25 points depending on the environmental conditions the child grows up in. Thus findings that black children score lower on IQ tests than do white children by as much as 15 points can be accounted for within Weinberg's suggestion of an environmentally determined 25-point range.

Controversial studies

The Bell Curve

The debate about genetic intelligence was revived in the mid-1990s by the publication of the highly controversial book *The Bell Curve* by Herrnstein and Murray (1994) in which it was reported that African American children consistently score lower than Euro-American children on IQ tests.

Despite the 12-point gap falling within the accepted Weinberg reaction range and despite substantial evidence of differences in the environmental conditions of the two groups, Herrnstein and Murray argued that the findings signified fundamental genetic differences in intelligence.

Their claims created a furore and a spate of research studies emerged to categorically refute them.

DNA, reading ability and socio-economic status

A very novel recent UK study by Jerrim et al. (2015) sought to determine whether genetic factors could account for the large socio-economic gap in children's reading scores.

Bio-molecular data were collected for over 10,000 mothers and primary school children and this was related to reading scores at ages 7, 9 and 11.

Only 2 per cent of the socio-economic gap in reading test scores could be attributed to genetic heritability, once again pointing to the greater effect of environmental factors.

Reader Reflection: IQ testing

Intelligence testing is attractive because it enables us to categorise and pigeonhole people and, despite years of critique of its theoretical foundations and its methodological weaknesses, some version of IQ testing is still used in many schools today to indicate potential. One of the major problems is being sure that it tests what it purports to.

If school type tasks are included, can training in those tasks help? Does reading ability play a part in the outcome? Do different cultural and linguistic experiences affect an individual's performance on the test?

In fact, it is very difficult to isolate underlying competence because the individual's experience, disposition, motivation and health on the day of the test will all impact on the outcome.

Take an IQ test yourself and reflect on it in the light of what you have read here.

Intelligence: final thoughts

Adey, who has conducted a considerable body of work on thinking skills and intelligence (see Chapter 9) makes the case for a general factor in intelligence (Adey, 2007; Adey et al., 2007). Nettelbeck and Wilson (2005) concluded from their review of intelligence theories that there is evidence of a general ability that can be tested by IQ tests. They cautioned, however, that such tests should sample a broad range of different intellectual domains in addition to general ability. MacBlain (2014) questions whether ability has any place at all in twenty-first century explanations of children's learning, urging instead an examination of what learners are capable of within a conducive environment. See Cooper (2010) for a fuller account of classic studies on intelligence and individual differences. In Chapter 9 the issue of intelligence is picked up again as the interest in this phenomenon is still intense and newer theoretical positions have been developed.

Cognitive-developmental theory

Piaget's maturational theory

The concept of maturation (genetically programmed sequential pattern of changing physical characteristics) was developed by Arnold Gessell in the USA in the 1920s (Gessell, 1925). The concept of maturation was applied to cognitive growth by Jean Piaget, a Swiss psychologist of the twentieth century, whose work has enjoyed very wide influence within education. Piaget (1932; 1952; 1954) explained cognitive growth as being driven by an internal need to understand the world. He saw intellectual and moral development as sequential with the child moving through stages of thinking.

Piaget's theory is one of maturation in which the learner's stage of thinking interacts with his experience of the world in a process of *adaptation*. Piaget used the term *operations* to describe the strategies, skills and mental activities used by the child in interacting with new experience. Thus adding 2 and 2 together, whether mentally or on paper, is an operation. Discoveries are made sequentially, for example adding and subtracting cannot be learned until objects are seen to be constant. Progress through the sequence of discoveries occurs slowly and at any one age the child has a particular general view of the world, a particular logic or structure that dominates the way they explore and manipulate the world. The logic changes as events are encountered which will not fit with the *schemata* (sets of ideas about objects or events) the child has constructed. When major shifts in the structure of the child's thinking occur, a new stage is said to be reached (see Table 8.1).

Central to Piaget's theory are the concepts of *assimilation* – taking in and adapting experience or objects to one's existing strategies or concepts – and *accommodation* – modifying and adjusting one's strategies or concepts as a result of new experiences or information (see Boyd and Bee, 2014, for a full outline of Piaget's theory).

Table 8.1   **Piaget's stages of cognitive development**

Stage	Age	Description
A Sensorimotor	Birth–2 years	The baby 'understands' the world in terms of what they can do with objects and of their sensory information. A block is how it tastes, feels to grasp, looks to the eye.
B Pre-operational	2–6 years	By about 18–24 months, the child can represent objects to themselves internally and begins to understand the classification of objects into groups and to be able to take others' perspectives. Fantasy play appears, as does primitive logic.
C Concrete operational	6–12 years	The child's logic takes a great leap forward with the development of powerful new internal mental operations, such as addition, subtraction, class inclusion and the like. The child is still tied to specific experience but can do mental manipulations as well as physical ones.
D Formal operational	12 years +	The child becomes able to manipulate ideas as well as events or objects in their head. They can imagine and think about things that they have never seen or that have not yet happened; they can organise systematically and exhaustively and think deductively.

Source: Bee, H. and Boyd, D. *The Developing Child,* 13th edn, © 2012, p. 138. Reprinted by permission of Pearson Education, Inc., New York.

The application of Piaget's theory to education

Piaget's stage theory provides a criterion-referenced rather than norm-referenced explanation of cognitive development (Shayer, 2008). The neatness of Piaget's theory rendered it appealing to educationalists. The 11-plus test fitted well, for example, with the age at which children were thought to begin abstract or formal operations. Investigative and experiential methods, often referred to as 'discovery learning', were readily inferred because they provided cognitive conflict – the jarring of cognitive structures or schemata to promote new learning. The Plowden Committee, which reported in 1967 on primary education, was influenced by such maturation theory, advocating child-centred, experiential approaches to learning. It is easy to see, however, that a theory which specifies stages of capability can set up expectations about learning readiness – that children only learn effectively if their educational experiences are suitably matched to their current level of understanding. This can then determine the content and pace of instruction. If a child has not reached the anticipated stage the teaching will be too advanced. If the child has gone beyond it the teaching could constrain potential achievement. In the same way that intelligence testing can establish an arbitrary ceiling on learning, the rigid application of Piaget's theory could also place limits on achievement.

Nevertheless Piagetian principles are still influencing research. A study in Slovenia, for instance, by Krnel et al. (2005) into the development of the concept of matter asked children aged 3–13 to describe objects and substances placed in front of them. Children's responses were coded and explored for patterns indicating development with age and analysed from a Piagetian perspective, which hypothesises that the epigenesis of concepts takes place through children acting on the world. The study found that through their actions children gradually develop more elaborated schema that enable them to distinguish between extensive and intensive properties, and hence between object and matter. There is no doubt that Piaget's work has been very influential across the world. Adey and Shayer (2013), citing a synthesis by Hattie (2009) of over 800 meta-analyses of the effect of various educational approaches on achievement, noted the remarkable fact that Piagetian approaches came second out of 138 approaches.

Criticisms of Piaget's work

Many have argued, however, that there are problems with Piaget's theory. It says nothing about individual differences, social context or modes of learning. The child is viewed as a system of developing logic, not as a social, emotional being. The importance of language to thinking, a significant component in any model of human development, is underplayed: other psychologists, such as Vygotsky and Bruner, demonstrated language and socio-cultural linguistic differences to be fundamental to learning, as we shall see in Chapter 9.

Piaget used clinical, decontextualised methods with a very limited sample of middle-class children, including his own. When experiments were repeated with account taken of the importance of context, the power of children's thinking was found to be in advance of Piaget's claims (Donaldson, 1978; Hughes, 1975; McGarrigle and Donaldson, 1974; Siegler and Alibali, 2005). The success rates among four to six year olds were much better when tasks were not disembedded from the context, were made relevant to children's experience and when the children understood what the experimenter wanted. These findings called into question Piaget's claims about young children's egocentricity, revealing a more precocious ability to decentre (to see things from another's point of view in space and time), and about their ability to 'conserve' understanding, for example that the volume of a liquid remained the same despite its movement to a differently shaped vessel.

Piaget's theory of stages has been seriously challenged too. Although he conceded that the structures or operations (coordinated principles, rules or strategies that are applied across problems or tasks) do not develop all at once, he did imply that all learning could be approached at the same operational level. However, we know that while, like now, we operate at a formal operational level dealing with abstract ideas, we very often operate in our day-to-day lives at a concrete level, needing actual objects or events to work our logic on, for example the use of diagrams. Bee claimed that the information we have does not show that children are very consistent in their level of performance across tasks and cited much research to support her (Bee, 1992: 273).

Piaget's legacy

John Flavell, a one-time student of Piaget, concluded that human cognitive growth is generally not very stage-like (in Bee, 1992). He did, however, attest to the sequential nature of learning, saying 'sequences are the very wire and glue of development. Later cognitive acquisitions build on or are otherwise linked to earlier ones, and in their turn similarly prepare the ground for still later ones' (Flavell, 1982: 18). Within any given task, then, there seem to be predictable sequences shared by most children. The key task for teachers is to examine the progress of individuals in order to determine readiness to deal with increased intellectual demand.

Piaget's work can be said to have influenced the ideas of some other psychologists. Kohlberg (1976) posited links between children's cognitive development and their moral reasoning, proposing a stage model of moral development. Selman (1980) was interested in the way children make relationships, describing a set of stages or levels they go through in forming friendships. The stress on the idea of 'stages' in Piaget's theory has thus been quite far-reaching but a rigidly staged model of development is probably less helpful than the features of development the various stage theories describe.

Cognitive psychology

Despite the pre-eminence of behaviourism in the USA during the first half of the twentieth century, an interest in cognitive psychology was maintained by

European psychologists such as Frederick Bartlett (1932) who developed the notion of schema.

Information-processing

The value of Bartlett's work was not recognised until 1975 when Minsky, a computer scientist, read his book and developed from it the notion of frames of knowledge within artificial intelligence (Brewer, 2001). Rumelhart and McClelland (1986) later related these connectionist models of schema and concepts to psychology. The correspondence between how computers and the human mind process information had fascinated researchers since the 1960s when the *information-processing* approach to explaining cognition became the dominant view. Connections had already been drawn between cognitive processes and neural mechanisms, and there was a renewal of interest in the processes of attention, perception and memory which paralleled the huge advances in computer intelligence. As early as 1943 the British psychologist Kenneth Craik likened the brain to a computer. Essentially, information-processing theorists proposed that sensory experience (sounds, sights, tastes, smells and tangibles) is perceived and selectively attended to, depending on the individual's motivation, other distractions or emotional state, analysed within a short-term memory (STM) and stored within a long-term memory (LTM). This process is usually presented graphically as:

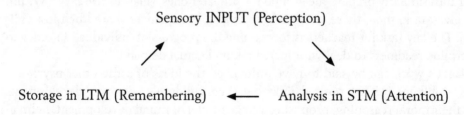

Sensory INPUT (Perception)

Storage in LTM (Remembering) ⟵ Analysis in STM (Attention)

Schema and concept development

Bartlett (1932) introduced the important idea of *schema* to account for the fact that we do not reproduce facts when we recall them, rather we reconstruct them. Schemata are the organising vehicles which we have built up in our minds from previous experience and knowledge which we then use to analyse new information. If you are presented with a new concept within your studies your tutor will probably attempt to explain it by reference to something you have already studied within that area, thus allowing you to employ the relevant schema. The material held in the long-term memory is stored as 'schemata' ('schema' is the singular) – mental structures abstracted from experience. They comprise sets of expectations which enable us to categorise and understand new stimuli. For example, our schema of higher education includes expectations of students, lecturers, the students' union and so on and is refined as we gain more experience and more information is categorised. Everyone's schemata are different; for instance, a teacher's schema of school will include expectations about hierarchies, pupil culture, staffroom behaviour and so on, while the experiences of parents are unlikely to have refined their schema of school to this extent.

A range of work on schema development and concept formation has been conducted since the 1950s. Collins and Quillian (1969) developed the notion that we store concepts hierarchically with general, overarching concepts being subdivided into more specific ones.

Reader Reflection: Developing concepts

Think about how, from an early age, you developed the concept of 'animal'.
   We define this concept by a range of criteria such as four legs, no language and so on. At this crude level our concept of animal does not differentiate between types of animal. Have you noticed, for instance, how small children sometimes refer to cats as 'doggies'?
   As we gain more experience we learn to discriminate between types of animal – we notice that cats are furry and dogs are hairy, cats purr and dogs bark.
   Animal is a superordinate concept to which dog and cat are subordinate.

Other models postulate linkages between concepts which are triggered via a logical association which is not necessarily hierarchical, for instance 'brainstorming' a topic produces many related ideas. Sometimes this is referred to as concept mapping. Anderson and Bower's (1973) model claimed that knowledge was stored as propositions about the world. Linkages between these propositions would constitute learning. Teachers encourage concept differentiation through comparison of objects or ideas and they usually introduce new ideas by reference to concrete examples. Even adults find new ideas easier to grasp if given concrete examples of them.

Schemata are thought to differ from concepts because they deal with larger phenomena like discourse structure and events which consist of their own particular concepts and interrelations. If you are presented with a bizarre drawing of a familiar object you will employ your schema of that object to make sense of it even though it does not conform entirely to the set of expectations the schema contains.

> Think, for example, of a bicycle drawn without handlebars and saddle and missing the back wheel. Although unrideable, you would still recognise it as a bicycle!

Similarly, when we see clouds which appear to be making recognisable shapes our schema are being involuntarily pressed into service to make sense of the shapes.

Implications of concept development for learning new knowledge

Psychologists interested in education have long argued that new knowledge should be linked to what is already known (Ausubel, 1968). The work of both Gagne (1977) and Ausubel indicated the need for material new to the learner to be structured in a hierarchical way which reflects the inherent conceptual structure of the topic, skill or information in order for assimilation to be effective. Ausubel distinguished between *reception* and *discovery* learning, explaining that most school knowledge is of the former type because there is so much to learn that there is not time for pupils to discover everything anew. However, a certain amount of discovery is involved in learning even pre-packaged information because the learner must engage with the material, by reading it or listening to it, and then make new connections with existing knowledge. The use of sequential procedures, moving from the general to the specific, and the recall of key words and ideas from previous lessons to cue the learner are all strategies which can aid retention and recall.

In mathematics, for example, we move from the general concepts of addition, subtraction and multiplication to more specific computations like calculating area, solving equations or estimating probabilities. If the teacher has given instruction based on the inherent hierarchical structure of the material, the assimilation and accommodation of schemata will be achieved at varying levels by learners. It could therefore be profitable to create cognitive environments which stimulate new and unique reconstructions of the taught material by individual learners through the use of open-ended tasks.

The clarification and extension of declarative or factual subject knowledge (facts, vocabulary, formulae) has traditionally taken precedence over the learning of procedural knowledge specific to each subject, for example the mechanics of performing calculations in mathematics, the process of writing for different genres in English or the steps taken to set up an experiment in science. Latterly, however, procedural knowledge has been recognised as important in school learning; tasks which facilitate the learning of procedural knowledge are likely to be of an investigative applied nature, possibly involving open-ended role-play or problem-solving.

An emphasis on structure and sequence is evidenced in the learning of modern foreign languages where pupils are taught to recognise and acquire discrete vocabulary items in order later to construct sentences, spoken or written. Knowledge from other subject areas which falls into this category is that of a formulaic nature, such as the periodic table from chemistry or logarithms from mathematics. Information of this kind is traditionally learned by rote but knowledge acquired in this way can have limited retention and is a rather uneconomic means of storing information. Material learned meaningfully, where the essence of something read, seen or heard is abstracted from the whole experience, is stored substantively rather than verbatim in the memory. Combining concrete examples with abstract instruction can assist this learning (Anderson et al., 1996), for instance the use of practical or visual 'props' in the teaching of languages or mathematics.

Rote learning is not inherently meaningful so cannot be stored in LTM with other related information. Rather it must be stored in its full form, taking up a lot of space in the memory. It is analysed only superficially in STM because the pupil does not have to make connections with other pieces of information.

Reader Reflection: Meaningful and rote learning

We can employ an example now to illustrate the difference between meaningful and rote learning. If you are asked the four times table you will probably recite 'one four is four, two fours are eight' and so on.

You probably will not explain the mathematical principle of multiplication by a factor of four. If, however, we ask you the meaning of the term 'standard deviation', you are unlikely to recite a verbatim answer.

Instead, your STM searches your LTM for your 'schemata' of statistical terms and relationships. You then articulate your abstracted understanding of the term.

The intellectual challenge involved in articulating the second answer is greater, although knowing one's tables can be very useful.

In the context of information-processing theory the teacher's role is to help learners apply their knowledge and skills by finding new ways of recalling previous knowledge, solving problems, formulating hypotheses and so on. Games and simulations are sometimes used to facilitate critical thinking and in turn encourage new connections to be made between areas of subject knowledge or experience.

Unpacking information-processing

Perception

Perception is deemed to be the first part in the information-processing mechanism. It is the interpretation by the brain of the signals received by the senses. As we have seen, gestalt psychology had revealed some important principles about perception and much research into visual illusion has helped elucidate our understanding of perceptual processes. Gibson (1979) emphasised the functional aspects of perception through his research into pilots landing aircraft. He identified the perceptual phenomenon of a constant aspect approach where the pilot sees the landing point as motionless with the land around it pulling away from that point. Thus the perceptual process assists the perceptual function to which it is harnessed. Neisser (1976) postulated a perpetual cycle of perception in which what we expect to see affects what we do see. The notion of 'perceptual set', where we can be predisposed to perceive something in a certain way, is of particular note to education. A simple illustration of this is when we cannot see the other interpretation within an ambiguous drawing, for example Rubin's vase/faces. When applied to more complex situations this perceptual set can inhibit or advance learning.

Often our emotional state can precipitate perceptual set, for instance if a child associates an event with a dissatisfied response from a parent or teacher they may be unable to perceive such an event in a positive way again. Conversely, a teacher may contrive perceptual set among a class of pupils in order that they are ready to learn a certain topic; if the topic is three-dimensional drawing in the natural environment pupils might be shown in previous lessons a number of artworks in which the three-dimensional perspective is particularly well drawn.

Attention

Broadbent (1958) developed a model of attention which held that stimuli are selectively filtered out because of the limited capacity of the short-term memory to analyse incoming stimuli. The effect of interruption, doing two things simultaneously and dividing one's attention, is well known to have a negative effect on knowledge retention or learning a new skill. The level of familiarity we have with a task will determine the extent to which we can be interrupted and still perform the task well. If you are a seasoned knitter you will be able to simultaneously engage in quite detailed discussion – not so for the novice! You may well be quite practised in the art of listening to two conversations at once, but in fact we do this by tuning in to one or the other at intervals and while attuned to one, we can only register very superficial signals from the other. This helps explain why there is increasing worry about the distracting effects of satellite navigation systems and mobile phones while driving, with legislation now banning the latter in the UK.

In learning environments gaining the attention of the learner is very important – huge tracts of guidance have been written for training teachers on this topic! Younger children are more susceptible to distraction; it is fascinating to note just how much more incidental learning they achieve than do adults while also performing the main task. This is learning that derives from attending to stimuli to which the teacher has not directed them. Long et al. (2011) explain that the ability to resist interference declines after puberty, citing a study by Dorfberger et al. (2007) in which 9 and 12 year olds outperformed 17 year olds on a motor sequence learning task after exposure to an interference task.

Reader Reflection: Interference test

You can do a simple experiment to show this.

Show a group of five year olds an interesting, lively picture for a couple of minutes and a group of fellow students the same picture for one minute (time varies to account for adults' understanding of need to attend to task).

It might be a picture of some animals in a farmyard. Tell them to concentrate on what the animals are doing. Afterwards ask them what the animals were doing and also ask a series of unrelated questions based on other information within the picture, such as: 'What was the farmhouse made of? How many windows did it have? What were the children doing? What colour was the farmer's jumper?'

You will probably find the children are better able to answer the questions relating to incidental learning than the students are but that both groups are able to answer the main question about what the animals were doing.

Teachers generally want their pupils to focus on the matter in hand rather than on incidentals, so they have to use cueing signals to direct attention, develop learning materials and tasks that are stimulating and interesting, use strong colours and sounds, and maintain variety of task and approach.

Memory

While Atkinson and Shiffrin (1968) contended that incoming sensations were analysed in the short-term memory and the organised or abstracted idea deposited with the relevant schema within the long-term memory, Craik and Lockhart (1972) suggested that it was the level of processing of the stimuli which determined the degree of permanence with which it was stored. Miller (1956) revealed our ability generally to remember up to seven chunks of information, plus or minus two. Studies have also shown that recalling later items in a list is more difficult when earlier ones have been learned and recall tested. The finding that we tend to recall the first and last sets of items heard when a list is read out is explained by the most recently heard items being retrieved from STM and the least recent items from LTM. The ones in the middle of the list tend to be lost because they have not been processed for storage in LTM and have been subject to decay from STM. Interference theory (Long et al., 2011) explains that the retrieval of newly learned information can be affected by its similarity to previously stored material. These and other findings have obvious implications for teaching and learning: the value of repetition, rehearsal and mnemonic strategies such as acronyms, rhymes or imagery; the danger of studying too much information at once; and the need to organise material in a conceptually coherent way which aids retrieval.

Tulving (1972) postulated two types of memory: episodic and semantic. Episodic memory is when we recall actual events and experiences, replaying conversations verbatim or 'seeing' actions that occurred. It often applies to major events – for example, many of you will be able to recall precisely where you were and what you were doing when the news of Michael Jackson's death or the 9/11 tragedy were announced – but we also have episodic memories of non-significant occurrences, such as feeding the cat or eating a meal. These fade within days as we have more and more experiences of a similar type but the episodic memories of significant events can remain for a very long time. If you talk to old people, although they might have become very forgetful, they will often be able to recount vivid descriptions of what they were doing at times of significant events which marked autobiographical, national or international historical turning points, even if they occurred 50 years ago. Semantic memory stores the abstractions from our experience, so if you read a book you will not recall its contents verbatim but will have a précised account of its meaning within your memory. Sometimes we can retrieve episodic memories which then enable us to retrieve a stored semantic memory. A huge amount has been written about memory which is quite fascinating and of obvious consequence for educational practitioners, but we do not have space to deal with it here (see Baddeley, 2007; Baddeley et al., 2014; or Tulving and Craik, 2000, for comprehensive texts). Ultimately, for the teacher and the learner, strategies for retention and recall are of primary importance.

Video Discussion

Visit https://study.sagepub.com/bartlettburton4e to watch a video discussion on:

Intelligence testing: Nature or nurture? Controversy or coherence?

This video clip discusses issues which are also relevant to Chapters 10 and 11.

Conclusion

This chapter has provided an overview of key psychological theories which illuminate our understanding of how educational attainment can differ from individual to individual. The legacy of ideas such as those of Piaget, of the behaviourists and of the cognitive psychologists is powerful and we have seen how their theories have impacted upon pedagogical trends. These psychologists give different explanations of mental ability and individual development. The emphasis of behaviourist theories on external stimuli to learning contrasts sharply with the maturational patterns revealed by Piaget or the information-processing approaches of cognitive psychologists. Certainly there has been heated discussion about how much of an individual's character and ability is due to genetic inheritance (nature) and how much to socialisation and environmental factors (nurture). The type of education deemed suitable has depended to a large extent on whether ability was considered to be innate or determined by experience. This rather simplistic dichotomy of nature/nurture has been rendered more complex by psychological studies of the past 35 years, which we will look at in Chapter 9 when we focus on how the interaction of these two influences affects learning development.

Student activities

1. Look at some of the experiments which Piaget used (Boyd and Bee, 2014). Try some of these with a couple of children you know. If possible, choose children of different ages so you can cover at least two of Piaget's stages. Discuss your results with a tutor or other students. Do you think the experiments are useful? Would you/did you alter them in any way?

2. Refer to a text which describes personality measures (Boyle et al., 2008, or Child, 2007, for instance). Most measures take the form of some sort of inventory of characteristics against which the subjects rate themselves. You might like to have a go. Discuss with other students the value of such inventories. Are there any problems with self-report measures?

Recommended reading

Boyd, D. and Bee, H. (2014) *The Developing Child*, 13th edn. Boston: Pearson Education. This excellent, readable text covers all aspects of human development. The latest edition of this classic brings the research right up to date.

Boyle, G. J., Matthews, G. and Saklofske, D. H. (2008) *The SAGE Handbook of Personality Theory and Assessment*. London: SAGE. This handbook reviews the major contemporary personality models and associated psychometric measurement instruments that underpin them.

Cooper, C. (2010) *Individual Differences and Personality*, 3rd edn, London: Hodder Education. Covering both personality theories and the methodological issues associated with personality and psychometric testing, this new edition has been expanded to include recent developments in the field.

Wentzel, K. R. and Brophy, J. E. (2014) *Motivating Students to Learn*, 4th edn, New York and Abingdon: Routledge. This text discusses specific classroom strategies in the context of contemporary schools, curriculum goals and classroom dynamics, laying out effective extrinsic and intrinsic strategies for practice, guidelines for adapting to group and individual differences and ways to reach disaffected learners.

Access the companion website to this book and find SAGE journal articles exploring this chapter topic in further detail: https://study.sagepub.com/bartlettburton4e.

CHAPTER 9

Education and psychological research

Chapter overview

In this chapter psychological developments that have been influential within education since the 1970s are examined, including social constructivism, multiple and emotional intelligences, situated cognition and metacognition. Research into individual learning styles, strategies and preferences is explored, so too the growing interest in brain functioning or 'neuroscience'. Although these are considered separately, they inevitably overlap with each other and with theories discussed in the previous chapter. This is inevitable as research into cognition, the brain and the emotions builds on previous research. Fundamentally it is accelerating our understanding of how learning works and can be enhanced.

Introduction

Psychologists' interest in how the mind works and how education affects individuals is as vibrant now as it has ever been. It might be argued that the theoretical and empirical work described in Chapter 8, although revealing a great deal about mental processes, also opened new avenues of enquiry. This chapter will examine psychological research which has become influential since the 1970s within education, including:

- constructivist theory which urges a focus on learners' existing conceptions
- social constructivist theory which stresses the importance of social interaction and scaffolded support in the learning process

- metacognitive theory which demonstrates the value of learners' understanding and controlling their learning strategies
- learning style theories which imply not better/poorer distinctions between ways of learning but the matching of learning tasks to a preferred processing style
- learning preferences and the implications for conducive environmental conditions for learning
- multiple intelligence theory which suggests a multidimensional rather than a singular intelligence
- emotional intelligence theory which emphasises the potency of the learner's emotional state
- situated cognition theory which explains all learning as context-bound
- the growing knowledge of brain functioning.

Interest in explanations for pupils' differential success rates in learning, which go beyond notions of static intelligence and learning readiness, continues to grow. Over ten years ago there were calls for learning opportunities to be 'personalised', to match work to pupils' needs (Miliband, 2004a). These pedagogical trends are examined in more detail in Chapter 11. As we have seen in Chapter 8, individual differences have traditionally been conceptualised as differences in intelligence as measured by IQ tests. In the contemporary context, however, richer explanations exist for how pupils learn. We begin by looking at research which stresses the individualised nature of constructing meaning.

Constructivism

Constructivism is predicated on the idea that people make their own sense of things in a unique way. It attaches great importance to the individualised nature of learners' conceptions. Information-processing theorists would probably attribute the differences between individuals' conceptions to the different ways stimuli are perceived or represented in their minds. But Driver and Bell (1986) argued that stimuli, or knowledge, are not that straightforward. New information is problematic for the learner, who must examine it in relation to prior conceptions and experiences and see to what extent it fits. Driver et al. (1996) referred to these as alternative frameworks. Little emphasis is placed on the role of instruction. Rather the teacher must create situations which facilitate individuals constructing their own knowledge. According to Liang and Gabel (2005) the teacher is expected to support, guide and facilitate rather than perform the functions of teaching, information-providing and information-transferring. Students synthesise new information according to their former knowledge, experiences, beliefs and attitudes and then shape the information and find their own meanings within it rather than simply receiving the information (Seker, 2008). If pupils harbour misconceptions they must be helped to take them apart at the root since long-held conceptions are very difficult to shake off and are resistant to change even when teachers and others explain the error. Constructivism emphasises the need to give learners responsibility for directing their own learning experiences (Seker, 2008).

Studies by Boghossian (2006) and Cronjé (2006) found the main characteristics of learning outcomes derived using constructivist approaches to be the generation of personal meanings through which the students develop their skills to find and process specific as well as general information they need in their lives. More recently Boghossian (2012) has argued that constructivist pedagogies cannot achieve their declared critical thinking ambitions because the teacher needs to be able to correct a student's propositions and cognitions against a shared, knowable world. He suggests using some form of meaningful synthesis that uses a corrective mechanism, for example, asking learners to articulate what unstated conclusions they could draw from what their classmates were saying, or not saying. The teacher could then challenge those conclusions either by counterexamples or by asking pupils for evidence and then challenging it. If no corrective feedback is given and one answer is as good as the next, the opportunity for critical thinking is reduced.

Social constructivist theories

Vygotsky

Since the 1970s educators have increasingly recognised the importance of the ideas of Lev Vygotsky, the Russian psychologist. Vygotsky's work dates from the 1920s and 1930s but did not become available in the West until the 1970s, which explains why his publications date from after this time despite his early death from tuberculosis in 1934 aged 38. The sociological ideas of Durkheim, Wundt's emphasis on cultural psychology, gestalt psychology, the early works of Jean Piaget and the new modernist theories of linguistics and literary theory emerging in the USSR in the 1920s influenced Vygotsky.

This eclecticism was denounced as anti-Marxist and Vygotsky's work went into oblivion. After the political rehabilitation of his work in the USSR and its delayed discovery in the West, his seminal work on the relationship between language and thought spawned studies of major importance in the former USSR and in the West.

Cole and Scribner's (1974) studies, focusing on Vygotsky's view that children's learning of scientific concepts depends on the interaction between these and the child's own spontaneous everyday concepts, revealed that school-based cognitive skills become more important where there is an increased demand for scholastic-type activities outside school.

Kozulin juxtaposed Piaget's and Vygotsky's theories, explaining their 'common denominators as a child centred approach, an emphasis on action in the formation of thought, and a systematic understanding of psychological functioning' and their biggest difference as their understanding of psychological activity (Kozulin, 1998: 34). For Vygotsky (1978), psychological activity has socio-cultural characteristics from the very beginning of development. Theoretical concepts are generative from a range of different stimuli, implying a problem-solving approach for the learner and a facilitator role for the teacher. Whereas Piaget (1959) considered language a tool of thought in the child's developing mind, for Vygotsky language was generated from the need to communicate and was central to the development of thinking. Vygotsky emphasised the functional value of egocentric speech to verbal reasoning and self-regulation, and the importance of socio-cultural factors in its development. In 'inner speech' the sense attached by the individual predominates over meaning but speech forms originating in external dialogues have to be internalised and internal thoughts translated into a form of speech comprehensible for others. Vygotsky likened this to there being two co-authors, where one accommodates their thoughts to the pre-existent system of meanings and the other immediately turns them into idiosyncratic senses, in simultaneous outbound and inbound conversations. In communicative talk, then, the development is not just in the language contrived to formulate the sentence since the process of combining the words to shape the sentence also shapes the thought itself.

Thus Vygotsky's work highlighted the importance of talk as a learning tool. Prompted by the influential Bullock Report (1975), the status of talk in UK classrooms has been reinforced since the 1980s, with reports highlighting its centrality to learning (Assessment of Performance Unit, 1986; Norman, 1992). The encouragement of pupil talk for the learning of both declarative and procedural knowledge has been increasingly acknowledged to be of value since it allows learners to refine what they know through the articulation of their thoughts (Withers and Eke, 1995). This has also been found in research into pupils' understanding of science. Howe et al. (2007) found the most productive interaction between learners was when they were explaining their reasons for their ideas to one another. The learning outcomes were greatest when the pupils held clearly opposing views to one another.

The concept of 'psychological tools' was a cornerstone of Vygotsky's theory (Kozulin, 2003): 'symbolic artefacts' such as signs, symbols, texts, formulae, and graphic symbolic devices which help learners accomplish their own 'natural' psychological functions of perception, memory, attention and so on. They serve as a 'bridge between individual acts of cognition and the symbolic socio-cultural prerequisites of these acts' (Kozulin, 1998: 1). Naturally existing signs, such as tracks, are replaced by artificial versions of the same and are dependent on the social environment. Vygotskian theory holds that intercultural cognitive differences are attributable to the variance in systems of psychological tools and in the methods of their acquisition practised in *different* cultures. His work has spawned much interest in socio-cultural theory (Mercer and Littleton, 2007) wherein thinking and learning are shaped by culture, and human development is understood by reference to its social and communicative form.

Kozulin explored the work of Feuerstein et al. (1991) who developed Vygotsky's notion of the human mediator in the interaction between child and environment. Charting the philosophical and sociological antecedents of mediated interaction, Kozulin cited Hegel's description of work as a mediated activity and Mead's view that the interaction between the individual and the environment is always mediated by meanings which originate through social relations. For Vygotsky, psychological tools mediate humans' own psychological processes. Feuerstein developed mediated learning experience (MLE) theory working with culturally different groups, culturally deprived individuals and learning-disabled children. MLE is achieved by the involvement of an adult between the stimuli of the environment and the child with the intention of modifying 'learner deficiencies'. This appears to be a deficit model of learners but Kozulin claims it can reveal hidden learning potential and can reorient parents and teachers from passive acceptance of children's 'deficiencies' to active modification of them. MacBlain (2014) suggests Feuerstein's belief that all children, irrespective of their difficulties, can become effective learners, with the appropriate support, liberates teachers from focusing on constraints upon an individual's achievement.

Bruner

Jerome Bruner, a US psychologist who has contributed a huge amount in a variety of areas of psychological research since the 1950s, also placed an emphasis on structured intervention within communicative learning models. He formulated a theory of instruction, central to which is the notion of systematic, structured pupil experience via a spiral curriculum where the learner returns to address increasingly complex components of a topic as they develop over time. Learners construct new ideas or concepts based upon their current/past knowledge. Thus in Year 5 at primary school tackling the problem of fractions will be approached using many

250 INTRODUCTION TO EDUCATION STUDIES

more concrete examples than when it is returned to in Year 7 at secondary school. For Bruner, learning involves the active restructuring of knowledge through experience with the environment. The learner selects and transforms information, constructs hypotheses and makes decisions, relying on an internal and developing cognitive structure to do so. Cognitive structure (schema, mental models) provides meaning and organisation to experiences and allows the individual to go beyond the information given.

As far as teaching is concerned, good pedagogy should try to encourage students to discover principles by themselves. The instructor and student should engage in an active dialogue, asking questions, presenting and testing hypotheses. Thus Bruner advocated discovery methods rather than the provision of pre-packaged materials. The teacher's job was to guide this discovery through structured support, for example, by asking focused questions or providing appropriate materials. A similar, but more systematic, approach could be seen in a method known as Direct Instruction (DI), a model of carefully planned instruction that originated in the 1960s and concentrates on incremental mastery of skills and knowledge, with the teacher giving substantial guidance to begin with and then gradually reducing it. Liem and Martin (2013) conclude from a review of several studies that student results achieved in DI programmes are consistently better than those achieved through discovery learning or problem-based learning. The notion of scaffolding of pupils' learning, how best this can be done and the degree to which support should be given has thus long been considered a key element in determining approaches to teaching and continues to feature in contemporary teacher education programmes.

The influence of social constructivist theories

The pedagogical implications of the work of Vygotsky and Bruner centre on the role of communication and structured intervention in thinking and problem-solving. Essentially, if pupils discuss with others what new ideas mean to them, further thinking is generated with more complex links between ideas afforded. The role of the teacher in facilitating learning situations involving talk is of critical importance. Judicious grouping of pupils for such talk is important. Ann Brown, an influential psychologist in America, developed Lave and Wenger's (1991) notion of communities of practice, whereby people collaborate to progress their learning within a common cause or profession, into learning communities which operate like research seminar groups. Taking a Vygotskian approach she argued that 'students navigate by different routes and at different rates. But the push is towards upper, rather than lower, levels of competence' (Brown, 1994: 7). See Hara (2009) for a full account of communities of practice and peer learning.

Homogeneous (same level of ability) grouping and pairing has been considered to have advantages in fostering learning, particularly in its promotion of argument and sharing of complex ideas (Gillies and Ashman, 2003; Rogoff, 1990; 1998). Fazey and Marton (2002) explain that one of the reasons why helping children to talk about their learning is so productive is that individual learners tend to assume that the reality which they experience is the reality that others experience too. Greenfield (1997) has shown how even the perceptions and interpretations of the same experiences by identical twins lead to unique sets of memories. Bruner's ideas about the power of systematic and well-structured pupil experiences to promote cognitive development are fundamental to a social constructivist approach.

Reader Reflection: Scaffolding learning

Maybin et al. (1992) used Bruner's (1983) ideas of 'scaffolding' in relation to classroom talk. The ideas of pupils emerging through their talk are scaffolded or framed by the teacher putting in 'steps' or questions at appropriate junctures.

A group of pupils might be discussing how to solve a problem. The teacher can intervene when they hear an idea emerge which will help pupils find the solution by asking a question which requires the pupils to address that idea explicitly. *You may wish to try this if you have a placement in a school.*

Is it easy to work out when to intervene?

How far does the influence of an idea reflect the strength of the pupil's personality or the validity of the idea?

How should a teacher handle this without demotivating the pupil/pupils?

Bruner argued that the scaffolding provided by the teacher should decrease in direct correspondence to the progress of the learner. Wood (1988) developed Bruner's ideas, describing five levels of support which become increasingly specific and supportive in relation to the help needed by the pupil:

1. general verbal encouragement
2. specific verbal instruction
3. assistance with pupil's choice of material or strategies
4. preparation of material for pupil assembly
5. demonstration of task.

Thus, having established the task the pupils are to complete, a teacher might give general verbal encouragement to the whole class, follow this up with specific verbal instruction to groups who need it and perhaps target individuals with guidance on strategies for approaching the task. Some pupils will need physical help in performing the task and yet others need to be shown exactly what to do, probably in small stages. Some researchers favour slight differences between partners in order to encourage 'cognitive conflict', which, as Webb (2013: 215) explains, 'arises when learners perceive contradiction between their existing understanding and what they hear and see in the course of interacting with others. To resolve the conflict, learners re-examine and question their own ideas and beliefs, seek additional information and try out new ideas, which leads to higher levels of reasoning and learning'. However, Webb (2013) cautions that too little or too much conflict can be detrimental. The research findings are by no means clear so it is not possible to conclude whether pupils matched on the basis of similar or of different previous performance is most advantageous; this is likely to vary according to the task and the learners. In terms of age differences, however, recent research seems to be more conclusive with Tymms et al. (2011) reporting that cross-age peer tutoring enhanced attainment in maths and reading in two different age groups for all the participants (pupil tutors and pupil tutees). Can and Ginsburg-Block (2013) provide a useful discussion of peer tutoring, drawing together conclusions from a number of studies.

The Vygotskian notion of 'zones of proximal development' (ZPDs) has application here. These zones describe the gap between a pupil's current level of learning and the level they could be functioning at given the appropriate learning experience and adult or peer support. Vygotsky claimed that 'self-supported competence is only possible if successful performance has been established through assisted learning' (Long et al., 2011: 187). Teachers are usually well aware of the extent to which these zones vary from pupil to pupil even if they do not use Vygotskian terminology; indeed, it is the extent of this variation which constitutes the challenge for the teacher. While many teachers are now trained to scaffold learning, the tyranny of target-driven national curriculum testing often leads them to seek to homogenise pupils' individual ZPDs in an effort to utilise a directive teaching style rather than targeted differentiated scaffolding. When struggling to deliver a crowded curriculum teachers may worry this approach is more time-consuming and difficult to manage because of the degree of control that transfers to the pupils within a more pupil-centred, discursive pedagogy, thus constraining an often genuine desire to incorporate such methodology.

Reader Reflection: Critiquing scaffolding

Studies have also warned of the dangers of casually incorporating 'scaffolding' into the professional lexicon as a proxy for generalised help or support rather than, as was originally intended, a very precise means of helping pupils master a specific task (Mercer and Littleton, 2007).

Perhaps it is for this reason (the need for very precise questioning) that, in direct contradiction to the espoused value of scaffolding and teacher intervention, Howe et al. (2007) found that when learners engaged in communicative talk it was actually most successful when teachers did not intervene.

However, a later study by Howe (Fung and Howe, 2014) into the effects of teacher-supported group work with 140 16–18 year olds in Hong Kong found the opposite, with students making considerably more progress with teacher assistance.

In the face of conflicting empirical evidence, we have to take a critical stance to our reading of results.

To what extent do you think the context of the research could account for the opposing outcomes of these studies? For instance, could the teachers in the 2007 study have been less adept at the need to question precisely for the scaffolding to be effective than those in the 2014 study?

To what extent might the notion of scaffolding as a pedagogy (the theoretical framework against which the evidence was collected) have been interpreted differently within each study, accounting for the different outcomes?

Discuss with your peers or tutor what other things could account for the different results.

Metacognition

The process of coming to know more about one's own learning strategies, such as strategies for remembering, ways of presenting information when thinking, approaches to problems and so on, is known as metacognition. Bruner (2006: 168) noted that a study by Brown (1975) 'illustrated how remembering strategies were profoundly changed by the child turning her inner eye on how she herself proceeded in attempting to commit something to memory'. It was Flavell who first proposed the notion of metacognition, arguing that becoming 'aware of one's own "cognitive machinery" is a vital component of intelligence' (1979: 907). It is interesting to note that the approach of the earliest modern psychologist, James, in 1890 was to focus on internal consciousness but he soon drew criticism for being too subjective (see Chapter 8). See Goswami (2008) for early research on metacognition and its relationship with reasoning, memory and cognitive development.

It has become fashionable to refer to metacognition as 'learning to learn' and whole systems explaining to teachers how to achieve it are available (see, for example, Guy Claxton's long established 'learning power' approach in Claxton, 2002 and Claxton et al., 2011 or a scheme for secondary schools by Best and O'Donnell, 2011). Researchers suggest that this concept has potential for moving learning away from a curriculum- and assessment-dominated education system (Hall et al., 2006) and for enabling learners to attain better outcomes (Hattie, 2009).

Metacognition is closely related to the idea of self-regulation, which refers to 'self-generated thoughts, feelings, and actions directed to reaching academic goals' (Zimmerman, 1998, cited by Schunk and Mullen, 2013). Hattie (2012) emphasises the need for learners to self-regulate, basing his advice on a huge synthesis of over 800 meta-analyses of research conducted with millions of learners over 15 years into what contributes to effective learning. It is argued that if pupils are helped by their teachers to become more reflective and aware of processes they are deploying, they will be more able to take control of their learning. Being metacognitively aware can be likened to having a commentator in the learner's mind who analyses and comments upon the methods they are using to learn a new concept or skill while the learning is happening. Learners should be encouraged to explore their own ways of knowing and remembering, to experiment with learning strategies, to appreciate teaching and learning techniques which help them learn best and to monitor their own learning.

Baker (2013) distinguishes between cognitive strategies (such as concept mapping, revising, summarising) and metacognitive strategies (for example, self-testing to check understanding and judging the effectiveness of one's own efforts).

Anderson et al. (1996) reported that studies show that transfer of learning between tasks is enhanced where the teacher cues learners into the specific skill being learned and encourages them to reflect on its potential for transfer. The role of the teacher is to provide the scaffolding for the pupils to think for themselves. An emphasis on critical thinking within problem-solving tasks, study skills development, and collaborative and innovative learning can help. Bruner (1966) argued that difficult ideas should be seen as a challenge and that, if properly presented, can be learned by most pupils. Adey and colleagues developed a system of cognitive acceleration in science education (CASE) which challenges pupils to examine the processes they use to solve problems (Adey, 1992, 2008; Shayer and Adey, 2002). In doing so it is argued that pupils are enhancing their thinking processes as the activities are designed to create the cognitive conflict we described earlier. Pupils are given problem-solving tasks which require them to justify their conclusions.

The teacher's role is to carefully question pupils so that each one rethinks the basis for their conclusions. Adey has argued that the activities are appropriate to mixed-ability classes because, although undifferentiated, they make intellectual demands at a range of levels. To substantiate this he cited the results of the project as being equally successful with both high and low scorers on initial measures of cognitive development. He claimed that a two-year programme of fortnightly CASE lessons with Year 7 and 8 pupils led to substantial gains for those pupils in science, mathematics and English GCSE results in Year 11.

The apparent transfer of higher-order cognitive skills beyond science suggests that a focus on pupils' metacognition is worthwhile. The CASE project is premised, then, on the notion of an underlying set of intellectual processes rather than domain-specific thinking skills. It is argued that, through discussing their views of, and solutions to, problem-solving tasks, 'students become accustomed to reflect on the sort of thinking they have been engaged in, to bring it to the front of their consciousness, and to make of it an explicit tool which is then more likely to be available for use in a new context' (Adey, 1992: 141). Adey and Shayer (2013) explain that CASE draws on both Piaget and Vygotsky. Applying a Vygotskian explanation, Adey (1992) has claimed that the encouragement of pupils to describe reasoning patterns using appropriate terminology, even when they do not fully understand the terms, aids their ability to reflect on how they are thinking because the more the terms are used and discussed with peers, the greater meaning they accrue.

A number of studies across the world indicate learning gains as a consequence of metacognitive training. Namrouti and Alshannag's (2004) research in Jordan identified statistically significant differences in seventh grade students' achievement in science. Black et al.'s (2002) study in London, in which mathematics and science teachers were trained to use structured questioning and to encourage pupils to discuss their understanding of concepts, led to pupils of all abilities scoring higher in their national assessment tests or GCSEs than pupils in ordinary lessons. Spada et al. (2006) found that taking a metacognitive approach with social science undergraduates reduced the tendency for their test anxiety to lead to a surface approach to their learning. Baker (2013: 421) confidently claims that '[w]orldwide educational policy makers now recommend attention to metacognition' because 'the evidence that metacognitive strategies impact academic achievement is too strong to ignore'.

As noted earlier, metacognition and self-regulated learning are often felt to be interchangeable but Thoutenhoofd and Pirrie (2015) caution against too readily linking the two, explaining that self-regulated learning focuses more on the individual and thus loses sight of the fundamental role of social interaction in the learning process. They attribute this development to the ascendancy of psychological research and its impact on education to the detriment of socio-logical analyses and a very necessary emphasis on the social dimension of learning to learn.

Learning styles, strategies, approaches and preferences

Research into learning styles and strategies has grown apace since the 1950s and some of the more easily understood categorisations have been popularised within both education and management studies. A fashionable way of identifying 'learn-ing style' has been to refer to learners' preferences for visual, auditory and kinaesthetic ways of working (see Burton, 2007). Contrary to popular belief, how-ever, this categorisation is just one way of describing learning style. Whatever construct of style we use, identifying a learner's habitual way of processing infor-mation is not a simple case of fixing on one descriptor within the construct to the exclusion of the others, for example identifying someone exclusively as a visual-iser, because we know that learning requires the use of different strategies according to the task and the context.

Curry (1983) developed a model which grouped learning style measures into strata which resemble the layers of an onion, distinguishing between a habitual and involuntary underlying feature of personality, the individual's intellectual approach to assimilating information and their instructional preference or choice of learning environment. Since Curry's model was presented, a great deal more research has been done. It is therefore helpful to define what is meant by the four main areas of research in this field.

1. *Learning or cognitive style*: habitual way of representing and processing informa-tion; innate to learner; not susceptible to change.
2. *Learning strategy*: way of approaching and tackling tasks; learned; capable of change.
3. *Learning approaches*: motivation for and attitude towards learning; largely sta-ble but can change according to task or purpose.
4. *Learning preferences*: environmental preferences for learning, such as place, light, atmosphere.

The important principle which characterises each of these research areas is that learning is not better or worse depending on style, strategy, approach or preference but is *different*. Whereas intelligence theory sets a limit on the capacity to learn, these theories describe the differences between learners' preferred or involuntary styles.

This implies that a match between a learner's preference and the learning task will remove any such limits on learning potential but Mayer (2011) claims the evidence for teaching to learners' styles is not convincing. Higgins (2013) says that the matching idea re-emerges every few years so that when teachers use such approaches they get positive feedback but that this is not due to the matching itself; it merely results indirectly from the changes teachers have made.

Many constructs could be used to illustrate these four areas. Below we look at the main or most researched ones but you will come across many more. The key is to be critical in considering them.

Learning or cognitive styles

Individual differences are thought to underlie a whole range of more readily observable differences. Learners bring to their studies a stable, involuntary mode of representing information during their thinking. Riding (1991) proposed that two overarching dimensions can be identified which subsume the various constructs of previous researchers. These are:

wholist-analytic style – whether an individual tends to process information in wholes or in parts

verbal-imagery style – whether an individual represents information during thinking verbally or in mental pictures.

Riding (1996) advocated advance organisers for wholists since they have difficulty seeing the structure and sections of learning material. A topic map indicating the hierarchically related separate areas would help them divide it into its parts. However, the wholist would have trouble disembedding particular information from tables and densely packed diagrams. For analytics an overview after the information has been presented would help learners to create an integrated picture of the topic. Analytics tend to focus on one part at a time, sometimes overemphasising an element of the whole. They are therefore likely to need help in seeing links and relationships between the parts of a topic and in establishing the appropriate balance between the significance of the parts. An overview in the form of a concept map would be highly relevant, as would tabulated information. Riding et al. (2003) found that, for the overall learning behaviour of 206 Year 8 pupils, there was an interaction between working memory capacity and cognitive style. With the wholist-analytic style dimension, memory made a marked difference for analytics but had little effect for wholists, and with the verbal-imagery dimension verbalisers were affected but not imagers.

The predominant coding style of verbalisers suits them for tasks involving texts and definitions so verbal versions of pictorial and diagrammatic material are helpful to them. The greater use now of technology in schools means that it should also be possible, during teacher exposition and questioning, to use interactive techniques involving virtual learning environments, webcams, digital interchange and high-spec recording. Since imagers are found to achieve best on material which can be visualised in mental pictures and which does not contain many acoustically complex and unfamiliar terms, it is suggested that verbal material should be converted into pictorial form for them. Imagers would also benefit from concrete analogies of abstract ideas. As they are superior to verbalisers on spatial and directional information, mapping tasks could be encouraged across subjects. Teacher exposition and questioning could be punctuated with pictures and artefacts or presented using computer graphics and video material. Storage of such learning activity will soon cease to be problematic because of the increasing adoption of 'cloud technology' which provides infinite web storage capacity.

Motivationally wholist-verbalisers will probably be less willing to focus for long periods on material or tasks which are not particularly stimulating, whereas imagers may well persevere with it. They are also likely to be happier working in groups while imagers usually prefer to work alone. Riding and Burton (1998) found that teachers rated the behaviour of wholist boys in Years 10 and 11 as significantly less good than that of analytic boys. They pointed out that a wholist style tends to be associated with a more sociable, outgoing personality which may, among some adolescent boys, present to teachers as deviant behaviour. Evans and Waring (2006) conducted research into the learning styles of 80 primary teacher trainees using Riding's construct. While they found that many of the differences reported in the literature between the different cognitive styles were not evident in this study, the interpersonal and intrapersonal characteristics of wholists and analytics, respectively, were evident and perceived to impact on the teachers' planning and delivery in the classroom. For a full account of style constructs which can be grouped with Riding's dimensions, see Riding and Cheema (1991).

Integrating assessment of wholist-analytic and verbal-imagery dimensions

Riding (1991) developed a computer-presented test which directly assesses both ends of the wholist-analytic and verbal-imagery dimensions. The Cognitive Styles Analysis (CSA) comprises three subtests and uses response time to determine the subject's position on each dimension. The validity of the instrument is supported by the finding of significant relationships between style and a range of school learning performance (Riding et al., 2003). For pupils who exhibit learning difficulties a mismatch between their preferred learning styles and the learning tasks can affect their achievement more than a mismatch would for competent learners. Long et al. (2011) discuss the implications for learning of several other studies by Riding and colleagues and suggest that if a pupil has a similar cognitive style to the teacher, the pupil will have a more positive learning experience.

A huge body of research has been generated using the various learning style constructs and their associated assessment instruments. A study using the Felder-Silverman Index of Learning Styles© (ILS) by Palou (2006) in Mexico found that an activity-based instructional approach improved the performance of 'actives' and 'sensors' found in previous studies to be disadvantaged in the science and engineering curricula. Conversely, a study in the USA by Smith et al. (2006) using Gregorc's (1982) style delineator found no significant effect of learning style on graduate health-care student performance when the medium of instruction in clinical skills was matched to style. For more information on these instruments see Riding and Rayner (1998), and for a systematic review of 71 different constructs see Coffield et al. (2004a and 2004b). Coffield (2008: 33) has complained that 'the learning styles movement has muddied the waters by producing endless dichotomies such as "pragmatists" v "theorists", "field independent" v "field dependent" learners, and "left" v "right brainers". Most of these terms have no scientific justification whatsoever; nevertheless too many tutors succumb to the intuitive appeal of these pseudo-scientific concepts'.

Learning strategies

David Kolb (2015) developed the idea of experiential learning 40 years ago but explains that its roots can be traced to ideas about discovery learning in the work of Dewey, Lewin and Piaget. Kolb's work (1976; 1985) is based on his ideas about what he calls learning style but which in our definitions above are more akin to learning strategies. He described two dimensions: perceiving and processing. The dimensions are bipolar with abstract and concrete thinking at the ends of the perceiving dimension and doing (active) and watching (reflective) at the ends of the processing dimension. Kolb said that these dimensions interact so that four types of learner can be identified:

1. *divergers* who perceive information concretely and process it reflectively, needing to be personally involved in the task
2. *convergers* who perceive information abstractly and process it reflectively, taking detailed, sequential steps
3. *assimilators* who perceive information abstractly and process it actively, needing to be set pragmatic problem-solving activities
4. *accommodators* who perceive information concretely and process it actively, taking risks, experimenting and needing flexibility in learning tasks.

Kolb's notion of experiential learning is a cyclical sequence through the four areas of learning mode implied by the interaction of the two dimensions. His descriptions of learning styles are therefore not to be seen as static but modifiable by the learner's training in the four sequences of the cycle. Learners will have a predilection for one of the stages, thus giving rise to the four styles. The idea is that if these learners experience all of the stages in the cycle, in addition to their preferred one, their learning strategies may be increased. In the 1980s Kolb's work influenced workplace management training (Honey and Mumford, 1986) and found favour in educational settings. The TVEI, funded by the Department for Employment in the mid-1980s, was very influential in developing 'flexible learning'; this used Kolb's work as its theoretical underpinning (Harris and Bell, 1990). Gibbs's (1992) work on adult learning was also influenced by Kolb. In further education, projects looking at the application of Kolb's learning styles to flexible, support-based pedagogy were developed.

A study by Kayes (2005) confirmed the reliability and validity of his assessment instrument, the Learning Style Inventory (LSI), and Jarvis et al. (2003) reported work adapted from Kolb with adult learners which demonstrated the influence of experience on learning and the role of this in andragogy, the science of adult teaching and learning. Kolb's work continues to be influential with a large number of very recent studies conducted. Typical of these is a study by Chen (2015) who applied Kolb's model to a very contemporary learning context. She investigated the learning outcomes of 134 twenty-one-year-old Taiwanese students when using mobile Facebook for learning. Results showed that those with 'assimilating' and 'diverging' styles performed better than those with 'accommodating' and 'converging' styles. The extent to which such studies are helpful in promoting more effective learning must be considered against the backdrop of increasing academic criticism of the theoretical basis of Kolb's work. Schenck and Cruickshank (2015) cite a number of such studies and call for a new model of experiential learning which embraces the role of the social environment and which engages explicitly with developments in neuroscience.

Reader Reflection: Experiential learning theory and metacognition

David Kolb has discussed the link between his experiential learning theory (ELT) and metacognition – see Kolb and Kolb (2009), available online at: http://sag.sagepub.com/cgi/content/abstract/40/3/297.

Locate this article and assess the extent to which it demonstrates robust links between ELT and metacognition. Discuss with others the reasons why Kolb may be developing this line of argument.

Learning approaches

Biggs' (1978; 1987a; 1987b; 2001) work on approaches to study was developed from Marton and Saljo's (1976) studies of 'deep' and 'surface' approaches to learning and was contemporary with Entwistle's (1981) work on learning orientations. Research on learning approaches has been conducted almost exclusively within the higher education sector. The massification of HE and student self-funding has triggered a greater imperative to provide effective and satisfying learning experiences for students, so advice on learning approaches (Biggs and Tang, 2011; Entwistle, 2009) is once again highly relevant. Entwistle et al. (2001) described four orientations to learning: 'meaning', 'reproducing', 'achieving' and 'holistic'. It was suggested that combinations of these orientations with extrinsic factors, such as the desire to pass examinations or a keen interest in a subject, generate certain approaches to study which employ different levels of thinking from 'deep' to 'surface'. Approaches to learning are thus a function of both motive and strategy and motives influence learning strategies (Biggs, 1993). An instrumental or surface motive engenders reproducing or rote-learning strategies. An intrinsic desire to learn is associated with deep motive and the use of learning strategies which emphasise understanding and meaning. An achieving motive might result from the need to pass examinations; from this can come strategies which stress time management and efficient organisation.

Students whose motives and strategies are compatible with the learning tasks are likely to perform well. Conversely, someone with a deep approach will be constrained by too superficial a task and a student who has an achieving motive will probably flounder if long-term, vague objectives are set. Young and Collins (2014) found that where tutors involved students in course design, deeper learning motivation and strategies were facilitated compared with traditionally taught courses.

Ausubel (1985) showed that the need to compete in public examinations can lead to the adoption of rote-learning techniques resulting in temporary, peripheral learning. The type of learning orientation which has been encouraged in many countries, including the USA, the UK and Japan, by the increased emphasis on performance testing and school comparability is that of the achieving type (Darling-Hammond, 1994; Madeus, 1994). This militates against deep approaches which require learners to enjoy few time constraints and full learner autonomy. Clearly the short-term practices of schools to improve results serve to cultivate, at best, an achieving orientation and, at worst, a surface orientation to learning.

It has been suggested that there are cultural differences in motivational approach. However, the findings of many studies about the effects of competition and testing on motivation appear to hold true for both Eastern *and* Western education settings.

Hardre et al. (2006) investigated the relationships between 404 teachers' self-reported classroom goal structures, instructional self-perceptions, teaching efficacy and perceptions of students' motivation in a developing East Asian nation. The teachers reported that their students' motivation was primarily extrinsic and per-formance-oriented and was influenced by external factors, predominantly exam pressure and social expectations. Similarly, in Hong Kong, Lam et al.'s (2004) study with 52 grade 7 secondary pupils found that competition led students to focus narrowly on learning outcomes rather than learning opportunities.

Purdie and Hattie (1996) compared the learning strategies employed by 16–18-year-old students in Australia and Japan. They found that the range of strate-gies used by three culturally diverse groups was the same but that the pattern of use differed for each group. Significantly, the range of strategies used was broadest among high achievers irrespective of cultural group. This might suggest that, where learners are free to determine their own strategy use, high achievers are those who have used their habitual style traits without any mediation of culturally bound learning strate-gies. The Japanese students made far greater use of memorisation by rote than the Australian students, as did the Japanese students who had studied in Australia. Effort and willpower were seen to be closely associated with this use of strategy in a bid to succeed. The cultural determinant of this can be said to lie in the Japanese view that repetition is a route to understanding (Hess and Azuma, 1991). Kember and Gow (1990) reported the same tendency among the Chinese, and Lim (1994) among the students of Singapore. However, two separate studies concerned with cross-cultural validation of Biggs's Study Process Questionnaire (Kong and Hau, 1996; Wong et al., 1996) revealed links between an achieving orientation and a deep approach to learn-ing among Chinese secondary age pupils. Salili's (1996) investigation of achievement motivation among British and Chinese students, using McClelland's (1985) Thematic Apperception Test (TAT), revealed the same tendency.

It is important not to over-generalise such findings and to examine the context within which they have been researched. Elbers (2010) points out that in classes where pupils are of mixed cultural heritage it is potentially limiting to ascribe stereotypical attributes to learners when, in fact, individuals and groups are engaged in a continual process of cultural adaptation. The key thing to remember about learners is that they are individuals, irrespective of their heritage.

Learning preferences

The Productivity Environmental Preference Survey (PEPS) (Price et al., 1991) derives from the work of Dunn et al. (1979; 1989) and is widely used in the USA to measure the 'learning styles' of adults. Learners are thought to possess biologically based physical and environmental learning preferences which combine with emotional traits, sociological preferences and psychological inclinations to make up an individual style profile. Measures include preferences relating to sound, light, temperature, seating design, motivation, structure, persistence, responsibility, sociological needs, physical needs (auditory, visual, kinaesthetic and tactile), best time of day for learning, mobility, intake of food and drink, processing styles, impulsivity/reflectivity and hemispheric dominance (see the section on the brain later in Chapter 9). The PEPS has been widely criticised (Englander et al., 2013) most notably by the systematic review, referred to earlier, by Coffield et al. (2004a and 2004b) who claim inadequate evidence is provided to support its validity; this is allegedly further compounded by missing data and the quality of citations, referencing and interpretations of statistics.

The LSI (Dunn et al., 1989), from which the PEPS was derived, uses similar factors to determine the preferences of younger learners. See Dunn and Griggs (2003) for a synthesis of the research into the LSI. An extensive website is also available at www.learningstyles.net. Dunn (1991) argued that instruction should be arranged which accommodates learners' preferences. The implications of this for a school classroom are quite profound since the potential range of factors a teacher would have to consider for a class of 30 pupils is enormous. Smith's (2006) research in Australia with 160 teachers and trainers of vocational learners found that teachers do make observations of learners' preferences, organising their ideas about preferences into those to do with mode of delivery and those to do with learning context differences. Smith notes, however, that the teachers responded to these differences pragmatically. It is clear that measuring preferences is better suited to adult self-use and, apart from possible application with small groups or with sixth-form students, it is not easy to see how teachers could reconcile the extent of instructional matching which it implies with curriculum requirements within a school's resource base.

Reader Reflection: Selecting the evidence

There is a vast array of research into learning conducted daily throughout the world so we have been able to introduce you to only a few.

Throughout this book we have encouraged our readers to take an enquiring, critical stance to the issues we discuss.

(Continued)

(Continued)

> *Think about why we have chosen the particular studies that we did when so many are available.*
>
> *Might we have chosen others that provided a different view?*
>
> *Think about the ways we have described the findings of the studies we chose and the specific language we used to discuss them.*

Make your own selection by conducting a review of some research studies into individual differences within learning in different countries of the world. Decide upon a few research terms and input them to an academic research database such as the British Education Index. Read the abstracts of studies that emerge from your search and identify the extent to which the evidence both conflicts and converges. You may want to conduct your own mini systematic review (see Chapter 3) to help you with your assignments.

Implications of research into learning styles, strategies, approaches and preferences for education

Rayner and Riding argued that a pupil's style profile will be 'a key consideration in curriculum design, assessment-based teaching and differentiated learning' (1997: 24), recognising, however, that such a profile needs to be manageable, accessible and geared to the real world of teaching. It is not necessary, even if it were possible within the constraints of organising and delivering a diverse curriculum, to know an individual's profile on the full range of style and strategy measures. Given that, unlike measurements of ability, learning styles, strategies and approaches are differentiated not by value but by function, acquiring a more definitive knowledge of individual style is less important than providing a diverse range of classroom approaches, resources, teaching styles and assessment media such that every learner has maximum access to the learning.

Reader Reflection: Too many constructs?

Perhaps the fact that there are apparently so many learning style, strategy, approach and preference constructs should alarm us.

> *Is it feasible that there can be so many different ways of describing aspects of learners' processing or thinking styles?*

Riding and Cheema (1991) claimed these were actually just different manifestations of (and labels for) the same construct, or at least different aspects of the same construct.

How helpful is it anyway to determine whether a learner is an innovator or an adaptor, reflective or pragmatic?

Most of the theorists deal in polar opposites and they acknowledge that individuals may lie anywhere along a respective dimension and not necessarily at either end of it.

Does the fact that they deal only in linear descriptions suggest a failure to acknowledge the multi-faceted, context-bound nature of learning?

Situated cognition

'Situatedness', the study of cognition within its natural context, grew out of dissatisfaction with the disembedded approach of traditional cognitive psychology. Both information-processing and constructivist approaches essentially depicted knowledge as an object located within learners who are isolated from one another. They emphasised rational, individual, abstract thought processes, the study of which could reveal universal principles generalisable to all individuals in any circumstances. In contrast, situated cognition theory (Greeno et al., 1993; Lave and Wenger, 1991; Suchmann, 1987) stressed that learning cannot be studied in isolation from its context without destroying its defining properties. To some extent this school of thought grew out of social constructivism because it emphasised the role of collaborative learning (Hara, 2009) but situated learning theorists go further than the Vygotskian approach by casting the individual learner as a subsystem to a series of increasingly complex systems (classroom, school, neighbourhood, culture and humanity) wherein learning exists as a part of those contexts. This placement of learners within more complex systems is not new, having been described by Bronfenbrenner in his ecological model of human development. Bronfenbrenner (1979) conceptualised human development as the process of understanding and restructuring our ecological environment at successively greater levels of complexity (Smith and Cowie, 2003; Boyd and Bee, 2014). His theory postulated four nested systems of development in context (see Figure 9.1):

- *microsystem* – the home, the classroom, friendships
- *mesosystem* – links between microsystems, for example no breakfast at home can lead to poor work at school

- *exosystem* – links between microsystems and settings in which the child does not participate but is affected by, for example a mother's stressful work environment may provoke intolerance with the child
- *macrosystem* – the ideology and organisations of society or subculture in which the child lives, such as unemployment levels, social taboos.

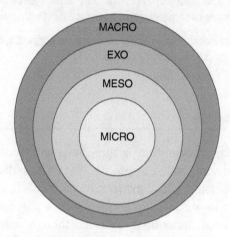

Figure 9.1   The four nested systems of development

Bronfenbrenner's model of ecological systems and subsystems helps explain the interconnectedness of environmental factors which impact on a child's learning, illustrating, for example, the effect of the interplay between a child's health, the state of the parents' relationship and a decision at national level to make budgetary cuts in education or social services.

The impact of this 'development in context' on the growth and measurement of intelligence cannot be ignored. Baltes (1996) emphasised the lifespan nature of development and the importance of historical influences, stressing that age-related trends are but one of three important influences each determined by an interaction of biological and environmental factors:

normative age-graded influences – for example, the advent of puberty (biological genesis) or starting school at five (environmental genesis)

normative history-graded influences – for example, famine (biological impact) or China's one-child policy (environmental genesis)

non-normative life events – for example, an accident causing brain damage (biological impact), divorce or job loss (environmental genesis).

Situated cognition theory goes further than Bronfenbrenner's and Baltes' analyses, espousing a collective knowledge which is embodied in 'the ongoing, ever-evolving interaction' between people (Davis and Sumara, 1997: 115) in real-life situations in the work or marketplace, or social or educational settings. Whereas a cognitive approach to investigating adult performance in mental arithmetic showed poor results as it was in a laboratory setting, Lave (1988) argued that asking the same questions in the context of grocery shopping in the supermarket produces more realistic results (Seifert, 1999). Think, for example, of how quickly darts players sum their scores in the pub!

Situated explanations of cognition generally dispute the transference of knowledge between learning activities because the situative perspective does not allow that knowledge can exist as a 'substance' within the learner (Greeno, 1997). Instead, 'generality of knowing' is preferred as a phrase to describe a learner's 'participation in interactions with other people and with material and representational systems' (Greeno, 1997: 11). From the situative perspective, context-bound learning is more effective than the abstract representation of phenomena which constitutes much classroom teaching. Greeno calls for school learning to become more beneficial beyond the classroom, 'providing students with general resources for reasoning both in and with the concepts of subject-matter domains' (1997: 14). In recent years, the English school curriculum has increasingly adopted the use of 'authentic' learning activities which seek to replicate real-life situations. However, the idea that transference of learning is not possible is not generally embraced by teachers.

Clear parallels can be drawn with the work of Vygotsky, given his emphasis on interaction promoting cognition. However, some forms of situated cognition theory deny the possibility of individual cognition, suggesting instead that all learning is embedded within its interactive context and that there is therefore only collective cognition. It is difficult to see how cognition can be said not to be occurring in an individual's mind irrespective of any form of group cognition. Nevertheless, it is now widely accepted that much value comes from emphasising collaborative classroom activity. Cooperative group approaches to teaching and learning in which no one person has the monopoly on the direction of the learning are inferred by the situative perspective. Greeno has called for the arrangement of 'complex, social activities' with an emphasis on enquiry where pupils are given opportunities to formulate and evaluate 'problems, questions, conjectures, conclusions, arguments and examples' (1997: 10).

Davis and Sumara (2012) tell us that learning is now broadly acknowledged as poorly understood and immensely complex. They describe their nested conception in which hundreds of learning theories and phenomena are enfolded and unfold from other learning phenomena. Rather than juxtaposing apparently competing or opposing ideas, this approach helps explain the relationships we discern between different theories and allows us to embrace the connections between them as psychological research expands our understanding of the complexity of learning.

A theory of learning cultures and a cultural theory of learning

The researchers leading the largest independent study of teaching and learning in further education in England (Hodkinson et al., 2007; James and Biesta, 2007) developed a theory of learning cultures and a cultural theory of learning. By the term 'learning cultures', the researchers mean the social practices through which tutors and students learn and not the contexts or environments in which they learn. Individuals are part of learning cultures and so exert their influence upon them and vice versa, so learning cultures are part of individuals and influence them in turn. Learning cultures permit, promote, inhibit or rule out certain kinds of learning.

So how do individuals learn through their participation in such learning cultures? The researchers use their second big idea, 'a cultural theory of learning', to explain the dynamic and reciprocal interplay between individuals and learning cultures. As they argue, 'the impact of an individual on learning culture depends upon a combination of their position within that culture, their dispositions towards that culture, and the various types of capital (social, cultural and economic) that they possess' (James and Biesta, 2007: 34). In this approach, learning is understood as something that is done; learning is practical and embodied, that is, it involves our emotions and our bodies as well as our brains. Moreover, learning is (in the main) done with others which means that it is 'a thoroughly social process' (James and Biesta, 2007: 34). Learning is also the process through which the learner's dispositions (e.g. attitudes to academic study) are confirmed, developed, challenged or changed.

Coffield (2008) noted that one of the values of this socio-cultural approach to learning is that it presents a holistic view of learning rather than the narrow, official view which is preoccupied with qualifications. Biesta (2011: 208) argued more recently 'that we need to move from learning cultures to educational cultures to highlight that in educational settings there is always the question of the purpose... where value judgements come in – judgements about what is considered educationally desirable – which, in turn, brings in the notion of the complexity of educational cultures, which has to do with the fact that the question of purpose in education is always multidimensional'. Educational cultures, as an approach, then, also integrates psychological and sociological views of learning and attempts to give equal weight to both. Finally, this cultural approach, because it stresses the complexity of all learning and the differing social, ethnic and gender positions of learners and tutors, argues that there can be no such thing as 'best practice' which can be universally applied in all classrooms and in all contexts. By considering this new perspective on learning we can see how previous studies and theoretical positions help generate new thinking that combines elements of existing approaches into a new way of envisioning learning and teaching. In this case we see resonances of social constructivism, metacognition and situated cognition.

Reader Reflection: Combining competing perspectives on learning

In acknowledging that the social world of the classroom is a crucial stage for learning, it is possible to consider two ostensibly competing perspectives on learning – the situated cognitive and the traditionally cognitive – coexisting as explanations of the learning process.

How might both be useful in their inferences for pedagogy?

The former could be said to be descriptive of the social contexts and interactions within which individual cognition, as explained from a cognitive perspective, occurs. The cognitive perspective can be used to explain phenomena about individual pupils' learning, personalities and behaviour implied by the analysis of empirical data.

But is it also helpful to do more than just describe these social, interactive contexts?

Learning environments can profitably be analysed from a situated perspective in order for researchers to understand, for example, the socio-political context and the educational, interactional settings within which the research takes place.

How could we make sense of the former without the latter?

It would be unbound by context and, as such, difficult to make sense of.

Can empirical validity and generalisability be claimed for a situated cognition research perspective?

The theoretical frameworks and constructs investigated within a traditional cognitive approach, for example the construct of learning style, intelligence or creativity, can be replicated but collectively constructed understandings which are bound by time and context are not replicable and therefore not amenable to empirical testing (Anderson et al., 1997).

Brain function

Koch et al. (2013) report that research in neuroscience, cognitive science, neuropsychology, and education has flourished in recent years. More is being learned all the time about the way the brain functions and this helps to elucidate our understanding of mental processes (see Stiles et al., 2015, for a detailed discussion of brain functioning and cognitive development). Goswami (2008) provides a helpful definition of the difference between cognitive psychology, which explains cognition via concepts and ideas held in the mind, and cognitive neuroscience, which is the study of neural networks in the brain that are active while the mind is active. Many would claim, however, that such research is still in its infancy as there remains a great deal for us to find out. Neuroscientists revealed many years ago the physiology of mental functioning. The Spanish neuroscientist Cajal studied the central nervous system (the brain and spinal cord which together control all human functioning), revealing the function of nerve cells (neurones) in transmitting information to and from the cerebral cortex (DeFelipe and Jones, 1991). The gaps between the neurones (synapses) are traversed and new connections made when thinking occurs.

Opportunities to grapple with ideas should therefore enable learners to 'grow' their brains by making new, strong connections. Information that is learned in a meaningful way will create longer-term connections that can be refreshed even after long periods of disuse, whereas rote learning is likely to lead to weak, temporary connections.

The advantage of neuroscience is that technological advances now enable us to create MRI (magnetic resonance imaging) scans of the active areas of the brain so that we can watch it while it performs a mental function, such as constructing a sentence or solving an equation. Few research studies use this technique with children; such research is mostly done with adults but in time it could become commonplace, allowing us to draw conclusions about the impact of certain types of cognitive task on the deployment of specific areas of the cortex and on subsequent neural development. To date most studies into cognition have conducted experiments to try to deduce why cognitive development follows a particular path but Goswami (2008) is confident that before very long causal explanations will also be drawn from neuroscience. Koch et al. (2013) make a strong plea for educators to work together to conduct and deploy research findings from MRI scans to improve teaching and learning, claiming that this has been derailed by a preoccupation with 'neuromyths' (see Chapter 11).

Research into hemispheric specificity indicates that the left side of the brain deals more with language and logic and the right side with spatial and visual awareness. It is also claimed that we can infer from electrical activity in the brain, measured using an EEG (electroencephalogram) while someone is asked to perform a variety of tasks, the different parts of the brain associated with the various processes of perception, attention, remembering, retrieval and language comprehension (Fodor, 1983; Hillyard, 1993). Brain scans have suggested that different brain patterns are activated when recalling facts learned by rote as opposed to in meaningful mode, which may explain why some rote learning, for example of arithmetical tables, persists but why problem-solving strategies appear to be transferable to new problems only following meaningful learning. This theory contrasts with the ideas of developmental psychologists and information-processing theorists who argue that mental processes are domain-general not domain-specific. There is still doubt, however, about modularity or localisation of brain functioning. Fodor (2000) queried his own claims for modularity and is sceptical about how much is actually known for certain about brain functioning. Greenfield (2000) also cast doubt on the modularity theory, suggesting instead 'neuronal assemblies' in which millions of brain cells compete to create elements of consciousness. She did not provide robust evidence for this theory though.

Blakemore and Frith (2005) explain that while the proliferation and pruning of brain cell connections in infancy encompasses most areas of the brain, the changes in the adolescent brain are specifically associated with regions of the cortex, including the prefrontal cortex. This is the area of the brain that deals with the higher-order activities of planning, self-awareness, selecting behaviour and certain types of memory – sometimes referred to as executive functions. Not only is there a dramatic reorganisation of connections related to the executive functions during this period, but there is also a significant increase in 'myelination'. Myelin is a white sheath of fat and protein that gradually develops around transmitter cells, insulating them and increasing the speed of interconnectivity. Myelination goes on into the twenties greatly increasing the speed of transmission between cells. These changes imply that there should be an improvement during the teens and early twenties in an individual's ability to focus attention, make decisions, exercise self-control and manipulate the memory to carry out more than one task at a time. There are also likely to be subtle but significant developments in awareness both of oneself and of others, including the ability to understand another person's viewpoint – although these changes in social cognition may be temporarily obscured or confused by the effects of hormonal changes during puberty.

Thus the brain continues to grow and change over the first 20 years of life, which suggests that teaching methods at different stages in the educational process should be sensitive to these changes. Brain development seems to be more generalised the younger the learner. As students reach adolescence, neural connections in most areas become well established, but those in the regions associated with the executive functions continue to be fragile and malleable (Blakemore and Frith, 2005). It may make sense, therefore, for primary teachers to concentrate on a more general, holistic approach to education, helping to establish the overall architecture of the brain. They should also take into account that their pupils' attention span is likely to be shorter than that of adults, decision-making more difficult and working memory less efficient. Some tasks that seem negligible to adults are quite taxing for children. At secondary age, teachers should be able to assume that overall interconnectivity is established and concentrate on the still fragile areas in the prefrontal cortex, helping students become steadily more capable of selective attention, decision-making, planning and multi-tasking. Buckler and Castle (2014) provide a helpful discussion of brain function and neurological development, drawing out implications for learning and teaching.

Psychologists and neuroscientists are still trying to find an answer to the 'hard problem' of how subjective thought and streams of consciousness are derived from brain matter. In the meantime the most persuasive parts of neuroscientific theory are cherry-picked for application within the classroom (see Chapter 11) which Koch et al. (2013) say has stalled progress in neuroscientists working with educators to develop and apply the necessary research findings to improve learning.

Research on brain functioning has impacted on education in a less superficial way when it comes to specific learning disorders such as dyslexia, a reading disorder thought to derive from sensory-perceptual processing delays which impede the brain's phonological representation.

Dyslexia is thought to affect 4–5 per cent of the school-age population, a not insignificant percentage. Problems about its definition and prevalence (more boys are reported to suffer from the condition but this may be because girls' better behaviour hides the problem) abound (Elliott, 2005) but explaining the condition using 'brain science' has reduced the stigma which attached to it when the cause was attributed to lower intelligence.

We must, as usual, take care though not to allow the expertness (and more than a little mystique) around neuroscience to dupe us into accepting its explanations unthinkingly. Weisberg et al.'s (2008) study found that people (both lay and expert) were easily led to believe bogus neuroscientific explanations!

Different views of intelligence

Triarchic and multiple intelligences

Debate about whether a single intelligence can be identified or whether intellectual power is better characterised as multiple intelligences continues to exercise contemporary theorists. Those who favour an information-processing explanation of human understanding, Robert Sternberg in the USA for example, describe intelligence in relation to its cognitive components. Sternberg (1985) proposed a triarchic model of intelligence comprising three major aspects which interact with one another: analytical, creative and practical thinking:

Analytical or *componential* intelligence is what is normally measured on IQ and achievement tests – planning, organising and remembering facts then applying them to new situations.

Creative or *experiential* intelligence is the ability to see new connections between things and to develop original ideas.

Practical or *contextual* intelligence is the ability to read situations and people, and manipulate them to best advantage.

Neither experiential nor practical intelligence are measured in IQ tests according to Sternberg (2011) and yet, beyond schooling, these are probably needed at least as much as analytical intelligence.

Much research effort has also been put into understanding genius, giftedness and creativity in relation to normal intelligence. Sternberg and O'Hara (1999) reviewed research into the relationship between intelligence and creativity, concluding that psychologists had not reached a consensus about the relation between creativity and intelligence nor even a shared understanding of what these two constructs are. Sternberg's later work (2003b; 2005) argued for a model of intelligence that involves synthesising wisdom, intelligence and creativity (WICS). He bemoaned the fact that Western society is organised around a closed system of selection that defines intelligence very narrowly. He counselled that giftedness is ultimately just expertise in development and that all measures of giftedness assess some kind of expertise to some extent. Research into creativity and its relationship with intelligence is vast and fascinating and we cannot begin to do justice to it here. It has been of particular interest to those studying special educational needs but is a very important area for all students of education, particularly intending teachers and would form a good dissertation or masters' level focus.

Howard Gardner (1983; 1995; 2011) is well known for shunning a unitary explanation of intelligence, developing instead his theory of multiple intelligences (MI). Eight distinct intelligences are said to exist independently of one another: linguistic, spatial, logical-mathematical, musical, bodily-kinaesthetic, interpersonal, intrapersonal and naturalist. Gardner explained that individuals have different entry points to learning depending on the strength of their various intelligences.

Sternberg (1999) pointed out that, although Gardner cited evidence to support his theory, he had not carried out research directly to test his model. Scott (2013) argues there is still very little hard research evidence available for MI theory, however, since we all recognise in ourselves some tendency to be better at some things than others, Gardner's theory seems intuitively to be relevant. However, if one sees cognition as the processing of information using fairly universal sets of mental strategies, it is difficult to conceive of separate, discrete intelligences. White (2005) critiqued Gardner's theory in detail, questioning the criteria on which the designation of an intelligence is based and pointing out that much intelligent behaviour can often rely on more than one of Gardner's intelligences at once. Hayes (2010) points out that Gardner drew much of his evidence from high-achieving people but ignored the effect on them of social influences which, as we will see in Chapter 10, can have a powerful impact on an individual's success or failure. Although he never intended its application to education (Cerruti, 2013), Gardner's work has become very popular in educational circles, possibly because it offers an alternative to the view of intelligence as unitary and fairly stable, encouraging instead a focus on developing particular individual capabilities to their highest potential.

Silver et al. (1997) advocated a synthesis of Gardner's MI theory with their own learning style theory, arguing that the former offers ideas about the content and context of learning while the latter elucidates the generalised processes of learning within which can be observed individual differences. Their integrated model of style and MI suggests how different combinations might translate into vocations, for example logical-mathematical intelligence within a person with a mastery learning style might lead to a job as an accountant. Where it combines with an interpersonal learning style it is suggested the vocation might be a tradesperson or homemaker. There can be dangers in being overly enthusiastic about such an approach, of course, since the integration of a *different* model of learning style with MI theory could elicit a whole range of other vocational trends!

The value of learning style theory, MI theory and other ideas we have looked at in this chapter is that they provide us with more questions with which to probe human behaviour and different ways of understanding it. Theoretical and empirical categorisations help us to make sense of our observations but attempting to characterise different types of learning or vocation too precisely can obscure our focus on the individual differences between people which make them unique.

Emotional intelligence

A popular construct within the field of intelligence research is that of *emotional intelligence* (EI) (Goleman, 1995; 2006; 2011; Mayer et al., 2004; Petrides, 2009;

Petrides et al., 2011; Salovey and Mayer, 1990). While there is debate about the existence of discrete brain structures (the limbic system) for emotional experience and behaviour, there can be no doubt that an individual's emotional state and ability to deal with their feelings can impact on their educational performance. Traditionally this 'affective' domain of experience has been little more than acknowledged by educators with their main focus being on the 'cognitive' domain. It is now receiving more attention as a result of Goleman's popular work. He has related the ability to control impulses, motivate oneself and regulate moods to improved thinking and learning.

EI projects tend to combine common sense and neuroscience. Research has focused on the role of the prefrontal cortex, the part of the brain just behind the forehead, which develops most rapidly between the ages of three and eight. This mediates our emotional impulses, which come from the amygdala. The amygdala, part of the limbic system that controls and processes emotional experience and behaviour, takes over when someone is frightened or stressed (this is the well-known fight or flight mechanism that ensures survival) (OECD, 2005). It directs some of our most powerful and primitive feelings, such as fear, straight to all the major centres of the brain before the neocortex – the site of more rational reactions – has time to react. The amygdala thus controls the routing of information to the cortex, where it is stored as long-term memory; if a learner is frightened, perhaps of failure or reprisals, this transfer stops and long-term learning is prevented. The job of the prefrontal cortex is to manage some of these instinctive emotions, dampening some of the signals generated by the amygdala and weighing up appropriate reactions.

Nettelbeck and Wilson (2005) concluded from their review of past and current intelligence theories that the existence of emotional intelligence cannot yet be confirmed. Petrides et al. (2011) examined the relationship between EI and personality factors but Cooper (2010) believes that EI questionnaires are themselves simply measuring familiar personality traits. In a 2002 DfES (see Clarke et al., 2015) commissioned study researchers found that schools developing programmes which fostered the emotional health of staff and pupils showed marked improvements in behaviour and learning, social cohesion, staff morale and confidence, and academic results. They did not, however, confirm a direct link between promoting emotional literacy and raising standards; this would be very difficult because isolating EI as the only variable making a difference would be almost impossible. However, Qualter et al. (2012) *did* establish a causal link between emotional intelligence and academic achievement. Notwithstanding the rather mixed nature of the research evidence, EI has become enormously influential within education, training and workplace settings. Banerjee et al. (2014: 720) reported that 'recent research has underlined the potential benefits of universal (i.e. not solely targeted at selected pupils known to have particular difficulties or vulnerabilities) work on social and emotional learning at school'. We will look at the application of EI in a little more detail in Chapter 11.

Video Discussion

Visit https://study.sagepub.com/bartlettburton4e to watch a video discussion on:

Psychological research and pedagogy

This video clip discusses issues which are also relevant to Chapter 11.

Conclusion

Research into the ecology of development, suggestions about different types of intelligence, new understandings about the brain and the effect of underlying cognitive style on learning approaches and strategies, and an acknowledgement of the impact of social and emotional factors on motivation and achievement all contribute to a richer understanding of individual development through education. The influence of social-constructivist ideas currently felt within institutions of education is very strong. These have built upon, rather than usurped, many of the ideas previously in favour. Even discredited notions of a single, measurable intelligence persist in our common-sense discourse of ability. The implications of more fluid ideas about intelligence, about the construction and site of knowledge and about the impact of greater learner autonomy through technologised forms of learning are beginning to impact on conventional wisdom about individual learning and achievement. Psychological research will continue to refine theoretical ideas about learning and, as students of education, you will enjoy a fascinating perspective on them. However, it is essential to adopt a critical stance when reviewing such research. This will be discussed further in Chapter 11.

Student activities

1. Find out what views your tutors and colleagues have about intelligence. What do they think about newer ideas of intelligence? Is there a tendency to think of intelligence as innate and fixed or do people conceptualise intelligence more fluidly? Try to explore this with any schoolteachers you know. How fundamental is their view of intelligence to the way they help pupils learn?

2. Think about your own learning style: do you write essays incrementally, piecing together the components one upon another, or do you like to have a generalised idea of the whole essay before you start writing? Do you see pictures and images when you are thinking or reading, or do you find yourself thinking in words? Relate this to a review of some of the learning styles literature (see Riding, 2002, for references).

3. Explore some of the emergent research into neuroscience – use Goswami's 2008 text as a way into the references and then seek out the very latest findings. To what extent does what we increasingly know about brain function alter the findings of cognitive psychology?

Recommended reading

Goleman, D. (2011) *The Brain and Emotional Intelligence: New Insights.* E-book: More Than Sound LLC. In this e-book Goleman reviews current knowledge about the brain basis of emotional intelligence. The authors aim is to deepen the reader's understanding and ability to apply the principles of EI. It is written in a style that makes it accessible to a wide readership.

Goswami, U. (2008) *Cognitive Development: The Learning Brain.* Hove and New York: Psychology Press. Written from the perspective of brain science this text shows how new discoveries in cognitive neuroscience force us to reconsider traditional theories of cognitive development. Goswami considers the established base of cognitive developmental psychology and demonstrates how new data from brain science require a new theoretical framework based on learning.

Long, M., Wood, C., Littleton, K., Passenger, T. and Sheehy, K. (2011) *The Psychology of Education.* Abingdon: Routledge. This second edition addresses key concepts from psychology which relate to education. It deals with a wide range of relevant issues affecting teachers and learners, cites many recent research studies and provides practical suggestions to improve learning outcomes.

Riding, R. (2002) *School Learning and Cognitive Styles.* London: David Fulton. Riding incorporates recent psychological developments on individual learning differences with practical classroom applications. These are central to the understanding of pupil differences and they affect our perception of how pupils can be helped to learn; why pupils find some aspects of their school work difficult; and why pupils behave as they do.

Wegerif, R., Li, L. and Kaufman, J. C. (eds) (2015) *The Routledge International Handbook of Research on Teaching Thinking.* Abingdon: Routledge. A comprehensive guide to research on teaching thinking, containing surveys and summaries of the latest international research on every aspect of teaching thinking in a range of contexts. Key topics include: approaches for teaching thinking; developing creative thinking; metacognition; and neuro-educational research on teaching thinking.

 Access the companion website to this book and find SAGE journal articles exploring this chapter topic in further detail: https://study.sagepub.com/bartlettburton4e.

CHAPTER 10

Social factors, gender, ethnicity and achievement

Chapter overview

This chapter explores the relationship between social factors and achievement in education. We have seen that factors such as intelligence and motivation are important in the success of individuals, but wider social influences are also highly significant. Research findings relating to class, ethnicity and gender are examined. The issue of equality of opportunity, which is so often taken for granted, is challenged. The assumption that schooling is one of the main determinants of a pupil's success is questioned in relation to the influence of wider social factors. The impact on education of discourses of class, gender and ethnicity is evaluated and current topical issues such as concerns about underachievement and school exclusion rates among specific groups are discussed.

Introduction

Social factors and their relationship to educational achievement remains a central concern of policy-makers. Perhaps the most significant and enduring achievement of recent studies in relation to social factors has been to put questions of class, culture, gender and ethnicity at the centre of descriptions of educational processes and systems.

A number of questions arise. How might the specific practices of education be exclusive and excluding? In what ways do the everyday activities of the classroom, for instance, alienate children from various different types of background? What is the general culture of the school? How can it be described? How does it affect children from different backgrounds? At the centre of these lines of inquiry is the big question about whether education is doomed to replicate the inequalities in society or whether it can be an engine for challenging inequality and for promoting social justice. This chapter examines these questions by reference to class, gender and ethnicity issues in education.

The state of educational achievement

According to official statistics from the DfE, overall educational achievement has increased steadily during the last two decades. End-of-key-stage assessment has shown increases in pupil attainment in the core subjects of English, mathematics and science. At every level of academic attainment more people hold qualifications and fewer people hold no qualifications. Over 90 per cent of 16 and 17 year olds are involved in education or training (www.education.gov.uk).

Educational achievement in higher education has also increased with the rapid expansion of HE since 1990. The Department for Business, Innovation and Skills (2014) statistics show that HE participation rates of English domiciled students climbed to over 45 per cent for three consecutive years prior to 2011/12. When fees increased in 2012/13 there was an initial reduction but this recovered to record levels of nearly 50 per cent participation in 2015 (www.hesa.ac.uk). It might seem that the benefits of educational qualifications and access to higher education have been made available to the population as a whole. There is some truth in this, although what the figures mean in terms of patterns of inequality in society in general needs to be closely examined. More education for all does not necessarily mean more equal education. There are issues to confront about the distribution of education resources and benefits throughout the population. Inequalities in provision and achievement exist between individuals for a host of complex reasons but also, significantly, between social groups and 'population categories'.

Pupils at different types of school achieve different levels of success in public examinations. Selective schools, whether in the private sector or the maintained sector, have much higher percentages of their pupils achieving top grades than non-selective schools, as one might expect. In addition, however, there are large, and fairly abiding, patterns of inequality associated with specific social groups. Social class, gender and ethnic group have been and remain key factors of inequality in education. The interaction between these three factors produces an even more powerful set of inequalities for many children.

Social class and achievement

Social class and economic background

Although social class is felt to be an important factor in educational achievement and has been on the 'agenda' of education studies for some time, it is not a category that is widely used in official statistics of education. This may perhaps be due to difficulties of defining social class or political sensitivities around not wishing to highlight social division (Wyness, 2015). It has also become unfashionable to consider traditional class categories.

Reader Reflection: Defining social class

Considering what you read in Chapter 3 on collecting research data.

Why do you think it is so difficult to use class as a category when measuring educational achievement?

Terms such as 'socio-economic status' (SES) and 'social advantage and disadvantage' are often used rather than class. Nevertheless, surveys which included class as a significant category have indicated that, by just about every criterion of achievement, middle-class pupils in maintained schools do better than working-class children. This imbalance was documented through a series of reports in the 1950s and 1960s when the question of class became a significant issue in education policy (Crowther Report, 1959; Gurney-Dixon Report, 1954; Newsom Report, 1963). These raised the issue of what kind of schooling was appropriate for a post-war democracy that created opportunities for all.

There has long been a relationship between wealth and education. In Victorian England the rich paid for the appropriate education of their sons as leaders and gentlemen at the expensive public schools. The poor and working class received little education at these times and what was given was largely provided by religious and capitalist benefactors in order to produce God-fearing, obedient and productive workers (see Chapter 4 for a history of the development of state schooling). Economic change led to the expansion of state education and greater social expectations of the people. This led to the liberal humanist view that Britain had become a meritocracy, in other words that achievement in society was based upon effort and ability rather than position and power. From the liberal perspective, education, while teaching us to live together, also offers the opportunity for individuals to develop in line with their ability and interests.

Studies of the earlier twentieth century pointed to the link between poverty and educational achievement (Halsey, 1978; 1995; 2013). It became clear that other social and cultural factors were linked to these economic conditions and these helped to explain why pupils from middle-class families continued to do better at school.

Although we may be tempted to assume that social change in the direction of equality has been significant, figures for Great Britain indicate that the link between social class, defined by parental occupation, and educational attainment remains strong. Goodman and Burton (2012) in a review of relevant literature, reported that national curriculum testing demonstrates that, by age seven, achievement gaps relating to socio-economic status, ethnicity and gender have *already* emerged. Such early gaps suggest that the factors that create and compound disadvantage begin to impact on a child's well-being and chances of educational success from a very early age, even before they start school. In a detailed study of the achievement gap in English primary school age children, Strand (2010) found that primary school pupils' performance on Key Stage 2 tests at age 11 in schools across the UK was substantially poorer for pupils entitled to free school meals, a common measure of socio-economic status, compared to non-FSM peers. The use of FSM actually underestimates the number of pupils in poverty as the figures only show those registered at the time and many pupils who are eligible do not apply or have left the register after being on it for much of their school career (Smith, 2012).

Gorard and Huat See (2013: 2) suggest that children start school with different levels of economic support and that they quickly display 'strong patterning of their attainment by family origin'. These same patterns are reflected at every subsequent stage of schooling and continue into post-compulsory education and then into opportunities for higher education. In an ethnographic study into white working-class achievement, Demie and Lewis (2011) suggest that this is the biggest underachieving group and that this problem has been masked by middle-class success in the education system. Smith and Smith (2014) note the lower educational performance in poor disadvantaged white neighbourhoods when compared to disadvantaged multicultural areas. While there are a number of factors combining to cause this low achievement, the main ones identified by Demie and Lewis were low aspirations of both parents and pupils combined with social deprivation.

Official figures (www.education.gov.uk) show that the gap in GCSE attainment levels by parental socio-economic group remains high. Also, 16 year olds with parents in higher professional occupations are more likely to remain in full-time education compared with those with parents in routine occupations. Similarly, participation in further or higher education is strongly influenced by people's social and economic background. Croll and Attwood (2013) suggest that this will only be altered with improved school performance of pupils from the lower socio-economic groups. The HE sector expanded significantly in the early 1990s so more places became available. Statistics do not distinguish between institutions of different status but Oxford and Cambridge remained socially powerful and there existed an important social distinction between so-called new universities that were previously polytechnics (prior to 1992) and the established universities. Mature students, those from low socio-economic backgrounds and those from minority ethnic groups have tended and continue to be concentrated in the newer post-1992 urban institutions (Tight, 2012). Hemsley-Brown (2015) found in her study of respondents with the same A level grades that those who had attended a private school were one and a half times more likely to attend a Russell Group (pre-1992) university than those who had attended a state-funded school.

Even though educational provision has expanded there remains a strong correlation between the type of education received, success in school, progression to university and parental occupation. Children of the upper and middle classes continue to do better in the education system. Whitty (2002) suggested that class differentials will only be overcome if policies that address wider economic inequalities are addressed in addition to changes to the education system. Reay (2013) says that middle- and upper-class parents 'heavily invest and constantly strategise to ensure that their children have a better chance of a fair chance than other peoples' children' (2013: 666). Thus middle-class parents have been able to use their understanding of education systems and their social skills to ensure that their children go to the 'best' schools and thereby benefit from educational advantage (see Chapter 6 on the effects of political policy on educational opportunity).

Reader Reflection: Inequality in achievement

Inequality in achievement was recognised by Michael Gove, when Secretary of State for Education, in the White Paper *The Importance of Teaching* in which he noted that:

> Children from poorer homes start behind their wealthier contemporaries when they arrive at school and during their educational journey they fall further and further back. The achievement gap between rich and poor widens at the beginning of primary school, gets worse by GCSE and is a yawning gulf by the time (far too few) sit A levels and apply to university. (DfE, 2010a: 7)

In what ways could you improve the achievement of those pupils from lower socio-economic groups in our society?

Can you foresee any difficulties in implementing such ideas?

In order to understand how these inequalities work in education it is helpful to consider some theoretical explanations of how social factors influence achievement.

Social theories of achievement

Social reproduction

Some theorists coming from a Marxist or social conflict perspective, such as Bourdieu and Passeron (1977) and Bowles and Gintis (1976), portrayed the education system as being one of several mechanisms of social reproduction. By this they meant the way in which those groups in the more privileged and powerful social positions maintain their place from generation to generation. Thus the social inequalities in society are constantly being reproduced over time. Social reproduction theorists considered the education system played a very important part in this process.

For Bowles and Gintis (1976) the education received corresponds to the future working environments that these pupils can expect and as such prepares young people to take their 'appropriate' place in society. The children of the wealthy go to private schools where they 'learn' how to be successful. Schools in poor areas with predominantly working-class intakes are more likely to suffer from teacher shortages or to be housed in poorer buildings. They tend to be low-attaining schools in terms of pupil achievements and most likely to be failing or put at risk by Ofsted in the current English education system. In schools where there is more of a social mix the middle-class pupils tend to be concentrated in the higher academic groups while the working-class pupils find themselves more likely to be placed in the lower teaching sets (Arnot and Reay, 2006; Parsons and Hallam, 2014). This reflects the future positions of pupils in society, which they come to see as 'normal' and expected as they replicate their positions within school.

How do pupils get separated onto different tracks like this? Officially they are grouped according to ability in order that they may be taught and learn more effectively. This grouping can begin at a very early stage in their school life with many primary schools in England, for instance, teaching pupils in ability groups for maths and English lessons (Hallam and Parsons, 2013). However, Bowles and Gintis (1976) suggested that actually there is often very little measurable difference between pupils initially and that they are grouped on the basis of very little evidence. In fact grouping can result as much from teacher perceptions as actual academic difference. The pupils who teachers perceive as more able or likely to do well in the future are those that display middle-class characteristics. As time goes on the difference between groups of pupils may be seen to widen and this is due to the increasing effects of being taught differently, experiencing differential teacher expectations and being offered different opportunities through the curriculum.

The 'hidden curriculum'

If the 'official' curriculum is considered to be what is formally taught in school through subjects on the timetable, the 'hidden curriculum' is all that is taught and learned unofficially through the process of schooling. This is often as significant for the individual pupil as the formal learning. Bowles and Gintis (1976) originally coined the term as a result of a major study in the USA in which they noted the prevalence of regulatory practices: uniform, time keeping, rowed seating in classrooms, rules for corridor movement, the countless injunctions to maintain order and so on. They point out the training in boredom represented by the majority of school time spent on passively being instructed or in actively performing tasks that have no obvious meaning or visible use. Effectively this is training in accepting relations of subordination, preparing the majority of pupils for a waged life working for a corporation or institution that will deploy similar tactics and practices for economic gain. What is fascinating is the similarities between the forms of control described in this study of 40 years ago and the rituals and routines that still prevail in schools today. A further form of control is exercised via the organisation of pupils into groups.

When pupils are put in different sets they are effectively being given a different 'value' depending upon whether they are in a top, middle or bottom group. Being placed in a high or low set is likely to be a very different experience for the individual pupil in terms of the enthusiasm and behaviour of their peers in the group, the attitude of the teachers, the type of work given and expectations of the amount and level of work they need to produce. The hidden curriculum message here is that pupils have a place in school (society) and the powers that be have mechanisms for keeping them in those places.

Finally, the hidden curriculum can be seen thriving within the apparently uncontrolled features of school life. Pupils learn how to survive on the corridors and in the toilets; they are aware of the pecking order that goes unnoticed by the official school system. There is a whole unofficial process of learning that these pupils go through. Thus school is good preparation for, and reflects, the communities that they will live in.

Social reproduction theory, then, demonstrates how the educational experiences of pupils correspond to their future employment. Schooling is in this way preparation for their future lives.

Cultural capital

Bourdieu and Passeron (1977) suggested that one main way in which education ensured the reproduction of society was by the passing on of cultural values from one generation to the next. Dominant culture is a set of properties, characteristics, behaviours, orientations that dominant class groups already have and that subordinate class groups must strive to acquire if they want to compete for educational success. As it is the dominant middle-class values that schools endorse it is the continued superior position of this group that is ensured. Middle-class children are already attuned to the codes and meanings of schooling, whereas for working-class children these are likely to be opaque.

Pupils who are used to these middle-class codes and 'live' them are able to take most advantage of the education system. Middle-class pupils are used, through their socialising experience as children in middle-class society, to conversing with adults in an appropriate manner. Middle-class children better understand how to speak, how to behave with books, how to sit at story-telling time and how to conduct themselves as good pupils in general. They have developed a wide, rich vocabulary, a social awareness and appropriate knowledge to a far greater degree than working-class pupils who have not had the same opportunities. Middle-class children are taught the importance of success at school for their future opportunities and have learned to practise deferred gratification at home (a belief that hard work now will lead to reward later) that is so important in creating this success. The whole process of schooling, as well as the institutional habits and demands, are likely to be much less amenable to working-class children's culture than to middle-class children's culture.

Social inequalities are not simply based on wealth. Bourdieu introduces the idea of cultural capital – the accumulation of cultural attributes that can be reinvested into education with a positive return for their holder. Bourdieu said that these attributes possessed by middle-class children help them to progress at school and give them an advantage over their working-class peers. Their cultural values are in effect an economic advantage to be realised in the future; they can be seen as a form of capital in the sense that an economist would use the term. They are cultural capital and of value to be invested in the same way as money is wealth to be invested for the future. As pupils progress through the various stages of schooling this cultural capital accumulates further and is ultimately high-value currency to trade for a well-paid, high-status role in society (Bourdieu and Passeron, 1977).

As Reay (2006) notes, contemporary theorists have been extensively influenced by the work of Bourdieu in developing new conceptualisations of class processes and practices that embrace the influence of everyday, largely unacknowledged social class practices. O'Donoghue (2012) for instance showed how working-class mothers were restricted in their ability to influence the schooling of their children as a result of their class position. Conversely Bathmaker et al. (2013) showed how middle-class students in HE were able to 'play the game' and use their social capital to enhance their future employment prospects by developing their personal profiles through securing attractive internships, involvement in sports clubs and other such voluntary and social activities.

Within such analyses class is seen as everywhere and nowhere, denied yet continually enacted, infusing the minutiae of everyday interactions while the privileged, for the most part, continue to either deny or ignore its relevance to lived experience. (Reay, 2006: 290)

Language

As language is such an important part of our means of communication the ability to use and understand language will be a significant factor in success in education. How we learn to read different genres and the range of vocabulary we develop will depend upon our exposure to different stimuli. This is particularly important in the early childhood years. The range of linguistic experience among children differs greatly, influenced largely by social background. Bernstein (1971; 1973) suggested that it was as though there are two different language codes in operation. The restricted code consists of short sentences with relatively simple words. This code gives basic description and relies on a tacit understanding of the area of conversation by all involved who make assumptions that are not verbalised. It relies on other communication apart from just verbal such as hand gestures and facial expressions. This is the sort of language that is used in brief everyday exchanges by everyone.

The elaborate code is, as the name implies, a much more sophisticated form of speech. It involves richer use of language with complex sentence construction and much more detailed explanation. This code does not rely on taken-for-granted assumptions or other non-verbal communication in transmitting the message. It is more applicable to polite social settings and gatherings. It may be portrayed as a more formal use of language. Due to its richness and more complex nature it is also more appropriate to formal learning situations. It is a form of language more familiar to the middle-class child who will have heard it in conversations between adults and also will have practised it with some of these adults as well as their own parents.

While being the formal language of the middle classes, the elaborate code is also the language used in school by teachers and textbooks. Pupils who are more used to hearing and using such language will not notice any difference in a school setting. Those pupils not used to such language and unable to use it feel less easy in the formal school learning situation, are unlikely to express themselves in the expected manner at school and are more likely to be perceived as less able generally by their teachers.

Bernstein suggested that working-class children were not used to hearing or using the elaborate code in their daily lives and so were at a disadvantage when they entered the formal learning environment of the primary school.

The use of the terms 'restricted' and 'elaborate' code imply that one form of speech is superior to another. Labov (1973) and Halliday (1979) make the case that different forms of speech may not necessarily be inferior but just different. It is the cultural dominance of standard forms that give middle-class pupils the advantage. In the USA, the question of language has consistently drawn much interest and analysis, especially in relation to the underachievement of large sections of the population, particularly African Americans who have consistently fared less well through state-funded education. Schools are constantly promoting linguistic norms but all pupils do not share these norms equally. Certain groups may actually have quite different linguistic norms as part of their upbringing or lived cultural heritage. This means that many children, black American children particularly, may experience the school as a linguistically and culturally alienating environment.

Rather than have their children and pupils suffer the kind of cultural negation that can come from being unrecognised by the official and unofficial language of the school, some activists adopted an alternative approach. They decided that the best way to ensure that the culture of the school was not alienating for the children from African American background was to use the language of black Americans, called 'Ebonics', as a medium of instruction. They took positive measures to celebrate the linguistic heritage of their charges and to teach the characteristics of Ebonics and draw comparisons with so-called standard English. Delpit (1995) and Smitherman (2000) have written about the need to make schools user-friendly, cultural, linguistic environments for African American pupils and have demonstrated how Ebonics may be used to effect changes in the rates of success for African American children in state schools. The Ebonics movement has been politically contentious, partly because it challenges the given order of things and partly because it has been misread as an attempt to offer a non-academic curriculum to African American children (Labov, 1997).

The Ebonics issue has many implications when examining the use of language in education, particularly concerning the school as a linguistic environment.

- It indicates the extent to which language is a significant factor in educational success and failure.
- It raises questions about the nature and social role of standard English in education, particularly in relation to practices of assessment.
- It highlights the tension between the cultures of pupils in schools and the culture expressed in the dominant practices of the school and the curriculum.

It is interesting to consider the development of the Ebonics movement in relation to the emergence of supplementary schools for black and ethnic minority youth in the UK. Parents uneasy about what they perceive to be the lack of achievement of their children in mainstream schooling have helped to establish these schools (see Maylor et al., 2013, for an evaluation of the impact of these schools on the achievement of ethnic minority pupils).

Labelling

Symbolic interactionists see individual existence as always being bounded and impinged on by external forces (see Chapter 2 for more details on this group of theorists). We are what we are by process rather than by fixed characteristics or identity. Identity is produced by the relation between your view of yourself and the way others view and react to you. Identity is always being worked on. It is in a state of flux and it may well vary considerably according to context. In addition, the institutions we inhabit impose social roles upon us like that of pupil or teacher. David Hargreaves' seminal study, *Social Relations in a Secondary School* (1967), indicates how the school effectively (and not always at a conscious level) defines pupils as conformist or non-conformist, successful or not successful. This sets up a dynamic of social relations that produces broadly differentiated subcultural groups in the pupil population. So pupils who find themselves being negatively defined in relation to the dominant values of the school in terms of behaviours, attitudes and academic work may themselves accept this definition. They may also transform it into a positive form of identity so that an alternative form of high status can be achieved by rule-breaking and general non-conformism. In *Deviance in Classrooms* (Hargreaves et al., 1975), factors such as appearance, attitudes to discipline, ability to work, 'likeability', relations with other pupils, personality and deviance rating were found to contribute to the way that teachers distinguish and define pupils.

Teachers 'size up' pupils using knowledge gained from their past experiences of teaching, for example whether a child is good, naughty, clever, low ability, a 'typical' boy or girl and so on, and then react appropriately to a range of classroom situations. Teachers will tend to apply a range of stereotypical experiences that will help them interpret each situation in order to decide how to act. The use of labels and stereotypes is like using an adaptable template to lay over social settings to aid understanding and guide actions. Pupils also need to make sense of classroom life and to find themselves a place in this social setting. They become quickly aware of the teacher's position in the classroom and how this varies from teacher to teacher. They will also make initial decisions about classmates. The decisions made by the teachers and pupils about all of those others in the classroom are initially provisional and open to change and negotiation but over time become clearer and more agreed.

Early on in classroom life certain behaviours, however casual, become noted and a label is attached to the 'actor'. It may be to do with such things as (lack of) intellectual ability, temperament, lack of concentration, poor attitude to school, 'coolness'. The label becomes reinforced if the appropriate behaviour is repeated, especially if other associated characteristics are also present, such as physical appearance of the pupil, how the pupil speaks to others, who the child's friends are, i.e. whether they are associated with a 'nice' or a rough crowd. The person being labelled is often not aware of a negative label that is being placed upon them until it has actually happened. Subsequent behaviour serves to reinforce the label and the expectations of others. Thus we expect naughty boys to behave badly, watch out for any signs of misbehaviour and punish it immediately. This may cause resentment and further difficult behaviour from these boys as they feel they are being picked on and treated differently from others. This surly response from them will further serve to confirm our opinion of their difficult behaviour and bad attitude. Any 'normal' behaviour by the boys, even if it takes up the majority of their time in the classroom, is unlikely to be noticed. We only really 'pick up' on behaviour that confirms the label. As labels become reinforced it becomes more difficult for the 'subject' to resist, escape, change or amend them, though not impossible.

Labelling theory suggests that as types get imposed upon pupils this affects their sense of themselves and their identity. In the long run this will influence their performance and potential to achieve. Labels will mean that others treat them according to their label. Certain pupils are 'policed' around the classroom and the whole school more than others as they are instantly recognised by other teachers and pupils. It then becomes even harder for these 'leopards to change their spots' and they will tend to develop a self-image that matches the label. They come to accept that they are 'not very good at school things'. Consider the following case study of how labelling works.

A case study of a group of pupils with learning difficulties

A number of reception class pupils, due to a range of reasons, do not initially take to reading and writing. As they move to Year 1 their classroom teacher identifies these pupils as needing extra support. In the classroom they are put in a group with other pupils who have been similarly identified as needing help and their table has a teaching assistant working with them for most of the time. Sometimes their whole table works with another teacher away from the rest of the class in a small room in what is called the special learning unit.

Their classmates soon see these pupils as different. They begin to be called names associated with low ability, are easily mocked by peers when they make mistakes and are laughed at when they express their opinions in class discussion. In a short time they become very unsure of themselves. They come to accept that they are not very clever at school and that most of their classmates are better than they are at everything. They stop volunteering for things and wish to be

(Continued)

(Continued)

left alone. They will begin to avoid writing, as this is where they can be further identified as fail-ures. Thus pupils become labelled and in the end behave in a way expected. For the pupils in this example the label will be reinforced as they do badly in each assessment throughout their school life and ultimately end up in the bottom sets in the secondary school. The difference between these pupils and those in the top sets will become greater over time.

The chance of being labelled and the ability to resist labels varies depending upon circumstances and also upon the social ability of the subject, or what we explained earlier as their cultural capital. Rist (1970), looking at interaction in American kin-dergartens, found that teachers quickly labelled and defined pupils as soon as they entered school and that the crucial factor in determining positive and negative identities was social class. Becker (1971), in researching school teachers and coun-cillors in Chicago, identified how they defined the 'ideal pupil' and how pupils from non-manual backgrounds most closely fitted this ideal whereas pupils from traditional working-class, manual backgrounds were furthest from it.

Middle-class pupils who are being naughty are more likely to be labelled high-spirited than disruptive pupils. They do not have the associated attributes of someone usually seen as disruptive or anti-school. It is more likely that other reasons for this behaviour will be identified and the problem can be 'solved'. However, once a label, such as lacking in ability, disruptive and naughty, has been assigned to a pupil it is difficult to resist. In fact the more a pupil reacts against sanctions and authority the stronger the label of 'problem pupil' becomes.

How pupils are labelled can also influence the learning opportunities made available to them. Smith (2001) explains that the labelling of African American boys in special education is influenced by a number of judgements. Access to knowledge by pupils depends on teachers' judgements about the ability of pupils to use knowledge and about their readiness. Social class has been found to be strongly influential in how teachers make judgements about pupils' relative 'abilities'. So it is that 'appropriate' knowledge is directed towards 'appropriate' pupils. Through a process of social construction pupils are classified and evaluated in schools.

Related to the labelling process, the concept of *self-fulfilling prophecy* indicates how the definitions that teachers make of pupils can powerfully influence how well they do and is a factor in determining their level of academic school success. Various studies have indicated how teachers react differently to pupils when given different types of information about them (Rosenthal and Jacobson, 1968).

Self-fulfilling prophecy

This concept was used by J. W. B. Douglas in his now classic study *The Home and the School* (1964) to describe the social process whereby working-class pupils came to underachieve. Douglas studied a sample of middle-class and working-class pupils and their progress through primary school.

There were material differences between middle- and working-class households that affected the schooling of the pupils noted by Douglas, such as the more overcrowded housing, fewer material possessions and poorer diet of many working-class pupils. He found that middle-class parents were more able to help their children achieve in the education system having been usually more successful themselves. They were able to 'push' their children and were more likely to contact the school and speak to the teachers about their children's progress. Working-class parents also wanted their children to do well at school but were less aware of how to achieve this. They were less confident when talking to the teachers about their children's progress, not having been successful at school themselves, and tended to ask more about their children's behaviour in lessons rather than academic progress. The teachers got to know their pupils quickly and formed expectations early on as to how well they could do. Douglas found that the teachers subconsciously expected more from the pupils with middle-class characteristics who, from their previous experience, were associated with success. It happened that it was these pupils that did in fact tend to do better. Douglas suggested that this could have been due to their ability and their better social circumstances but also to what he called a self-fulfilling prophecy.

This implied that if you expect students/pupils to do well then they will often fulfil expectations. This may be due to the teachers helping them and encouraging them more; also, the student may work harder because they believe they are able to do what others expect of them. Conversely, if you don't expect pupils to succeed, as a teacher you may not stretch them as much and will almost prepare them to do less well. As a pupil you will become resigned to others doing better than you. Douglas suggested that the expected low achievement of working-class pupils and the expected high achievement of middle-class pupils became effectively a self-fulfilling prophecy.

Reay claims that, despite government rhetoric on both sides of the Atlantic about equity, freedom and choice, very little progress has been made towards social justice and equality in education for the working classes over the past 100 years (2006: 304). She cites evidence from a number of studies that indicate that social class continues to exert a significant influence upon the educational achievement of pupils and students but has little impact on educational policy. Brown (2013) suggests that it is difficult for education to equalise life chances as it cannot compensate for wider social inequalities. We now turn our attention to gender, another important influence on educational achievement.

Gender and achievement

Sex and gender

Defining terms

It is important to first examine the terms 'sex' and 'gender' that are used to categorise and identify us all. Sex refers to our biological make-up. It identifies us as male or female. Biological differences include chromosomes, hormones and physical sexual characteristics such as sexual organs, body hair, physique, etc. Gender refers to the social construction of masculine and feminine. It is what we expect males and females to be 'like' in terms of behaviour, appearance, beliefs and attitudes. There has been a continuing debate as to how much of our maleness and femaleness is biologically determined and how much is socially constructed.

A biological determinist or essentialist position purports that, even though we are subject to social constraints, it is our biological make-up that plays the major part in determining who we are and how we behave. This viewpoint suggests that even in modern industrial societies our biological sex still to a large extent determines our behaviour, so that the two sexes relate to each other in a way that maintains human survival. The functionalist perspective of some early sociologists such as Parsons (1959) and Davis and Moore (1967), while exploring the influence of cultural factors on the development of societies, still have a biological underpinning to their theories. The family was seen as a functional prerequisite to the maintenance of any society and the conjugal roles of the male breadwinner and the female homemaker/child-rearer are presented as being the most appropriate. Though alternatives are seen as possible, there is a view promulgated by these functionalists that the 'normal' roles of men and women, with their biological basis, provide the best 'fit' for any kind of society. So, while in some, often traditional, communities these sociologists could point to large extended families and in others, usually modern industrial societies, to nuclear families, the role of women is seen essentially as domestically based in both.

The physical differences between males and females, while less apparent in young children, become more obvious as we grow up and move through adolescence and into adulthood. However, there is a wide variation both within and across the genders in terms of individual physical characteristics. What is deemed as attractive to the opposite sex is different from society to society and changes over time with fashion. Clothing, diet and body building/reducing exercises to change our appearance are all used and with advances in medical science people can radically alter their physical characteristics and even biological sex. In modern societies and across a range of cultures any presentation of a clear uncomplicated sexual divide would constitute an oversimplification.

Differentiating between notions of sex and gender became more important when early feminist writers such as Oakley (1975) wished to highlight the significance of cultural as opposed to biological factors in explaining the ongoing socially inferior position of women in society. Their argument was that although there are biological differences between the sexes, it was social constructions of gender and sexuality that led to the oppression of women. The biological arguments were seen as part of the male hegemony that perpetuated the myth of male superiority. The whole notion of masculinity and femininity could be seen to be socially rather than biologically determined and could thus be challenged. What still remains unclear is the dividing line between biological and social influences on an individual's gender construction.

Influences upon the creation of gender

If we were to consider different societies in history and around the world we see many differences in gender roles. In her now classic anthropological account, Mead (1935) found great variation in the roles of men and women in a study of three tribes in New Guinea. In one tribe both men and women were gentle and submissive with little clear division between the sexes while in another men were more aggressive with women being more submissive. In the third, women were more involved in leadership of the group and were more aggressive whereas the males were responsible for domestic tasks, were more 'fussy' about their appearance and tended to gossip. For Mead this illustrated the significance of social expectations upon male and female behaviour.

The representation of gender as a binary split between masculine and feminine makes them appear as opposites with everyone falling either side of the sexual binary line. In this way stereotypes of male and female can be presented as diametrically opposed, for example male versus female, hard versus soft, rational versus emotional. Kehily (2001) suggests that the dualist creation of gender by society can have a direct bearing on our sexuality and sexual identity. Thus from birth we begin to be male or female and to be mistaken for being of the opposite sex from that with which you identify is a significant concern as we seek to maintain our self-identity.

Gender characteristics that stereotype appropriate physical appearance and behaviour can cause pressure to conform, particularly on young people who are coming to terms with themselves as they develop. To be identified as different or 'other' can have a significant effect upon the self-image of young people. Smith and Chambers (2015) examine the issues of sexuality in school and how identities are negotiated and created. Pupil interaction and perceptions are significant in the 'othering' process. Labels become attached to pupils and some are more difficult to resist or counter than others. Language plays a very powerful part in this process and use of sexual insults such as 'gay' or 'slag' have lasting repercussions on the identities, future interactions and sexual behaviour of the young people involved. Use of such terms, while causing conformity among many for fear of being seen as different, may actually serve to distance and create outsiders of others. Vicars (2006) drew upon autobiographical accounts to show the implications of being identified as 'queer' within schools and the effects of homophobic language on such pupils. Guasp (2012) reported that over half of lesbian, gay and bisexual young people have experienced homophobic bullying at school.

Masculinities and femininities

If we carefully examine groups of young people and consider the broad range that exists in terms of behaviour, beliefs, values, preferred appearance, etc. we see that it becomes difficult to place them all into too rigid a definition of what constitutes female or male behaviour. The majority of boys are not disruptive in the classroom and all girls do not get on with their work quietly. For this reason some writers, such as Swain (2004) and Connell (2006), speak of masculinities and femininities that allow for greater variation. Paechter (2006) suggests that as children grow older, they move through successive overlapping communities as they develop their understanding of what it means to be an adult man or woman. Swain says that pupils live within the context of their own communities and that these wider contexts influence the local school policies.

> Each school has its own *gender regime* which consists of . . . individual personnel expectations, rules, routines and a hierarchical ordering of particular practices. (2004: 182)

Although there is a great deal of commonality between schools there is also variation. Harber (2014: 162) suggests that while there are many forms of masculinity there are some 'dominant or hegemonic forms of male identity internationally which have traditionally preserved patriarchal power and privilege'. These promote perceptions and so reinforce realities of male dominance and female subordination in many societies.

Marshall (2014) points out that many girls in the developing world face significant barriers in accessing education resulting from traditional cultural beliefs linked at the same time to economic poverty. Key factors adversely affecting girls are things such as boy's education being more valued, girls being kept at home for household chores, married at a young age and being perceived as having a home-based future and not worth educating. In some regions girls report violence and sexual harassment on the way to and from school and also in school and so are more likely to stay at home. For such reasons Marshall (2014) suggests that girls in various geographical areas are unlikely to receive an education equivalent to boys and in some cases any significant formal education at all. However, Harber (2014) does note that in a number of areas, Honduras for example, it is the boys who are more likely to drop out of school as they are needed to earn a wage to supplement the family income while girls are not expected to work outside the home. Once again poverty is a key factor in influencing gender and schooling.

Reader Reflection: Gender in school life

Since schools are a key part of the wider socialisation process, they both influence and are influenced by gender relationships (Liu, 2006; Mellor and Epstein, 2006).

Consider the integral part that gender relationships play in school life and how these vary depending upon the ethos of the school.

Policy approaches to gender differences

Historical developments in gender relations and the schooling of boys and girls

The roles of men and women and their relationships are not fixed and have varied over time. This can be illustrated by considering the comparatively short period from Victorian England to the present day. In the early 1800s Britain was very much a patriarchal society. Women were not able to vote, own property or obtain a divorce. Within the middle classes it was considered essential for a young woman to marry so they effectively moved from being controlled by their father to being controlled by their husband. It was men who governed the empire and the society; men ran businesses and supported the family. Women did not work and were confined to a life that revolved around the home. Boys from the more affluent classes would be educated at public and grammar schools but the education of girls would be primarily left to governesses, would be conducted in the home and would revolve around acquiring the skills and knowledge suitable for a lady. For the working classes life was much harder and both men and women worked, though women did the more menial factory work and were paid less than men. In the early educational provision for the working classes girls were able to attend school as well as boys, with each taught according to the social expectations of the time.

It took years of pressure and steady change in social attitudes for women to achieve legal equality with men. They gained the right to divorce and, importantly, to retain their own property upon divorce. After years of campaigning, women were enfranchised in 1918 for those over 30 but not on equal age terms with men until 1928. For many years to come it was still legally possible to discriminate in terms of gender. Women could be paid less than men for the same job and it was possible to refuse someone employment because they were female and therefore considered unsuitable. It was also possible to refuse entry to social gatherings on gender grounds so many public houses had male-only bars where women were only allowed at the weekends. Remarkably, it was not until the Sex Discrimination Act of 1975 that discrimination on gender grounds was outlawed.

From this date women, legally at least, had equality with men. However, there were still economic and social differences that were strongly influenced by gender. It was still largely accepted that a woman's place was really in the home and that the man was the breadwinner. In this way women's employment was largely seen as a temporary occupation before they raised children or as a way of supplementing the main income of the husband when the children were older. In employment terms women remained very under-represented in many, usually more highly paid, professions and the average earnings of women remained well below those of men. The term 'glass ceiling' was coined to illustrate the invisible but powerful constraints upon the progression of women upwards in society. Until relatively recently, it has actually been very difficult for women to 'break into' male dominated areas such as medicine, law and engineering and even now reports of pay and promotion differentials still exist at the highest levels of organisations with women still under-represented in the top posts and on boards of directors. Changes in attitude, employment rights, maternity and paternity leave have gradually made it more possible for a woman to pursue her career and have children and more men are now employed in occupations that were previously considered suitable for women only, such as nursing. However, while there has been a change in social attitudes and lifestyles, it is still not a level playing field. Women's average earnings still lag behind those of men and in many households women still undertake most of the domestic chores despite having full-time jobs.

Social and political attitudes are reflected in education. State education has been provided since the end of the nineteenth century to all pupils regardless of gender. The introduction of the tripartite system saw the development of single-sex grammar schools and often, though not always, single-sex secondary modern schools. It was the development of new large comprehensive schools from the 1960s onwards that saw boys and girls taught together for their secondary education. However, being taught in the same school did not necessarily mean that they had equal opportunity or that gender did not have a significant effect upon a pupil's experiences. This was the time when the women's liberation movement was highlighting gender inequality in society. These inequalities were reflected in the classroom where teachers, peers and parents treated boys and girls very differently. At that time it was not considered politically incorrect to have gender-specific stereotypical expectations of pupils so curricular activities were unashamedly contrived around them, for example needlework for girls and metalwork for boys.

In the 1970s and 1980s much feminist research in education was concerned with the perceived underachievement of girls and how the education process worked to maintain this through discrimination and marginalisation. The gender differences were maintained and highlighted through the processes of schooling that involved the separation of the genders, differences in uniform, a gender-specific curriculum and differential expectations of behaviour. This was further enforced through the attitude of teachers, peers, parents and later their – usually male – employers. Feminist researchers were interested to show how the ambitions of female students remained low and how they were discouraged in a variety of ways from choosing the 'hard' mathematical and scientific subjects so important to future employment prospects in favour of the more 'feminine' arts and humanities.

Oakley (1975) looked at the socialisation of young children and how they acquired their gender roles from home, school and peers. Children learn gender expectations from the society around them and these lessons are reinforced through play. Whyte (1983) looked at gender stereotyping and bias in the primary school curriculum. This was displayed through reading schemes and lesson content that emphasised the different positions of men and women in society. Sharpe (1976) considered the influence of gender stereotypes in secondary schools and how this encouraged teenage girls to behave in 'feminine' ways and to develop gendered career aspirations. Spender (1982) investigated interaction in the classroom, language and the curriculum. She noted the marginal position of girls in the classroom and the message this gave about their future roles in society. Interestingly, Francis (2010) has more recently shown how toys and other resources available to children are still a significant part of the gendering process.

Curriculum changes

Strategies were developed to make the curriculum more girl-friendly in response to such concerns and there have been many initiatives designed to raise the achievement of girls by raising awareness, altering attitudes and increasing ambition. Consideration was given to the curriculum and teaching methods. A seminal example is the Girls into Science and Technology Project (GIST), a four-year project from 1979 to 1983 that investigated the reasons for girls' underachievement in science and technology and encouraged teachers to develop classroom strategies to change this. Similarly, Genderwatch was a practical evaluation pack that enabled teachers to monitor gender in all areas of school life with a view to raising awareness and taking positive anti-discriminatory action (Myers, 1987; updated version, *Genderwatch – Still Watching*, Myers at al., 2007). These initiatives tended to be individual rather than coordinated and although they could be said to have worked for many, mainly middle-class, girls, they may have provoked a male backlash.

This raising of awareness and development work was based on the underachievement of girls relative to boys but the actual figures show that the reality was not that straightforward. Even in the 1970s girls were outperforming boys in English and modern foreign languages. Also, more girls were achieving five or more O level passes (equivalent to A*–C GCSE) than boys. However, because these included subjects that were seen as low status such as home economics and because boys were doing better at maths and sciences regarded as 'hard' subjects of high status, girls were perceived as underachieving. Also, it should be noted that the tripartite system, in operation before the widespread development of the comprehensive system, had favoured boys due to the larger number of places available in boys' grammar schools as opposed to those admitting girls. Thus boys did not need to score as highly as girls in the 11-plus to secure a grammar school education.

The Conservative government came to power in 1979 emphasising competition, individual achievement and success. The Tories did not trust the liberal education establishment and sought to reform the education system. While not being particularly concerned with the promotion of equal opportunities, one of their reforms, the introduction of the national curriculum, had what is now often regarded as a significant impact on the achievements of girls. From its inception all pupils were required to take the whole curriculum so it was no longer possible for boys or girls to 'drop' some subjects in favour of others.

The league tables of GCSE and A level results, introduced by the Conservatives to judge overall school performance, made the achievements of boys and girls more transparent than ever. Over the years these tables have shown how the performance of both boys and girls has steadily improved but girls' improvement has outstripped that of boys. While continuing to outperform boys in language subjects, girls have caught up with boys in maths and the sciences so policy concern now focuses on the performance of boys.

Reader Reflection: International focus on gender differences

Go to the PISA website (www.oecd.org/pisa/keyfindings/pisa-2012-results.htm).
   Read the country specific overviews for the UK and three other countries such as Brazil, Germany and Norway. Compare the gender differences in maths, reading and science for the four countries.

   How does the UK compare to this wider international picture?

Relationship between gender and achievement

Explanations for boys' achievements

Since the late 1990s we have shifted from debates about equal opportunities and improving the educational experiences of girls to those concerning notions of underachievement and male disadvantage (Bartlett and Burton, 2015). Moral panic developed over boys' underachievement, particularly in the popular press. This was perhaps rather an over-reaction. After all, overall results of both boys and girls improved. Girls' improvement has been greater but not by a great deal. The media portrayed boys as falling behind and homed in on the apparent growth of a 'laddish' culture among teenage boys that is anti-study, against school values and leads to underachievement.

   Various reasons have been offered to explain why girls are performing better than boys, with the motivations, attitudes and performance of boys particularly highlighted. Current DfE figures (www.gov www.gov.uk/government/statistics/gcse-and-equivalent-attainment-by-pupil-characteristics-2014) of GCSE performance show that girls attain a higher percentage of five or more passes at A*–C than boys. They outperform boys in the majority of subjects, the gap being particularly noticeable in English language. There is, however, little statistical difference between the performance of boys and girls in the areas of maths and science. At A level, pass rates and grades are comparable for boys and girls but what still remains significant is that, apart from biology, far fewer girls are taking the STEM subjects than boys.

   Along with the increasing number of students taking A levels, higher education has expanded since the mid 1980s and become more accessible to a wider proportion of the population. As the number of students has steadily increased women now make up the largest proportion of those studying for both undergraduate and postgraduate degrees. In 2013/14 women made up 54.7 per cent of full time undergraduate students (HESA, 2015), a significant change from when university study was largely the preserve of a minority of privileged males. Women entrants now outnumber men in the majority of undergraduate courses including medicine and dentistry, subject areas previously dominated by males. However men remain over-represented in most STEM subjects, most notably engineering. Adams (2015) suggests that the success of female applicants into higher education mirrors the trend at GCSE and A-level, with girls performing well but still being under-represented in the STEM subjects. Thus, while this expanding education participation creates the possibility of wider career access for women, this is still not the case in areas such as construction and engineering that require high level qualifications in the STEM subjects. Even with the comparable academic performance of females gender may still be having an impact upon behaviour, subject and ultimately career choices. Francis et al. (2014) noted that many students, male and female, still tended to use stereotypical constructions of gender difference even while rejecting the notion that gender and other structural differences impact upon their experiences.

Genetic differences

In previous times it has been the assumption, due to male hegemony, that women were the weaker inferior sex and needed to be protected. This was considered to be in all aspects, not just muscular strength. It is interesting that the consistently higher level of achievement by girls academically can now lead us to the conclusion that this is due to genetic differences, i.e. the intellectual superiority of women. However, we know of no neurological evidence to suggest that boys' cognitive processing approaches or ways of learning are any different from girls', or that any particular learning or thinking styles could be gender specific. In fact DCSF (2009b) suggests that any learning preferences that are gendered are likely to be due to social rather than biological pressures. Feminist analysts would suggest that the 'moral panic' that has accompanied this perceived failure of boys and the demand to rectify the situation is a reflection of the fear within the male-dominated political establishment that there may be some basis to the genetics argument.

Changes in society and the masculine image

There have in recent decades been enormous changes in the economy that have had repercussions on how people earn their living, the organisation of the family and the amount of leisure time and disposable income available. The traditional occupations based upon heavy industry, dominated by male workers, which involved strength and training in traditional skills have disappeared. This has had significant effects upon communities based around these industries such as mining, shipbuilding, steel and deep-sea fishing. Newer forms of employment are service based and seen as being more traditionally female. The male is no longer the only, or even the major, breadwinner. Thus the traditional masculine image in working-class communities is no longer applicable as it was even 20 years ago.

It is suggested that, while many families have more leisure time with more disposable income to spend upon home luxuries, holidays, clothes, etc. and women play more of an active role in society, many working-class boys see no particular role for themselves. They see no need to work hard at school as it will make little difference to their future. At the same time these boys emphasise and play out their masculinities at school where it is important to be seen as 'hard', 'cool', not a 'poof' or a 'swot' (Ward, 2014a). Francis (2009) and Ward (2014a) looked at how high achievement can be stigmatised by pupils through the assigning of labels such as 'boffin' or 'geek'. This can affect all pupils but boys are particularly prone to marginalisation through such bullying behaviour. Of course it can be argued that working-class boys could always get labouring jobs in the past and so have never really had reason to work hard at school. Skelton et al. (2010) suggest that girls can also experience tensions between achieving in education and general perceptions of what it means to be a 'proper girl'. Perhaps, as Connolly suggests, forms of masculinities and femininities that exist are not just about gender alone but are combinations with social class and ethnicity that 'produce differing and enduring forms of identity' (2006: 15).

School culture

It is suggested that the school culture works against the achievement of boys and in favour of girls (Smith, 2012, and Stahl and Dale, 2013 discuss these arguments). There are a number of strands to this point of view.

- It is assumed that assessment regimes have developed to favour girls with more emphasis on coursework rather than final exams. However, this trend has reversed in recent years with no significant falling back of girls' performance.
- The curriculum is said to favour girls with little to excite boys but this point ignores the many areas of the curriculum where the content has been specifically chosen to attract boys. DCSF (2009b) suggested that there is no evidence that the content of the secondary curriculum reflects particularly gendered interests. Changing the curriculum to make it boy-friendly appears to have little effect on boy's achievements; in fact such changes may involve gender stereotyping that could actually limit the choices that boys and girls make (Keddie and Mills, 2008).
- It is argued that boys prefer a more competitive environment than exists in schools. DCSF (2009b) again suggests that this is a myth. In fact, if they are not succeeding, an emphasis on competition may actually be counter-productive. It also appears to be a fallacy that introducing single-sex classes is a way to improve achievement in secondary schools. While, in some cases, single-sex

classes may benefit girls, the evidence for boys is much more mixed. Carrington and McPhee (2008) note that the evidence for the introduction of more male teachers in primary education in order to raise boys' motivation remains inconclusive while McGrath and Sinclair (2013) suggest that more male teachers in primary schools may be something that benefits girls as well as boys.

Reader Reflection: Theoretical understandings of differential achievement

After reading about the achievements of girls and boys, how helpful are the concepts of self-fulfilling prophecy and labelling in explaining differential achievement in terms of gender?

In summarising the arguments concerning gender and achievement at GCSE we can say that the performance of boys and girls overall has improved since the 1990s, that girls outperform boys in many subjects and are at least performing more or less equally in all. However, to portray girls as achieving and boys as underachieving is too simplistic a view (Bartlett and Burton, 2015; DCSF, 2009b; Richards and Posnett, 2012). It should be noted that the differences in overall performance of boys and girls are not that great. It is the improvement in performance of girls from the more middle-class backgrounds in all subjects that has caused the rise in girls' performance overall. Boys from middle-class backgrounds continue to generally perform well. Boys and girls from the lower socio-economic groups continue to underperform when compared to their more affluent peers. The interrelationships of gender, social class and ethnicity continue to present a complex picture of pupil achievement (Skelton et al., 2010).

Ethnicity and achievement

'Race' and ethnicity

A further social factor that influences educational achievement is that of 'race' or ethnicity. Bloch and Solomos (2010: 5) suggest that:

> Over the past decade or so the shifting boundaries of race and ethnicity as categories of social analysis have become ever more evident . . . In this environment ideas about race, racism and ethnicity have become the subject of

intense debate and controversy. Yet it is paradoxically the case that there is still much confusion about what it is that we mean by such notions, as evidenced by the range of terminological debates that have tended to dominate much discussion in recent years.

'Race'

'Race' is a form of classification whereby individuals are grouped according to certain genetically inherited physical characteristics. People are categorised by 'racial' groupings in matter-of-fact ways and in daily conversation the term 'race' is applied as though the labels given are straightforward. However, apart from being a socially loaded concept, the use of 'race' as a means of categorisation is fraught with problems.

Using the term 'race' assumes the existence of a number of clear physical 'types' into which all humans fall. It is these inherited physical characteristics that are then used to identify the races to which people(s) belong; skin colour, hair type and body shape are used to define 'race'. The concept of 'race' portrays certain groups of people as naturally different and represents a biologically determinist view of human development. It creates a justification for not treating 'them' the same as 'us' or not feeling guilty about such different treatments. Implicit in theories of 'race' is often an unstated belief that certain mental as well as physical characteristics can also be attributed to 'racial' groups.

Racial classification came to the fore as European powers expanded their colonial empires. The Victorian English (British?) ruled many parts of the globe, convincing themselves it was because of their *supposed* British national characteristics, moral fibre and racial superiority. In effect the empire was seen as the natural order of things. The colonists had a duty to guide and care for *their* colonial peoples whom they regarded as inferior. This idea of 'racial' superiority has been used to justify the inhumane treatment and physical domination of one group over others throughout history. Consider how past empires have maintained their power over and treated their conquered peoples, for example the Roman, British, Spanish and Portuguese empires, the apartheid system in South Africa or Hitler's Germany.

Reader Reflection: Racial stereotypes

Throughout history theories of 'racial' difference, with the implication of superiority of one 'racial' group over another (eugenics), have been espoused. Jensen (1973), for example, theorised about the difference in IQ of black and white Americans.

(Continued)

(Continued)

Eysenck (1971) looked at differences between traits, physical and intellectual, of different racial groups. However, these theories failed to take into account social factors that led to differences in educational achievement, for instance sporting success was used as a major route out of poverty for black youth in educational regimes that assumed they were intellectually inferior. The same value was not placed on sporting prowess so black people were not fighting against the label they had been assigned by succeeding in sport. This, in turn, fed the stereotype that black people are good at sport.

How powerful do you think racial stereotypes are today in influencing people's attitudes and behaviour by comparison with the past?

While 'race' was used as a means of social categorisation, scientists down the years have been unable to establish a clear biological basis to the concept. Creating lists of 'races' proved impossible because mutually exclusive characteristics could not be identified. Even grouping everyone into one of three broad groups of Caucasoid, Negroid and Mongoloid proved problematic. Any physical characteristics identified are never totally exclusive to a single group. Whatever categorisation for 'race' is used there is both a range of differences within each group and at the same time overlap between the categories. Thus the idea of 'race' is effectively a social construction based on prejudiced stereotypes. For that reason many writers, when they use it, put the term 'race' in inverted commas as we do in this text.

Ethnicity

Rather than 'race', the terms 'ethnic group' or 'ethnic minority' are now more frequently used with 'ethnic minorities' referring to all groups making up the overall minority. The term 'ethnicity' includes cultural and religious beliefs as well as physical similarities and so is felt to be a more appropriate term that is adaptable to social as well as physical variations. Tizard and Phoenix (2001: 128) suggest that

> ethnicity refers to a collectivity or community that makes assumptions about shared common attributes to do with cultural practices and shared history.

As such they suggest that it is largely 'insider' defined. However, both of the terms 'race' and 'ethnic group' can be seen as social constructions whose meaning and applications change over time. They are often used as a means of boundary maintenance (Anthias and Yuval-Davis, 1992) and to categorise and emphasise the differences between groups of people (Stanley, 2015). The terms 'race' or 'ethnicity' should be seen as being used and evolving within the economic, political and social power relationships of any society at the time.

Confusion is maintained by the use of a range of racially/racist-based terms in any documentation or analysis. A range of people(s) from many different origins are included, or conversely excluded, when categories such as 'Asian' are created. The same can be said of the use of the term 'black', which can be used to include African, African-Caribbean and sometimes Asian. What many official monitoring documents now encourage is self-categorisation whereby they include a wide range of categories and allow people to place themselves in the one they feel they belong to or even to add a relevant category for themselves.

Migration

Human history is one of continuous migration around the globe driven by a variety of causes – wars, trade, employment, escape from natural disasters such as flood, famine, earthquake, etc. The history of the British Isles certainly reflects this world picture with population movements of those born within the islands, both voluntary and forced, from rural areas to towns and cities and also away into other parts of the world; peoples that have arrived as conquerors from the northern Scandinavian countries, Rome and France; and refugees fleeing political and economic persecution such as the Huguenots, Jews, Poles, Hungarians and Irish. Post-Second World War Britain, until recently, has largely been in an official position of net emigration, with more people leaving the country to live than entering. There was immigration from the Caribbean in the 1950s and 1960s and from India, Pakistan and Bangladesh in the 1960s and 1970s. More recently there has been immigration from parts of Africa, Eastern Europe and the Near East driven by the linked forces of political instability and global economic pressures.

Gundara (2000) points out that although these communities and groups share common experiences of racism and have often struggled against this in similar ways, sometimes coming together in this process, they are very different communities and their diversity must be realised. Indian, Pakistani and Bangladeshi communities are often classified as Asian and so regarded as the same by a frosty white majority but they are very different in culture, religion, language and economic circumstances. Furthermore, the younger generations within these communities are, like all adolescents, adapting; developing their own ambitions, lifestyles and leisure pursuits that at times cause conflict with their parents. They face the same conflicts as the majority of youth, striving for independence from their family, but with the added complexity of needing the support and solidarity of their traditional communities in the face of racism. Gundara, in talking about multiple identities, suggests that black youth are engaged in defining themselves in the context of dominant British identity as well as their identity as Black persons in Britain. (2000: 44)

The ethnic make-up of Britain has changed throughout its history and continues to do so, rendering it an impossible task to identify a British culture. It also makes the use of the term 'ethnic' unsafe in any more than a very general sense.

Policy approaches to combating racism

Gillborn (2008), while warning against the dangers of making over simplistic generalisations, expanded on an earlier typology of Tomlinson (1977) to show the recent history of policy on race since the Second World War. He divided the period up into eight policy phases:

1. Ignorance and neglect (1945 to late 1950s)
2. Assimilation (late 1950s to mid-1960s)
3. Integration (mid-1960s to late 1970s)
4. Cultural pluralism and multiculturalism (late 1970s to late 1980s)
5. Thatcherism: the new racism and colour-blind policy (mid-1980s to 1997)
6. Naive multiculturalism: New Labour and the Blairite project (1997 to 2001)
7. Cynical multiculturalism: from 9/11 to 7/7 (2001 to 2005)
8. Aggressive majoritarianism (2005 onwards)

Ignorance, assimilation and integration

In the period of ignorance and neglect the official response to migration from the Caribbean and Indian subcontinent was to ignore it and do nothing. By default this was supporting the traditional colonialist views on racial inequality. The assumption was immigrants would do menial, low-paid work that reflected their racial status.

The late 1950s to the mid-1960s was a period of assimilation followed by integration (mid-1960s to late 1970s). During the first part of this period it was assumed that any immigrants would become part of British society. It was expected that 'they' would dress, talk and live like 'us' and over time would become assimilated into British life. This was very much perceived as a one-way process of 'them' becoming more like 'us' (Modood, 2014). 'Racial incidents' were presented as part of a 'colour problem', i.e. the failure of 'coloured' people to fully assimilate. Clearly any issues were seen as emanating from the minority group and not the white majority whose home this had always been. The integrationists realised the impracticality of this policy and that differences in appearance could not be eradicated just by making migrant groups conform in social behaviour terms. They emphasised equal opportunity and began to call for more tolerance of cultural diversity. It is worth noting that the Race Relations Act was passed in 1976 outlawing discrimination on the basis of 'race'.

Multicultural education

The multiculturalism and anti-racist phase (late 1970s to late 1980s) arose during a period of social unrest when ethnic minority groups protested more openly about the social and economic oppression they faced – high unemployment, poor housing, lack of opportunity. The resistance of ethnic minority youth grew in the form of difficult and disruptive behaviour at school, increasing truancy and disturbance on the streets. The result, in the summer of 1981, was a period of significant rioting in a number of urban centres such as Handsworth in Birmingham and Toxteth in Liverpool.

In response to this growing urban unrest and based on the initial findings in the Rampton Report (DES, 1981), the Conservative government set up the Swann Commission. The Swann Report (DES, 1985b) stressed the pluralistic make-up of British society. This was seen as a strength and the cultural richness it brought needed to be recognised as leading to a vibrant developing society. However, the report also pointed to the inequality and prejudice that minority groups faced in all areas of their lives. Swann felt that, if not addressed, this inequality would lead to greater tension and civil unrest. The report wanted racism in all its guises to be addressed but particularly what it called institutional racism. This, it stated, was where the official institutions in society, such as the education system, the health service and the police, operate in a way that automatically discriminates against and disadvantages certain groups. The procedures and processes of such institutions needed to be monitored carefully for such practices. The Swann Report also stated that racism should not be seen as primarily a minority issue but rather a white problem. It was members of the white majority who were engaged in racism and discriminatory practices. It was this group that needed to be educated. Swann made the point that education about and against racism was as, if not more, important in areas that were predominantly white.

The report itself was largely ignored politically in favour of a bland summary accompanying it by Lord Swann that failed to draw attention to the issues of racism raised in the actual report. This summary caused a split among different groups involved in writing the report. It was felt by some that Lord Swann had been influenced by the Conservative government of the day, which was seeking to avoid criticism. However, the sentiments of the actual Swann Commission could be seen in the notion of multicultural education that grew in schools and LEAs across Britain.

Multicultural education involved understanding and celebrating difference through education. Thus diversity was reflected in the curriculum by educating about different cultures through, for example, awareness of different forms of music, religious ceremonies and beliefs, languages and diet. This approach also involved the scrutinising of classroom texts to make them more representative. However, although regarded as a move forward from assimilationism, the multi-cultural approach has been criticised for being condescending. Multicultural programmes came to be seen as naive and inadequate, largely in terms of how they ignored institutional racism in education (Williams, 1981). Some even suggested multiculturalism was itself racist and a cause of disaffection (Mullard, 1981). It was argued that multiculturalism was nothing more than a form of social control, a misguided form of tokenism designed to integrate rather than to enable serious cultural differences to be properly expressed. In spite of these protests, multicul-turalism remained (and remains) a position adopted by institutions at different levels of the education system.

Anti-racist education

The anti-racist movement, whose proponents believed that a more active stance needed to be taken to oppose racism, took a more radical approach. Racist atti-tudes needed to be vigorously opposed and policies that emphasised a belief in equality of opportunity clearly and forcefully stated. This approach was adopted by a number of LEAs and local authorities and became associated with left-wing administrations that were targeted for attack by the Conservative government in the 1980s. Consequently, it soon became discredited as extremist.

The Conservative governments of Thatcher and later John Major (1979–97) emphasised individualism and the use of the market as a means to economic and social success. At the same time there was a resurgence in emphasis on national identity, seen clearly in the international conflict in the Falklands, and reaction against perceived high levels of immigration that were changing the 'British' way of life.

It was in the late 1980s and early 1990s that the national curriculum was introduced along with policies that encouraged parents' choice of school for their children. While the rhetoric was one of raising standards, Gillborn (2001) noted that this was a 'colour-blind' reform taking no account of ethnic diversity. Differences in culture and language were not considered when imposing a rigid curriculum for all. The assumption that curriculum content was 'neutral' hid the bias towards traditional white British values. This can be seen when examining the content of the history, literature and modern foreign language (only European languages were considered as appropriate at this time) parts of the national curriculum programmes. Not only were ethnic minority pupils not reflected in the curriculum they were taught, they were further alienated by a rigid testing regime that took no account of language differences. Gillborn (2001) suggests that by stressing individualism, the market and choice, 'race' inequalities were effectively 'removed from the agenda'.

Naive multiculturalism

From 1997 to 2001 is a period Gillborn (2001) calls 'naive multiculturalism'. In examining the policy of the Labour government from this time he suggests that although 'racial' inequality and achievement were acknowledged as needing to be tackled, there were no policies that actually addressed this specific issue. The murder of a black teenager, Stephen Lawrence, in a racist attack in London and the lack of response by the police, fuelled by their initial assumptions that it was likely to have been the black boy's fault, led to accusations of institutional racism echoing those raised by Swann nearly 20 years earlier. The Macpherson Report (1999) that followed an inquiry into the murder highlighted a need for positive changes in education to tackle racism. Gillborn (2008) noted that the Labour government responded, as had the Conservative administration at the time of the Swann Report, with tokenistic gestures calling for greater tolerance and understanding. There was rhetoric rather than serious action. It was assumed that such issues could be 'covered' in the introduction of citizenship into the curriculum. We can conclude from this lack of an anti-racist approach and the will to change things that little had changed in terms of government policy towards 'race'.

Cynical multiculturalism

The period after the 11 September attacks on the twin towers in New York in 2001 saw a shift towards what Gillborn (2008) calls 'cynical multiculturalism'. There was a mood of public anger and a desire for retribution against those who had been responsible for such acts that were clearly associated with specific ethnic and religious groups. Gillborn (2008) suggests that while it retained its public commitment to ethnic diversity and equality, the Labour rhetoric and policy resembled the earlier assimilation/integration phases. Such policy included proposals to restrict marriages of convenience that allowed migration into the country, arrangements to speed up the deportation of illegal immigrants and an emphasis on acquisition of English language skills by migrants. Attention was also focused on schools with a high proportion of students from minority backgrounds. The media hype was of the education of white pupils suffering due to 'swamping' by children of asylum seekers.

Aggressive majoritarianism

The policy position and public rhetoric further hardened into what Gillborn (2008) termed 'aggressive majoritarianism' after a series of disturbances involving large ethnic minority communities in towns such as Oldham and Bradford and the London bombings of 7 July 2005 that became known as 7/7. Gillborn suggests that from this time there were more white disciplinary agendas and more aggressive assimilationism. The media and politicians highlighted the separating of ethnic minority communities from majority white ones. Bates et al. (2011) cite Islamophobia as a moral panic of the time. According to Bloch and Solomos (2010) the Islamophobic discourse on community cohesion was about the maintaining of foreign cultures and failed integration rather than exclusion and discrimination. The wearing of the veil was criticised openly as illustrating female oppression within these Muslim communities and clothing that may accentuate the segregation of pupils in schools was disallowed. Multicultural policies of the past were portrayed as having failed and diversity was now seen as destabilising.

Aggressive majoritarianism seems to have continued into the Coalition and subsequent Conservative administrations, as illustrated in a speech in 2011 by Prime Minister Cameron about radicalisation and the causes of terrorism in which he said that state multiculturalism had failed and argued the need for a stronger identity in the UK to prevent people turning to all kinds of extremism. He called for 'a lot less of the passive tolerance of recent years and much more active, muscular liberalism' (www.bbc.co.uk/news/ukCameron, 2015). Hills (2015) contends that within this discourse multiculturalism is being compared unfavourably to 'British values' on the basis of its supposed relativism and passivity. Cameron warned Muslim groups that they would lose government funding if they failed to endorse women's rights or promote integration. This was a clear reference to the previous disturbances of 2001 and the veil debate that began under Labour. He also reiterated the previous government's policy that immigrants to Britain should speak English and that schools teach a common culture (Wright and Taylor, 2011). The term 'multicultural' was no longer considered useful and integration was the way forward when dealing with cultural diversity and immigration (Race, 2014). Modood (2014) suggests that even today when some politicians use the term 'integration' they are actually talking about assimilation. Concerns about multiculturalism and its association with social fracture have, according to Keddie (2014: 540), led to a change in governance approaches that 'reflect a civic rebalancing agenda, where greater social harmony can be realised through emphasising a stronger commitment to Britishness as a core identity'.

Reviewing this analysis it would appear that we have almost returned to policies of assimilation adopted in the 1950s which, according to Gillborn (2008), has never been far from the surface.

Achievement of ethnic groups

Much of the research in the second half of the twentieth century and the early years of the twenty-first focused on the underachievement of black pupils in the education system. This was seen as largely influenced by the experiences of these pupils in a racist society and education system.

In the 1970s and early 1980s attention was drawn to the curriculum in which black faces did not appear except as part of topics involving slavery. Ethnic minorities were presented in the media and also the classroom in negative ways. Thus many areas of the world were portrayed as being 'primitive' and as jungle or desert and certainly in poverty. Large parts of the Indian subcontinent and Sub-Saharan Africa, for example, only appeared in the media when suffering famine. In this way young ethnic minority pupils could find few, if any, positive images of themselves or people like themselves. It was suggested in some early studies (Coard, 1971; Milner, 1975) that this may have led to lack of self-esteem and, in turn, underperformance. Others said that this actually led to cultures of resistance and ethnic minority pupils forming their own, alternative, views of self that brought them into conflict with the establishment (Mac an Ghaill, 1988; Sewell, 1997).

The racism ethnic minority pupils faced in the education process has been pointed out by many studies (Majors, 2000; Wright et al., 1999). Black pupils, boys in particular, were more likely to get into trouble at school, to be labelled as 'difficult' pupils by teachers and to be excluded from school. Black pupils were seen as less academic and more likely to be in the lower academic sets. Attempts were made to address these issues during the multicultural and anti-racist movements that developed in the 1970s onwards. The curriculum was adapted to include more positive images of ethnic minorities and curriculum materials were made more inclusive in terms of the appearance of different ethnic groups in textbooks. However, the introduction of the national curriculum from 1988 onwards and the colour-blind approach taken to education, which made no allowances for ethnic differences in curriculum content, assessment or first language of the pupils, can be said to have put back the development of equality of opportunity for ethnic minority pupils to before the 1970s.

Strand (2011; 2014) found that the low attainment and poor progress of black Caribbean students could not be explained in terms of social class alone and pointed to other factors such as teacher expectations, institutional racism and cultural differences as potentially having an influence. Tomlinson (2008) suggests that policies which promote market forces and encourage parents and pupils to compete for places at 'good' schools will continue to legitimate inequalities and ensure that ethnic minorities remain largely in those schools that are heavily criticised as underperforming. This, she says, will do little to promote social justice.

Crozier (2005) said that institutional racism continues to have a significant impact upon the achievements of young black people who experience cumulative negative experiences throughout their education. She suggests that the school system holds a pathological view of the black child that works against his or her success. Thus, the pressures of league tables, together with the need to maintain the facade of good discipline and high pupil performance, have led to more exclusions of pupils with behavioural problems and, by extension, the number of black pupils excluded. This view is supported by Gillborn and Rollock (2010: 160) who show how race inequality has been influenced by the drive to improve 'standards' as defined in official policy. They state that

> education policy appears to be actively implicated in the processes that sustain, and in some cases extend, race inequality.

While much of the literature explained the poor performance of black children in schools and related this to their experiences of schooling, Demie (2005), Zanoni and Mampaey (2013) and Forsman and Hummelstedt-Djedou (2014) show how some schools are able to develop cultures that value all pupils and in which all ethnic groups can be successful.

It is pertinent to consider school exclusion rates among different pupil groups. The 2013/14 statistics for England (https://www.gov.uk/government/statistics/permanent-and-fixed-period-exclusions-in-england-2013-to-2014) show that boys are three times more likely to be excluded than girls. Pupils on free school meals are four times more likely to be permanently excluded and three times more likely to be excluded for a fixed term than those not on free school meals. Pupils of black Caribbean and white and black Caribbean ethnic groups are three times more likely to be excluded than the school population as a whole. If we turn our attention to pupil achievement in terms of GCSE results for the same year (www.gov.uk/government/statistics/gcse-and-equivalent-attainment-by-pupil-characteristics-2014) we can see a very similar if complex picture. Taking five GCSEs at A*–C as our measure, girls achieve better than boys in every ethnic category. Chinese, Indian and Bangladeshi children have the highest percentage, achieving five GCSEs at A*–C, while a much smaller percentage of black Caribbean boys and white and black Caribbean boys obtain five GCSEs at A*–C than any other ethnic group. What must be acknowledged, however, are the vast differences in the size of each ethnic group that make up these statistics. It should also be noted that pupils on free school meals have the lowest percentage obtaining the five GCSE grades at A*–C in *every* ethnic category, with white boys on free school meals performing lowest of all. Strand (2014) notes in a study examining pupil achievement at age 11 that the groups with the lowest educational attainment and the poorest progress are both black Caribbean (high and low SES) and white British low SES pupils. Certainly ethnicity is a significant factor to be taken into account when explaining pupil achievement. However, as pointed out previously in our discussions of class and gender, in order to appreciate these social processes and how they affect the individual, we need to be aware of the complex interrelationship between ethnicity, gender and economic circumstances in the form of social class (Smith, 2012; Crozier, 2014). Vincent et al. (2013) suggest that race cannot simply be 'added on' to class. The two intersect in complex ways.

Reader Reflection: Statistics on student achievement

Consider the official figures for permanent exclusions (https://www.gov.uk/government/statistics/permanent-and-fixed-period-exclusions-in-england-2013-to-2014) and on the GCSE achievement of different ethnic groups (www.gov.uk/government/statistics/gcse-and-equivalent-attainment-by-pupil-characteristics-2014).

What do you think are the difficulties of compiling such figures in terms of their accuracy?

Do you think that publishing such figures on pupil achievement (categorised according to ethnicity and gender) identifies issues to be resolved or does it further highlight and exacerbate social division?

Video Discussion

Visit https://study.sagepub.com/bartlettburton4e to watch a video discussion on:

Education: creating equal opportunity or reinforcing inequality?

This video clip discusses issues which are also relevant to Chapters 4 and 6.

Conclusion

There is no doubt that the processes and effects of education can and do influence the life opportunities of individuals and particular social groups. In the past, alternative forms of education were openly provided for different social groups. It seemed reasonable to educate the children of the labouring classes to fulfil their future roles effectively. Likewise the sons of the middle classes needed to be equipped to take decisions fitting to their future station in life. Economic life and working conditions have changed greatly and today the emphasis by politicians is more on individual opportunity and social mobility. However, the existence of opportunity and social mobility for individuals does not necessarily lead to reductions in social and economic inequality. As Reay (2013: 665) points out:

> Britain in the 2010s is more unequal than Britain in the 1970s. And social mobility becomes even more important symbolically as inequalities worsen in societies. In deeply unequal societies such as the United Kingdom and the United States it operates as … a justification for growing levels of inequality. In the 2010s a majority of British people acquiesce in sharp distinctions of wealth and power on the basis that as individuals they are free to scale the heights.

Rising GCSE and A level results, increasing percentages of pupils staying in full-time education post 16, improved performance at all levels by females and ethnic minorities, and greater participation in FE and HE all seem to point to the opening up of opportunity. But inequalities in education persist with the continued lower achievement and effective exclusion of significant sections of the population. This continuing state of affairs may have a profound effect upon the future of our democracy. Janmaat and Green (2013: 7) suggest that there

> is a mismatch between the cherished ideal of meritocracy and the reality of a stratified society, both objectively and perceived. This is … likely to contribute to the political alienation of disadvantaged groups.

Class, gender and ethnicity thus remain significant factors that operate at different levels and in various ways to influence educational outcomes.

Student activities

1. Discuss with others your different experiences of growing up and the influence that social factors such as class, ethnicity and gender had upon you. Particularly consider:

   - your primary and secondary school experiences
   - any paid employment you have undertaken
   - your life as a student
   - your future aspirations.

2. Find the gender balance for a number of courses at your university/college. Has this changed over a number of years? Discuss the findings and reasons for any significant results.

3. Visit the Higher Education Statistics Agency website (www.hesa.ac.uk) and chart the number of places in HE taken by students according to socio-economic status, gender and ethnicity over the last five years. What trends, if any, can you identify from these statistics?

Recommended reading

Gillborn, D. (2008) *Racism and Education: Coincidence or Conspiracy?* London: Routledge. Written by one of the leading academics in this area this text uses critical race theory to analyse racism across the education system. Through clear argument and evidence it is able to challenge much of the rhetoric surrounding current race policy.

Race, R. and Lander, V. (eds) (2014) *Advancing Race and Ethnicity in Education.* Basingstoke: Palgrave Macmillan. This collection of chapters considers contemporary issues on race, ethnicity and inclusion in relation to teaching and learning using domestic and international education research.

Richards, G. and Armstrong, F. (eds) (2015) *Teaching and Learning in Diverse and Inclusive Classrooms.* 2nd edn. London: Routledge. This is an edited book that addresses issues relating to inclusive education. The book focuses on social diversity, teaching and learning. Chapters look specifically at ethnicity, gender and special needs as well as many other areas.

Smith, E. (2012) *Key Issues in Education and Social Justice.* London: SAGE. This book has been specifically written for education studies students and we highly recommend it as a detailed introduction to the field. It outlines the whole area of social justice and inequality in relation to education. It considers all age phases and takes the reader from childhood through to higher education and the learning society.

Access the companion website to this book and find SAGE journal articles exploring this chapter topic in further detail: **https://study.sagepub.com/bartlettburton4e.**

CHAPTER 11
Organising teaching and learning

Chapter overview

Our discussion in Chapter 4 demonstrated how historical narratives can shed light on different aspects of education. Some historical reflection will help us now to examine how current pedagogical trends have evolved. This historical narrative, informed by our overview of psychological research and information about how class, ethnicity and gender can impact on educational achievement, provides us with a set of perspectives with which to analyse issues about how pupils and other learners are grouped and taught and how learner attainment is conceptualised. The chapter will consider pedagogical trends since the 1950s from setting and streaming of learners through mixed-ability teaching and differentiation, the early twenty-first century vogue for personalised learning, and the influence of 'psycho-pedagogy'.

Introduction

This chapter first embarks on a review of the different ways learning groups have been organised since the start of the comprehensive system, which is a key pedagogic issue. Tracing historical precedents and analysing them within their contemporary social, economic and political contexts allows us to better understand current developments in pedagogy. Teaching and learning approaches of the early twenty-first century have been influenced by what we might refer to as 'psycho-pedagogy' – the basing of pedagogical approaches on popular ideas from psychological research. As with everything we have examined in this text, it is not possible to appreciate what this means without also looking at the ideological context that has spawned it. It is of fundamental importance that educators and students of education apply a questioning approach to the plethora of teaching and learning techniques that seem so easily to gain favour through our globalised, media-rich modern communication systems. This chapter explores some of these pedagogical trends, inviting readers to think back to their research bases discussed in Chapter 9 and the extent to which they might legitimately be applied in practice.

Grouping pupils for learning

The traditional notion that individual differences in how people learn can be explained by differences in a single intelligence as measured by IQ tests has been shown to be sterile. Commentary from the 1960s and 1970s (Ball, 1981; Hargreaves, 1972; Jackson, 1964) was very sceptical of the ceiling effect on pupil attainment that such a view implied. This was referred to as the self-fulfilling prophecy where pupils meet the expectations set of them and no more and has been discussed in Chapter 10. A look back at the various ways of organising learners demonstrates that the conditions responsible for encouraging this ceiling effect, namely setting by ability, are directly related to prevailing ideological forces, in particular to the strength of emphasis on conventional, publicly comparable assessment data.

Streamed groups

In 1964 a seminal study was produced in England by Brian Jackson (Jackson, 1964), who wrote from the heart as an experienced teacher disenchanted with an education system which he had taken for granted but later found to be wanting. His investigation into the effects of streaming children into groups, on the basis of mathematical or literacy competence, within primary schools was highly influential. It came at a time politically and economically ripe for consciousness to be raised about perceived social and educational injustices. Jackson found that 'A'-stream teachers were more experienced and better qualified, that children with autumn birthdays were over-represented in 'A' streams, that working-class children were underestimated and relegated to the 'C' stream where they stayed and that over a third of parents had no idea what streaming meant.

Jackson adopted a teaching approach as a result of his findings that put no ceiling on his expectations of pupils which, in turn, liberated them from simply meeting specified goals. He also developed teaching resources that caught the interest and met the needs of his pupils. What Jackson was breaking down was the much discussed self-fulfilling prophecy (Rosenthal and Jacobson, 1968) wherein teachers' expectations of pupils were said to limit their achievement. There was serious worry about this phenomenon when the Plowden Report (CACE, 1967) confirmed that, at as young an age as seven, a child's life chances were fixed because there was seldom any transfer between streams. This phenomenon may have drawn a spurious legitimacy from stage theories of development such as Piagetian theory (see Chapter 8). Widely adopted as applicable to an educational context, these theories did tend to generate ideas about learning readiness which suggested that it was not sensible to expect certain capabilities from children until they were maturationally ready. Teachers may have considered that the concept of learning readiness could be applied to 'ability' equally well as to age, serving as a justification for the stability of streamed groups.

Hargreaves (1972) argued that believing in the child's potential for improvement, often in the face of contradictory evidence, and the communication of this belief to the child was the key to releasing this potential. In 1967 he had studied the effects of streaming on pupils in a secondary modern school, pointing to the development of subcultures within the lower streams. Sporting norms and values at variance with those of the school, these groups became alienated from the mainstream aims. Disenfranchised from status positions within school, which were bound up in high achievement, pupils in the lower streams gained status instead from deviant behaviour. This perpetuated the lack of movement between streams.

Mixed-ability teaching

When comprehensive schooling was introduced in the late 1960s it was hoped that the problems created by using streaming as a form of differentiation would abate. Initially, however, a certain resistance to change and a lack of experience in teaching pupils of all abilities together simply led to a replication of the secondary modern/grammar groupings of pupils on a smaller scale within the comprehensives. The DES (1978a) stressed the social arguments for mixed-ability groupings: for the individual there would be increased equality of opportunity, less rejection and classification; for the teacher there would be greater control since mixed grouping avoids the emergence of a sink mentality and promotes group cooperation, better relationships and a reduction in competitive/aggressive behaviour; and, for society, class differences would be counteracted helping to create a non-competitive, non-elitist society.

Keddie (1971), observing the introduction of a new humanities curriculum within a comprehensive school, found a relationship between perceived ability and social class. She argued that teachers classified children in terms of an ideal type of pupil even though the classes were of mixed ability. Pupils meeting the teachers' stereotype of an 'A'-stream type pupil were given access to higher-grade knowledge, even though all pupils were supposed to be taught the material in the same way. The result was the differentiation of an undifferentiated curriculum.

By the late 1970s mixed-ability grouping had become widespread but neither research nor HMI reports could find evidence to support the strategy because the grouping, whether banded, setted, streamed or mixed, did not in itself appear to improve teaching and learning (Bourne and Moon, 1994; Slavin, 1990). The findings of HMI school inspections (DES, 1978a) indicated that in the main teachers were teaching to the middle via whole-class teaching with the needs of the less and more able pupils being ignored. Both HMI and a study by Kerry (1984) found little evidence of task differentiation. Where attempts had been made to cater for the range of abilities in one class, these had of necessity to be so teacher directed that they limited the extent to which the pupil could be intellectually challenged. 'Death by a thousand worksheets' is a phrase with which many teachers of the 1970s identified. It described the overuse of differentiated worksheets within mixed-ability classrooms (Toogood, 1984).

Ball (1981) reported on the change from banding (where pupils are placed in broad-ability bands on the basis of results in English and mathematics and then setted further into ability groups for each subject) to mixed-ability grouping in one comprehensive school in the 1970s. Later, in 1987, he commented that:

> At Beachside the implementation of mixed-ability as a teaching problem was left almost entirely to the teaching departments to cope with. Each department was asked by the head-teacher to produce a report outlining their intended responses, but there was no follow-up to the reports, and in several cases the teaching strategies actually employed bore no resemblance to original stated intentions. (Ball, 1987: 40)

The political heat generated by the introduction of mixed-ability methods was such that much energy was employed engineering and safeguarding them (Toogood, 1984). Clearly thought-out school policies for the teaching of these groups were rare; Toogood's text provides a retrospective explanation of the approach taken at one 'progressive' school and Kelly's (1975) collection of case studies describes the methods employed in five schools. Despite some innovative developments by individual teachers (Hart, 1996), there were few systematised approaches within either schools or LEAs to galvanise these strengths and disseminate good practice. Along with political pressure, this helped seal the fate of mixed-ability teaching which declined in the 1980s, to be replaced by setting within each subject.

Setting versus collaboration

The introduction of the national curriculum with its differentiated attainment levels led to changes in grouping policy (Bourne and Moon, 1994). This was explicitly encouraged by the government White Paper *Excellence in Schools* (DfEE, 1997) for both secondary and primary schools. The publishing of examination results forced the hand of many stalwart supporters of mixed-ability teaching because of the risk of a perceived association between mixed-ability teaching and poor examination results (Boaler, 1997). The very public arena in which schools increasingly functioned encouraged further abandonment of mixed-ability teaching in favour of setting rather than efforts to develop more appropriate teaching strategies to support it (Weston, 1996).

Boaler's (1997) review of the research found that while there was a small but not statistically significant advantage for the most able pupils if they were setted, the losses for the less able were large if they were setted. Their attainment was significantly lower than the attainment of the less able who were in mixed-ability groups.

Boaler (1996) conducted her own three-year study comparing the GCSE mathematics results of 310 pupils in two schools, one of which set the pupils while the other taught pupils in mixed-ability groups. She found that results were significantly better among the latter group even though test results from Year 7 indicated the pupils were performing at the same levels. When she asked Year 11 pupils in the setted school about mathematics lessons the responses revealed a dissatisfaction with the fixed pace of progress. Some pupils, especially girls, found the pace too fast which occasioned them to become anxious; more of the boys reported that the pace was too slow. This was the case across the eight sets which is a striking finding, given that one would assume a limited range of ability within each set.

The pupils preferred the arrangements lower down the school when they had been able to work at their own pace in mixed-ability groups because they gained a better understanding. Many of the pupils who were negatively affected by setting were the most able. Boaler concluded that 'a student's success in their set had relatively little to do with their ability, but a great deal to do with their personal preferences for learning pace and style' (1996: 585).

A number of studies suggest that attempting to match tasks to learners' abilities may be less effective than providing differentiated, individualised teacher support to pupils working on the same task (see Burton, 2003, for a review).

Where pupils remained in mixed-ability groups, for instance at primary level and in some 'progressive' comprehensives, the standard collaborative learning method was heterogeneous grouping. High-ability pupils were felt to benefit from having to organise their thoughts in order to explain them to their less able partners and from having studied new material more carefully in order to explain it later. Low-ability pupils were said to learn from these explanations, which were often more accessible than those given by a teacher. Conversely, Bennett and Dunne (1992) and Jones and Carter (1994) found that within setted systems for older pupils, lower-ability groups were unable to collaborate or stimulate each other sufficiently to make progress. The academic rationale for a mixed approach is significantly different from the social benefits advocated for mixed-ability grouping in the 1970s. Indeed social problems were found to exist *within* mixed groups: Dowrick (1996) found evidence in Mulryan's (1992) study that low-ability pupils were looked down on by their partners. In Japan, studies indicated that ability was a much less central concern than effort (Purdie and Hattie, 1996). The Western notion of ability is turned on its head, hence 'intelligence is viewed as an expression of achievement; it results from experience and education' (Purdie and Hattie, 1996: 848).

Townsend and Hicks (1997) examined the relationship between academic task values (for mathematics and language) and perceptions of social satisfaction for 162 12- and 13-year-old pupils in New Zealand using a cooperative, interactive learning structure and in ordinary classrooms. Task values for engagement in learning activities were found to be higher in classrooms using a cooperative goal structure and to be associated with higher social satisfaction among pupils. The authors suggested that these findings imply a need to examine the coordination of multiple goals which extend beyond the academic domain. Brown, describing the learning communities she espoused, aimed at:

> non-conformity in the distribution of expertise and interests so everyone can benefit from the subsequent richness of available knowledge. Teams composed of members with homogeneous ideas and skills are denied access to such richness. (1994: 10)

There seemed, then, to be a complex relationship between grouping structures, pedagogical strategy, academic achievement and social satisfaction. It is possible to conclude that the classroom strategies employed were of greater significance to the quality of learning than the organisation of the teaching groups. Slavin suggested the need for a better understanding of how to choose teaching methods which work at appropriate times with particular pupils in different group structures, since:

it does not move the discussion forward at all to note that students differ and then to assume that all achievement differences must be dealt with through some sort of grouping. (1993: 13)

Nevertheless, the preoccupation with group organisation has been a feature of British education for a very long time and by 2008 Abraham (2008: 855) claimed that 'in the last 10–15 years setting has become the dominant form of organising secondary schooling in Britain in most subjects and the preferred approach by governments'. Within primary education setting took longer. In a 1999 survey of 2,000 London primary schools Hallam et al. (2004) found that within-class ability grouping was the most common arrangement in the core subjects of mathematics and English, with setting far less common and streaming negligible. However, by 2008, extensive studies across the UK involving nearly 9,000 children showed that both setting and streaming in primary schools were enjoying a revival (Hallam, 2012; Hallam and Parsons, 2013). In a study involving over 5,000 primary school children, Campbell (2014) notes that the already disproportionate tendency of teachers to judge autumn born children as more able than summer born children is more pronounced when children are grouped by ability in class than when they are not. This has obvious implications for children's later success given what we discussed earlier about the effect of teacher expectations and labelling.

Reader Reflection: Research into mixed-ability versus setted groups

In recent years a number of major studies have been conducted into the effects of mixed and setted ability groupings within both primary and secondary schools by Judith Ireson and Susan Hallam and their research team at the London Institute of Education (Hallam et al., 2004; Ireson and Hallam, 2005).

In 2007 they reported the findings of a study into pupils' satisfaction with their class placements within their sets or mixed-ability groups (Hallam and Ireson, 2007). The study was extensive, covering 45 schools and 5,000 Year 9 (13–14-year-old) pupils and the data were collected via a self-report questionnaire. At secondary level the majority of pupils reported preferring ability grouping structures (setting). The reason they gave was that ability grouping enables work to be set at an appropriate level (Hallam and Ireson, 2006). The findings indicated that when ability grouping structures were in place, for a substantial proportion of pupils work was perceived to be too difficult or, more commonly, too easy. The authors argued that if pupils moved freely between ability groups this issue might be resolved but the evidence from the pupils in their study and previous research studies suggested that this generally does not happen (Hallam and Ireson, 2007: 41).

Abraham (2008), in an article responding to Hallam and Ireson's study, suggested that their findings could have been interpreted differently and contended that the majority preference for setting among the pupils from these 45 schools might be an expression of conformity to the dominant ideology found in the schools. He explained this by reference to the powerful ideology of an 'ability hierarchy' within our schools and wider culture, especially pupil/student culture, noting that such ideology has been promoted by successive governments in the UK since the early 1980s, if not before (see also Araujo, 2007). For context, it is worth noting that evidence from international comparisons suggests that where there is *less* differentiation between schools and classes educational inequality is reduced (Green and Wiborg, 2004).

Here we have an interesting juxtaposition of views which demonstrates how far from straightforward conducting research is. Think about the impact of ideological positions on these authors' perspectives. Consider how, even in a study conducted on such a large scale, there can be methodological questions raised – what might these be? (Think about the data collection tool, for instance.)

Differentiated learning

Key principles

Irrespective of whether pupils were set or in mixed-ability classes, in the 1990s the common pedagogical approach was to differentiate learning experiences, tasks and materials for learners. Two principles that informed the concept of a differentiated approach to learning can be identified. The first lies in changing notions of the rather nebulous term 'ability' which we see became 'abilities' in the National Curriculum Council's definition of differentiation:

> the matching of work to the abilities of individual children, so that they are stretched, but still achieve success. (NCC, 1993: 78)

This suggested a shifting, wide-ranging set of skills, interests and talents rather than a singular ability which is stable across a range of contexts. The idea of responding to or matching work to this range of abilities was the natural corollary of adopting this definition of ability. Thus Visser defined differentiation as 'the process whereby teachers meet the need for progress through the curriculum by selecting appropriate teaching methods to match the individual child's learning strategies, within a group situation' (1993: 15). By this definition the common-sense notion of an all-embracing ability derived from IQ theory had been replaced by a more finely tuned, diagnostic assessment of what each child is capable of at a particular time, with a particular teacher, in a particular subject, using a particular learning strategy. This has echoes of Howard Gardner's explanations of the proclivities learners have for different aspects of their learning (Gardner, 1983) and foregrounds the need for subject-specific identification of ability, eschewing the global IQ testing approach. Leo and Galloway (1996) highlighted the impact of children's own conceptions of ability on their goal orientations, citing the work of Dweck (1991) and Nicholls (1989). These studies indicated a tendency for adolescents to conceive of ability as stable and fixed, which led to performance-oriented goals which in turn affected the effort they made in class; if they felt their efforts would not have an effect on their achievement they reasoned there was no point. Younger children were found to be more likely to conceive of ability as changeable, something which is affected by effort; this can orient them towards learning goals.

> Teachers' conceptualisations of ability affect the way they teach pupils. Those holding a view of ability as a fixed, stable entity 'might behave in ways which impede effective development of mastery learners' (Leo and Galloway, 1996: 43).

The second principle of differentiated learning lay in the emphasis on process. Thus 'differentiation is a planned process of intervention in the classroom to max-imise potential based on individual needs' (Dickinson and Wright, 1993: 1). Tubbs placed the teacher at the centre of this intervention, defining differentiation as 'the means by which a teacher intervenes in every pupil's education in order to provide effective and relevant access for them to the curriculum' (1996: 49). Stradling et al. identified teacher–pupil dialogue as one manifestation of this intervention pro-cess: 'The commonest characteristics of differentiation between individual learners tend to be an emphasis on dialogue in the form of regular review between teachers and individual pupils about their progress and their learning needs' (1991: 11).

Groups of pupils, whether setted or mixed ability, will display differences in their interest in the topic, presentation skills, ability to work cooperatively or inde-pendently, listening skills, parental support, learning styles, gender, ethnic group, cultural background and so on. These differences have an impact on scholastic achievement (Maqsud, 1997). In responding to these differences by differentiating the learning the teacher's aim is itself to make a difference – the difference between where a pupil is now and where they have the potential to be. This reso-nates clearly with Vygotsky's (1978) work on zones of proximal development as he explained that what a child does at first in cooperation with others, they will then learn to do alone. The clear implication of this social constructivist approach is that the teacher's intervention will vary from child to child; as Warnock had explained in the 1970s: 'The purpose of education for all children is the same; the goals are the same. But the help that individual children need in progressing towards them will be different' (DES, 1978b: 5).

We would argue that two principles which characterise a differentiated approach to facilitating learning can be summarised as follows:

1. Pupil performance is not a function of a simply defined ability, but of a range of interrelated internal and external factors; it is more helpful to use the notion of contextually dependent sets of skills and aptitudes as the underpinning to achievement.
2. The teacher's focus will be on the learning process rather than on the learning product.

Differentiation and attainment

These principles are manifestly more complex than those identified by the National Curriculum Council (NCC, 1990) which explained that the national curriculum would help teachers to:

- assess what each pupil knows, understands and can do
- use their assessment and the programmes of study to identify the learning needs of individuals
- plan programmes of work which take account of their pupils' attainments and allow them to work at different levels
- ensure that all children achieve their maximum potential. (Hart, 1996: 21)

While committed to the potential of individuals, the NCC, in linking differentiation to an assessment of attainment, placed the same ceiling on expectations as that occasioned by the streaming of the 1960s. In contrast, our two principles outlined above embrace the complex nature of attainment, and in pursuing process rather than product, encourage a liberation of learner potential.

In the 1990s the publication of examination results led to schools adopting tactics such as cramming sessions for pupils on the C/D grade boundary of GCSEs to boost results. This strategy was even extended to pupils in the final year of primary school in order to boost a school's percentage of level 4s in the core subjects' end-of-key-stage tests. The culture of national benchmarks based on assessment and other performance indicators along with parental and employer pressure are recurring features of school life and since 1998, following

Labour endorsement of these ideas, benchmarking data have been published annually for schools to determine their examination targets in relation to the achievements of schools in similar situations. Thus the ramifications of individual differences in attainment are more far-reaching than a single child's performance in examinations. It goes hand in hand with the implications that each single child's performance has for the aggregated results of a school.

Differentiation and ideology

In its broadest sense differentiation is a construct which describes a whole host of educational phenomena, from the ways in which schooling systems are organised within societies, how learners are divided up for teaching and assessment, the extent to which teachers observe policies of inclusion, right through to the particular teaching and learning strategies a teacher employs with individual pupils.

These various manifestations of differentiation are inextricably bound up with the socio-political and ideological contexts in which they exist. The 1960s was a time of largesse, economic boom and social conscience wherein the drive was for equality of treatment through comprehensive schooling, social opportunity, gender and ethnic rights. After difficult economic times in the 1970s, the late 1980s and early 1990s were again a time of economic progress but the prevailing ideological ethic was one of personal enterprise, endeavour and resourcefulness, and not state responsibility (Thatcherism). Equality of opportunity in education was ostensibly provided by creating the appearance of choice of schools. This choice was promoted by an expectation that schools should be more publicly accountable for their 'performance' through comparative league tables of examination results. In fact the choice for low-income families had actually been reduced since, unlike high-income families, they could not transport their children to the schools with the best results.

As you read in Chapter 6, a change of government did not alter the emphasis on choice although the New Labour rhetoric used to support it became one of 'social justice'. In 2001 the government White Paper *Schools Achieving Success* (DfES, 2001), set out how diversity of provision would be achieved through different types of schools such as Specialist Schools, which demonstrated a particular subject competence, and Beacon Schools, chosen for their exhibition and dissemination of best practice (see Burton, 2003, for a fuller discussion of this). This was extended first through a commitment within Labour's *Five-Year Strategy for Children and Learners* (DfES, 2004b) to create 200 independently managed academies and later within the Education and Inspections Act (2006) to develop new 'trust schools' which would be independent of local authority control and would (ostensibly) create even greater choice for parents and pupils. The commitment to independent trust schools was a further step in Labour's strategy that emphasised how selective and differentiated provision could, in its view, meet everyone's needs.

Yet the political and popular backlash against the partial selective admissions processes for such schools took the government by surprise and this element of the Act's provision was changed. The key point here is that neither structural nor pedagogical change can be achieved if the appropriate political conditions do not pertain. So what changed in five years? A host of issues that were nothing to do with education, most significantly the war on Iraq, combined to erode confidence in the prime minister and his government such that the hitherto benign back-bench and public acceptance of New Labour spin gave way to a healthier questioning of so-called 'social justice' education policies. The rhetoric that creating choice and diversity in schooling served to advance the opportunities for every pupil and not just those with the human, physical and cultural capital to access it lost its credibility.

At all levels of the education system, then, differentiation – of pedagogy, of assessment, even of school type – took hold throughout the 1990s and into the new century, buoyed along by Labour ideology of 'choice and diversity' and 'social justice'. Significant by its absence in government guidance towards the end of the 1990s, however, was any mention of *how* classroom learning was to be enhanced (Reynolds, 1997). Decisions about what strategies to deploy within a differentiated pedagogy were still the preserve of teachers. This changed with the implementation in England of what became known as the national strategies for literacy, for numeracy and later for primary education and Key Stage 3 more generally (see Chapter 5 for details). These gave prescriptive guidance on the format and content of lessons and, although not compulsory, were adopted by the majority of schools because of the force of the official support and government documentation behind them. The strategies were criticised for their straitjacket approach to learning, which was thought to stifle creativity, and questions were raised regarding the rigour and provenance of the research underpinning them with several studies registering concern that they elicited limited learning gains (Brown et al., 2003; Kyriacou, 2005; Wyse, 2003). This entrée of government and its advisers into the very heart of the teaching and learning process continued so that by the middle of the first decade of the new millennium they were taking a great deal of interest in the methods that teachers and learners might employ to effect 'personalised learning' (Leadbeater, 2004). Thus the control of the curriculum exercised by a number of governments across the world via national curricula began to be further extended via an even more insidious form of control, that of pedagogical approaches. For instance, increasing control of pedagogy was also found to be happening in Australia (Bates, 2005).

Personalised learning

Much of the psychological research described in Chapter 9 has been drawn on internationally in the development of psycho-pedagogic approaches embraced within the trend for personalised learning which began under the last Labour government. Burton (2007) argued that PL has its pedagogical and political roots in the 1990s vogue for differentiated learning. Weston (1996) described differentiation as a shorthand for the methods teachers use to enable each pupil to achieve their intended learning targets. The pedagogical discourse of the 1990s established 'differentiation' as a seminal term and this definition resonates with its successor, 'personalised' or 'tailored' learning, promoted by the UK Labour government. The DfES (2004a) described personalised learning as having its roots in the best practices of the teaching profession:

> It has the potential to ensure that every child or young person reaches the highest possible standards by tailoring learning and teaching. Personalised learning by its very nature cannot be prescriptive and has to be developed within a given context. (http://www.essexprimaryheads.co.uk/sites/essexprimaryheads.co.uk/files/A%20National%20Conversation%20about%20Personalised%20Learning.pdf)

Despite this lack of prescription five components of personalised learning were identified by the incumbent education minister, David Miliband (2004b) as: assessment for learning, teaching and learning strategies, curriculum choice, school organisation and community links. To these were added ICT, advice and guidance, mentoring and student voice. PL would appear, then, to embrace most of what goes on in schools and was actually not terribly new or different. There was also an obvious policy tension in pursuing a personalised curriculum because personal choice does not sit easily with the notion of a broad and balanced curriculum entitlement enshrined within the national curriculum.

The White Paper referred to earlier (DfES, 2001) described a range of ways in which pedagogical diversity was to be pursued. These included the use of different types of adults in classrooms, for example classroom assistants and learning mentors, investment in ICT equipment, an on-line curriculum 'catering for children of all abilities' (DfES, 2001: 5) and the facility for the most able pupils to progress at a faster pace. These initiatives were later implemented via an initiative known as 'Workforce Remodelling' in England (DfES, 2003a). There was also much more emphasis placed in schools and colleges worldwide on developing the learning technologies and software to support personalised learning. Sophisticated hyper-media systems could identify learners' interests, preferences and needs and adapt the content of pages and the links between them to the needs of that user (Triantafillou et al., 2004).

There is some evidence that blended learning, which involves a variety of instructional media, leads to better motivation to learn (Klein et al., 2006). We saw in Chapter 9, however, that social constructivist research (Bruner, 1983; Vygotsky, 1978) has repeatedly demonstrated the necessity for group interaction and adult intervention in consolidating learning and extending thinking. Although many teachers are familiar with these key ideas, Kutnick et al. (2002) cautioned that they may not think strategically about the size and composition of groups in relation to the tasks assigned and reminded educationalists to pay attention to the social pedagogy of pupil grouping. Running counter to social constructivist (and personalised) approaches at this time was the UK government's requirement for whole-class teaching within the national literacy and numeracy strategies. Whole-class teaching tends to place the emphasis for talking with the teacher through whom all interactions are routed, thus reducing the emphasis on collaborative learner talk. Myhill's (2006) extensive research demonstrated that teacher dis-course can sometimes impede pupil learning because cognitive or conceptual connections are not made sufficiently clear. Conversely, Smit et al. (2013), invok-ing Vygotsky, have argued that it is possible to develop whole-class scaffolding which enables effectively scaffolded teacher–pupil interaction and ultimately leads to pupil independence.

Personalised learning was further promoted in the subsequent White Paper (DfES, 2005a) with an explicit call for the setting of pupils, the implicit assump-tion being that setting enhances personalisation. Yet, as we saw earlier, research provides no clear evidence that setting creates greater learning gains for pupils. In an extensive study that followed 6,000 Year 9 pupils in 45 secondary comprehen-sive schools through to Year 11, Ireson et al. (2005) found no significant effects of setting on GCSE achievement in English, mathematics or science.

PL, or at least several of its elements, is now a fairly well established school pedagogy. In a study from Australia, where UK education initiatives are often subsequently adopted, Prain et al. (2013) discuss the origins of and rationales for personalised learning and the challenges of introducing PL programmes in four Australian secondary schools. Winstanley (2016) provides guidance on the princi-ples of personalised learning and strategies for its practical application. She makes the very salient point that, for effective teachers, PL should not require a radical shift in their practice, though it may require them to make more space for the pupil voice.

A decade after Frith's (2005) predictions about the implanting of microchips to enhance cognitive functioning and techniques to track an individual's learning within the developing brain in order to match teacher or teaching method to learner, such developments appear to be a long way off.

Until then, teachers will continue to need detailed knowledge of each learner's progress, strengths and challenges in a particular learning context.

Whether we call it personalised learning, differentiation or a learner-centred approach, the issue is not one that can be simply dealt with by governmental injunctions to setting, since in both set and mixed-ability groups the individualised nature of pupil learning and teacher response is paramount.

The drive towards personalised learning was fuelled in the UK and beyond by an approach towards the professional development of teachers that increasingly took the form of 'edutainment'. Charismatic, high-profile education consultants delivered courses on new pedagogies such as those embraced within Smith's accelerated learning (AL) (Smith, 1996; Smith and Call, 2002). High-energy presentations drew eclectically from a range of research findings thought to have practical benefits for learning. These were presented with a theatrical fervour and missionary zeal that was compelling. Teachers generally enjoyed these stimulating sessions and the recipe approach to pedagogic techniques but they were seldom encouraged to look deeper into the research that may or may not underpin them. Many teachers were keen to trial these techniques, tending initially to accept them at face value rather than to question their theoretical or empirical validity (Bartlett and Burton, 2006b).

In the UK, government money was directed at such trends so head teachers encouraged their staff to explore their application in what was often an overly simplistic, mechanistic way, where short-term gains, possibly in the form of end-of-term test results, were the goal. When teachers met for professional purposes within local, national or virtual communities of practice the new trends were discussed and the shorthand terms used to describe these ideas became generic, passing into educational discourse with a legitimacy and authority borne of practitioners' enthusiasm and partial application of the constructs. Consequently, a tendency developed for education dissertations to focus on the practical application of an increasingly narrow set of the latest popular ideas, where the construct itself was not the focus of the investigation for its legitimacy was taken for granted. In this way the corpus of pedagogical research work became self-referential and based on taken-for-granted assumptions with little attempt made to refer back to the original psychological research on which those assumptions may have been loosely based.

As we embark on a Conservative administration it will be interesting to assess how pedagogical proclivities differ from those of the erstwhile Coalition government but during that administration there was no major break with what went before under Labour. While the Coalition government did not, for political reasons, wish to perpetuate language used by its Labour predecessors, its ideas on pedagogy seemed not radically different at first, but a creeping traditionalism soon became evident. We have discussed in Chapter 5 the way in which ministerial pronouncements on effective pedagogy seem to be born of a neo-liberal desire to return to educational practices of yesteryear. These ideas are likely to strengthen now that the Conservatives have a full mandate but it is more than a little concerning that the school lives of generations of learners are at the mercy of changing ideological perspectives rather than being consequent on the application of thoroughly researched educational practices.

Psychological research and pedagogical developments

This somewhat unscholarly approach to developing and justifying pedagogical techniques reveals why there is some scepticism about the robustness of the research bases underpinning new trends such as personalising learning. Examining further the context in which such psycho-pedagogy has grown up helps explain why this less than rigorous approach to the research and development of new ideas holds sway. Educational research had been criticised for its apparent lack of relevance to practical teaching and learning situations. As discussed in Chapter 3, governments were calling for research that would have a direct impact on practice in classrooms and for teaching approaches to be supported by practitioners' own research into 'what works' with learners. The utilitarian value of research was sought and attempts made to define 'evidence-based practice' (EBP). The basic tenet of EBP, that is without evidence we cannot trust professionals, has, however, been shown to be overly simplistic (Pring, 2015). In a recent analysis, Kvernbekk (2016) concedes that using EBP generally makes good sense but concludes that it is far more complicated than *either* advocates *or* critics realise. Hammersley (2004) suggested that EBP had the effect of undermining opposition to politically favoured standpoints. This in turn, of course, served to reinforce policy positions.

As we saw in Chapter 9, research that has been increasingly popularised within educational pedagogy includes studies on learning or thinking styles, learning strategies, approaches and preferences, metacognition, brain functioning and thinking skills, emotional intelligence and multiple intelligences. Accelerated learning (Smith and Call, 2002) became an umbrella term for a series of pedagogical approaches that draws from a range of theories including many of those listed above. It might be said to cohere a set of principles that have governed effective teaching and learning for some time. Motivating learners is a key precept of this approach as is the expectation that all learners can achieve at a level normally considered beyond them. AL practitioners focused on the need to understand how learning happens rather than what is learned and gave assurances that all their suggestions were based on sound research despite allowing very little time within the sessions for an examination of that research.

Within the AL approach reference was made to VAK (see Dryden and Vos, 2001), the construct that there are predominantly three learning styles – visual, auditory and kinaesthetic – that pupils can be categorised into, with appropriate tasks matched to their individual styles. The emphasis on this single style construct was an example of the tendency to adopt the easiest or most attractive construct on offer rather than to properly examine the range of ideas available and their respective research bases. Easy to understand and internalise, VAK appeared to become synonymous with learning styles, virtually replacing it as the generic term (Burton and Bartlett, 2006b). As Chapter 9 demonstrates, this is simply inaccurate since a whole host of style constructs have been generated from a range of research, each predicated to differing degrees on empirical research. Despite attracting considerable criticism from the academic world, largely for its crude simplifications and lack of research base (see Sharp and Murphy, 2014, for instance), VAK was easy to assess and useful as a labelling device to justify treating pupils in particular ways or having certain expectations of them. Such popular pedagogical ideas tend to be promoted through universal media on a global stage with one or two references to an original source providing the appearance of rigorous research legitimacy.

The power of endorsement from government and global education media was grotesquely demonstrated by the scale and speed of schools' uptake of VAK, with pupils even walking around with labels identifying their VAK style. This should concern us on many levels, from the teachers' lack of critical engagement in allowing such practice, to the stultifying effect of labelling, and thereby limiting, learners' potential and opportunities. Certainly a great deal of money has been made from the commercial application of style instruments in schools. Coffield et al. (2004a; 2004b) reviewed 71 of these, concluding that most, including resources advocated by the DfES, were unreliable and of negligible pedagogical value. Teachers are probably better off providing varied pedagogy that reflects the host of ways in which learners interact with and process information rather than matching tasks to individuals that simply serve to reinforce the stereotypes assigned to them. Coffield has suggested that with older learners 'learning styles could be the starting point for a dialogue with students about how they learn and fail to learn, as long as the knowledgeable tutor quickly moves the discussion away from a narrow preoccupation with learning styles to conceptions of learning, learning strategies and the purposes of learning' (2008: 40).

Reader Reflection: Kinaesthetic learning

It is interesting to consider how the exclusive use of kinaesthetic forms of learning could possibly facilitate pupils' learning of the curriculum.

If we labelled pupils in this way would it mean they would never be expected to interact with visual or auditory stimuli in the form of reading a book or listening to one another? Emphasis on the identification of a single style attribute would certainly lead to this odd conclusion.

Is it actually possible, though, to use just one mode – don't we employ an interaction of seeing, hearing and doing in most things we learn?

Think about how your own learning requires the use of different strategies according to the task and the context.

Should teachers attempt to train learners not to use particular learning strategies or to need particular environmental preferences? The business of basing pedagogy on learning styles in their more multifarious forms is complex. Should educators define each learner across a range of style constructs and match tasks accordingly?

A similar tendency to oversimplification pertains to ideas about metacognition, which, as we saw, has a sound basis in research (see Adey and Shayer, 2013, for instance). In our knowledge-rich society it might be argued that there is a surfeit of information generated together with ever more technological ways of accessing it. This requires people generally and learners in particular to develop more sophisticated ways of finding things out and greater confidence in filtering them for relevance and reliability. Claxton (2002) has argued that learners need above all to learn to learn and that teachers' main focus should be teaching them how. This metacognitive approach has in some circles been dubbed 'learnacy', a product perhaps of the tendency to think that ideas are only accessible if they are reduced to sound bites or tabloid shorthand. This tendency is reinforced in some education texts by authors' preoccupation with gratuitous alliterative devices and metaphors to communicate their ideas as if they would not otherwise be understood. Thus Claxton talks about pupils needing to 'build learning power' (Claxton et al., 2011), to exercise their 'learning muscles' and to become 'resourceful, resilient, reflective learners', using these terms as organising vehicles for his arguments. This approach can lead to the publishing of polemic rather than detailed research accounts and can divert students of education from wrestling with the central research proposition.

Research into brain functioning, though relatively speaking in its infancy, has caught the imagination of both the general public and the education sector. There is a tendency to alight on elements of the research that appear to lend themselves to innovative pedagogic techniques. Novelty claims that are well known but not well substantiated by research include the apparently beneficial effects of listening to music while learning, sipping water to 'hydrate the brain' and using neuro-linguistic programming to reveal how the brain codes experience in order to improve communication. Many researchers decry this misappropriation of small elements of research findings which are taken out of context and misunderstood (Howard-Jones, 2016).

Brain gym is a good example of this tendency but it has a longer legacy than most of the novelty psycho-pedagogic practices that have infected schools. Brain gym is a popular brain improvement tool developed by the American Paul Dennison in the late 1960s. As a dyslexic, Dennison was interested in the connection between physical activity and learning ability. It comprises a set of exercises designed to improve concentration, reading ability and hand–eye coordination and it has been suggested that using such simple movements improves learning. Exercise sessions usually last for a few minutes and are often used at the beginning of lessons to focus pupils' attention. They are sometimes related to the work that is being taught, for example letter sounds, arithmetical functions or handwriting; they may be used to break up passive learning or to refresh pupils, particularly those with attention difficulties. It is suggested that brain gym can help children become calm, alert and ready to concentrate by stimulating neurological pathways so that both sides of the brain work together. Mind mapping is a strategy copyrighted by Tony Buzan (2004) to facilitate this dual hemispheric functioning, which in turn enhances problem-solving, the generation of creative ideas and the organisation of thoughts. It has been suggested that stress causes people to overuse the right side of the brain leading to emotions obscuring understanding so attempts to balance this would be considered effective pedagogical strategy. Studies authenticating long-term benefits, however, are not well known.

In terms of pedagogic influence, emotional intelligence continues to be prevalent, with most professional development courses and management textbooks drawing on its maxims (see Killick, 2006; Zins et al., 2004). Indeed the social and emotional aspects of learning (SEAL) were officially endorsed and promulgated through government education policies (DfES, 2005b; 2007).

Goleman's popular work (1995; 2006; 2011) related the ability to control impulses, motivate oneself and regulate moods to improved thinking and learning and to better self- and people management. We might agree this seems sensible enough but not all subscribe to the elevation of emotions above or on a par with cognitive goals within education. Ecclestone (2004) criticised the trend, arguing that it detracts from risk-taking, and points to a lack of systematic research evidence to support claims made about the damaging effects of poor emotional literacy.

Subjecting emotional intelligence to research is indeed problematic because it is not easy to isolate and measure such a nebulous variable within a research context. Nevertheless, by 2010 the uptake of SEAL had been extensive with 90 per cent of primary and 70 per cent of secondary schools engaging to some extent with SEAL resources with similar programmes promoted internationally (Evans et al., 2015). Results are mixed.

Wood and Warin's (2014) case study on the use of SEAL in three north of England primary schools found somewhat worryingly (but perhaps unsurprisingly) that teachers were influenced by their perceptions of parents' ability to develop social, emotional and behavioural skills in their children and that these perceptions were influenced by the parents' social class. The SEAL scheme was used to complement the practices of those parents perceived as middle-class parents and to counter those of minority-ethnic and working-class parents, which helped to 're-affirm the practices of the dominant culture whilst serving to marginalise the values of the less powerful groups in society' (Wood and Warin, 2014: 937).

A case study by Evans et al. (2015) of four secondary schools in Wales found unintended consequences of targeting individual pupils for social and emotional learning (SEL) interventions. For instance, the SEL label was used as a form of social capital to enhance a pupil's status with their peers which thus exacerbated rather than reduced deviancy.

This finding accords with those of an extensive study by Banerjee et al. (2014) which found that SEAL was most effective when it was applied to all pupils, was aligned with the overall school ethos and delivered in a coordinated rather than a piecemeal way.

Finally, we turn to the vexed subject of how intelligence theory influences pedagogy. We have seen that IQ theory had a far-reaching effect on pupil life chances within the tripartite selective secondary school system set up after the Second World War. Since then attention has turned to multiple forms of describing, developing and assessing intelligence. We considered Gardner's theory of multiple intelligences and Sternberg's work on triarchic categorisations of intelligences in Chapter 9. Clearly these models are significantly different from one another and although developed around the same time, fewer educators have heard of Sternberg's model than Gardner's. Sternberg (2003a) argued that schools undervalue creativity and think it is no different from general intelligence. For Sternberg (2012) creativity, which he argues can be fostered by educators, should be a vital, standard component of learners' education and assessment but that accountability cultures militate against its inclusion.

Reader Reflection: Multiple intelligences

It is easy to see how Gardner's model could gain currency at a common-sense level since people often display particular talents or tendencies. Indeed the school curriculum and Hirst's (1975) forms of knowledge use similar categorisations.

But can we really believe that these constitute discrete and differently processed forms of intelligence? Do we have evidence that learners use different thinking and processing techniques across eight areas of experience and activity in the way the existence of discrete forms of intelligence might suggest?

Think about how you might approach the understanding of an educational ideology within your course and contrast this with the processes you use to determine your weekly household finances. Does your brain employ different processing techniques to do these two things or is it just the context that is different?

White (1998; 2005) has heavily critiqued Gardner's work but many educators across the globe still rely on Gardner's problematic explanation of intelligence.

There was insufficient scepticism about the provenance of psycho-pedagogic approaches among the educational community at first but this has increasingly been replaced by greater circumspection and a questioning of their theoretical and empirical bases. Nevertheless, it is fascinating to see the impact of economic considerations in relation to the popularising of such work, wherein ideas become commercialised and branded, often kept alive by reissuing the original ideas in a 'new' text or applying them in a new context. Much of Goleman's work has been applied to leadership contexts in recent years and Gardner's original 1993 text was republished with co-authors in 2011 with only a new introduction added by Gardner himself.

Conclusion

Psychological research has for many years facilitated new understandings among educators about how people learn, from which pedagogical implications have been derived. The varying influence of these theories is linked to shifts within both policy imperatives and pedagogical 'trends' and the extent to which these are championed by an increasingly sophisticated global media. Psychological research continues to develop and refine theoretical ideas about learning but educators must resist reductionist attempts to produce neat, digestible, commercialised chunks of pedagogy from them. Teachers, students and education professionals will enjoy a fascinating perspective on psycho-pedagogy as long as a critical, enquiring approach is taken to their theoretical or empirical basis and to their political provenance.

Edgar Stones, an influential educational psychologist, railed against the ready adoption of populist terms (2000; 2002) and the increasingly fluid and amorphous perceptions of pedagogy. He argued for an unequivocal expression of the concept and alluded to the influence of fashion on the communication of educational ideas. It may be that you, as students of education, will be the ones that expose the 'emperor's new clothes' syndrome that besets education, where constructs such as 'learnacy' and 'personalised', 'tailored' or 'brain-based' learning become accepted sound bites within the educational lexicon, having been used in ministers' speeches or government documents without anyone sharing an understanding of what they mean, much less a knowledge of their research basis.

Student activities

Think of examples to illustrate how the age of the students, their academic ability, the resources available and the number of students in the group may influence how a teacher plans a lesson.

Recommended reading

Arthur, J. and Cremin, T. (eds) (2014) *Learning to Teach in the Primary School*, 3rd edn. Abingdon: Routledge.

Capel, S., Leask, M. and Turner, T. (eds) (2016) *Learning to Teach in the Secondary School: A Companion to School Experience*, 7th edn. Abingdon: Routledge.

These are comprehensive, up-to-date texts outlining a wide range of pedagogical issues and approaches in an accessible way.

Hattie, J. (2012) *Visible Learning for Teachers: Maximising Impact on Learning*. Abingdon: Routledge. Based on a synthesis of the results of thousands of research studies over 15 years into the effects of various educational approaches on achievement, Hattie offers advice on the most successful interventions and gives practical guidance on implementing them.

Tomlinson, P., Dockrell, J. and Winne, P. (eds) (2005) *Pedagogy – Teaching for Learning*, British Journal of Educational Psychology Monograph Series II: Psychological Aspects of Education – Current Trends. Leicester: British Psychological Society. This text is a collection of papers taken from conferences organised by the British Psychological Society on aspects of education. Now offering a slightly more historical perspective, its aim was to disseminate the latest developments in psychological research among educators and also students of education. As such it links psychological theories to education practice aiming to counterbalance the often shallow approach that was taken to such issues by practitioners.

Access the companion website to this book and find SAGE journal articles exploring this chapter topic in further detail: https://study.sagepub.com/bartlettburton4e.

CHAPTER 12

Conclusion: education – a contested enterprise

Chapter overview

It is argued in this chapter that to study education in any meaningful way requires an awareness of the interrelationship between the different disciplines involved, that is, it requires a multidisciplinary approach. Education is presented as the result of continual conflict and interaction between competing ideologies at many levels. The chapter suggests that, inevitably, the ideologically charged area of education will always be at the heart of the development of any society and will remain a focus of political debate and struggle. Some reference is made to broader areas of education study that readers should also investigate which are beyond the remit of this book.

Introduction

The aim of this book has been to introduce the study of education. The approach has highlighted the value-laden nature of education and how both its policies and its practices are informed by different sets of beliefs. These ideologies can be seen to permeate every part of the education process. Their various proponents bring them to bear on the principles and practices of education through the often politicised processes of developing theory to determine practice and extrapolate theory out of practice. As a subject, Education Studies is able to apply an eclectic range of research questions and analytical tools to reveal and explore these theories from a number of perspectives.

Common-sense perceptions often represent theory as being quite distinct from practice. This is sometimes the case in education where the classroom or 'chalk-face' is set against what are felt to be the vague irrelevancies of the academic world. In fact, this common-sense view is *itself* a theory of how things are and – as with all theories – represents a particular way of looking at the world. In accepting that we are all interpretively situated, Carr suggests that education theory itself is 'the product of the educational theorist's own interpretive assumptions; that educational theory is just one more discursive practice' (2006: 155). He sees such theory as not necessarily causing educational change but being used to justify it.

The influence of ideology on a study of education

Reader Reflection: Education and public debate

Education is a central force within society and is likely to play a significant part in the shaping of future generations. Being such a contested enterprise it is at the heart of the public political process.

This process is played out at national level, in law-making and parliamentary debate, and at the local level of the school and individual teacher, in terms of day-to-day classroom-based decisions.

An understanding of how different sets of beliefs and values compete in this process is central to the analysis. At any one time a number of ideological influences can be identified as seeking to influence policy.

Consider how frequently education issues appear prominently in the media and the controversies surrounding them.

We have seen the impact of disparate ideological perspectives on education as an area of study:

- from the functionalist view of education existing to prepare citizens for society to the Marxist view of education acting as an agency of the state in the reinforcement of class differentials
- from the view of education as ensuring social order to Rousseau's view of self-development through education.

We also looked at how, in using particular educational ideologies, the emphasis can be on the development of the individual, the significance of particular knowledge or the importance of inculcating economic and social skills. Sometimes the emphasis is clear, as in the case of certain vocational courses and practical instruction. Often, however, the aims and objectives of a curriculum are broad, involving all three of these educational ideologies, as we saw in the case of the national curriculum. This inevitably leads to difficult decisions and compromises in terms of appropriate content, pedagogy and assessment.

While in daily classroom life the complexity of competing ideologies which seek to influence education may not be very apparent, there are tensions and conflicts inherent in even the simplest curriculum and educational policy decisions. These are a consequence of the different belief systems which pervade the education system at every level. We have referred to the compulsory sector when analysing the relevance of these ideologies to education but the analysis is of course applicable to other sectors of education, such as post-compulsory and higher education.

Through our discussion we have demonstrated the deep conflicts in ideas about knowledge, the curriculum and the school. Acknowledging the power of the curriculum to be a purveyor of beliefs and values raises important issues about the purpose and nature of education. Although a number of Western nation states have adopted national curricula that are similar in content and structure, there remain big questions about the utilitarian value of subject knowledge and its cultural authority. Also significant is the way the curriculum acts as a vehicle for socialisation and the different motives ascribed to this by competing ideologies of education. We illustrated how structural features can facilitate this via a case study of the English national curriculum.

Reader Reflection: Revealing ideology through structure

The 'story' surrounding the implementation of the national curriculum is a fascinating example of ideological power struggles. We have only been able, in Chapter 5, to introduce its development but an in-depth study would facilitate an analysis from philosophical, psychological, sociological and historical perspectives.

Consider how an examination of certain structural features of the national curriculum can serve to reveal its underpinning ideological position. Examples might include:

*   *the value of core subjects in relation to the rest of the curriculum or*
*   *the effects of publishing test results on an individual school's future.*

The kind of learning promoted and cultivated by any curriculum reveals much about a society's fundamental premises and culture.

Education and individuals

In focusing our attention on the views of policy-makers, curriculum planners, researchers and teachers, it is important not to forget that pupils and students are not simply passive recipients in the education process. Learners of all ages may be subject to various forms of teacher control. Frightened by the ogre, mesmerised or motivated by the raconteur or enthusiast, they generally accept the power differential between themselves and the teacher and agree to conform at least to a certain extent. However, it should not be assumed that they have no say. Their power varies and depends upon a number of factors in the relationship between themselves and their teachers. Learners of any age use strategies to cause disruption during the teaching session. At least one of the authors has found it particularly disconcerting to find a student doing an essay for another subject during a lecture. When challenged, the student simply replied that the essay was more important. Learners are thus able to exercise at least some degree of autonomy in many ways. In some situations the learner is granted 'legitimate' autonomy. For example, in higher education it is usual for students to design their own projects and independent programmes of learning with supervised help as part of their degree course. In pursuing 'off-task' behaviour in school or university learners are, of course, exercising 'unlegitimated' forms of autonomy which often involve resisting the official goals of the curriculum, school or college.

When considering individuals in education and influences upon their achievement we face a number of complex issues which are only resolvable from different perspectives. When we measure success in education what factors are we looking at? Achievement could be seen in academic terms measured in examination scores, it could be physical ability assessed by coordination and strength or it could be social skills in terms of being able to cooperate with others or demonstrate leadership. Ultimately different institutions and agencies, including government, schools, colleges and universities, determine what should be measured and this is based upon what attributes are valued most highly.

Thus, as researchers of education, we are still interested in whether the education system develops individuals and gives them the opportunity to progress or whether it perpetuates inequalities. In Britain the question remains about the extent to which the education system is a meritocracy or whether such a concept is a myth designed to legitimate and help maintain inequality. Paradoxically, the education system can be shown to reproduce existing inequalities while simultaneously extending opportunities and access for all.

Education studies and the 'disciplines'

Education studies, then, draws on particular disciplines to provide explanations and to inform research. In this book we have emphasised philosophy, sociology, psychology and history, but sometimes it is difficult to determine which of these discourses of knowledge is most relevant to the question in hand. In recent times the strict divisions of the curriculum and of different areas of knowledge, study and research have been challenged. Claims for official forms of knowledge and truth have been challenged by such discourses as feminism, deconstructionism and postmodernism, which have deliberately sought to problematise the nature of truth and knowledge. They have begun to influence the way that theorists of education think about and define systems, institutions, policies and practices. Education as a focus of study offers opportunities for the interaction between discourses and this can give rise to 'hybrid' forms of knowledge – as with gender studies and social geography, for example. This often means that the boundaries of education study are not fixed, which can have highly beneficial effects in terms of the construction of interdisciplinary forms and examples of knowledge.

A number of traditional and emerging disciplines contribute to our understanding of education. We contend that on their own the disciplines would be unable to deal with the issues in such a cohesive manner. While drawing on the theories and research of the traditional disciplines, education studies is an increasingly significant area of study in its own right which can benefit too from analyses drawn from newer discourses. What remains to the fore of any study is the contested nature of education itself and how beliefs and values permeate every aspect of it.

The breadth of education studies

In this volume we have been unable to examine the full range of topics covered within education studies courses. Instead we have concentrated on outlining some of the major questions and issues with which education studies is concerned, using mainly schools and the compulsory education sector to illustrate where appropriate. Readers will be aware that this is just one sector of formal education and that even this could be examined in greater depth. Some of the other important areas which warrant further study as significant topics within the field of education studies are outlined below. The fundamental questions raised in this volume concerning beliefs, values and purpose remain appropriate in respect of these topics.

Further and higher education

We briefly discussed the current funding issues of HE in Chapter 6 when examining the education policies of New Labour, the Coalition and Conservative administrations. The post-16 sectors of further and higher education have expanded rapidly since the late 1980s. These post-compulsory sectors have become increasingly significant arenas for education as, in England at least, students must now remain in some form of education or training from the ages of 16 to 18.

Traditionally, higher education was regarded as an elitist sector for public school and grammar school pupils. Universities were for a minority of academically successful pupils. The 1960s saw the development of polytechnics run by LEAs which were designed to give an alternative to the traditional subject approach. They were to provide more applied courses at degree level that would be appropriate to meeting the needs of industry. However, over time, they also began to offer degree courses similar to those run by the traditional universities. In the Education Reform Act 1988 polytechnics were given their independence from LEAs. The binary line, which separated them from the traditional universities, was later abolished altogether and they became full universities in 1992 (Ward, 2014b).

The Robbins Report (1963) had suggested that as society benefits from the quality of university graduates then society should pay the cost of their education. This was affordable when only a small proportion of the population partook of higher education. As the numbers entering higher education rapidly expanded a new view emerged – that since graduates benefit most from higher education they should bear at least some of the cost. In Chapter 6 we looked at how over a period of ten years the student grant system was dismantled and student fees were introduced alongside loans until we reached the current point where students now incur fees of up to £9,000 per annum (paying these back to the government over a 30-year period when earning a sufficient amount). Currently, the only direct government funding of universities is for some of the costs of students taking STEM subjects. Thus the balance has swung completely to graduates footing the whole cost of their university education. These changes have been difficult to reconcile with a desire to expand participation in HE and widen access to students from backgrounds that have not traditionally entered HE.

Funding shortfalls over this period also led to a focus on the nature of teaching and learning by the HEFCE and within the higher education institutions themselves. Students were encouraged to be more self-directing with a growing emphasis on independent study and distance learning. This was presented as increasing student autonomy but it can be viewed more sceptically as a means of reducing the quality of provision as students' contact time with tutors decreased.

At the same time lecturers were given greater teaching loads and larger groups. This might be considered ironic in the context of the introduction of increasingly higher fees. The quality of higher education became an issue with the government promising to maintain standards while increasing student numbers and reducing costs. Universities are monitored by the Quality Assurance Agency and increasingly by the media, which compiles university league tables based on a range of indicators including employment rates of students, staff–student ratios, library spend, research income and so on. As universities are forced to compete even harder in the marketplace for students such comparative tables take on greater significance for them and the notion of students as customers forces them into a new service culture.

The newly created market for students and research funding in the HE sector has threatened to widen the gulf between the traditional Russell Group of universities (the established 'old' prestige universities including, for example, Oxford and Cambridge) and the post-1992 universities. The government's removal of the cap on the numbers of students a university can recruit from 2015 could lead to annual increases of 60,000 students per year. Students can go to a university of their choice so universities will raise their entry grade requirements, recreating the divide dispensed with by the abolition of the binary line. Thus issues of student access, individual achievement, teaching and learning methods, and the nature of the curriculum apply just as much to higher education as to the compulsory sector. Ideological conflict is, as it always has been, an important force within developments in higher education.

The experience of further education in many ways mirrors that of higher education. Further education institutions have faced similar changes since they were given their 'independence' from LEAs and have become responsible for their own finances. This development was an important part of creating the market within further education provision. The introduction of this demand-led approach, coupled with a decline in central funding, meant colleges had to become more flexible with increasing proportions of staff employed on part-time and temporary contracts. Both the further and higher education sectors have witnessed the development of management cultures in a similar form to that of business and industry.

Lifelong learning

The whole issue of lifelong learning and the development of a learning society enjoyed a high profile in political debate under Labour. Changes in the economy with the development of modern communications technology and the obsolescence of traditional skills put an end to the notion of training for a job for life. The government (DfEE, 1998b) noted that people would need to be adaptable, continually learning and updating their skills as employees would probably follow several different careers during their working lives. This concept of lifelong learning does not only apply to the workforce. Prolonged life expectancy means that citizens will remain active for longer and will want to develop a wide range of interests and skills throughout their lives. The notion developed of a 'third age' of learning in which retired people would study new things for pleasure rather than for economic or career expediency.

Reader Reflection: Lifelong learning – liberation or control?

There are interesting issues to consider when thinking about how lifelong learning will take place. While it may involve traditional forms of teaching and learning in the classroom, this approach is unlikely to be appropriate for all, or even the majority, of the adult population. The emphasis is likely to be on information and communications technology with the development of flexible and distance learning modes.

There is debate, however, as to whether we *are* actually moving towards a learning society or whether the whole concept is just political rhetoric designed to create images of new opportunities.

Some would see lifelong learning as a liberating process, increasing learner autonomy and helping to create a more socially democratic society. Others portray it as just another, though perhaps more sophisticated, form of control developed through modern technology (Bartlett and Burton, 2009).

To what extent do you think the relationship between lifelong learning and modern modes of employment is open to question?

Is there genuine practical and financial support for voluntary education and lifelong learning across all sectors in society ?

After being at the forefront of Labour rhetoric throughout the first decade of the new millennium the phrase 'lifelong learning' has hardly been mentioned by the Coalition and Conservative governments. It is perhaps significant that in 2015 the National Institute of Adult and Continuing Education (NIACE), the 'national voice for lifelong learning', and the Centre for Economic and Social Inclusion (CESI), 'dedicated to tackling disadvantage and promoting social inclusion in the labour market', announced their intention to become one organisation, placing the emphasis on championing employment and skills for the unemployed rather than support for the 'leisure learning' of the third age.

Our aim is that next year a new organisation will be born that will champion employment, skills and learning for all – especially for the unemployed and those on low incomes. Together we will build a new organisation that has a strong policy voice, high standards of research and will be stronger and more sustainable. (Dave Simmonds, CEO of CESI)

The skills and employment agendas are critical for us as a nation: we have an ageing population, immense technological change, too many people without the skills to participate fully in life and a tough labour market for young people and older adults. As Government, LEPs and Combined Authorities focus more on employment support and employer engagement in skills, we will be able to provide solutions to the current challenges of low pay, low productivity, the need for higher labour market participation and skills short-ages at all levels, from basic to specialised. (David Hughes, CEO of NIACE)

Source: www.niace.org.uk/our-thinking/news/niace-and-cesi-merge (accessed 14 July 2015)

While the claims about education providing access to a fairer labour market are robust, it is clear that a decision to merge saves money. Consequently, some aspects of provision will be lost, most likely support for non-vocational learning such as that pursued by the older sections of society. It would appear, then, that lifelong learning beyond the employment imperative is less of a priority when there is high unemployment and low-paid job prospects generally.

Early childhood education

At the other end of the educational spectrum early childhood studies has rapidly become an area of study in its own right (Maynard and Powell, 2014). Early child-hood studies considers physiological, psychological, sociological and legal aspects of child development. Interest in this area has increased with the expansion of educational provision for younger children in schools, nurseries and playgroups. Hotly debated issues about the appropriateness of particular educational early years' experiences, coupled with differing theories of child development, create a rich source of study.

Nutbrown et al. (2014) point out how early childhood education has been transformed in recent years. The growth of early years' provision formed a central policy plank of the previous Labour government. A significant development in this area was the incorporation of the foundation stage into the national curricu-lum and the creation of early learning goals. The Children Act of 2004 and the publication of *Every Child Matters: Change for Children* (DfES, 2004c) had a far-reaching impact on services working with children.

The Coalition government also took an interest in early years' provision by drastically reducing Labour's Sure Start scheme while later introducing an early years' pupil premium. It went on to introduce a revised EYFS (DfE, 2014b) and a final EYFS profile report for each child which, while substantially slimmer than its predecessor, remarkably still requires four to five year olds to be assessed against 17 early learning goals with a short commentary on their learning characteristics. Clearly, then, curriculum tensions remain in this rapidly developing sector around the need for children to play and discover at their own pace while also being prepared in the foundation stage to be 'school ready' by the time they enter Year 1.

Citizenship and social justice

Rapid social change in society due to, among other things, advances in technology and developing global economic pressures, has led to concern about increasing social fragmentation. This has resulted in an emphasis on the importance of citizenship education which involves, variously, consideration of individual rights and responsibilities, notions of active involvement by citizens in society, the promotion of social justice and an understanding of global and environmental issues.

Separating the educational rationale from the political rhetoric constructed to justify educational developments such as citizenship education is an interesting task. The early twenty-first century Labour mantra of social justice was replaced in the second decade by the Conservative-led Coalition's talk of social mobility with very little distinction (rhetorically at least) between the goals of each. If both are about improving one's life chances through education, how is it possible to fully meet the needs of each individual learner while also ensuring the group ('society') enjoys equal access to opportunity and 'betterment'? The current Conservative administration persists with this rhetoric while dismantling the services, benefits and housing infrastructure which enables children from poor families to have access to education and employment. Ironically, against this backdrop, citizenship teachers are to teach pupils about the very processes of democracy which lead to governments being in a position to pursue such policies and to inculcate ideas about being a good citizen. Thus, the concept of citizenship itself is open to varying definitions and is ideologically loaded (Dunn and Burton, 2011).

Furthermore, tension can be seen between citizenship education being an empowering experience for students and, through emphasising social cohesiveness, a form of social control. Faulks (2006) argued there was a strong case for including citizenship in the curriculum but that diversity of secondary school provision, social exclusion, changing conceptions of what counts as political and lack of consideration of appropriate forms of delivery rendered the provision of citizenship education precarious. By 2013, Faulks and colleagues claimed the UK government was still cautious about recognising children and young people as citizens (Bacon et al., 2013). The extant statutory guidance for citizenship programmes of study at Key Stages 3 and 4 (DfE, 2013c) states that:

> A high-quality citizenship education helps to provide pupils with knowledge, skills and understanding to prepare them to play a full and active part in society. In particular, citizenship education should foster pupils' keen awareness and understanding of democracy, government and how laws are made and upheld. Teaching should equip pupils with the skills and knowledge to explore political and social issues critically, to weigh evidence, debate and make reasoned arguments. It should also prepare pupils to take their place in society as responsible citizens, manage their money well and make sound financial decisions.

Under Labour, teachers were trained specifically to deliver citizenship education as a discrete curriculum area. The success of this was limited as the subject only became a statutory part of the national curriculum in 2002 and then only at secondary level so its status relations with other subjects were poor. Following a period where students could study for a half GCSE in citizenship, which adversely affected perceptions about its worthwhileness, full course GCSEs for citizenship studies were introduced in 2009 and the numbers of candidates being entered rose steadily. The Association for Citizenship Education (ACT, 2015) anticipates further rises as schools increasingly use citizenship to meet the Ofsted-inspected requirement to promote 'British values' through their responsibility for SMSC (spiritual, moral, social and cultural) development.

Reader Reflection: Citizenship education in the curriculum

Rumours that the subject could be dropped by the Coalition government in the 2014 curriculum changes were foiled when citizenship education was confirmed as a compulsory subject (DfE, 2014a) with a reformed GCSE available from 2016.

The key difference in the GCSE is that assessment will be by 100 per cent examination, which appears a remarkable development given that 'Active Citizenship' remains a key part of

(Continued)

> *(Continued)*
>
> each qualification wherein students plan, undertake and evaluate their own active citizenship projects.
>
> *Citizenship persists in the English education curriculum but does it do so as the highly politicised subject area it has the potential to be or as a benign means of inculcating so-called 'British values' and developing 'good' citizens for the perpetuation of a stable society?*

Education and globalisation

This book has limited itself to a consideration of the English education system. This, of course, can make us blind to alternatives and may lead us to assume that other parts of the world have had similar experiences to our own. It also encourages a distorted view of our own significance. We introduced the idea of comparative education in Chapter 7 and, if we had space in the book to take in a wider range of education systems, similar issues about how purpose and ideology shape curriculum design and models of learning would arise. In addition the impact and pressures of globalisation on education systems and their pedagogy has generated a great deal of interest among educators. Globalisation is a significant factor in shaping both policy and practice across the world as systems 'interfere' with one another and ideas, research, ideologies and institutions take on different shape and form.

It is interesting to see how the impact of fashions and trends is as keenly felt in education as on the high street. The power of the media to advertise, promote and interpret these trends is as significant in relation to 'new' educational phenomena as it is to consumer goods. Latterly this 'tabloiding' of education policy, pedagogy and practice has led to ideas becoming popularised and even sensationalised within the education media itself. The backdrop for this is an increasingly 'media-ised' and 'celebretised' notion of success within society in general and education in particular. Many countries have annual teacher and lecturer awards ceremonies, often fronted by a media celebrity and sponsored by quality newspapers. Teachers and educators become the consumers of, and the audience for, this mediated expression of pedagogical or policy developments, whether through the educational press, dedicated teachers' television channels or via a proliferation of government websites.

As a manifestation of globalisation this social phenomenon is fascinating but it is important to understand the impact of it. The speed with which the internet and television can transmit ideas and information and appear to afford them (often spurious) validation should concern us as educators. We need to be interested in the way in which these ideas are researched and justified and not just in their utilitarian application. A Marxist interpretation of this phenomenon is likely to lie in constructs of power and control wherein sections of society are able to sustain and reproduce their position through the control and packaging of what people are taught and how they are taught it.

Conclusion

This volume has argued for a critical multidisciplinary approach to the study of education. It also demonstrates the importance of treating education as a field of study in its own right. This enables us to look at the major issues, structural features and sources of controversy in education and to ask critical questions. The last question we would put to you is the same as the first:

'What exactly is education?'

To answer this question we need to go back to the beginning!

 Access the companion website to this book and find SAGE journal articles exploring this chapter topic in further detail: https://study.sagepub.com/bartlettburton4e.

References

Abraham, J. (2008) 'Pupils' perceptions of setting and beyond – a response to Hallam and Ireson', *British Educational Research Journal*, 34 (6): 855–63.

ACT (Association for Citizenship Teaching) (2015) 'More schools to use new GCSEs in Citizenship Studies – ACT GCSE guide'. Online at: www.teachingcitizenship.org.uk/news/24072015–1339/more-schools-use-new-gcses-citizenship-studies-act-gcse-guide (accessed 13 October 2015).

Adams, J. (2013) 'Editorial: the English baccalaureate: a new philistinism', *The International Journal of Art and Design Education*, 32 (1): 2.

Adams, R. (2015) 'Gender gap in university admissions rises to record level', *The Guardian*, Wednesday 21st January 2015.

Adey, P. (1992) 'The CASE results: implications for science teaching', *International Journal of Science Education*, 14: 137–46.

Adey, P. (2007) 'The CASE for a general factor intelligence', in M. J. Roberts (ed.), *Integrating the Mind Domain: General versus Domain Specific Processes in Higher Cognition*. Hove: Psychological Press.

Adey, P. (2008) *Let's Think Handbook: Cognitive Acceleration in the Primary School*. London: NFER Nelson.

Adey, P., Csapo, B., Demeteriou, A., Hautamaki, J. and Shayer, M. (2007) 'Can we be intelligent about intelligence? Why education needs the concept of plastic general ability', *Educational Research Review*, 2 (2): 75–97.

Adey, P. and Shayer, M. (2013) 'Piagetian approaches', in J. Hattie and E. M. Anderman (eds), *International Guide to Student Achievement*. Abingdon and New York: Routledge.

Albert, R. S. and Runco, M. A. (1999) 'A history of research on creativity', in R. Sternberg (ed.), *Handbook of Creativity*. Cambridge: Cambridge University Press.

Alexander, R. (ed.) (2009) *Children, Their World, Their Education: Final Report and Recommendations of the Cambridge Primary Review*. London: Routledge.

Aliyu, A., Bello, M., Kasim, R. and Martin, D. (2014) 'Positivist and non-positivist paradigm in social science research: conflicting paradigms or perfect partners?', *Journal of Management and Sustainability*, 4 (3): 79–95.

Althusser, L. (1984) *Essays on Ideology*. London: Verso.

Anderson, J. and Bower, G. (1973) *Human Associative Memory*. Washington, DC: Winston.

Anderson, J. R., Reder, L. M. and Simon, H. A. (1996) 'Situated learning and education', *Educational Researcher*, 25: 5–11.

Anderson, J. R., Reder, L. M. and Simon, H. A. (1997) 'Situative versus cognitive perspectives: form versus substance', *Educational Researcher*, 26: 18–21.

Anthias, F. and Yuval-Davis, N. (in association with H. Cain) (1992) *Racialized Boundaries: Race, Nation, Gender, Colour and Class and the Anti-Racist Struggle*. London: Routledge.

Anyon, J. (2011) *Marx and Education*. London: Routledge.

Apple, M. (1988) 'Work, class and teaching', in J. Ozga (ed.), *Schoolwork: Approaches to the Labour Process of Teaching*. Milton Keynes: Open University Press.

Araujo, M. (2007) '"Modernising the comprehensive principle": selection, setting and the institutionalisation of educational failure', *British Journal of Sociology of Education*, 28 (2): 241–57.

Armstrong, F. (2015) 'Inclusive education: school cultures, teaching and learning', in G. Richards and F. Armstrong (eds), *Teaching and Learning in Diverse and Inclusive Classrooms*, 2nd edn. London: Routledge, pp. 7–18.

Arnot, M. and Reay, D. (2006) 'The framing of performance pedagogies: pupil perspectives on the control of school knowledge and its acquisition', in H. Lauder, P. Brown, J. Dillabough and A. H. Halsey (eds), *Education, Globalisation and Social Change*. Oxford: Oxford University Press.

Arnove, R. (2013) 'Introduction: reframing comparative education: the dialectic of the global and the local', in R. Arnove, A. Torres and S. Franz (eds), *Comparative Education: The Dialectic of the Global and the Local*, 4th edn. Plymouth: Rowman & Littlefield.

Arthur, J. and Cremin, T. (eds) (2014) *Learning to Teach in the Primary School*, 2nd edn. Abingdon: Routledge.

Assessment of Performance Unit (1986) *Speaking and Listening: Assessment at Age 11*. Windsor: NFER-Nelson.

Assessment Reform Group (2002) *Assessment for Learning: 10 Principles – Research Based Principles to Guide Classroom Practice*. Online at: http://www.aaia.org.uk/content/uploads/2010/06/Assessment-for-Learning-10-principles.pdf (accessed: 30 October 2015).

Atkinson, J. W. (1964) *An Introduction to Motivation*. Princeton, NJ: Van Nostrand.

Atkinson, R. C. and Shiffrin, R. M. (1968) 'Human memory: a proposed system and its control processes', in K. Spence and J. Spence (eds), *The Psychology of Learning and Motivation*, Vol. 2. London: Academic Press.

Auld, E. and Morris, P. (2014) 'Comparative education, the New Paradigm and policy borrowing: constructing knowledge for educational reform', *Comparative Education*, 50 (2): 129–55.

Auld, R. (1976) *William Tyndale Junior and Infant Schools Public Inquiry: A Report of the Inner London Education Authority* (The Auld Report). London: ILEA.

Ausubel, D. P. (1968) *Educational Psychology: A Cognitive View*. New York: Holt, Rinehart & Winston.

Ausubel, D. P. (1985) 'Learning as constructing meaning', in N. Entwistle (ed.), *New Directions in Educational Psychology: 1. Learning and Teaching*. Lewes: Falmer Press.

Ayoubi, R. M. and Ustwani, B. (2014) 'The relationship between student's MBTI, preferences and academic performance at a Syrian university', *Education & Training*, 56 (1): 78–90.

Bacon, K., Frankel, S. and Faulks, K. (2013) 'Building the "Big Society": exploring representations of young people and citizenship in the National Citizen Service', *The International Journal of Children's Rights*, 21 (3): 488–509.

Baddeley, A. D. (2007) *Working Memory, Thought and Action*. Oxford: Oxford University Press.

Baddeley, A. D., Eysenck, M. and Anderson, M. (2014) *Memory*, 2nd edn. Hove: Psychology Press.

Baker, L. (2013) 'Metacognitive strategies', in J. Hattie and E. M. Anderman (eds), *International Guide to Student Achievement*. Abingdon and New York: Routledge.

Ball, S. J. (1981) *Beachside Comprehensive: A Case Study of Secondary Schooling*. Cambridge: Cambridge University Press.

Ball, S. J. (1987) *The Micro-Politics of the School: Towards a Theory of School Organisation*. London: Methuen.

Ball, S. J. (1993) *The Micro-Politics of the School*. London: Routledge.

Ball, S. (2003) *Class Strategies and the Education Market: The Middle Classes and Social Advantages*. London: RoutledgeFalmer.

Ball, S. (2011) 'Back to the 19th century with Michael Gove's education bill', *The Guardian*, 31 January.

Ball, S. (2013) *The Education Debate*, 2nd edn. Bristol: Policy Press.

Baltes, P. B. (1996) *Interactive Minds: Life-Span Perspectives on the Social Foundations of Cognition*. Cambridge: Cambridge University Press.

Bandura, A. (1977) *Social Learning Theory*. Englewood Cliffs, NJ: Prentice-Hall.

Bandura, A. (2008) 'Reconstrual of "free will" from the agentic perspective of social cognitive theory', in J. Baer, J. Kaufman and R. Baumeister (eds), *Are We Free? Psychology and Free Will*. New York: Oxford University Press.

Banerjee, R., Weare, K. and Farr, W. (2014) 'Working with "Social and Emotional Aspects of Learning" (SEAL): associations with school ethos, pupil social experiences, attendance, and attainment', *British Educational Research Journal*, 40: 718–42.

Bartlett, F. C. (1932) *Remembering*. Cambridge: Cambridge University Press.

Bartlett, S. and Burton, D. (eds) (2003) *Education Studies: Essential Issues*. London: SAGE.

Bartlett, S. and Burton, D. (2006a) 'The growth of the "New Education Studies"', *Escalate Newsletter*, 5: 6–7.

Bartlett, S. and Burton, D. (2006b) 'Practitioner research or descriptions of classroom practice? A discussion of teachers investigating their classrooms', *Educational Action Research*, 14 (3): 395–405.

Bartlett, S. and Burton, D. (2009) 'Lifelong learning', in J. Sharp, S. Ward and L. Hankin (eds), *Education Studies: An Issues-Based Approach*, 2nd edn. Exeter: Learning Matters.

Bartlett, S. and Burton, D. (2015) 'The influence of gender in the classroom: How boys and girls learn', in G. Richards and F. Armstrong, *Teaching and Learning in Diverse and Inclusive Classrooms*, 2nd edn. London: Routledge.

Bartram, B. (2010) *Attitudes to Modern Foreign Language Learning: Insights from Comparative Education*. London: Continuum Press.

Bash, L. and Coulby, D. (1989) *The Education Reform Act: Competition and Control*. London: Cassell.

Bassey, M. (1990) 'On the nature of research in education (Part 2)', *Research Intelligence*, 37: 39–44.

Bates, J., Lewis, S. and Pickard, A. (2011) *Education Policy, Practice and the Professional*. London: Continuum.

Bates, R. (2005) 'On the future of teacher education: challenges, context and content', *Journal of Education for Teaching: International Research and Pedagogy*, 31 (4): 301–5.

Bathmaker, A., Ingram, N. and Waller, R. (2013) 'Higher education, social class and the mobilisation of capitals: recognising and playing the game', *British Journal of Sociology of Education*, 34 (5): 723–43.

British Broadcasting Corporation (BBC) (2010) 'Gove puts focus on traditional school values', 24 November. Online at: http://www.bbc.co.uk/news/education-11822208 (accessed 29 October 2015).

Beaman, R. and Wheldall, K. (2010). 'Teachers' use of approval and disapproval in the classroom', in K. Wheldall (ed.), *Developments in Educational Psychology*, 2nd edn. London: Routledge.

Beck, U. (1992) *The Risk Society: Towards a New Modernity*. London: SAGE.

Becker, H. S. (1971) 'Social class variations in the teacher pupil relationship', in B. R. Cosin, I. R. Dale, G. M. Esland and D. F. Swift (eds), *School and Society*. London: Routledge & Kegan Paul.

Bee, H. (1985) *The Developing Child*, 4th edn. New York: Harper & Row.

Bee, H. (1992) *The Developing Child*, 6th edn. London: HarperCollins.

Bee, H. L., Barnard, K. E., Eyres, S. J., Gray, C. A., Hammond, M. A., Speitz, A. L., Snyder, C. and Clark, B. (1982) 'Predication of IQ and language skill from perinatal status, child performance, family characteristics, and mother–infant interaction', *Child Development*, 53: 1135–56.

Bee, H. and Boyd, D. (2010) *The Developing Child*, 12th edn. Boston: Pearson Education.

Beech, M. (2006) *The Political Philosophy of New Labour*. London: I. B. Tauris.

Bell, J. with Waters, S. (2014) *Doing Your Research Project: A Guide for First-time Researchers in Education, Health and Social Science*, 6th edn. Maidenhead: Open University Press.

Bennett, N. and Dunne, E. (1992) *Managing Classroom Groups*. Hemel Hempstead: Simon & Schuster.

Benton, T. and Craib, I. (2011) *Philosophy of Social Science: The Philosophical Foundations of Social Thought*, 2nd edn. Basingstoke: Palgrave.

BERA (British Educational Research Association) (2011) *Ethical Guidelines for Educational Research*. Online at: https://www.bera.ac.uk/researchers-resources/publications/ethical-guidelines-for-educational-research-2011 (accessed 30 October 2015).

Bernstein, B. (1971) *Class, Codes and Control*. London: Routledge & Kegan Paul.

Bernstein, B. (ed.) (1973) *Class, Codes and Control*, Vol. 2. London: Routledge & Kegan Paul.

Best, B. and O'Donnell, G. (2011) *Learning to Learn Toolkit*. London: Optimus Education Bookshop.

Biesta, G. (2011) 'From learning cultures to educational cultures: values and judgements in educational research and educational improvement', *International Journal of Early Childhood*, 43 (3): 199–210.

Biesta, G. (2015) 'Thinking philosophically about education; thinking educationally about philosophy', in D. Matheson (ed.), *An Introduction to the Study of Education*, 4th edn. London: Routledge.

Biggs, J. B. (1978) 'Individual and group differences in study processes', *British Journal of Educational Psychology*, 48: 266–79.

Biggs, J. B. (1987a) *The Study Process Questionnaire (SPQ) Manual*. Hawthorne, Victoria: Australian Council for Educational Research.

Biggs, J. B. (1987b) *Student Approaches to Learning and Studying*. Hawthorne, Victoria: Australian Council for Educational Research.

Biggs, J. B. (1993) 'What do inventories of students' learning processes really measure? A theoretical review and clarification', *British Journal of Educational Psychology*, 63: 3–19.

Biggs, J. B. (2001) 'Enhancing learning: a matter of style or approach?', in R. J. Sternberg and L. F. Zhang (eds), *Perspectives on Thinking, Learning, and Cognitive Styles*. Mahwah, NJ: Lawrence Erlbaum Associates.

Biggs, J. B. and Tang, C. S. (2011) *Teaching for Quality Learning at University*, Society for Research into Higher Education. Maidenhead: Open University Press.

Birks, M. and Mills, J. (2015) *Grounded Theory: A Practical Guide*. London: SAGE.

Birney, D. and Sternberg, R. (2011) 'The development of cognitive abilities', in M. Bornstein and M. Lamb (eds), *Developmental Science: An Advanced Textbook*, 6th edn. New York: Psychology Press.

Black, P., Harrison, C., Lee, C., Marshall, B. and Wiliam, D. (2002) *Working Inside the Black Box: Assessment for Learning in the Classroom*. London: King's College, University of London.

Blakemore, S.-J. and Frith, U. (2005) *The Learning Brain. Lessons for Education*. London: Blackwell.

Blaxter, L., Hughes, C. and Tight, M. (2010) *How to Research*, 4th edn. Maidenhead: Open University Press.

Bliss, T., Robinson, G. and Maines, B. (1995) *Coming Round to Circle Time*. Bristol: Lame Duck Publishing.

Bloch, A. and Solomos, J. (eds) (2010) *Race and Ethnicity in the 21st Century*. Basingstoke: Palgrave Macmillan.

Boaler, J. (1996) 'A case study of setted and mixed ability teaching', paper presented at the British Education Research Association Conference, Lancaster University, September.

Boaler, J. (1997) 'Setting, social class and survival of the quickest', *British Educational Research Journal*, 23: 575–95.

Bochel, H. (ed.) (2011) *The Conservative Party and Social Policy*. Bristol: Policy Press.

Boghossian, P. (2006) 'Behaviourism, constructivism, and Socratic pedagogy', *Educational Philosophy and Theory*, 38 (6): 713–22.

Boghossian, P. (2012) 'Critical thinking and constructivism: mambo dog fish to the banana patch', *Journal of Philosophy of Education*, 46: 73–84.

Bouchard, T. J. and McGue, M. (1981) 'Familial studies of intelligence: a review', *Science*, 212: 1055–9.

Bourdieu, P. and Passeron, J. (1977) *Reproduction in Education, Society and Culture*. London: SAGE.

Bourne, J. and Moon, B. (1994) 'A question of ability?', in B. Moon and A. Shelton Mayes (eds), *Teaching and Learning in the Secondary School*. London: Routledge.

Bowles, S. and Gintis, H. (1976) *Schooling in Capitalist America: Educational Reform and the Contradictions of Economic Life*. London: Routledge & Kegan Paul.

Boyd, D. and Bee, H. (2014) *The Developing Child*, 13th edn. Boston: Pearson Education.

Boyle, G. J. and Helmes, E. (2009) 'Methods of personality assessment', Humanities and Social Sciences Paper 327. Online at: http://epublications.bond.edu.au/hss_pubs/327 (accessed 12 October 2015).

Boyle, G. J., Matthews, G. and Saklofske, D. H. (2008) *The SAGE Handbook of Personality Theory and Assessment*. London: SAGE.

Brewer, W. F. (2001) 'Bartlett, Frederic Charles', in R. A. Wilson and F. C. Keil (eds), *The MIT Encyclopedia of the Cognitive Sciences*. Cambridge, MA: MIT Press.

Broadbent, D. (1958) *Perception and Communication*. London: Pergamon Press.

Bronfenbrenner, U. (1979) *The Ecology of Human Development*. Cambridge, MA: Harvard University Press.

Brook, A. (2001) 'Kant, Emmanuel', in R. A. Wilson and F. C. Keil (eds), *The MIT Encyclopedia of the Cognitive Sciences*. Cambridge, MA: MIT Press.

Brown, A. (1975) 'The development of memory: knowing, knowing about knowing, and knowing how to know', in H. W. Reese (ed.), *Advances in Child Development and Behaviour*, Vol 10. New York: Academic Press.

Brown, A. L. (1994) 'The advancement of learning', *Educational Researcher*, 23: 4–12.

Brown, M., Askew, M., Millett, A. and Rhodes, V. (2003) 'The key role of educational research in the development and evaluation of the national numeracy strategy', *British Educational Research Journal*, 29 (5): 655–67.

Brown, P. (2013) 'Education, opportunity and the prospects for mobility', *British Journal of Sociology of Education*, 34 (5): 678–700.

Browne, Lord J. (2010) *Securing a Sustainable Future for Higher Education* (The Browne Report). Online at: https://www.gov.uk/government/publications/the-browne-report-higher-education-funding-and-student-finance (accessed 30 October 2015).

Bruner, J. (1966) *Towards a Theory of Instruction*. New York: Norton.

Bruner, J. S. (1972) *The Relevance of Education*. London: Allen & Unwin.

Bruner, J. (1983) *Child's Talk: Learning to Use Language*. Oxford: Oxford University Press.

Bruner (2006) *In Search of Pedagogy Volume II: The Selected Works of Jerome S. Bruner.* London and New York: Routledge.

Bruun, H. and Whimster, S. (eds) (2013) *Max Weber: Collected Methodological Writings*. London: Routledge.

Bryman, A. (2012) *Social Research Methods*, 4th edn. Oxford: Oxford University Press.

Buckler, S. and Castle, P. (2014) *Psychology for Teachers*. London: Sage.

Buckler, S. and Dolowitz, D. (2009) 'Ideology, party identity and renewal', *Journal of Political Ideologies*, 14 (1): 11–30.

Bullock Report (1975) *A Language for Life*. London: HMSO.

Burt, C. (1935) *The Subnormal Mind*. London: Oxford University Press.

Burt, C. (1955) 'The evidence for the concept of intelligence', *British Journal of Educational Psychology*, 25: 158–77.

Burton, D. (2003) 'Differentiation of schooling and pedagogy', in S. Bartlett and D. Burton (eds), *Education Studies: Essential Issues*. London: SAGE.

Burton, D. (2007) 'Psycho-pedagogy and personalised learning', *Journal of Education for Teaching*, 33 (1): 5–17.

Burton, D. and Bartlett, S. (2005) *Practitioner Research for Teachers*. London: Paul Chapman.

Burton, D. and Bartlett, S. (2006a) 'The evolution of Education Studies in higher education in England', *The Curriculum Journal*, 17 (4): 383–96.

Burton, D. and Bartlett, S. (2006b) 'Shaping pedagogy from psychological ideas', in D. Kassem, E. Mufti and J. Robinson (eds), *Education Studies*. Maidenhead: Open University Press.

Burton, D. and Bartlett, S. (2009) *Key Issues for Education Researchers*. London: SAGE.

Buzan, T. (2004) *Mind maps for kids: study skills*. London: Thorsons.

Cabinet Office (2010) *The Coalition: Our Programme for Government*. London: Cabinet Office. Online at: http://programmeforgovernment.hmg.gov.uk/schools (accessed 30 October 2015).

CACE (Central Advisory Council for Education) (1967) *Children and Their Primary Schools* (The Plowden Report). London: HMSO.

Cameron, D. (2015) Speech on plans to address extremism. Given at Ninestiles school, Birmingham on 20 July 2015. Online at: https://www.gov.uk/government/speeches/extremism-pm-speech (accessed 30 October 2015).

Campbell, T. (2014) 'Stratified at seven: in-class ability grouping and the relative age effect', *British Educational Research Journal*, 40 (5): 749–71.

Can, D. D. and Ginsburg-Block, M. (2013) 'Peer tutoring school-age children', in J. Hattie and E. M. Anderman (eds), *International Guide to Student Achievement*. Abingdon and New York: Routledge.

Canter, L. (2009) *Assertive discipline: Positive behaviour management for today's classroom*, 4th edn. Publisher: Author.

Canter, L. and Canter, M. (1977) *Assertive Discipline*. Los Angeles: Lee Canter Associates.

Capel, S., Leask, M. and Turner, T. (eds) (2016) *Learning to Teach in the Secondary School: A Companion to School Experience*, 7th edn. London: Routledge.

Carpentier, V. (2008) 'Sources and interpretations: quantitative sources for the history of education', *History of Education*, 37 (5): 701–20.

Carr, W. (2006) 'Education without theory', *British Journal of Educational Studies*, 54 (2): 136–59.

Carr, W. and Hartnett, A. (1996) *Education and the Struggle for Democracy: The Politics of Educational Ideas*. Buckingham: Open University Press.

Carr, W. and Kemmis, S. (1986) *Becoming Critical: Education, Knowledge and Action Research*. London: Falmer.

Carrington, B. and McPhee, A. (2008) 'Boys' "underachievement" and the feminization of teaching', *Journal of Education for Teaching*, 34 (2): 109–20.

Cattell, H. E. P. and Mead, A. D. (2008) 'The sixteen personality factor questionnaire (16PF)', in G. Boyle, G. Matthews and D. H. Saklofske (eds), *The SAGE Handbook of Personality Theory and Assessment, Vol. 2 Personality Measurement and Testing*. London and Los Angeles: SAGE.

Cattell, R. B. (1963) 'Theory of fluid and crystallized intelligence: a critical experiment', *Journal of Educational Psychology*, 54: 1–22.

Cattell, R. B. (1970) *The Technical Handbook to the 16 PF*. Champaign, IL: Institute for Personality and Achievement Tests.

CCCS (Centre for Contemporary Cultural Studies) (1981) *Unpopular Education*. London: Hutchinson.

CCCS (Centre for Contemporary Cultural Studies) (1991) *Education Limited*. London: Unwin Hyman.

Cerruti, C. (2013) 'Building a functional multiple intelligences theory to advance educational neuroscience', *Frontiers in Psychology*, 4: 950–6.

Chen, Y. C. (2015) 'Linking learning styles and learning on mobile Facebook', *International Review of Research in Open and Distributed Learning*, 16 (2): 94–114.

Chikoko, V., Gilmour, J., Harber, C. and Serf, J. (2011) 'Teaching controversial issues and teacher education in England and South Africa', *Journal of Education for Teaching*, 37 (1): 5–19.

Child, D. (2007) *Psychology and the Teacher*, 8th edn. London: Continuum.

Chitty, C. (2008) 'The UK National Curriculum: an historical perspective', *Forum*, 50 (3): 343. Online at: www.wwwords.co.uk/FORUM (accessed 12 October 2015).

Chitty, C. (2014) *Education Policy in Britain*, 3rd edn. Basingstoke: Palgrave Macmillan.

Chitty, C. and Dunford, J. (1999) *State Schools: New Labour and the Conservative Legacy*. London: Woburn Press.

Chomsky, N. (1965) *Aspects of the Theory of Syntax*. Cambridge, MA: MIT Press.

Clarke, A.M., Morreale, S., Field, C.A., Hussein, Y., & Barry, M.M. (2015) What works in enhancing social and emotional skills development during childhood and adolescence? A review of the evidence on the effectiveness of school-based and out-of-school programmes in the UK. *A report produced by the World Health Organization Collaborating Centre for Health Promotion Research*, National University of Ireland Galway.

Clarkson, J. (2009) 'What is comparative education?', in W. Bignold and L. Gayton (eds), *Global Issues and Comparative Education*. Exeter: Learning Matters.

Claxton, G. (2002) *Building Learning Power: Helping Young People Become Better Learners*. Bristol: TLO.

Claxton, G., Chambers, M., Powell, G. and Lucas, B. (2011) *The Learning Powered School: Pioneering 21st Century Education*. Bristol: TLO.

Clough, P. and Nutbrown, C. (2012) *A Student's Guide to Methodology*, 3rd edn. London: SAGE.

Coard, B. (1971) *How the West Indian Child Is Made Educationally Subnormal in the British School System*. London: New Beacon Books.

Cocco, F. (2015) 'Education: the pupil premium had one job – it failed', *The Mirror*, 5 February. Online at: www.mirror.co.uk/news/ampp3d/education-pupil-premium-one-job-5108809 (accessed 12 October 2015).

Coffield, F. (2008) *Just Suppose Teaching and Learning Became the First Priority*. London: Learning and Skills Network. Online at: www.itslifejimbutnotasweknowit.org.uk/files/Coffield_IfOnly.pdf (accessed 12 October 2015).

Coffield, F., Moseley, D., Hall, E. and Ecclestone, K. (2004a) *Learning Styles and Pedagogy in Post-16 Learning: A Systematic and Critical Review*. London: Learning and Skills Research Centre/Learning and Skills Development Agency.

Coffield, F., Moseley, D., Hall, E. and Ecclestone, K. (2004b) *Should We Be Using Learning Styles? What Research Has to Say to Practice*. London: Learning and Skills Research Centre/Learning and Skills Development Agency.

Cole, M. and Scribner, S. (1974) *Culture and Thought*. New York: Wiley.

Collins, A. M. and Quillian, M. R. (1969) 'Retrieval time from semantic memory', *Journal of Verbal Learning and Verbal Behaviour*, 8: 240–8.

Colucci-Gray, L., Das, S., Gray, D., Robinson, D. and Spratt, J. (2013) 'Evidence-based practice and teacher action-research: a reflection on the nature and direction of change', *British Educational Research Journal*, 39 (1): 126–47.

Connell, R. W. (2006) 'Understanding men: gender sociology and the new international research on masculinities', in C. Skelton, B. Francis and L. Smulyan (eds), *The SAGE Handbook of Gender and Education*. London: SAGE.

Connolly, P. (2006) 'The effects of social class and ethnicity on gender differences in GCSE attainment: a secondary analysis of the Youth Cohort Study of England and Wales 1997–2001', *British Educational Research Journal*, 32 (1): 3–21.

Conway, D. (2010) *Liberal Education and the National Curriculum*. London: Civitas.

Cooley, C. H. (1902) *Human Nature and the Social Order*. New York: Scribner.

Cooper, C. (2010) *Individual Differences and Personality*, 3rd edn. London: Hodder Education.

Counsell, C. (2011) 'Disciplinary knowledge for all: the secondary history curriculum and history teachers' achievement', *Curriculum Journal*, 22 (2): 201–25.

Covington, M. (1998) *The Will to Learn: A Guide for Motivating Young People*. Cambridge: Cambridge University Press.

Cowen, R. (2014) 'Ways of knowing, outcomes and "comparative education": be careful what you pray for', *Comparative Education*, 50 (3): 282–301.

Cox, C. B. and Boyson, R. (1975) *Black Paper 1975: The Fight For Education*. London: Dent.

Cox, C. B. and Boyson, R. (1977) *Black Paper 1977*. London: Maurice Temple Smith.

Cox, C. B. and Dyson, A. E. (eds) (1969a) *Fight for Education: A Black Paper*. Manchester: Critical Quarterly Society.

Cox, C. B. and Dyson, A. E. (eds) (1969b) *Black Paper Two: The Crisis in Education*. Manchester: Critical Quarterly Society.

Cox, C. B. and Dyson, A. E. (1970) *Black Paper Three: Goodbye Mr. Short*. London: Critical Quarterly Society.

Craik, F. and Lockhart, R. (1972) 'Levels of processing: a framework for memory research', *Journal of Verbal Learning and Verbal Behaviour*, 11: 671–84.

Craik, K. (1943) *The Nature of Explanation*. Cambridge: Cambridge University Press.

Creemers, B. and Kyriakides, L. (2012) *Improving Quality in Education: Dynamic Approaches to School Improvement*. Abingdon: Routledge.

Creswell, J. W. (2014) *Research Design: Qualitative, Quantitative and Mixed Methods*, 4th edn. London: SAGE.

Croll, P. and Attwood, G. (2013) 'Participation in higher education: Aspirations, attainment and social background', *British Journal of Educational Studies*, 61(2): 187–202.

Cronjé, J. (2006) 'Paradigms regained: toward integrating objectivism and constructivism in instructional design and the learning sciences', *Association for Educational Communications and Technology ETR&D*, 54 (4): 387–416.

Crowther Report (1959) *15 to 18*. London: HMSO.

Crozier, G. (2005) 'There's a war against our children: Black educational underachievement revisited', *British Journal of Sociology of Education*, 26 (5): 585–98.

Crozier, G. (2014) 'Foreword', in R. Race and V. Lander (eds), *Advancing Race and Ethnicity in Education*. Basingstoke: Palgrave Macmillan.

Curry, L. (1983) 'An organisation of learning style theory and constructs', in L. Curry (ed.), *Learning Style in Continuing Education*. Halifax, Nova Scotia: Dalhousie University.

Curtis, W. (2011) 'The philosophy of education', in B. Dufour and W. Curtis (eds), *Studying Education: An Introduction to the Key Disciplines in Education Studies*. Buckingham: Open University Press.

Dadds, M. and Hart, S. (2001) *Doing Practitioner Research Differently*. London: RoutledgeFalmer.

Darling-Hammond, L. (1994) 'Performance-based assessment and educational equity', *Harvard Educational Review*, 64: 5–30.

Darwin, C. (1859) *On the Origin of Species by Means of Natural Selection*. London: Murray.

Davies, I. and Hogarth, S. (2004) 'Perceptions of educational studies', *Educational Studies*, 30 (4): 425–39.

Davis, B. and Sumara, D. J. (1997) 'Cognition, complexity and teacher education', *Harvard Educational Review*, 67: 105–21.

Davis, B. and Sumara, D. J. (2012) 'Fitting teacher education in/to/for an increasingly complex world', *Complicity: An International Journal of Complexity & Education*, 9 (1): 30–40.

Davis, K. and Moore, W. E. (1967) 'Some principles of stratification', in R. Bendix and S. M. Lipset (eds), *Class, Status, and Power*. London: Kegan Paul.

DCSF (Department for Children, Schools and Families) (2007) *The Children's Plan: Building Brighter Futures*. London: DCSF/HMSO.

DCSF (Department for Children, Schools and Families) (2008) *Pupil Characteristics and Class Sizes in Maintained Schools in England*, Statistical First Release 09/2008 (provisional). London: DCSF.

DCSF (Department for Children, Schools and Families) (2009a) *Independent Review of the Primary Curriculum: Final Report*. Online at: http://www.educationengland.org.uk/documents/pdfs/2009-IRPC-final-report.pdf (accessed 30th October 2015).

DCSF (Department for Children, Schools and Families) (2009b) *Gender and Education – Mythbusters. Addressing Gender and Achievement: Myths and Realities*. London: Department for Children, Schools and Families.

DCSF (Department for Children, Schools and Families) (2009c) *200th Academy Opens a Year Early as Ministers Set Out New Plans to Open Up Programme to New Sponsors*. Online at: www.education.gov.uk/schools/leadership/typesofschools/academies/a0061222/academies-act-2010 (accessed 17 November 2010).

Dearden, L., Machin, S. and Vignoles, A. (2009) 'Economics of education research: a review and future prospects', *Oxford Review of Education*, 35 (5): 617–32.

Dearing, R. (1994) *The National Curriculum and Its Assessment: Final Report* (The Dearing Report). London: School Curriculum and Assessment Authority.

Deci, E., Koestner, R. and Ryan, R. (1999) 'A meta-analytic review of experiments examining the effects of external rewards on intrinsic motivation', *Psychological Bulletin*, 125: 627–68.

DeFelipe, J. and Jones, E. G. (1991) *Cajal's Degeneration and Regeneration of the Nervous System.* New York: Oxford University Press.

Delpit, L. (1995) *Other People's Children: Cultural Conflict in the Classroom.* New York: New Press.

Demie, F. (2005) 'Achievement of Black Caribbean pupils: good practice in Lambeth schools', *British Educational Research Journal*, 31 (4): 481–508.

Demie, F. And Lewis, K. (2011) 'White working-class achievement: an ethnographic study of barriers to learning in schools', *Educational Studies*, 37 (3): 245–64.

Denscombe, M. (2014) *The Good Research Guide*, 5th edn. Maidenhead: Open University Press.

Department for Business, Innovation and Skills (2014) *Participation Rates in Higher Education: Academic Years 2006/2007–2012/2013 (Provisional).* London: DBIS.

Derrida, J. (1987) *Positions.* London: Athlone.

DES (Department of Education and Science) (1965) *The Organisation of Secondary Education*, Circular 10/65. London: HMSO.

DES (Department of Education and Science) (1978a) *Mixed Ability Work in Comprehensive Schools*, HMI Matters for Discussion 6. London: HMSO.

DES (Department of Education and Science) (1978b) *Report of the Committee of Enquiry into the Education of Handicapped Children and Young People* (The Warnock Report). London: HMSO.

DES (Department of Education and Science) (1981) *West Indian Children in our Schools* (The Rampton Report). London: HMSO.

DES (Department of Education and Science) (1985a) *The Curriculum from 5 to 16.* London: HMSO.

DES (Department of Education and Science) (1985b) *Education for All* (The Swann Report). London: HMSO.

DES (Department of Education and Science) (1987) *The Secondary Schooling Staffing Survey – Data on the Curriculum in Maintained Secondary Schools in England*, Statistical Bulletin 10/87. London: HMSO.

DES (Department of Education and Science) (1988) *The Education Reform Act.* London: HMSO.

DES (Department of Education and Science) (1989a) *National Curriculum: From Policy to Practice.* London: HMSO.

DES (Department of Education and Science) (1989b) *The Task Group on Assessment and Testing: A Report.* London: HMSO.

DfE (Department for Education) (2010a) *The Importance of Teaching. The Schools White Paper.* Online at: www.gov.uk/government/publications/the-importance-of-teaching-the-schools-white-paper-2010 (accessed 12 October 2015).

DfE (Department for Education) (2010b) *The Academies Act 2010.* Online at: http://services.parliament.uk/bills/2010-12/academieshl/documents.html (accessed 30 October 2015).

DfE (Department for Education) (2011) 'National curriculum review launched', press release, 20 January. Online at: www.gov.uk/government/news/national-curriculum-review-launched (accessed 12 October 2015).

DfE (Department for Education) (2012) *Early Years Foundation Stage (EYFS) framework.* Online at: www.gov.uk/government/publications/early-years-foundation-stage-framework. (accessed 20 November 2012).

DfE (Department for Education) (2013a) *The National Curriculum in England: Framework Document*, July. Online at: www.gov.uk/government/uploads/system/uploads/attachment_data/file/210969/NC_framework_document_-_FINAL.pdf (accessed 12 October 2015).

DfE (Department for Education) (2013b) 'New TechBacc will give vocational education the high status it deserves', press release, 22 April. Online at: www.gov.uk/government/

news/new-techbacc-will-give-vocational-education-the-high-status-it-deserves (accessed 12 October 2015).

DfE (Department for Education) (2013c) *Statutory Guidance: National Curriculum In England: Citizenship Programmes of Study*. Online at: www.gov.uk/government/publications/national-curriculum-in-england-citizenship-programmes-of-study (accessed 12 October 2015).

DfE (Department for Education) (2014a) *The National Curriculum in England Framework Document*. Online at: www.gov.uk/government/uploads/system/uploads/attachment_data/file/381344/Master_final_national_curriculum_28_Nov.pdf (accessed 12 October 2015).

DfE (Department for Education) (2014b) *Early Years (Under Fives) Foundation Stage Framework (EYFS)*. Online at: www.gov.uk/government/publications/early-years-foundation-stage-framework—2 (accessed 12 October 2015).

DfE (Department for Education) (2014c) *Children and Families Act*. London: HMSO.

DfE (Department for Education) (2015a) *Policy Paper: The English Baccalaureate* (22 June). Online at: www.gov.uk/government/publications/english-baccalaureate-ebacc/ (accessed 12 October 2015).

DfE (Department for Education) (2015b) *Policy Paper: 2010 to 2015 Government Policy: Education of Disadvantaged Children*. Online at: www.gov.uk/government/publications/2010-to-2015-government-policy-education-of-disadvantaged-children/ (accessed 12 October 2015).

DfE (Department for Education) (2015c) *Policy Paper: 2010 to 2015 Government Policy: Academies and Free Schools*. Online at: www.gov.uk/government/publications/2010-to-2015-government-policy-academies-and-free-schools (accessed 12 October 2015).

DfEE (Department for Education and Employment) (1997) *Excellence in Schools*. London: Stationery Office.

DfEE (Department for Education and Employment) (1998a) *The National Literacy Strategy: Framework for Teaching*. London: DfEE.

DfEE (Department for Education and Employment (1998b) *The Learning Age: A Renaissance for a New Britain*. London: Stationery Office.

DfEE (Department for Education and Employment) (1999) *The National Numeracy Strategy: Framework for Teaching*. London: DfEE.

DfEE/QCA (Department for Education and Employment/Qualifications and Curriculum Authority) (2000) *Curriculum Guidance for the Foundation Stage*. London: DfEE.

DfES (Department for Education and Skills) (2001) *Schools Achieving Success*. London: DfES Publications.

DfES (Department for Education and Skills) (2003a) *Every Child Matters*. London: Stationery Office/DfES.

DfES (Department for Education and Skills) (2003b) *Excellence and Enjoyment: A Strategy for Primary Schools*. London: DfES/HMSO.

DfES (Department for Education and Skills) (2004a) *A National Conversation About Personalised Learning*. Online at: http://www.essexprimaryheads.co.uk/sites/essexprimary-heads.co.uk/files/A%20National%20Conversation%20about%20Personalised%20Learning.pdf (accessed 30 October 2015).

DfES (Department for Education and Skills) (2004b) *Five-Year Strategy for Children and Learners*. London: DfES.

DfES (Department for Education and Skills) (2004c) *Every Child Matters: Change for Children*. London: HMSO.

DfES (Department for Education and Skills) (2005a) *Higher Standards, Better Schools for All*. Norwich: Stationery Office.

DfES (Department for Education and Skills) (2005b) *Excellence and Enjoyment: Social and Emotional Aspects of Learning.* Nottingham: DfES Publications.

DfES (Department for Education and Skills) (2007) *Social and Emotional Aspects of Learning for Secondary Schools (SEAL).* Nottingham: DfES Publications.

Dick, M. M. (2008) 'Discourses for the new industrial world: industrialisation and the education of the public in late eighteenth-century Britain', *History of Education*, 37 (4): 567–84.

Dickinson, C. and Wright, J. (1993) *Differentiation: A Practical Handbook of Classroom Strategies.* Coventry: NCET.

Donaldson, M. (1978) *Children's Minds.* London: Fontana.

Dorfberger, S., Adi-Japha, E. and Karni, A. (2007) 'Reduced susceptibility to interference in the consolidation of motor memory before adolescence', *PLoS ONE*, 2 (2): e240.

Douglas, J. W. B. (1964) *The Home and the School.* St Albans: Panther.

Dowrick, N. (1996) '"But many that are first shall be last": attainment differences in young collaborators', *Research in Education*, 55: 16–28.

Driver, R. and Bell, J. (1986) 'Students' thinking and learning of science: a constructivist view', *School Science Review*, 67 (240): 443–56.

Driver, R., Leach, J., Millar, R. and Scott, P. (1996) *Young People's Images of Science.* Buckingham: Open University Press.

Dryden, G. and Vos, J. (2001) *The Learning Revolution: To Change the Way the World Learns.* Stafford: Network Educational Press in association with Learning Web.

Dufour, B. (2011) 'The history of education', in B. Dufour and W. Curtis (eds), *Studying Education: An Introduction to the Key Disciplines in Education Studies.* Buckingham: Open University Press.

Dunn, A. and Burton, D. (2011) 'New Labour, communitarianism and citizenship education in England and Wales', *Education, Citizenship and Social Justice*, 6 (2): 169–80.

Dunn, R. (1991) 'How learning style changes over time', presentation at the 14th Annual Leadership Institute: Teaching Students Through Their Individual Learning Styles, New York, 7–13 July.

Dunn, R., Dunn, K. and Price, G. (1979) 'Identifying learning styles', in J. W. Keif (ed.), *Student Learning Styles: Diagnosing and Prescribing Programmes.* Reston, VA: National Association of Secondary School Principals.

Dunn, R., Dunn, K. and Price, G. E. (1989) *The Learning Style Inventory.* Lawrence, KS: Price Systems.

Dunn, R. and Griggs, S. (2003) *Synthesis of the Dunn and Dunn Learning Styles Model Research: Who, What, When, Where and So What – The Dunn and Dunn Learning Styles Model and Its Theoretical Cornerstone.* New York: Learning Styles Network/St John's University.

Durkheim, E. (1947) *The Division of Labour in Society* [1893]. New York: Free Press.

Durkheim, E. (1964) *The Rules of Sociological Method.* New York: Free Press.

Durkheim, E. (1970) *Suicide: A Study in Sociology.* London: Routledge & Kegan Paul.

Durkheim, E. (2014) *The Division of Labor in Society*, ed. S. Lukes. New York: Simon and Schuster.

Dweck, C. S. (1991) 'Self-theories and goals: their role in motivation, personality and development', in R. Dienstbier (ed.), *Nebraska Symposium on Motivation.* Lincoln, NE: University of Nebraska Press.

Eagleton, T. (2000) *The Idea of Culture.* Oxford: Blackwell.

Ebbinghaus, H. (1964) *Memory: A Contribution to Experimental Psychology Refurbished* [1885]. New York: Dover.

Ecclestone, K. (2004) 'Learning or therapy? The demoralisation of education', *British Journal of Educational Studies*, 57 (3): 127–41.

Edwards, R. and Usher, R. (2000) *Globalisation and Pedagogy: Space, Place and Identity*. London: Routledge.

Eisenberger, R. and Cameron, A. (1996) 'The detrimental effects of reward: myth or reality?', *American Psychologist*, 51: 1153–6.

Elbers, E. (2010) 'Learning and social interaction in culturally diverse classrooms', in K. Littleton, C. Wood and J. Kleine Staarman (eds), *The International Handbook of Psychology in Education*. Bingley: Emerald.

Elliott, J. (1991) *Action Research for Educational Change*. Milton Keynes: Open University Press.

Elliott, J. (1993) 'What have we learned from action research in school-based evaluation?', *Education Action Research*, 1 (1): 175–86.

Elliott, J. (1998) *The Curriculum Experiment: Meeting the Social Challenge*. Buckingham: Open University Press.

Elliott, J. (2003) 'Interview with John Elliott, December 6, 2002', *Educational Action Research*, 11 (2): 169–80.

Elliott, J. (2005) 'Dyslexia myths and the feel-bad factor', *Times Educational Supplement*, 2 September.

Elliott, J. (2006) 'Educational research as a form of democratic rationality', *Journal of Philosophy of Education*, 40 (2): 169–86.

Engestrom, Y. (1993) 'Developmental studies of work as a testbench of activity theory', in S. Chaiklin and J. Lave (eds), *Understanding Practice: Perspectives on Activity and Context*. Cambridge: Cambridge University Press.

Englander, F., Terregrossa, R. A. and Wang, Z. (2013) 'Testing the construct validity of the Productivity Environmental Preference Survey Learning Style Inventory instrument', *International Journal of Education Research*, 8 (1): 107–15.

Entwistle, N. J. (1981) *Styles of Learning and Teaching*. Chichester: Wiley.

Entwistle, N. J. (2009) *Teaching for Understanding at University: Deep Approaches and Distinctive Ways of Thinking*. Basingstoke: Palgrave Macmillan.

Entwistle, N., McCune, V. and Walker, P. (2001) 'Conceptions, styles and approaches within higher education: analytic abstractions and everyday experience', in R. J. Sternberg and L. F. Zhang (eds), *Perspectives on Thinking, Learning, and Cognitive Styles*. Mahwah, NJ: Lawrence Erlbaum Associates.

Erikson, E. H. (1980) *Identity and the Life Cycle*. New York: Norton.

Evans, C. and Waring, M. (2006) 'Towards inclusive teacher education: sensitising individuals to how they learn', *Educational Psychology*, 26 (4): 499–518.

Evans, K. and King, D. (2006) *Studying Society: The Essentials*. Oxford: Routledge.

Evans, R., Scourfield, J. and Murphy, S. (2015) 'The unintended consequences of targeting: young people's lived experiences of social and emotional learning interventions', *British Education Research Journal*, 41: 381–97.

Exley, S. and Ball, S. (2011) 'Understanding Conservative policy', in H. Boschel (ed.), *The Conservative Party and Social Policy*. Bristol: Policy Press.

Eysenck, H. J. (1947) *Dimensions of Personality*. London: Routledge.

Eysenck, H. J. (1967) *The Biological Basis of Personality*. Springfield, IL: Thomas.

Eysenck, H. J. (1971) *Race, Intelligence and Education*. London: Temple-Smith.

Fallan, L. (2006) 'Quality reform: personality type, preferred learning style and majors in a business school', *Quality in Higher Education*, 12 (14): 193–206.

Faulks, K. (2006) 'Education for citizenship in England's secondary schools: a critique of current principle and practice', *Journal of Educational Policy*, 21 (1): 59–74.

Fazey, J. A. and Marton, F. (2002) 'Understanding the space of experiential variation', *Active Learning in Higher Education*, 3 (3): 234–50.

Festinger, L. (1957) *A Theory of Cognitive Dissonance*. Evanston, IL: Row, Peterson.

Feuerstein, R., Klein, P. and Tannenbaum, A. (eds) (1991) *Mediated Learning Experience*. London: Freund.

Flavell, J. H. (1979) 'Metacognition and cognitive monitoring', *American Psychologist*, 34: 906–11.

Flavell, J. H. (1982) 'Structures, stages, and sequences in cognitive development', in W. A. Collins (ed.), *The Concept of Development: The Minnesota Symposia on Child Psychology*, 15: 1–28.

Flick, U. (2015) *Introducing Research Methodology*, 2nd edn. London: SAGE.

Flynn, J. (2007) *What Is Intelligence? Beyond the Flynn Effect*. New York: Cambridge University Press.

Fodor, J. (1975) *The Language of Thought*. Cambridge, MA: Harvard University Press.

Fodor, J. (1983) *The Modularity of Mind*. Cambridge, MA: MIT Press.

Fodor, J. (2000) *The Mind Doesn't Work That Way: The Scope and Limits of Computational Psychology*. Cambridge, MA: MIT Press.

Forsman, L. and Hummelstedt-Djedou, I. (2014) 'The identity game: constructing and enabling multicultural identities in a Finland–Swedish school setting', *British Educational Research Journal*, 40 (3): 501–22.

Foucault, M. (1977) *The Archaeology of Knowledge*. London: Tavistock.

Foucault, M. (1988) *Technologies of the Self*. London: Tavistock.

Fowler, F. J. (2014) *Survey Research Methods*, 5th edn. London: SAGE.

Francis, B. (2009) 'The role of The Boffin as abject Other in gendered performances of school achievement', *Sociological Review*, 57 (4): 645–69.

Francis, B. (2010) 'Gender, toys and learning', *Oxford Review of Education*, 36 (3): 325–44.

Francis, B., Burke, P. and Read, B. (2014) 'The submergence and re-emergence of gender in underground accounts of university experience', *Gender and Education*, 26 (1): 1–17.

Fransella, F. (2005) *The Essential Practitioner's Handbook of Personal Construct Psychology*. London: John Wiley.

Freud, S. (1901) 'The psychopathology of everyday life', republished in 1953 in J. Strachey (ed.), *The Standard Edition of the Complete Psychological Works of Sigmund Freud*, Vol. 6. London: Hogarth.

Frick, B. (2013) 'Fostering student creativity in the era of high stakes testing', in J. Hattie and E. M. Anderman (eds), *International Guide to Student Achievement*. Abingdon and New York: Routledge.

Frith, U. (2005) 'Teaching in 2020: the impact of neuroscience', *Journal of Education for Teaching: International Research and Pedagogy*, 31 (4): 289–91.

Fung, D. and Howe, C. (2014) 'Group work and the learning of critical thinking in the Hong Kong secondary liberal studies curriculum', *Cambridge Journal of Education*, 4 (2): 245–70.

Furlong, J. (2005) 'New Labour and teacher education: the end of an era', *Oxford Review of Education*, 31 (1): 119–34.

Gagne, R. M. (1977) *The Conditions of Learning*. New York: Holt International.

Galton, F. (1869) *Hereditary Genius*. New York: Macmillan.

Gardner, H. (1983) *Frames of Mind: The Theory of Multiple Intelligences*. New York: Basic Books.

Gardner, H. (1995) 'Reflections on multiple intelligences: myths and messages', *Phi Delta Kappan*, 77: 200–3, 206–9.

Gardner, H. (2011) *Frames of Mind: The Theory of Multiple Intelligences*. New York: Basic Books.

Gervis, M. and Capel, S. (2016) 'Motivating pupils', in S. Capel, M. Leask and S. Younie (eds), *Learning to Teach in the Secondary School: A Companion to School Experience*, 7th edn. London: Routledge.

Gessell, A. (1925) *The Mental Growth of the Preschool Child*. New York: Macmillan.

Gibbs, G. (1992) *Improving the Quality of Student Learning*. Bristol: Technical and Educational Services.

Gibson, J. (1979) *The Ecological Approach to Visual Perception*. Boston, MA: Houghton Mifflin.

Gibson, S. (2014) 'SEN and the question of inclusive education', in W. Curtis, S. Ward, J. Sharp, and L. Hankin (eds), *Education Studies: An Issues Based Approach*, 3rd edn. Exeter: Learning Matters.

Giddens, A. (1985) *The Constitution of Society*. Cambridge: Polity Press.

Giddens, A. (1998) *The Third Way: The Renewal of Social Democracy*. Cambridge: Polity Press.

Giddens, A. (2000) *The Third Way and Its Critics*. Cambridge: Polity Press.

Giddens, A. and Sutton, A. (2013) *Sociology*, 7th edn. Cambridge: Polity Press.

Gillard, D. (2011) *Education in England: A Brief History*. Online at: www.educationengland.org.uk/history (accessed 12 October 2015).

Gillborn, D. (2001) 'Racism, policy and the (mis)education of Black children', in R. Majors (ed.), *Educating Our Black Children: New Directions and Radical Approaches*. London: RoutledgeFalmer.

Gillborn, D. (2008) *Racism and Education: Coincidence or Conspiracy?* London: Routledge.

Gillborn, D. and Rollock, N. (2010) 'Education', in A. Bloch and J. Solomos (eds), *Race and Ethnicity in the 21st Century*. Basingstoke: Palgrave Macmillan.

Gillies, R. M. and Ashman, A. F. (2003) *Co-operative Learning: The Social and Intellectual Outcomes of Learning in Groups*. London: RoutledgeFalmer.

Gipps, C. (1993) 'The structure for assessment and recording', in P. O'Hear and J. White (eds), *Assessing the National Curriculum*. London: Paul Chapman.

Gipps, C. and Stobart, G. (1993) *Assessment*. London: Hodder & Stoughton.

Glaser, B. and Strauss, A. (1967) *The Discovery of Grounded Theory*. Chicago: Aldane.

Goldthorpe, J. H., Lockwood, D., Bechhofer, F. and Platt, J. (1968) *The Affluent Worker: Industrial Attitudes and Behaviour*. Cambridge: Cambridge University Press.

Goleman, D. (1995) *Emotional Intelligence*. New York: Bantam.

Goleman, D. (2006) *Emotional Intelligence: Why It Can Matter More Than IQ*, 10th anniversary edn. New York: Bantam Books.

Goleman, D. (2011) *The Brain and Emotional Intelligence: New Insights* [e-book]. More Than Sound LLC.

Goodman, J. and Grosvenor, I. (2009) 'Educational research – history of education a curious case?', *Oxford Review of Education*, 35 (5): 601–16.

Goodman, R. and Burton, D. (2012) 'The academies programme: an education revolution', *Educationalfutures: BESA Journal*, 4 (3): 3–12.

Gorard, S. (2009) 'What are academies the answer to?', *Journal of Education Policy*, 24 (1): 101–13.

Gorard, S. (2010) 'Serious doubts about school effectiveness', *British Educational Research Journal*, 36 (5): 745–66.

Gorard, S. (2011) 'Doubts about school effectiveness exacerbated – by attempted justification', *Research Intelligence*, 114: 26.

Gorard, S. (2014) 'The link between academies in England, pupil outcomes and local patterns of socio-economic segregation between schools', *Research Papers in Education*, 29 (3): 268–84.

Gorard, S. and Huat See, B. (2013) *Overcoming Disadvantage in Education*. London: Routledge.

Goswami, U. (2008) *Cognitive Development: The Learning Brain*. Hove and New York: Psychology Press.

Gove, M. (2007) 'It's time for modern compassionate Conservative education policy', speech, 1 October at the Conservative Party Conference in Blackpool. Available at: http://conservative-speeches.sayit.mysociety.org/speech/599789 (accessed 2 December 2015).

Gove, M. (2009) 'A comprehensive programme for state education', speech, 6 November at the Centre for Policy Studies.

Gove, M. (2010) 'Schools are promised an education revolution', interview, *BBC News*, 26 May.

Gramsci, A. (1985) *Selections from Cultural Writings*. London: Lawrence & Wishart.

Gramsci, A. (1991) *Prison Notebooks*. New York: Columbia University Press.

Green, A. and Wiborg, S. (2004) 'Comprehensive schooling and educational inequality: an international perspective', in M. Benn and C. Chitty (eds), *A Tribute to Caroline Benn: Education and Democracy*. London: Continuum.

Greenfield, S. (1997) *The Human Brain: A Guided Tour*. London: Weidenfeld & Nicolson.

Greenfield, S. (2000) *Brain Story*. London: BBC Worldwide.

Greeno, J. G. (1997) 'On claims that answer the wrong questions', *Educational Researcher*, 26: 5–17.

Greeno, J. G., Smith, D. R. and Moore, J. L. (1993) 'Transfer of situated learning', in D. K. Detterman and R. J. Sternberg (eds), *Transfer on Trial: Intelligence, Cognition and Instruction*. Norwood, NJ: Ablex.

Gregorc, A. R. (1982) *Style Delineator*. Maynard, MA: Gabriel Systems.

Guasp, A. (2012) *The School Report: The Experiences of Gay Young People in Britain's Schools in 2012*. London: Stonewall and University of Cambridge: Online at: www.stonewall.org.uk/search/school%20report%202012 (accessed 12 October 2015).

Guilford, J. P. (1950) 'Creativity', *American Psychologist*, 5: 444–54.

Guilford, J. P. (1967) *The Nature of Human Intelligence*. New York: McGraw-Hill.

Gundara, J. (2000) *Interculturalism, Education and Inclusion*. London: Paul Chapman.

Gunter, H. and McGinity, R. (2014) 'The politics of the academies programme: natality and pluralism in education policy making', *Research Papers in Education*, 29 (3): 300–14.

Gurney-Dixon Report (1954) *Early Leaving*. London: HMSO.

Hadow Report (1926) *The Education of the Adolescent*. London: Board of Education, HMSO.

Hall, E., Leat, D., Wall, K., Higgins, S. and Edwards, G. (2006) 'Learning to learn: teacher research in the zone of proximal development', *Teacher Development*, 10 (2): 149–66.

Hall, J., Eisenstadt, N., Sylva, K., Smith, T., Sammons, P., Smith, G., Evangelou, M., Goff, J., Tanner, E., Agur, M. and Hussey, D. (2015) 'A review of the services offered by English Sure Start Children's Centres in 2011 and 2012', *Oxford Review of Education*, 41 (1): 89–104.

Hall, K. and Sheehy, K. (2014) 'Assessment and learning: summative approaches', in T. Cremin and J. Arthur (eds), *Learning to Teach in the Primary School*, 3rd edn. London and New York: Routledge.

Hallam, S. (2012) 'Streaming and setting in UK primary schools: evidence from the Millennium Cohort Study', *FORUM*, 54 (1): 57–63.

Hallam, S. and Ireson, J. (2006) 'Secondary school pupils' preferences for different types of structured grouping practices', *British Educational Research Journal*, 32 (4): 583–99.

Hallam, S. and Ireson, J. (2007) 'Secondary school pupils' satisfaction with their ability grouping placements', *British Educational Research Journal*, 33 (1): 27–45.

Hallam, S., Ireson, J. and Davies, J. (2004) 'Primary pupils' experiences of different types of grouping in school', *British Educational Research Journal*, 30 (4): 515–33.

Hallam, S. and Parsons, S. (2013) 'Prevalence of streaming in UK primary schools: evidence from the Millennium Cohort Study', *British Educational Research Journal*, 39 (3): 514–44.

Halliday, M. A. K. (1979) *Language as Social Semiotic*. London: Arnold.

Halsey, A. H. (1978) *Change in British Society*. Oxford: Oxford University Press.

Halsey, A. H. (1995) *Change in British Society from 1900 to the Present Day*, 4th edn. Oxford: Oxford University Press.

Halsey, A. H. (2013) 'Reflections on education and social mobility', *British Journal of Sociology of Education*, 34 (5): 644–59.

Halsey, A. H., Heath, A. F. and Ridge, J. M. (1980) *Origins and Destinations*. Oxford: Clarendon Press.

Halsey, A. H., Lauder, H., Brown, P. and Wells, A. (1997) *Education: Culture Economy Society*. Oxford: Oxford University Press.

Hammersley, M. (2004) 'Some questions about evidence-based practice in education', in G. Thomas and R. Pring (eds), *Evidence-based Practice in Education*. Maidenhead: Open University Press.

Hammersley, M. and Atkinson, I. (2007) *Ethnography: Principles in Practice*, 3rd edn. London: Routledge.

Hara, N. (2009) *Communities of Practice: Fostering Peer to Peer Learning and Informal Knowledge Sharing in the Workplace*. Berlin: Springer.

Harber, C. (2014) *Education and International Development: Theory, Practice and Issues*. Oxford: Symposium Books.

Hardre, P., Huang, S., Hua, C., Ching, H., Chiang, C., Ting, J., Fen, L. and Warden, L. (2006) 'High school teachers' motivational perceptions and strategies in an East Asian Nation', *Asia-Pacific Journal of Teacher Education*, 34 (2): 199–221.

Hargreaves, D. (1967) *Social Relations in a Secondary School*. London: Routledge & Kegan Paul.

Hargreaves, D. (1972) *Interpersonal Relations and Education*. London: Routledge & Kegan Paul.

Hargreaves, D., Hestor, S. and Mellor, F. (1975) *Deviance in Classrooms*. London: Routledge & Kegan Paul.

Hargreaves, E., Gipps, C. and Pickering, A. (2014) 'Assessment for learning: formative approaches', in T. Cremin and J. Arthur (eds), *Learning to Teach in the Primary School*, 3rd edn. London and New York: Routledge.

Harlen, W. (ed.) (2008) *Student Assessment and Testing*, 4 vols. London: SAGE.

Harlen, W. and Qualter, A. (2014) *The Teaching of Science in Primary Schools*, 6th edn. London: Fulton.

Harris, A. (2009) *Equity and Diversity: Building Community. Improving Schools in Challenging Circumstances*. London: Institute of Education.

Harris, A. and Ranson, S. (2005) 'The contradictions of education policy: disadvantage and achievement', *British Educational Research Journal*, 31 (5): 571–87.

Harris, D. and Bell, C. (1990) *Evaluating and Assessing for Learning*. London: Kogan Page.

Hart, S. (ed.) (1996) *Differentiation and the Secondary Curriculum: Debates and Dilemmas*. London: Routledge.

Hatcher, R. (2008) 'Academies and diplomas: two strategies for shaping the future workforce', *Oxford Review of Education*, 34(6): 665–76.

Hattie, J. (2009) *Visible Learning: A Synthesis of Over 800 Meta-analyses Relating to Achievement*. London and New York: Routledge.

Hattie, J. (2012) *Visible Learning for Teachers Maximising Impact on Learning*. London and New York: Routledge.

Hayes, D. (2006) *Primary Education: Key Concepts*. London: Routledge.

Hayes, N. (2010) *Understand Psychology*. London: Hodder Education.

Haylock, D. (2014) *Mathematics Explained for Primary Teachers*, 5th edn. London: SAGE.

Hebb, D. O. (1949) *The Organisation of Behaviour*. New York: Wiley.

Hemsley-Brown, J. (2015) 'Getting into a Russell Group university: high scores and private schooling', *British Educational Research Journal*, 41 (3): 398–422.

Henderson-King, D. and Smith, M. (2006) 'Meanings of education for university students: academic motivation and personal values as predictors', *Social Psychology of Education*, 9 (2): 195–221.

Herrnstein, R. J. and Murray, C. (1994) *The Bell Curve: Intelligence and Class Structure in American Life*. New York: Free Press.

Higher Education Statistics Agency (HESA) (2015) Overview of student data 2009/10 to 2013/14. Online at: https://www.hesa.ac.uk/free-statistics (accessed 30 October 2015).

Hess, R. D. and Azuma, M. (1991) 'Cultural support for schooling: contrasts between Japan and the United States', *Educational Researcher*, 20: 2–8.

Higgins, S. (2013) 'Matching style of learning', in J. Hattie and E. M. Anderman (eds), *International Guide to Student Achievement*. Abingdon and New York: Routledge.

Higham, R. (2014) 'Free schools in the Big Society: the motivations, aims and demography of free school proposers', *Journal of Education Policy*, 29 (1): 122–39.

Hills, P. (2015) 'A normative approach to the legitimacy of Muslim schools in multicultural Britain', *British Journal of Educational Studies*, 63 (2): 179–96.

Hillyard, S. A. (1993) 'Electrical and magnetic brain recordings: contributions to cognitive neuroscience', *Current Opinion in Neurobiology*, 3: 217–24.

Hirst, P. H. (1975) *Knowledge and the Curriculum*. London: Routledge & Kegan Paul.

HMI (Her Majesty's Inspectorate) (1977) *Curriculum 11–16: A Contribution to Current Debate*. London: HMSO.

HMI (Her Majesty's Inspectorate) (1994) 'The entitlement curriculum', in B. Moon and S. Mayes (eds), *Teaching and Learning in the Secondary School*. London: Routledge.

Hodkinson, A. (2016) *Key Issues in Special Educational Needs and Inclusion*, 2nd edn. London: SAGE.

Hodkinson, P., Biesta, G. and James, D. (2007) 'Learning cultures and a cultural theory of learning', *Educational Review*, 59 (4): 415–27.

Honey, P. and Mumford, A. (1986) *Using Your Learning Styles*. Maidenhead: Honey.

Hopkins, D., Stringfield, S., Harris, A., Stoll, L. and Mackay, T. (2014) 'School and system improvement: a narrative state-of-the-art review', *School Effectiveness and School Improvement: An International Journal of Research, Policy and Practice*, 25 (2): 257–81.

Hopkins, E. (1994) *Childhood Transformed: Working-Class Children in Nineteenth-Century England*. Manchester: Manchester University Press.

Howard-Jones, P. (2016) 'Neuro-education: the emergence of the brain in education', in S. Capel, M. Leask and S. Younie (eds), *Learning to Teach in the Secondary School: A Companion to School Experience*, 7th edn. London: Routledge.

Howe, C., Tolmie, A., Thurston, A., Topping, K., Christie, D., Livingston, K., Jessiman, E. and Donaldson, C. (2007) 'Group work in elementary science: towards organizational principles for supporting pupil learning', *Learning and Instruction*, 17: 549–63.

Hughes, M. (1975) 'Egocentricity in children', unpublished PhD thesis, Edinburgh University.

Hurst, D. (2014) 'National curriculum review premature, say parents and teachers', *Guardian*, 13 January. Online at: www.theguardian.com/world/2014/jan/13/national-curriculum-review-premature-say-parents-and-teachers (accessed 12 October 2015).

Husbands, C. (2012) 'Models of the curriculum', in V. Brooks, I. Abbott and P. Huddleston (eds), *Preparing to Teach in Secondary Schools: A Student Teacher's Guide to Professional Issues in Secondary Education*, 3rd edn. Maidenhead: Open University Press.

Ireson, J. and Hallam, S. (2005) 'Pupils' liking for school: ability grouping, self-concept and perceptions of teaching', *British Journal of Educational Psychology*, 75 (2): 297–311.

Ireson, J., Hallam, S. and Hurley, C. (2005) 'What are the effects of ability grouping on GCSE attainment?', *British Educational Research Journal*, 31 (4): 443–58.

Jackson, B. (1964) *Streaming: An Education System in Miniature*. London: Routledge & Kegan Paul.

Jackson, B. and Marsden, D. (1962) *Education and the Working Class*. Harmondsworth: Penguin.

James, D. and Biesta, G. (2007) *Improving Learning Cultures in Further Education*. London: Routledge.

James, W. (1890) *The Principles of Psychology*, 2 vols. New York: Dover reprint 1950.

Janmaat, J. and Green, A. (2013) 'Skills inequality, adult learning and social cohesion in the United Kingdom', *British Journal of Educational Studies*, 61 (1): 7–24.

Jarvis, P., Holford, J. and Griffin, C. (2003) *The Theory and Practice of Learning*, 2nd edn. London: Kogan Page.

Jenkins, D. and Shipman, M. D. (1976) *Curriculum: An Introduction*. London: Open Books.

Jenkins, S. (2010) 'Napoleon Gove can dictate its terms but the school curriculum is bogus', *The Guardian*, 25 November.

Jensen, A. R. (1969) 'How much can we boost IQ and scholastic achievement?', *Harvard Educational Review*, 33: 1–23.

Jensen, A. R. (1973) *Educational Differences*. London: Methuen.

Jerrim, J., Vignoles, A., Lingam, R. and Friend, A. (2015) 'The socio-economic gradient in children's reading skills and the role of genetics', *British Education Research Journal*, 41 (1): 6–29.

Jones, G. and Carter, G. (1994) 'Verbal and non-verbal behaviour of ability-grouped dyads', *Journal of Research in Science Teaching*, 31: 603–19.

Jones, K. (2016) *Education in Britain: 1944 to the Present*, 2nd edn. Oxford: Polity Press.

Kavanagh, S. (2000) 'A total system of classroom management: consistent, flexible, practical and working', *Pastoral Care in Education*, 18 (1): 17–21.

Kayes, D. (2005) 'Internal validity and reliability of Kolb's Learning Style Inventory Version 3 (1999)', *Journal of Business and Psychology*, 20 (2): 249–57.

Keddie, A. (2014) 'The politics of Britishness: multiculturalism, schooling and social cohesion', *British Educational Research Journal*, 40 (3): 539–54.

Keddie, A. and Mills, M. (2008) *Teaching Boys*. Crows Nest, NSW: Allen & Unwin.

Keddie, N. (1971) 'Classroom knowledge', in M. F. D. Young (ed.), *Knowledge and Control*. London: Collier-Macmillan.

Kehily, M. J. (2001) 'Issues of gender and sexuality in schools', in B. Francis and C. Skelton, *Investigating Gender: Contemporary Perspectives in Education*. Buckingham: Open University Press.

Kelly, A. (2012) 'Measuring "equity" and "equitability" in school effectiveness research', *British Educational Research Journal*, 38 (6): 977–1003.

Kelly, A. V. (1975) *Case Studies in Mixed Ability Teaching*. London: Harper & Row.

Kelly, A. V. (2009) *The Curriculum: Theory and Practice*, 6th edn. London: SAGE.

Kelly, G. A. (1955) *The Psychology of Personal Constructs*. New York: Norton.

Kember, D. and Gow, L. (1990) 'Cultural specificity of approaches to learning', *British Journal of Educational Psychology*, 60: 356–63.

Kemmis, S. and Wilkinson, M. (1998) 'Participatory action research and the study of practice', in B. Atweh, S. Kemmis and P. Weeks (eds), *Action Research in Practice*. London: Routledge.

Kerry, T. (1984) 'Analysing the cognitive demands made by classroom tasks in mixed ability classes', in E. C. Wragg (ed.), *Classroom Teaching Skills*. Beckenham: Croom Helm.

Khalaila, R. (2015) 'The relationship between academic self-concept, intrinsic motivation, test anxiety, and academic achievement among nursing students: mediating and moderating effects', *Nurse Education Today*, 35 (3): 432–8.

Killick, S. (2006) *Emotional Literacy at the Heart of the School Ethos*. London: Paul Chapman.

Klein, H. J., Noe, R. A. and Wang, C. (2006) 'Motivation to learn and course outcomes: the impact of delivery mode, learning goal orientation, and perceived barriers and enablers', *Personnel Psychology*, 59 (3): 665–702.

Koch, K. R., Timmerman, L., Peiffer, A. M. and Laurienti, P. J. (2013) 'Convergence of two independent roads leads to collaboration between education and neuroscience', *Psychology in the Schools*, 50 (6): 577–88.

Koffka, K. (1935) *Principles of Gestalt Psychology*. New York: Harcourt Brace.

Kohlberg, L. (1976) 'Moral stages and moralization: the cognitive-developmental approach', in T. Lickona (ed.), *Moral Development and Behaviour: Theory, Research, and Social Issues*. New York: Holt, Rinehart & Winston.

Kohler, W. (1940) *Dynamics in Psychology*. New York: Liveright.

Kolb, A. Y. and Kolb, D. A. (2009) 'The learning way: meta-cognitive aspects of experiential learning', *Simulation and Gaming*, 40 (3): 297–327.

Kolb, D. A. (1976) *The Learning Style Inventory: Technical Manual*. Boston: McBer & Co.

Kolb, D. A. (1985) *The Learning Style Inventory: Technical Manual*, revised edn. Boston: McBer & Co.

Kolb, D. A. (2015) *Experiential Learning: Experience as the Source of Learning and Development*, 2nd edn. New Jersey: Pearson Education.

Kong, C. K. and Hau, K. T. (1996) 'Students' achievement goals and approaches to learning: the relationship between emphasis on self-improvement and thorough understanding', *Research in Education*, 55: 74–85.

Koshy, V. (2010) *Action Research for Improving Educational Practice*, 2nd edn. London: SAGE.

Kowalski, R. (2014) *Paradox in the Contrivance of Human Development*. Bloomington: iUniverse.

Kozulin, A. (1998) *Psychological Tools. A Sociocultural Approach to Education*. Cambridge, MA: Harvard University Press.

Kozulin, A. (2003) 'Psychological tools and mediated learning', in A. Kozulin, B. Gindis, V. Ageyev and S. Miller (eds), *Vygotsky's Educational Theory in Cultural Context*. Cambridge: Cambridge University Press.

Krnel, D., Watson, R. and Glazar, S. (2005) 'The development of the concept of "matter": a cross-age study of how children describe materials', *International Journal of Science Education*, 27 (3): 367–83.

Kubina, R. and Yurich, K. (2009) 'Developing behavioral fluency for students with autism: a guide for parents and teachers', *Intervention in School and Clinic*, 44 (3): 131–8.

Kutnick, P., Blatchford, P. and Baines, E. (2002) 'Pupil groupings in primary school classrooms: sites for learning and social pedagogy?', *British Educational Research Journal*, 28 (2): 187–206.

Kvernbekk, T. (2016) *Evidence-based Practice in Education: Functions of Evidence and Causal Presuppositions*. Abingdon, Oxon and New York: Routledge.

Kyriacou, C. (2005) 'The impact of daily mathematics lessons in England on pupil confidence and competence in early mathematics: a systematic review', *British Journal of Educational Studies*, 52 (2): 168–86.

Kyriakides, L., Creemers, B., Anatoniou, P. and Demetriou, D. (2010) 'A synthesis of studies searching for school factors: implications for theory and research', *British Educational Research Journal*, 36 (5): 807–30.

Labov, W. (1973) 'The logic of nonstandard English', in J. Young (ed.), *Tinker, Tailor: The Myth of Cultural Deprivation*. Harmondsworth: Penguin.

Labov, W. (1997) Testimony submitted by William Labov, Professor of Linguistics at the University of Pennsylvania, 23 January. Online at:. http://www.ling.upenn.edu/~wlabov/Papers/Ebonic%20testimony.pdf (accessed 12 January 2000).

Lacey, C. (1970) *Hightown Grammar: The School as a Social System*. Manchester: Manchester University Press.

Lam, S., Yim, P., Law, J. S. F. and Cheung, R. W. Y. (2004) 'The effects of competition on achievement motivation in Chinese classrooms', *British Journal of Educational Psychology*, 74 (2): 281–96.

Laming, S. (2003) *The Victoria Climbié Inquiry Report*. London: DfES.

Lave, J. (1988) *Cognition in Practice: Mind, Mathematics and Culture in Everyday Life*. Cambridge: Cambridge University Press.

Lave, J. and Wenger, E. (1991) *Situated Learning: Legitimate Peripheral Participation*. Cambridge: Cambridge University Press.

Lawn, M. and Furlong, J. (2009) 'The disciplines of education in the UK: between the ghost and the shadow', *Oxford Review of Education*, 35 (5): 553–68.

Lawrence, D. (2006) *Enhancing Self-Esteem in the Classroom*, 3rd edn. London: Paul Chapman.

Lawton, D. (1975) *Class, Culture and the Curriculum*. London: Routledge & Kegan Paul.

Lawton, D. (1992) *Education and Politics in the 1990s: Conflict or Consensus?* London: Falmer Press.

Lawton, D. (1999) *Beyond the National Curriculum*. London: Hodder & Stoughton.

Lawton, D. (2005) *Education and Labour Party Ideologies 1900–2001 and Beyond*. London: RoutledgeFalmer.

Lawton, D. (2008) 'The National Curriculum since 1988: panacea or poisoned chalice?', *Forum*, 50 (3): 337–42.

Lawton, D. and Chitty, C. (eds) (1988) *The National Curriculum*, Bedford Way Paper 33. London: Institute of Education, University of London.

Leadbeater, C. (2004) *Personalisation Through Participation: A New Script for Public Services*. London: DEMOS/DFES Innovations Unit.

Leo, E. L. and Galloway, D. (1996) 'Evaluating research on motivation: generating more heat than light?', *Evaluation and Research in Education*, 10: 35–47.

Lewin, K. (1946) 'Action research and minority problems', *Journal of Social Issues*, 2: 34–6.

Liang, L. and Gabel, D. (2005) 'Effectiveness of a constructivist approach to science instruction for prospective elementary teachers', *International Journal of Science Education*, 27 (10): 1143–62.

Liem, G. D. and Martin, A. J. (2013) 'Direct instruction', in J. Hattie and E. M. Anderman (eds), *International Guide to Student Achievement*. Abingdon and New York: Routledge.

Lim, T. K. (1994) 'Relationships between learning styles and personality types', *Research in Education*, 52: 99–100.

Liu, F. (2006) 'School culture and gender', in C. Skelton, B. Francis and L. Smulyan (eds), *The SAGE Handbook of Gender and Education*. London: SAGE.

Long, M., Wood, C., Littleton, K., Passenger, T. and Sheehy, K. (2011) *The Psychology of Education*. London and New York: Routledge.

Lumby, J. (2009) 'Performativity and identity: mechanisms of exclusion', *Journal of Education Policy*, 24 (3): 353–69.

Lund, B. (2008) 'Major, Blair and the third way in social policy', *Social Policy and Administration*, 42(1): 43–58.

Lupton, R. (2005) 'Social justice and school improvement: improving the quality of schooling in the poorest neighbourhoods', *British Educational Research Journal*, 31 (5): 589–604.

Lyotard, J.-F. (1986) *The Postmodern Condition*, 2nd edn. Manchester: Manchester University Press.

Mac an Ghaill, M. (1988) *Young, Gifted and Black*. Milton Keynes: Open University Press.

MacBlain, S. (2014) *How Children Learn*. London: SAGE.

McClelland, D. C. (1955) *Studies in Motivation*. New York: Appleton-Century-Crofts.

McClelland, D. C. (1985) *Motives, Personality and Society*. New York: Praeger.

McCormick, B. and Burn, K. (2011) 'Reviewing the National Curriculum 5–19 two decades on', *Curriculum Journal*, 22 (2): 109–15.

McCulloch, G. (2001) 'The reinvention of teacher professionalism', in R. Phillips and J. Furlong (eds), *Education, Reform and the State: Twenty-five Years of Politics, Policy and Practice*. London: RoutledgeFalmer.

McCulloch, G. (2002) 'Disciplines contributing to education? Educational studies and the disciplines', *British Journal of Educational Studies*, 50 (1): 100–19.

McCulloch, G. (2012) 'The Standing Conference on Studies in Education: sixty years on', *British Journal of Educational Studies*, 60 (4): 301–16.

McGarrigle, J. and Donaldson, M. (1974) 'Conservation accidents', *Cognition*, 3 (3): 41–50.

McGrath, K. and Sinclair, M. (2013) 'More male primary-school teachers? Social benefits for boys and girls', *Gender and Education*, 25 (5): 531–47.

McGregor, D. (1960) *The Human Side of Enterprise*. New York: McGraw-Hill.

McKenzie, J. (2001) *Changing Education: A Sociology of Education Since 1944*. Harlow: Prentice Hall.

McKernan, J. (2013) 'The origins of critical theory in education: Fabian socialism as social reconstructionism in nineteenth century Britain', *British Journal of Educational Studies*, 61 (4): 417–33.

McLoughlin, C. and Lee, M. J. (2010) 'Personalised and self regulated learning in the Web 2.0 era: International exemplars of innovative pedagogy using social software', *Australasian Journal of Educational Technology*, 26 (1): 28–43.

McNiff, J. (1988) *Action Research. Principles and Practice*. London: Macmillan.

McNiff, J. (2013) *Action Research. Principles and Practice*, 3rd edn. Oxon: Routledge.

McNiff, J. with Whitehead, J. (2002) *Action Research: Principles and Practice*, 2nd edn. London: RoutledgeFalmer.

McNiff, J. and Whitehead, J. (2010) *You and Your Action Research Project*, 3rd edn. London: Routledge.

McNiff, J. and Whitehead, J. (2011) *All You Need to Know About Action Research*, 2nd edn. London: SAGE.

Macpherson, W. (1999) *The Stephen Lawrence Inquiry* (The Macpherson Report), CM 4262–I. London: Stationery Office.

Madeus, G. F. (1994) 'A technological and historical consideration of equity issues associated with proposals to change the nation's testing policy', *Harvard Educational Review*, 64: 76–95.

Maguire, M., Brooks, R. and te Riele, K. (2014) *Ethics and Education Research*. London and New York: SAGE.

Majors, R. (2000) *The Black Education Revolution: 'Race' and Culture in Britain and America*. London: Routledge.

Maqsud, M. (1997) 'Effects of metacognitive skills and non-verbal ability on academic achievement of high school pupils', *Educational Psychology*, 17: 387–97.

Marsh, C. J. (2009) *Key Concepts for Understanding Curriculum*, 4th edn. London: RoutledgeFalmer.

Marshall, J. (2014) *Introduction to Comparative and International Education*. London: SAGE.

Martin, G. (2008) 'A brief history of state intervention in British schooling', in D. Matheson (ed.), *An Introduction to the Study of Education*, 3rd edn. London: David Fulton.

Martin, J. (2007) 'Thinking education histories differently: biographical approaches to class politics and women's movements in London, 1900s to 1960s', *History of Education*, 36 (4–5): 515–33.

Marton, F. and Saljo, R. (1976) 'On qualitative differences in learning, 1: outcome and process', *British Journal of Educational Psychology*, 46: 4–11.

Maslow, A. H. (1954) *Motivation and Personality*. New York: Harper.

Matheson, D. (ed.) (2015) *An Introduction to the Study of Education*, 4th edn. London: Routledge.

Maybin, J., Mercer, N. and Stierer, B. (1992) 'Scaffolding learning in the classroom', in K. Norman (ed.), *Thinking Voices: The Work of the National Oracy Project*. London: Hodder & Stoughton.

Mayer, J. D., Salovey, P. and Caruso, D. R. (2004) 'Emotional intelligence: theory, findings, and implications', *Psychological Inquiry*, 15 (3): 197–215.

Mayer, R. E. (2011) 'Does styles research have useful implications for educational practice?', *Learning and Individual Differences*, 21: 319–20.

Maylor, U., Rose, A., Minty, S., Ross, A., Issa, T. and Kuyok, K. (2013) 'Exploring the impact of supplementary schools on Black and Minority Ethnic pupils', *British Educational Research Journal*, 39 (1): 107–25.

Maynard, T. and Powell, S. (2014) *An Introduction to Early Childhood Studies*, 3rd edn. London: SAGE.

Meacham, M. L. and Allen E. W. (1969) *Changing Classroom Behavior: A Manual for Precision Teaching*. Scranton, PA: International Textbook Company.

Mead, G. H. (1934) *Mind, Self and Society*. Chicago: University of Chicago Press.

Mead, M. (1935) *Sex and Temperament in Three Primitive Societies*. London: Routledge & Kegan Paul.

Meighan, R. and Harber, C. (2007) *A Sociology of Educating*, 5th edn. London: Continuum.

Mellor, D. and Epstein, D. (2006) 'Appropriate behaviour? Sexualities, schooling and hetero-gender', in C. Skelton, B. Francis and L. Smulyan (eds), *The SAGE Handbook of Gender and Education*. London: SAGE.

Menter, I., Gallagher, C., Hayward, L. and Wyse, D. (2015) 'Compulsory education in the United Kingdom', in D. Matheson (ed.), *An Introduction to the Study of Education*, 4th edn. London: Routledge.

Mercer, N. and Littleton, K. (2007) *Dialogue and the Development of Children's Thinking: A Socio-cultural Approach*. London: Routledge.

Merrett, F. (1998) 'Helping readers who have fallen behind', *Support for Learning*, 13 (2): 59–63.

Miles, M. and Huberman, M. (1994) *Qualitative Data Analysis*. London: SAGE.

Miliband, D. (2004a) 'What does personalised learning mean to you?', speech delivered at North of England Conference, January.

Miliband, D. (2004b) 'Personalised learning: building a new relationship with schools', speech given at North of England Education Conference, Belfast, 8 January.

Millar, R. (2011) 'Reviewing the National Curriculum for science: opportunities and challenges', *Curriculum Journal*, 22 (2): 167–85.

Miller, D. J. and Moran, T. R. (2007) 'Theory and practice in self-esteem enhancement: circle time and efficacy based approaches, a controlled evaluation', *Teacher and Teaching: Theory and Practice*, 13 (6): 601–15.

Miller, G. (1956) 'The magical number seven plus or minus two: some limits on our capacity for processing information', *Psychological Review*, 63: 81–97.

Milner, D. (1975) *Children and Race*. Harmondsworth: Penguin.

Modood, T. (2014) 'Multiculturalism and integration', in R. Race and V. Lander (eds), *Advancing Race and Ethnicity in Education*. Basingstoke: Palgrave Macmillan.

Moon, B. and Mayes, A. S. (eds) (1994) *Teaching and Learning in the Secondary School*. London: Routledge.

Moran, S. (2008) 'After behaviourism, navigationism?', *Irish Educational Studies*, 27 (3): 209–21.

Morgan, N. (2015a) 'Why knowledge matters', speech delivered 27 January to the Carlton Club, London. Online at: www.gov.uk/government/speeches/nicky-morgan-why-knowledge-matters (accessed 12 October 2015).

Morgan, N. (2015b) 'Free schools drive social justice', DfE press release 22 May. Online at: www.gov.uk/government/news/free-schools-drive-social-justice-nicky-morgan (accessed 12 October 2015).

Morrison, K. and Ridley, K. (1989) 'Ideological contexts for curriculum planning', in M. Preedy (ed.), *Approaches to Curriculum Management*. Milton Keynes: Open University Press.

Moylett, H. (2003) 'Early years education and care', in S. Bartlett and D. Burton (eds), *Education Studies: Essential Issues*. London: SAGE.

Mullard, C. (1981) *Racism in School and Society*. London: University of London, Institute of Education Centre for Multicultural Studies.

Mulryan, C. (1992) 'Student passivity during co-operative small groups in mathematics', *Journal of Educational Research*, 85: 261–73.

Myers, K. (1987) *Genderwatch: Self-Assessment Schedules for Use in Schools*. London: Schools Curriculum Development Council.

Myers, K. and Taylor, H. with Adler, S. and Leonard, D. (eds) (2007) *Genderwatch – Still Watching*. Stoke-on-Trent: Trentham.

Myers Briggs, I., Kirby, L. K. and Myers, K. D. (1998) *Introduction to TYPE. A Guide to Understanding Your Results on the Myers-Briggs Type Indicator*, 6th edn. Oxford: Oxford Psychologists Press.

Myhill, D. (2006) 'Talk, talk, talk: teaching and learning in whole class discourse', *Research Papers in Education*, 21 (1): 19–41.

NAGCELL (1997) *Learning for the Twenty-First Century: First Report of the National Advisory Group for Continuing Education and Lifelong Learning* (The Fryer Report). London: NAGCELL.

Namrouti, A. and Alshannag, Q. (2004) 'Effect of using a metacognitive teaching strategy on seventh grade students' achievement in science', *Dirasat*, 31 (1): 1–13.

NCC (National Curriculum Council) (1990) *The Whole Curriculum: Curriculum Guidance Three*. York: NCC.

NCC (National Curriculum Council) (1993) *Teaching Science at Key Stage 1 and 2*. York: NCC.

NCIHE (National Committee of Inquiry into Higher Education) (1997) *Education in the Learning Society: Report of the National Committee* (The Dearing Report). London: HMSO.

Neisser, U. (1976) *Cognition and Reality*. San Francisco: Freeman.

NESS (2008) *The Impact of Sure Start Local Programmes on Three Year Olds and Their Families*. London: National Evaluation of Sure Start.

Nettelbeck, T. and Wilson, C. (2005) 'Intelligence and IQ: what teachers should know', *Educational Psychology*, 25 (6): 609–30.

Newsom Report (1963) *Half our Future*. London: Ministry of Education, HMSO.

Newton, P. (2009) 'The reliability of results from national curriculum testing in England', *Educational Research*, 51 (2): 181–212.

Nguyen, P.-M., Terloum, C. and Pilot, A. (2006) 'Culturally appropriate pedagogy: the case of group learning in a Confucian Heritage Culture context', *Intercultural Education*, 17 (1): 1–19.

Nicholls, J. G. (1989) *The Competitive Ethos and Democratic Education*. London: Harvard University Press.

Norman, K. (ed.) (1992) *Thinking Voices: The Work of the National Oracy Project*. London: Hodder & Stoughton.

Norwood Report (1943) *Curriculum and Examinations in Secondary Schools*. London: Board of Education, HMSO.

Nutbrown, C., Clough, P. and Selbie, P. (2014) *Early Childhood Education: History, Philosophy and Experience*, 2nd edn. London: SAGE.

Oakley, A. (1975) *Sex, Gender and Society*. London: Temple Smith.

Oates, T. (2011) 'Could do better: using international comparisons to refine the National Curriculum in England', *Curriculum Journal*, 22 (2): 121–50.

O'Donoghue, M. (2012) 'Putting working-class mothers in their place: social stratification, the field of education, and Pierre Bourdieu's theory of practice', *British Journal of Sociology of Education*, 34 (2): 190–270.

OECD (Organisation for Economic Cooperation and Development) (2005) *Learning Sciences and Brain Research Project*. Online at: http://www.oecd.org/edu/ceri/centreforeducational-researchandinnovationceri-brainandlearning.htm (accessed 30 October 2015).

Ofsted (Office for Standards in Education) (2000) *The Annual Report of Her Majesty's Chief Inspector of Schools, Standards and Quality in Education 1998/99*. London: Stationery Office.

Ofsted (Office for Standards in Education) (2010) *The National Strategies: A Review of Impact*. Manchester: Ofsted.

Oliver, E. J., Mawn, L., Stain, H. J., Bambra, C. L., Torgerson, C., Oliver, A. and Bridle, C. (2014) 'Should we "hug a hoodie"? Protocol for a systematic review and meta-analysis of interventions with young people not in employment, education or training (so-called NEETs)', *Systematic Reviews*, 3 (1): 73.

Olssen, M., Codd, J. and O'Neill, A. (2004) *Education Policy: Globalisation, Citizenship and Democracy*. London: SAGE.

Ozga, J. (1995) 'Deskilling a profession', in H. Busher and R. Saran (eds), *Managing Teachers in Schools*. London: Kogan Page.

Paechter, C. (2006) 'Constructing femininity/constructing femininities', in C. Skelton, B. Francis and L. Smulyan (eds), *The SAGE Handbook of Gender and Education*. London: SAGE.

Page, R. (2014) 'Progressive turns in post 1945 Conservative social policy', *Political Studies Review*, 12 (1): 17–28.

Palou, E. (2006) 'Learning styles of Mexican food science and engineering students', *Journal of Food Science Education*, 5 (7): 51–7.

Parsons, S. and Hallam, S. (2014) 'The impact of streaming on attainment at age seven: evidence from the Millennium cohort study', *Oxford Review of Education*, 40 (5): 567–89.

Parsons, T. (1959) 'The social structure of the family', in R. N. Anshen (ed.), *The Family: Its Functions and Destiny*. New York: Harper & Row.

Parsons, T. (1964) *Social Structure and Personality*. New York: Free Press.

Pavlov, I. P. (1927) *Conditioned Reflexes: An Investigation of the Physiological Activity of the Cerebral Cortex*. New York: Dover.

Peters, R. S. (1966) *Ethics and Education*. London: Allen & Unwin.

Peters, R. S. (1967) 'What is an educational process?', in R. S. Peters (ed.), *The Concept of Education*. London: Routledge & Kegan Paul.

Peters, R. S. (2010) 'What is an educational process?', in R. S. Peters (ed.), *The Concept of Education* (International Library of the Philosophy of Education). London: Routledge.

Peters, R. S. (2015) *Ethics and Education* (Routledge Revivals). London: Routledge.

Petrides, K. V. (2009) *Technical Manual for the Trait Emotional Intelligence Questionnaires (TEIQue)*. London: London Psychometric Laboratory.

Petrides, K. V., Vernon, P. A., Aitken Schermer, J. and Veselka, L. (2011) 'Trait emotional intelligence and the dark triad traits of personality', *Twin Research and Human Genetics*, 14 (1): 35–41.

Petty, G. (2014) *Teaching Today: A Practical Guide*, 5th edn. Oxford: Oxford University Press.

Phillips, D. and Schweisfurth, M. (2007) *Comparative and International Education. An Introduction to Theory, Method and Practice*. London: Continuum.

Phillips, R. (2001) 'Education, the state and the politics of reform: the historical context', in R. Phillips and J. Furlong (eds), *Education, Reform and the State: Twenty-five Years of Politics, Policy and Practice*. London: RoutledgeFalmer.

Piaget, J. (1932) *The Moral Judgment of the Child*. New York: Macmillan.

Piaget, J. (1952) *The Origins of Intelligence in Children*. New York: International University Press.

Piaget, J. (1954) *The Construction of Reality in the Child*. New York: Basic Books.

Piaget, J. (1959) *The Thought and Language of the Child*. London: Routledge & Kegan Paul.

Pinxten, M., Wouters, S., Preckel, F., Niepel, C., De Fraine, B. and Verschueren, K. (2015) 'The formation of academic self-concept in elementary education: A unifying model for external and internal comparisons', *Contemporary Educational Psychology*, 41: 124–32.

Pollard, A., Black-Hawkins, K. and Cliff Hodges, G. (2014) *Reflective Teaching in Schools*, 4th edn. London: Bloomsbury Academic.

Porter, J. (2009) 'Extravagant aims, distorted practice', *Forum*, 51 (3): 287–98.

Postman, N. and Weingartner, C. (1969) *Teaching as a Subversive Activity*. Harmondsworth: Penguin.

Prain, V., Cox, P., Deed, C., Dorman, J., Edwards, D., Farrelly, C., Keeffe, M., Lovejoy, V., Mow, L., Sellings, P., Waldrip, B. and Yager, Z. (2013) 'Personalised learning: lessons to be learnt', *British Education Research Journal*, 39: 654–76.

Price, G. E., Dunn, R. and Dunn, K. (1991) *Productivity Environmental Preference Survey (PEPS Manual)*. Lawrence, KS: Price Systems.

PricewaterhouseCoopers (2008) *Academies Evaluation Fifth Annual Report*. Online at: www.standards.dfes.gov.uk/academies/pdf/academies5thannualreport.pdf?version=1 (accessed 12 November 2010).

Pring, R. (1989) *The New Curriculum*. London: Cassell.

Pring, R. (2012) '60 Years on: the changing role of government', *British Journal of Educational Studies*, 60 (1): 29–38.

Pring, R. (2013) 'Another reform of qualifications – but qualifying for what?', *The Political Quarterly*, 84 (1): 139–43.

Pring, R. (2015) *Philosophy of Educational Research*, 3rd edn. London and New York: Bloomsbury Academic.

Punch, K. and Oancea, A. (2014) *Introduction to Research Methods in Education*, 2nd edn. London: SAGE.

Purdie, N. and Hattie, J. (1996) 'Cultural differences in the use of strategies for self-regulated learning', *American Educational Research Journal*, 33: 845–71.

QAA (Quality Assurance Agency) (2015) *Benchmarking Academic Standards: Education Studies*. Online at: http://www.qaa.ac.uk/en/Publications/Documents/SBS-education-studies-15.pdf (accessed 30 October 2015).

Qualter, P., Gardner, K. J., Pope, D. J., Hutchinson, J., M. and Whiteley, H. E. (2012) 'Ability, emotional intelligence, trait emotional intelligence, and academic success in British secondary schools: a 5 year longitudinal study', *Learning and Individual Differences*, 22 (1): 83–91.

Race, R. (2014) 'The multicultural dilemma, the integrationist consensus and the consequences for advancing race and ethnicity within education', in R. Race and V. Lander (eds), *Advancing Race and Ethnicity in Education*. Basingstoke: Palgrave Macmillan.

Rayner, S. and Riding, R. J. (1997) 'Towards a categorisation of cognitive styles and learning styles', *Educational Psychology*, 17: 5–27.

Reay, D. (2006) 'The zombie stalking English schools: social class and educational inequality', *British Journal of Educational Studies*, 54 (3): 288–307.

Reay, D. (2008) 'Tony Blair, the promotion of the "active" educational citizen, and middle-class hegemony', *Oxford Review of Education*, 34 (6): 639–50.

Reay, D. (2013) 'Social mobility, a panacea for austere times: tales of emperors, frogs, and tadpoles', *British Journal of Sociology of Education*, 34 (5): 660–77.

Reisz, M. (2011) 'Disciplinary tribalism "is stifling creativity"', *THE*, 23–29 June, p. 16. Online at: www.timeshighereducation.com/news/disciplinary-tribalism-is-stifling-creativity/416549.article (accessed 20 October 2015).

Reynolds, D. (1997) 'Now we must tackle social inequality not just assess it', *Times Educational Supplement*, 21 March.

Richards, G. and Armstrong, F. (eds) (2015) *Teaching and Learning in Diverse and Inclusive Classrooms*, 2nd edn. London: Routledge.

Richards, G. and Posnett, C. (2012) 'Aspiring girls: great expectations or impossible dreams?', *Educational Studies*, 38 (3): 249–59.

Richards, L. (2015) *Handling Qualitative Data: A Practical Guide*, 3rd edn. London: SAGE.

Riding, R. J. (1991) *Cognitive Styles Analysis*. Birmingham: Learning and Training Technology.

Riding, R. J. (1996) *Learning Styles and Technology-Based Training*. Sheffield: DfEE.

Riding, R. (2002) *School Learning and Cognitive Styles*. London: David Fulton.

Riding, R. J. and Burton, D. (1998) 'Cognitive style, gender and behaviour in secondary school pupils', *Research in Education*, 59: 38–49.

Riding, R. J. and Cheema, I. (1991) 'Cognitive styles: an overview and integration', *Educational Psychology*, 11: 193–215.

Riding, R. J., Grimley, M., Dahraei, H. and Banner, G. (2003) 'Cognitive style, working memory and learning behaviour and attainment in school subjects', *British Journal of Educational Psychology*, 73 (21): 149–69.

Riding, R. J. and Rayner, S. (1998) *Cognitive Styles and Learning Strategies*. London: Fulton.

Rist, R. (1970) 'Student social class and teacher expectations: the self-fulfilling prophecy in ghetto education', *Harvard Educational Review*, 40: 441–51.

Ritzer, G. (2001) *Explorations in Social Theory. From Metatheorizing to Rationalisation*. London: SAGE.

Robbins Report (1963) *Higher Education: A Report of the Committee Appointed by the Prime Minister Under the Chairmanship of Lord Robbins, 1961–63*, Cmnd 2154. London: HMSO.

Roberts, W. and Norwich, B. (2010) 'Using precision teaching to enhance the word reading skills and academic self-concept of secondary school students: a role for professional educational psychologists', *Educational Psychology in Practice*, 26 (3): 279–98.

Robertson, L. and Hill, D. (2014) 'Policy and ideologies in schooling and early years education in England: implications for and impacts on leadership, management and equality', *Management in Education*, 28 (4): 167–74.

Rogers, C. R. (1983) *Freedom to Learn for the 80s*. New York: Macmillan.

Rogoff, B. (1990) *Apprenticeship in Thinking: Cognitive Development in Social Context*. Oxford: Oxford University Press.

Rogoff, B. (1998) 'Cognition as a collaborative process', in D. Kuhn and R. S. Seigler (eds), *Cognition, Perception and Language*, Vol. 2 of W. Damon (ed.), *Handbook of Child Psychology*, 5th edn. New York: John Wiley.

Rosenthal, R. and Jacobson, L. (1968) *Pygmalion in the Classroom*. New York: Holt, Rinehart & Winston.

Rotter, J. B. (1966) *Generalised Expectancies for Internal Versus External Control of Reinforcement*, Psychological Monographs, 80 (609).

Rumelhart, D. E. and McClelland, J. L. (1986) *Parallel Distributed Processing: Explorations in the Microstructure of Cognition*. Cambridge, MA: MIT Press.

Rutter, M., Maughan, B., Mortimore, P. and Oulston, J. (1979) *Fifteen Thousand Hours: Secondary Schools and Their Effects on Children*. London: Open Books.

Sahlberg, P. (2015) 'Britain should be wary of borrowing education ideas from abroad', *The Guardian*, 27 April.

Salili, F. (1996) 'Achievement motivation: a cross-cultural comparison of British and Chinese students', *Educational Psychology*, 16: 271–9.

Salovey, P. and Mayer, J. D. (1990) 'Emotional intelligence', *Imagination, Cognition, and Personality*, 9: 185–211.

Salthouse, T. (2001) 'Aging and cognition', in R. A. Wilson and F. C. Keil (eds), *The MIT Encyclopedia of the Cognitive Sciences*. Cambridge, MA: MIT Press.

Sammons, P., Hillman, J. and Mortimore, P. (1995) *Key Characteristics of Effective Schools: A Review of School Effectiveness Research*. London: Office for Standards in Education.

Schenck, J. and Cruickshank, J. (2015) 'Evolving Kolb: experiential education in the age of neuroscience', *Journal of Experiential Education*, 38 (1): 73–95.

Schonell, F. (1924) *Backwardness in the Basic Subjects*. London: Oliver and Boyd.

Schunk, D. H. and Mullen, C. A. (2013) 'Study skills', in J. Hattie and E. M. Anderman (eds), *International Guide to Student Achievement*. Abingdon and New York: Routledge.

Scott, C. (2013) 'The search for the key for individualised instruction', in J. Hattie and E. M. Anderman (eds), *International Guide to Student Achievement*. Abingdon and New York: Routledge.

Scott, D. and Usher, R. (2011) *Researching Education: Data, Methods and Theory in Educational Enquiry*, 2nd edn. London: Continuum.

Scrimshaw, P. (1983) *Educational Ideologies. Unit 2 E204. Purpose and Planning in the Curriculum*. Milton Keynes: Open University Press.

Seifert, K. (1999) *Child and Adolescent Development*. Boston: Houghton Mifflin.

Seker, H. (2008) 'Will the constructivist approach employed in science teaching change the "grammar" of schooling?', *Journal of Baltic Science Education*, 7 (3): 175–84.

Selman, R. L. (1980) *The Growth of Interpersonal Understanding*. New York: Academic Press.

Sewell, T. (1997) *Black Masculinities and Schooling*. Stoke-on-Trent: Trentham.

Sharp, J. and Murphy, B. (2014) 'The mystery of learning', in W. Curtis, S. Ward, J. Sharp and L. Hankin (eds), *Education Studies: An Issues-Based Approach*, 3rd edn. London: SAGE/ Learning Matters.

Sharpe, S. (1976) *Just Like a Girl: How Girls Learn to Be Women*. Harmondsworth: Penguin.

Shaw, M. (2003) 'Warnock calls for rethink'. *Times Educational Supplement*. 19 September 2003.

Shayer, M. (2008) 'Intelligence for education: as described by Piaget and measured by metrics', *British Journal of Educational Psychology*, 78 (1): 1–29.

Shayer, M. and Adey, P. (eds) (2002) *Learning Intelligence: Cognitive Acceleration Across the Curriculum from 5 to 15 years*. Buckingham and Philadelphia: Open University Press.

Siegler, R. S. and Alibali, M. W. (2005) *Children's Thinking*, 4th edn. Upper Saddle River, NJ: Pearson/Prentice Hall.

Sigal, M. J. and McKelvie, S. J. (2012) 'Is exposure to visual media related to cognitive ability? Testing Neisser's hypothesis for the Flynn effect', *Journal of Articles in Support of the Null Hypothesis*, 9 (1): 23–49.

Silver, H., Strong, R. and Perini, M. (1997) 'Integrating learning styles and multiple intelligences', *Educational Leadership*, 55 (1): 22–7.

Silverman, D. (2013) *Doing Qualitative Research*, 4th edn. London: SAGE.

Simons, H. (2009) *Case Study Research in Practice*. London: SAGE.

Simonsen, B. and Sugai, G. (2013) 'PBIS in alternative education settings: positive support for youth with high-risk behavior', *Education & Treatment of Children*, 36 (3): 3–14.

Skelton, C., Francis, B. and Read, B. (2010) 'Brains before "beauty"? High achieving girls, school and gender identities', *Educational Studies*, 36 (2): 185–94.

Skinner, B. (1957) *Verbal Behavior*. New York: Appleton-Century-Crofts.

Skourdoumbis, A. and Gale, T. (2013) 'Classroom teacher effectiveness research: a conceptual critique', *British Educational Research Journal*, 39 (5): 892–906.

Slavin, R. E. (1990) 'Achievement effects of ability grouping in secondary schools: a best evidence synthesis', *Review of Educational Research*, 60: 471–99.

Slavin, R. E. (1993) 'Students differ: so what?', *Educational Researcher*, 22: 13–14.

Smit, J., van Eerde, H. and Bakker, A. (2013) 'A conceptualisation of whole-class scaffolding', *British Education Research Journal*, 39 (5): 817–34.

Smith, A. (1996) *Accelerated Learning in the Classroom*. London: Network Educational Press.

Smith, A. (2001) 'The labelling of African-American boys in special education: a case study', in G. Hudak and P. Kihn (eds), *Labelling, Pedagogy and Politics*. London: RoutledgeFalmer.

Smith, A. and Call, N. (2002) *The ALPS Approach*. London: ALITE.

Smith, A. R., Cavanaugh, C., Jones, J., Venn, J. and Wilson, W. (2006) 'Influence of learning style on graduate student cognitive and psychomotor performance', *Journal of Allied Health*, 35 (3): 182–203.

Smith, E. (2012) *Key Issues in Education and Social Justice*. London: SAGE.

Smith, G. and Smith, T. (2014) 'Targeting educational disadvantage by area: continuity and change in urban areas of England, 1968–2014', *Oxford Review of Education*, 40 (6): 715–38.

Smith, M. and Chambers, K. (2015) 'Half a million unseen, half a million unheard: inclusion for gender identity and sexual orientation', in G. Richards and F. Armstrong (eds), *Teaching and Learning in Diverse and Inclusive Classrooms*, 2nd edn. London: Routledge.

Smith, P. (2006) 'Identifying learning preferences in vocational education and training classroom settings', *Journal of Vocational Education and Training*, 58 (14): 257–70.

Smith, P. K. and Cowie, H. (2003) *Understanding Children's Development*, 4th edn. London: Blackwell.

Smitherman, G. (2000) *Talkin' That Talk: Language, Culture and Education in African America*. London: Routledge.

Spada, M., Nikcevic, A., Moneta, G. and Ireson, J. (2006) 'Metacognition as a mediator of the effect of test anxiety on a surface approach to studying', *Education Psychology*, 26 (5): 615–24.

Spearman, C. (1927) *The Abilities of Man*. London: Macmillan.

Spender, D. (1982) *Invisible Women: The Schooling Scandal*. London: Writers and Readers.

Stahl, G. and Dale, P. (2013) 'Success on the decks: working-class boys, education and turning the tables on perceptions of failure', *Gender and Education*, 25 (3): 357–72.

Stanley, J. (2015) '"Race" and education: the English experience', in D. Matheson (ed.), *An Introduction to the Study of Education*, 4th edn. London: David Fulton.

Steiner, R. (2008) *The Four Temperaments*. Forest Row: Sophia Books.

Stenhouse, L. (1975) *An Introduction to Curriculum Research and Development*. Oxford: Heinemann Educational.

Stenhouse, L. (1983) *Authority, Education and Emancipation*. London: Heinemann.

Sternberg, R. J. (1985) *Beyond IQ: A Triarchic Theory of Human Intelligence*. New York: Cambridge University Press.

Sternberg, R. J. (1999) 'Intelligence', in R. P. Wilson and F. C. Keil (eds), *The MIT Encyclopedia of the Cognitive Sciences*. Cambridge, MA: MIT Press.

Sternberg, R. J. (2003a) 'Creative thinking in the classroom', *Scandinavian Journal of Education Research*, 47 (3): 325–38.

Sternberg, R. J. (2003b) 'WICS as a model of giftedness', *High Ability Studies*, 14 (2): 109–37.

Sternberg, R. J. (2005) 'WICS: a model of positive educational leadership comprising wisdom, intelligence, and creativity synthesised', *Educational Psychology Review*, 17 (3): 191–262.

Sternberg, R. J. (2011) 'The theory of successful intelligence', in R. J. Sternberg and S. Kaufman (eds), *The Cambridge Handbook of Intelligence*. Cambridge: Cambridge University Press.

Sternberg, R. J. (2012) 'The assessment of creativity: an investment-based approach', *Creativity Research Journal*, 24 (1): 3–12.

Sternberg, R. J. and O'Hara, L. A. (1999) 'Creativity and intelligence', in R. J. Sternberg (ed.), *The Cambridge Handbook of Creativity*. Cambridge: Cambridge University Press.

Stewart, H. (2015) 'Nicky Morgan is wrong – the evidence for academies doesn't add up', *The Guardian*, 3 June. Online at: www.theguardian.com/commentisfree/2015/jun/03/nicky-morgan-wrong-evidence-academies-bill (accessed 30 October 2015).

Stiles, J. B., Brown, T. T., Haist, F. and Lernigan, T. L. (2015) 'Brain and cognitive development', in R. M. Lerner, L. S. Liben and U. Mueller (eds), *Handbook of Child Psychology and Developmental Science, Cognitive Processes*. New Jersey: Wiley.

Stobart, G. (2008) *Testing Times: The Uses and Abuses of Assessment*. Abingdon: Routledge.

Stobart, G. (2009) 'Determining validity in national curriculum assessments', *Educational Research*, 51 (2): 161–79.

Stones, E. (2000) 'Iconoclastes: poor pedagogy', *Journal of Education for Teaching: International Research and Pedagogy*, 26 (1): 93–5.

Stones, E. (2002) '*JET*: directions for the future', *Journal of Education for Teaching: International Research and Pedagogy*, 28 (3): 207–10.

Stradling, R., Saunders, L. and Weston, P. (1991) *Differentiation in Action: A Whole School Approach for Raising Attainment*. London: NFER/HMSO.

Strand, S. (2010) 'Do some schools narrow the gap? Differential school effectiveness by eth-nicity, gender, poverty and prior achievement', *School Effectiveness and School Improvement*, 21 (3): 289–314.

Strand, S. (2011) 'The limits of social class in explaining ethnic gaps in educational attainment', *British Educational Research Journal*, 37 (2): 197–229.

Strand, S. (2014) 'School effects and ethnic, gender and socio-economic gaps in educational achievement at age 11', *Oxford Review of Education*, 40 (2): 223–45.

Suchmann, L. (1987) *Plans and Situated Actions: The Problem of Human–Machine Communication*. Cambridge: Cambridge University Press.

Svennberg, L., Meckbach, J. and Redelius, K. (2015) 'Exploring PE teachers' "gut feelings": an attempt to verbalise and discuss teachers' internalised grading criteria', *European Physical Education Review*, 20 (2): 199–214.

Swain, J. (2004) 'The resources and strategies that 10–11-year-old boys use to construct mascu-linities in the school setting', *British Educational Research Journal*, 30 (1): 167–85.

Swarbrick, A. (2011) 'Languages: building on firm foundations', *Curriculum Journal*, 22 (2): 227–41.

Taylor, C., Fitz, J. and Gorard, S. (2005) 'Diversity, specialisation and equity in education', *Oxford Review of Education*, 31 (1): 47–69.

Taylor, R. (2005) 'Lifelong: learning and the Labour governments 1997–2004', *Oxford Review of Education*, 31 (1): 101–18.

Teddlie, C. and Reynolds, D. (2000) *International Handbook of School Effectiveness Research*. London: Falmer Press.

Terman, L. M. (1924) 'The mental tests as a psychological method', *Psychological Review*, 31: 93–117.

Thomas, G. (2015) *How to Do Your Case Study*, 2nd edn. London: SAGE.

Thorndike, E. L. (1911) *Animal Intelligence: Experimental Studies*. New York: Macmillan.

Thoutenhoofd, E. D. and Pirrie, A. (2015) 'From self-regulation to learning to learn: observations on the construction of self and learning', *British Education Research Journal*, 41: 72–84.

Thrupp, M. and Lupton, R. (2006) 'Taking school contexts more seriously: the social justice challenge', *British Journal of Educational Studies*, 54 (3): 308–28.

Thurstone, L. L. (1938) *Primary Mental Abilities*. Chicago: University of Chicago Press.

Tight, M. (2012) 'Widening participation: a post war scoreboard', *British Journal of Educational Studies*, 60 (3): 211–26.

Tizard, B. and Phoenix, A. (2001) *Black, White or Mixed Race? Race and Racism in the Lives of Young People of Mixed Parentage*. London: Routledge.

Tomlinson, M. (2004) *14–19 Curriculum and Qualifications Reform: Final Report of the Working Group on 14–19 Reform*. Online at: http://webarchive.nationalarchives.gov.uk/20130401 151715/http://www.education.gov.uk/publications/standard/publicationDetail/Page1/DfE-0976-2004 (accessed 30 October 2015).

Tomlinson, P., Dockrell, J. and Winne, P. (eds) (2005) 'Pedagogy – teaching for learning', *British Journal of Educational Psychology*, Monograph Series II: Psychological Aspects of Education – Current Trends. Leicester: British Psychological Society.

Tomlinson, S. (1977) 'Race and education in Britain 1960–77: an overview of the literature', *Sage Race Relations Abstracts*, 2 (4): 3–33.

Tomlinson, S. (2005) *Education in a Post-Welfare Society*, 2nd edn. Maidenhead: Open University Press.

Tomlinson, S. (2008) *Race and Education. Policy and Politics in Britain*. Maidenhead: Open University Press.

Toogood, P. (1984) *The Head's Tale*. Ironbridge: Dialogue Publications.

Townsend, M. A. R. and Hicks, L. (1997) 'Classroom goal structures, social satisfaction and the perceived value of academic tasks', *British Journal of Educational Psychology*, 67: 1–12.

Townsend, T. (ed.) (2007) *International Handbook of School Effectiveness and Improvement*. Dordrecht: Springer.

Triantafillou, E., Pomportsis, A., Demetriadis, S. and Georgiadou, E. (2004) 'The value of adaptivity based on cognitive style: an empirical study', *British Journal of Educational Technology*, 35 (1): 95–106.

Trowler, P. (2003) *Education Policy*, 2nd edn. London: Routledge.

Troyna, B. and Carrington, B. (1990) *Education, Racism and Reform*. London: Routledge.

Tubbs, N. (1996) *The New Teacher: An Introduction to Teaching in Comprehensive Education*. London: Fulton.

Tulving, E. (1972) 'Episodic and semantic memory', in E. Tulving and W. Donaldson (eds), *Organisation of Memory*. New York: Academic Press.

Tulving, E. and Craik, F. (eds) (2000) *The Oxford Handbook of Memory*. Oxford: Oxford University Press.

Tymms, P., Merrell, C., Thurston, A., Andor, J., Topping, K. and Miller, D. (2011) 'Improving attainment across a whole school district: school reform through peer tutoring in a randomised controlled trial', *School Effectiveness and School Improvement*, 22: 265–89.

Tymms, P., Merrell, C. and Wildy, H. (2015) 'The progress of pupils in their first year across classes and educational systems', *British Educational Research Journal*, 41 (3): 365–80.

Vicars, M. (2006) 'Who are you calling queer? Sticks and stones can break my bones but names will always hurt me', *British Educational Research Journal*, 32 (3): 347–61.

Vincent, C., Ball, S., Rollock, N. and Gillborn, D. (2013) 'Three generations of racism: Black middle-class children and schooling', *British Journal of Sociology of Education*, 34 (5): 929–46.

Visser, J. (1993) *Differentiation: Making It Work; Ideas for Staff Development*. Stafford: NASEN.

Vygotsky, L. S. (1978) *Mind in Society: The Development of Higher Psychological Processes*. London: Harvard University Press.

Walford, G. (2005) 'Introduction: education and the Labour Government', *Oxford Review of Education*, 31 (1): 3–9.

Walford, G. (2006) *Markets and Equity in Education*. London: Continuum.

Walford, G. (2009) 'For ethnograph', *Ethnography and Education*, 4 (3): 271–82.

Walford, G. (2014) 'Academies,free schools and social justice', *Research Papers in Education*, 29(3) 263–7.

Ward, M. (2014a) "'I'm a geek I am": academic achievement and the performance of a studious working-class masculinity', *Gender and Education*, 26 (7): 709–25.

Ward, S. (2014b) 'The nature of higher education', in W. Curtis, S. Ward, J. Sharp and L. Hankin (eds), *Education Studies: An Issues Based Approach*, 3rd edn. Exeter: Learning Matters.

Ward, S. and Eden, C. (2009) *Key Issues in Educational Policy*. London: SAGE.

Warnock, M. (2005) *Special educational needs: A new look*. London: Philosophy Society of Great Britain.

Watson, J. (1913) 'Psychology as the behaviorist views it', *Psychological Review*, 20: 159–77.

Webb, N. M. (2013) 'Collaboration in the classroom', in J. Hattie and E. M. Anderman (eds), *International Guide to Student Achievement*. Abingdon and New York: Routledge.

Weber, M. (1958) *The Protestant Ethic and the Spirit of Capitalism*. New York: Charles Scribner's Sons.

Weber, M. (1963) *The Sociology of Religion*. Boston: Beacon Press.

Weber, M. (2002) *The Protestant Ethic and the Spirit of Capitalism: and other writings*. Ed. and trans. P. Baehr and G. C. Wells. London: Penguin.

Weber, M. (2009) *From Max Weber: Essays in Sociology*. Ed. and trans. H. H. Gerth and C. W. Mills. London: Routledge.

Webster, R. and Blatchford, P. (2015) 'Worlds apart? The nature and quality of the educational experiences of pupils with a statement for special educational needs in mainstream primary schools', *British Educational Research Journal*, 41 (2): 324–42.

Wegerif, R., Li, L. and Kaufman, J. C. (eds) (2015) *The Routledge International Handbook of Research on Teaching Thinking*. London and New York: Routledge.

Weinberg, R. A. (1989) 'Intelligence and IQ: landmark issues and great debates', *American Psychologist*, 44: 98–104.

Weiner, B. J. (1972) *Theories of Motivation*. Chicago: Markham.

Weinstock, A. (1976) 'I blame the teachers', *Times Educational Supplement*, 23 January.

Weisberg, D. S., Keil, F. C., Goodstein, J., Rawson, E. and Gray, J. R. (2008) 'The seductive allure of neuroscience explanations', *Journal of Cognitive Neuroscience*, 20: 470–7.

Wentzel, K. R. and Brophy, J. E. (2014) *Motivating Students to Learn*, 4th edn. New York and Abingdon: Routledge.

Wentzel, K. R. and Wigfield, A. (2009) *Handbook of Motivation at School*. New York and Abingdon: Routledge.

Wertheimer, M. (1923) 'Untersuchungen zur Lehre von der Gestalt', *Psychologische Forschung*, 4: 301–50.

West, A. and Bailey, E. (2013) 'The development of the Academies Programme: "privatising" school-based education in England 1986–2013', *British Journal of Educational Studies*, 61 (2): 137–51.

West, A., Roberts, J., Lewis, J. and Noden, P. (2015) 'Paying for higher education in England: funding policy and families', *British Journal of Educational Studies*, 63 (1): 23–45.

Weston, P. (1996) 'Learning about differentiation in practice', *TOPIC*, 16 (4).

Wheldall, K. (2006) 'Positive uses of behaviourism', in D. McInerney and V. McInerney (eds), *Educational Psychology: Constructing Learning*, 4th edn. Sydney: Pearson-Prentice Hall.

Wheldall, K. and Merrett, F. (1985) *The Behavioural Approach to Teaching Package*. Birmingham: Positive Products.

Whetton, C. (2009) *A Brief History of a Testing Time: National Curriculum Assessment in England 1989–2008*. London: NFER.

White, J. (1998) *Perspectives on Education Policy: Do Howard Gardner's Multiple Intelligences Add Up?* London: Institute for Education.

White, J. (2005) *Howard Gardner: The Myth of Multiple Intelligences*, Viewpoint No. 16. London: Institute of Education.

Whitty, G. (2002) *Making Sense of Education Policy*. London: Paul Chapman.

Whitty, G. (2012) 'A life with the sociology of education', *British Journal of Educational Studies*, 60 (1): 65–75.

Whyte, J. (1983) *Beyond the Wendy House: Sex-Role Stereotyping in Primary Schools*. York: Longman.

Wiles, R. (2013) *What Are Quantitative Research Ethics?* London: Bloomsbury.

Williams, J. (1981) 'Race and schooling', *British Journal of Sociology*, 2 (2): 221.

Willis, P. (1979) *Learning to Labour*. Aldershot: Gator.

Wilson, R. A. (ed.) (1999) *Species: New Interdisciplinary Essays*. Cambridge, MA: MIT Press.

Winstanley, C. (2016) 'Personalising and individualising learning', in S. Capel, M. Leask and S. Younie (eds), *Learning to Teach in the Secondary School: A Companion to School Experience*, 7th edn. London: Routledge.

Winter, D. A. (2013) 'Still radical after all these years: George Kelly's *The Psychology of Personal Constructs*', *Clinical Child Psychology and Psychiatry*, 18 (2): 276–83.

Wintour, P. (1994) 'Blair gives "modern voice to Labour views"', *The Guardian*, 24 June.

Withers, R. and Eke, R. (1995) 'Reclaiming "Match" from the critics of primary education', *Educational Review*, 47: 59–73.

Wolf, A. (2011) *Review of Vocational Education* (The Wolf Report). London: Department for Education. Online at: www.gov.uk/government/publications/review-of-vocational-education-the-wolf-report (accessed 12 October 2015).

Wong, N. Y., Lin, W. Y. and Watkins, D. (1996) 'Cross-cultural validation of models of approaches to learning: an application of confirmatory factor analysis', *Educational Psychology*, 16 (3): 317–27.

Wood, D. (1988) *How Children Think and Learn*. Oxford: Blackwell.

Wood, P. and Warin, J. (2014) 'Social and emotional aspects of learning: Complementing, compensating and countering parental practices', *British Educational Research Journal*, 40(6): 937–51.

Woods, P. (2006) *Successful Writing for Qualitative Researcher*, 2nd edn. London: Routledge.

Wright, C., Weekes, D. and McGlaughlin, A. (1999) *'Race', Class and Gender in Exclusion from School*. London: Routledge.

Wright, O. and Taylor, J. (2011) 'Cameron: my war on multiculturalism', *The Independent*, 5 February. Online at: www.independent.co.uk/news/uk/politics/cameron-my-war-on-multi culturalism-2205074.html (accessed 12 October 2015).

Wright, T. (2003) 'Education for development', in S. Bartlett and D. Burton (eds), *Education Studies: Essential Issues*. London: SAGE.

Wyness, M. (2015) 'Schooling and social class', in D. Matheson (ed.), *An Introduction to the Study of Education*, 4th edn. London: Routledge.

Wyse, D. (2003) 'The National Literacy Strategy: a critical review of empirical evidence', *British Educational Research Journal*, 29 (6): 903–16.

Wyse, D. and Torrance, H. (2009) 'The development and consequences of national curriculum assessment for primary education in England', *Educational Research*, 51 (2): 213–28.

Yerkes, R. and Dodson, J. (1908) 'The relation of strength of stimulus to rapidity of habit-formation', *Journal of Comparative Neurology and Psychology*, 18: 459–82.

Yin, R. (2014) *Case Study Research: Design and Methods*, 5th edn. London: SAGE.

Young, M. (1971) *Knowledge and Control*. London: Collier-Macmillan.

Young, M. (2011) 'The return to subjects: a sociological perspective on the UK Coalition government's approach to the 14–19 curriculum', *Curriculum Journal*, 22 (2): 265–78.

Young, M. (2013) 'Overcoming the crisis in curriculum theory: a knowledge-based approach', *Journal of Curriculum Studies*, 45 (2): 101–18.

Young, M. and Collins, M. K. (2014) 'Value co-creation through learning styles segmentation and integrated course design', *Journal of Instructional Pedagogies*, 13: 1–9. Online at: www. aabri.com/manuscripts/131740.pdf (accessed 12 October 2015).

Zanoni, P. and Mampaey, J. (2013) 'Achieving ethnic minority student's inclusion: A Flemish school's discursive practices countering the quasi-market pressure to exclude', *British Educational Research Journal*, 39 (1): 1–21.

Zimmerman, B. J. (1998) 'Academic studying and the development of personal skill: a self-regulatory perspective', *Educational Psychologist*, 33: 73–86.

Zins, J. E., Weissberg, R. P., Wang, M. C. and Walberg, H. J. (2004) *Building Academic Success on Social and Emotional Learning. What Does the Research Say?* New York: Teachers College, Columbia University.

Author index

Subject index